ACCA

Paper P7 INT

Advanced audit and assurance

Complete text

British library cataloguing-in-publication data

A catalogue record for this book is available from the British Library.

Published by:
Kaplan Publishing UK
Unit 2 The Business Centre
Molly Millars Lane
Wokingham
Berkshire
RG41 2QZ

ISBN 978-1-84710-960-6

Printed in the UK by CPI William Clowes Beccles NR34 7TL.

Acknowledgements

We are grateful to the Association of Chartered Certified Accountants and the Chartered Institute of Management Accountants for permission to reproduce past examination questions. The answers have been prepared by Kaplan Publishing.

Contents

chapter

troduction

Paper Introduction

How to Use the Materials

These Kaplan Publishing learning materials have been carefully designed to make your learning experience as easy as possible and to give you the best chances of success in your examinations.

The product range contains a number of features to help you in the study process. They include:

(1) Detailed study guide and syllabus objectives

(2) Description of the examination

(3) Study skills and revision guidance

(4) Complete text or essential text

(5) Question practice

The sections on the study guide, the syllabus objectives, the examination and study skills should all be read before you commence your studies. They are designed to familiarise you with the nature and content of the examination and give you tips on how to best to approach your learning.

The **complete text or essential text** comprises the main learning materials and gives guidance as to the importance of topics and where other related resources can be found. Each chapter includes:

- The **learning objectives** contained in each chapter, which have been carefully mapped to the examining body's own syllabus learning objectives or outcomes. You should use these to check you have a clear understanding of all the topics on which you might be assessed in the examination.
- The **chapter diagram** provides a visual reference for the content in the chapter, giving an overview of the topics and how they link together.
- The **content** for each topic area commences with a brief explanation or definition to put the topic into context before covering the topic in detail. You should follow your studying of the content with a review of the illustration/s. These are worked examples which will help you to understand better how to apply the content for the topic.
- **Test your understanding** sections provide an opportunity to assess your understanding of the key topics by applying what you have learned to short questions. Answers can be found at the back of each chapter.

- **Summary diagrams** complete each chapter to show the important links between topics and the overall content of the paper. These diagrams should be used to check that you have covered and understood the core topics before moving on.
- **Question practice** is provided at the back of each text.

Icon Explanations

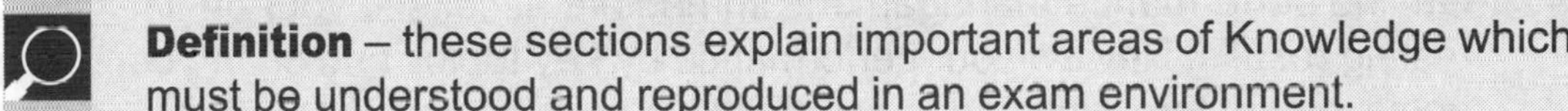

Definition – these sections explain important areas of Knowledge which must be understood and reproduced in an exam environment.

Key Point – identifies topics which are key to success and are often examined.

New – identifies topics that are brand new in papers that build on, and therefore also contain, learning covered in earlier papers.

Expandable Text – within the online version of the work book is a more detailed explanation of key terms, these sections will help to provide a deeper understanding of core areas. Reference to this text is vital when self studying.

Test Your Understanding – following key points and definitions are exercises which give the opportunity to assess the understanding of these core areas. Within the work book the answers to these sections are left blank, explanations to the questions can be found within the online version which can be hidden or shown on screen to enable repetition of activities.

Illustration – to help develop an understanding of topics and the test your understanding exercises the illustrative examples can be used.

Exclamation Mark – this symbol signifies a topic which can be more difficult to understand, when reviewing these areas care should be taken.

Tutorial note – included to explain some of the technical points in more detail.

Footsteps – helpful tutor tips.

On-line subscribers

Our on-line resources are designed to increase the flexibility of your learning materials and provide you with immediate feedback on how your studies are progressing. Ask your local customer services staff if you are not already a subscriber and wish to join.

If you are subscribed to our on-line resources you will find:

(1) On-line reference ware: reproduces your Complete or Essential Text on-line, giving you anytime, anywhere access.

(2) On-line testing: provides you with additional on-line objective testing so you can practice what you have learned further.

(3) On-line performance management: immediate access to your on-line testing results. Review your performance by key topics and chart your achievement through the course relative to your peer group.

Paper introduction

Paper background

The aim of ACCA Paper P7 (INT), Advanced audit and assurance, is to analyse, evaluate and conclude on the assurance engagement and other audit and assurance issues in the context of best practice and current developments.

Objectives of the syllabus

- Recognise the legal and regulatory environment and its impact on audit and assurance practice;
- Demonstrate the ability to work effectively on an assurance or other service engagement within a professional and ethical framework;
- Assess and recommend appropriate quality control policies and procedures in practice management and recognise the auditor's position in relation to the acceptance and retention of professional appointments;
- Identify and formulate the work required to meet the objectives of audit and non-audit assignments and apply the International Standards on Auditing;
- Evaluate findings and the results of work performed and draft suitable reports on assignments;
- Understand the current issues and developments relating to the provision of audit related and assurance services.

Core areas of the syllabus

- Regulatory environment.
- Professional and ethical considerations.
- Practice management.
- Assignments.
- Reporting.
- Current issues and developments.

Syllabus objectives

We have reproduced the ACCA's syllabus below, showing where the objectives are explored within this book. Within the chapters, we have broken down the extensive information found in the syllabus into easily digestible and relevant sections, called Content Objectives. These correspond to the objectives at the beginning of each chapter.

Syllabus learning objective	Chapter reference
A REGULATORY ENVIRONMENT	
1 International regulatory frameworks for audit and assurance services	
(a) Explain the need for laws, regulations, standards and other guidance relating to audit, assurance and related services.[2]	1
(b) Outline and explain the need for the legal and professional framework including:[2]	1
(i) the international standard-setting process	
(ii) the authority of national and international standards	
(iii) public oversight and principles of corporate governance	
(iv) the role of audit committees.	
(c) Discuss the effectiveness of the different ways in which the auditing profession and audit markets are regulated.[2]	1
2 Money laundering	
(a) Define 'money laundering'.[1]	7
(b) Explain how international efforts seek to combat money laundering.[2]	7
(c) Explain the scope of criminal offences of money laundering and how professional accountants may be protected from criminal and civil liability.[2]	7
(d) Explain the need for ethical guidance in this area.[2]	7
(e) Describe how accountants meet their obligations to help prevent and detect money laundering including record keeping and reporting of suspicion to a financial intelligence unit (FIU).[2]	7
(f) Explain the importance of customer due diligence (CDD).[2]	7
(g) Recognise potentially suspicious transactions and assess their impact on reporting duties.[2]	7
(h) Describe, with reasons, the basic elements of an anti-money laundering programme.[2]	7

3 Laws and regulations

(a) Compare and contrast the respective responsibilities of management and auditors concerning compliance with laws and regulations in an audit of financial statements.[2] 8

(b) Describe the auditors' considerations of compliance with laws and regulations and plan audit procedures when possible non-compliance is discovered.[2] 8

(c) Discuss how and to whom non-compliance should be reported.[2] 8

(d) Recognise when withdrawal from an engagement is necessary.[2] 8

B PROFESSIONAL AND ETHICAL CONSIDERATIONS

1 Code of ethics for professional accountants

(a) Explain the fundamental principles and the conceptual framework approach.[1] 2

(b) Identify, evaluate and respond to threats to compliance with the fundamental principles.[3] 2

(c) Discuss and evaluate the effectiveness of available safeguards.[3] 2

(d) Recognise and advise on conflicts in the application of fundamental principles.[3] 2

2 Fraud and error

(a) Define and clearly distinguish between the terms 'error', 'irregularity', 'fraud' and 'misstatement'.[2] 8

(b) Compare and contrast the respective responsibilities of management and auditors for fraud and error.[2] 8

(c) Describe the matters to be considered and procedures to be carried out to investigate actual and/or potential misstatements in a given situation.[2] 8

(d) Explain how, why, when and to whom fraud and error should be reported and the circumstances in which an auditor should withdraw from an engagement.[2] 8

(e) Discuss the current and possible future role of auditors in preventing, detecting and reporting error and fraud.[2] 8

3 Professional liability

(a) Recognise circumstances in which professional accountants may have legal liability.[2] 8

(b) Describe the factors to determine whether or not an auditor is negligent in given situations.[2] 8

(c) Explain the other criteria for legal liability to be recognised (including 'due professional care' and 'proximity') and apply them to given situations.[2] 8

(d) Compare and contrast liability to client with liability to third parties. [3] 8

(e) Comment on precedents of case law.[2] 8

(f) Evaluate the practicability and effectiveness of ways in which liability may be restricted, including professional indemnity insurance (PII).[3] 8

(g) Discuss how audit and other opinions may be affected by limiting auditors' liability.[2] 8

(h) Discuss the advantages and disadvantages of claims against auditors being settled out of court.[2] 8

(i) Discuss and appraise the principal causes of audit failure and other factors that contribute to the 'expectation gap' (e.g. responsibilities for fraud and error).[3] 8

(j) Recommend ways in which the expectation gap might be bridged. [2] 8

C PRACTICE MANAGEMENT

1 Quality control

(a) Explain the principles and purpose of quality control of audit and other assurance engagements.[1] 4

(b) Describe the elements of a system of quality control relevant to a given firm.[2] 4

(c) Select and justify quality control procedures that are applicable to a given audit engagement.[3] 4

(d) Assess whether an engagement has been performed in accordance with professional standards and whether reports issued are appropriate in the circumstances.[3] 4

2 Advertising, publicity, obtaining professional work and fees

(a) Explain the need for guidance in these areas.[2] 5

(b) Recognise situations in which specified advertisements are acceptable.[2] 5

(c) Discuss the restrictions on practice descriptions, the use of the ACCA logo and the names of practising firms.[2] 5

(d) Discuss the extent to which reference to fees may be made in promotional material.[2] 5

(e) Outline the determinants of fee-setting and justify the bases on which fees and commissions may and may not be charged for services.[3] 5

(f) Discuss the ethical and other professional problems involved in establishing and negotiating fees for a specified assignment.[3] 5

3 Tendering

(a) Discuss the reasons why entities change their auditors/professional accountants.[2] 6

(b) Recognise and explain the matters to be considered when a firm is invited to submit a proposal or fee quote for an audit or other professional engagement.[2] 6

(c) Identify the information required for a proposal.[2] 6

(d) Prepare the content of an engagement proposal document.[2] 6

(e) Discuss and appraise the criteria that might be used to evaluate tenders received from audit firms in a given situation.[3] 6

(f) Discuss reasons why audit fees may be lowered from the previous year's fees.[2] 6

(g) Explain 'lowballing' and discuss whether or not it impairs independence.[2] 6

4 Professional appointments

(a) Explain the matters to be considered and the procedures that an audit firm/professional accountant should carry out before accepting a specified new client/engagement including:[3] 3

(i) client acceptance

(ii) engagement acceptance

(iii) agreeing the terms of engagement.

(b) Recognise the key issues that underlie the agreement of the scope and terms of an engagement with a client.[2] 3

(c) Outline the procedures for the transfer of books, papers and information following a new appointment.[1] 3

D ASSIGNMENTS

1 The audit of historical financial information

(a) Describe the key features of the following audit methodologies:[1] 9

- (i) risk-based auditing
- (ii) 'top down' approach
- (iii) systems audit
- (iv) balance sheet approach
- (v) transaction cycle approach
- (vi) directional testing.

(b) Justify an appropriate approach to a given assignment and recognise when an approach is unsuitable.[3] 9

1 (i) Planning, materiality and assessing the risk of misstatement

(a) Specify the matters that should be considered in planning a given assignment including:[3] 10

- (i) logistics (e.g. staff and client management, multiple locations, deadlines)
- (ii) use of IT in administration
- (iii) time budgets
- (iv) assignment objectives and reports required
- (v) client interface (e.g. communication methods)
- (vi) preliminary materiality assessment
- (vii) key financial statement risks
- (viii)an overall audit strategy.

(b) Define materiality and demonstrate how it should be applied in financial reporting and auditing.[2] 10

(c) Apply the criteria that determine whether or not a matter is material and discuss the use and limitations of prescriptive rules in making decisions about materiality.[3] 10

(d) Identify and explain business risks in given situations.[2] 10

(e) Describe the factors that influence the assessment of a specified risk (e.g. inherent risk, financial statement risk) for a given assignment.[2] 10

(f) Explain how and why the assessments of risks and materiality affect the nature, timing and extent of auditing procedures in a given situation.[2] 10

(g) Select and apply appropriate risk assessment procedures, including analytical procedures, to obtain an understanding of a given entity and its environment.[3] 10

(h) Assess the risk of misstatement at the financial statement level and assertion level and design audit procedures in response to assessed risks.[3] 10

(i) Recognise and assess the implications of a specified computer system (e.g. network) on an assignment.[2] 10

1 (ii) Evidence

(a) Evaluate the appropriateness and sufficiency of different sources of audit evidence and the procedures by which evidence may be obtained including:[3] 12

- (i) analytical procedures
- (ii) management representations
- (iii) the work of others
- (iv) audit sampling
- (v) external confirmations
- (vi) audit automation tools.

(b) Specify audit procedures to obtain sufficient audit evidence from identified sources.[2] 12

(c) Apply the criteria for assessing the extent to which reliance can be placed on substantive analytical procedures and recognise situations in which analytical procedures may be used extensively.[3] 12

(d) Apply analytical procedures to financial and non-financial data.[2] 12

(e) Identify and evaluate the audit evidence expected to be available to:[3] 12

- (i) verify specific assets, liabilities, transactions and events; and
- (ii) support financial statement assertions and accounting treatm (including fair values).

(f) Explain the reasons for preparing and retaining documentation and the importance of reviewing working papers.[1] 12

(g) Explain the specific audit problems and procedures concerning related parties and related party transactions.[2] 12

(h) Recognise circumstances that may indicate the existence of unidentified related parties and select appropriate audit procedures.[2] 12

(i) Demonstrate the use of written management representations as the primary source of audit evidence and as complementary audit evidence.[2] 12

(j) Discuss the implications of contradictory evidence being discovered.[2] 12

(k) Recognise when it is justifiable to place reliance on the work of an expert (e.g. a surveyor employed by the audit client).[2] 12

(l) Assess the appropriateness and sufficiency of the work of internal auditors and the extent to which reliance can be placed on it.[2] 12

1 (iii) Evaluation and review

(a) Explain review procedures (including the use of analytical procedures and checklists) and assess their role in detecting material misstatements.[3] 13

(b) Evaluate findings quantitatively and qualitatively, e.g.:[3] 13

- (i) the results of audit tests and procedures
- (ii) the effect of actual and potential misstatements.

(c) Compare and contrast how the auditor's responsibilities for corresponding figures, comparative financial statements, 'other information', subsequent events and going concern are discharged.[3] 13

(d) Apply the further considerations and audit procedures relevant to initial engagements.[2] 13

(e) Discuss the courses of action available to an auditor if a material inconsistency or misstatement of fact exists.[2] 13

(f) Specify audit procedures designed to identify subsequent events that may require adjustment to, or disclosure in, the financial statements of a given entity.[2] 13

(g) List indicators that the going concern basis may be in doubt and recognise mitigating factors.[2] 13

(h) Evaluate the evidence that might be expected to be available and assess the appropriateness of the going concern basis in given situations.[3] 13

(i) Assess the adequacy of disclosures in financial statements relating to going concern and explain the implications for the auditor's report with regard to the going concern basis.[3] 13

(j) Evaluate the matters (e.g. materiality, risk, relevant accounting standards, audit evidence) relating to:[3] 13

(i) inventory

(ii) standard costing systems

(iii) cash flow statements

(iv) changes in accounting policy

(v) construction contracts

(vi) taxation

(vii) segment information

(viii) non-current assets

(ix) fair value

(x) leases

(xi) revenue recognition

(xii) employee benefits

(xiii)government grants and assistance

(xiv) borrowing costs

(xv) related parties

(xvi) earnings per share

(xvii) impairment

(xviii) provisions, contingent liabilities and contingent assets

(xix) goodwill

(xx) brands

(xxi) research and development

(xxii) other intangible assets

(xxiii) capital instruments

(xxiv) financial instruments

(xxv) investment properties

(xxvi) transition to International Financial Reporting Standards (IFRS)

(xxvii) share-based payment transactions

(xxviii) business combinations

(xxix) discontinued operations

(xxx) held for sale non-current assets

2 Group audits

(a) Recognise the specific matters to be considered before accepting appointment as principal auditor to a group in a given situation.[3] 11

(b) Compare and contrast the organisation, planning, management and administration issues specific to group audits with those of joint audits.[2] 11

(c) Recognise the specific audit problems and describe audit procedures in a given situation relating to:[3] 11

(i) the correct classification of investments

(ii) differing accounting policies and frameworks

(iii) fair values on acquisition

(iv) intangibles

(v) taxation

(vi) goodwill on consolidation

(vii) intra-group balances, transactions and profits

(viii) related parties

(ix) share options

(x) post balance sheet events

(xi) entities in developing countries.

(d) Discuss letters of support ('comfort letters') as audit evidence.[2] 11

(e) Identify and describe the matters to be considered and the procedures to be performed when a principal auditor uses the work of other auditors in a given situation.[3] 11

(f) Explain the implications for the auditor's report on the financial statements of an entity where the opinion on a component is qualified or otherwise modified in a given situation.[2] 11

3 Audit-related services

(a) Describe the nature of audit-related services, the circumstances in which they might be required and the comparative levels of assurance provided by professional accountants.[2] 16

(b) Distinguish between:[2] 16

(i) audit-related services and an audit of historical financial stater

(ii) an attestation engagement and a direct reporting engagement.

(c) Plan review engagements, for example:[2] 16

(i) a review of interim financial information

(ii) a 'due diligence' assignment (when acquiring a company, bus or other assets).

(d) Explain the importance of enquiry and analytical procedures in review engagements and apply these procedures.[2] 16

(e) Describe and apply the general principles and procedures relating to a compilation engagement (e.g. to prepare financial statements).[2] 16

(f) Explain why agreed-upon procedures and compilation engagements do not (usually) meet the requirements for an assurance engagement.[1] 16

(g) Illustrate the form and content of:[2] 16

(i) a report of factual findings

(ii) a compilation report.

4 Assurance services

(a) Describe the main categories of assurance services that audit firms can provide and assess the benefits of providing these services to management and external users:[3] 17

(i) risk assessments

(ii) business performance measurement

(iii) systems reliability

(iv) electronic commerce.

(b) Justify a level of assurance (reasonable, high, moderate, limited, negative) for an engagement depending on the subject matter evaluated, the criteria used, the procedures applied and the quality and quantity of evidence obtained.[3] 17

(c) Recognise the ways in which different types of risk (e.g. strategic, operating, information) may be identified and analysed and assess how management should respond to risk.[3] 17

(d) Recommend operational measures and describe how the reliability of performance information systems is assessed (including benchmarking).[2] 17

(e) Describe a value for money audit and recommend measures of economy, efficiency and effectiveness.[2] 17

(f) Explain the demand for reliable and more timely reporting on financial information and the development of continuous auditing. [2] 17

(g) Select procedures for assessing internal control effectiveness.[2] 17

(h) Describe how entities are using core technologies (e.g. EDI, e-mail, Internet, World Wide Web) and explain how e-commerce affects the business risk of a given entity.[2] 17

5 Prospective financial information

(a) Define 'prospective financial information' (PFI) and distinguish between a 'forecast', a 'projection', a 'hypothetical illustration' and a 'target'.[1] 18

(b) Explain the principles of useful PFI.[1] 18

(c) Identify and describe the matters to be considered before accepting a specified engagement to report on PFI.[2] 18

(d) Discuss the level of assurance that the auditor may provide and explain the other factors to be considered in determining the nature, timing and extent of examination procedures.[1] 18

(e) Describe examination procedures to verify forecasts and projections relating to:[2] 18

- (i) revenue
- (ii) capital expenditure
- (iii) revenue expenditure
- (iv) profits
- (v) cash flows
- (vi) working capital.

(f) Compare the content of a report on an examination of PFI with reports made in providing audit-related services.[2] 18

6 Forensic audits

(a) Define the terms 'forensic accounting', 'forensic investigation' and 'forensic audit'.[1] 19

(b) Describe the major applications of forensic auditing (e.g. fraud, negligence, insurance claims) and analyse the role of the forensic auditor as an expert witness.[2] 19

(c) Apply the fundamental ethical principles to professional accountants engaged in forensic audit assignments.[2] 19

(d) Select investigative procedures and evaluate evidence appropriate to determining the loss in a given situation.[3] 19

(e) Explain the terms under which experts make reports.[2] 19

7 Internal audit

(a) Compare the objectives and principal characteristics of internal audit with other assurance engagements.[2] 20

(b) Compare and contrast operational and compliance audits.[2] 20

(c) Justify a suitable approach (e.g. cyclical compliance) to specified multi-site operations.[3] 20

(d) Discuss outsourcing internal auditing services.[2] 20

8 Outsourcing

(a) Explain the different approaches to 'outsourcing' and compare with 'insourcing'.[2] 21

(b) Discuss and conclude on the advantages and disadvantages of outsourcing finance and accounting functions including:[3] 21

- (i) data (transaction) processing
- (ii) pensions
- (iii) information technology (IT)
- (iv) internal auditing
- (v) due diligence work
- (vi) taxes.

(c) Recognise and evaluate the impact of outsourced functions on the conduct of an audit.[3] 21

E REPORTING

1 Auditor's reports

(a) Critically appraise the form and content of a standard unmodified auditor's report.[3] 14

(b) Recognise and evaluate the factors to be taken into account when forming an audit opinion in a given situation.[3] 14

(c) Justify audit opinions that are consistent with the results of audit procedures relating to the sufficiency of audit evidence and/or compliance with accounting standards (including the going concern basis).[3] 14

(d) Draft extracts suitable for inclusion in an audit report.[3] 14

(e) Discuss the implications for the auditor's report on financial statements that report compliance with IFRSs.[2] 14

(f) Assess whether or not a proposed audit opinion is appropriate.[3] 14

(g) Discuss 'a true and fair view'.[2] 14

(h) Describe special purpose auditors' reports (e.g. on summarised financial statements) and analyse how and why they differ from an auditor's report on historical financial information.[2] 14

2 Reports to management

(a) Draft suitable content for a report to management, on the basis of given information, including statements of facts, their potential effects and appropriate recommendations for action.[3] 15

(b) Critically assess the quality of a management letter.[3] 15

(c) Advise on the content of reports to those charged with governance in a given situation.[3] 15

(d) Explain the need for timely communication, clearance, feedback and follow up.[2] 15

(e) Discuss the relative effectiveness of communication methods.[2] 15

3 Other reports

(a) Analyse the form and content of the professional accountant's report for an assurance engagement with an auditor's report.[2] 15

(b) Draft the content of a report on examination of prospective financial information.[2] 15

(c) Discuss the effectiveness of the 'negative assurance' form of reporting and evaluate situations in which it may be appropriate to express a reservation or deny a conclusion.[3] 15

F CURRENT ISSUES AND DEVELOPMENTS

Discuss the relative merits and the consequences of different standpoints taken in current debates and express opinions supported by reasoned arguments.

1 Professional, ethical and corporate governance

(a) Discuss the relative advantages of an ethical framework and a rulebook.[2] 2

(b) Evaluate the adequacy of existing ways in which objectivity may be safeguarded and suggest additional measures to improve independence.[3] 2

(c) Identify and assess relevant to emerging ethical issues and evaluate the safeguards available.[3] 2

(d) Discuss IFAC developments including:[2] 1

(i) the implementation and adoption of International Standards on Auditing (ISAs)

(ii) significant current assurance issues being dealt with by IAASB.

(e) Assess the relative advantages and disadvantages of partnership status, limited liability partnerships and incorporation of audit firms.[2] 1

(f) Discuss current developments in the limitation of auditors' liability and the practical ways in which the risk of litigation and liability can be reduced in a given situation.[3] 8

(g) Discuss innovations in corporate governance (e.g. enterprise-wide risk management) and their impact on boards of directors, audit committees and internal auditors.[3] 1

2 Information technology

(a) Describe recent trends in IT and their current and potential impact on auditors (e.g. the audit implications of 'cyberincidents' and other risks).[2] 17

(b) Explain how IT may be used to assist auditors and discuss the problems that may be encountered in automating the audit process.[2] 17

3 Transnational audits

(a) Define 'transnational audits' and explain the role of the Transnational Audit Committee (TAC) of IFAC.[1] 11

(b) Discuss how transnational audits may differ from other audits of historical financial information (e.g. in terms of applicable financial reporting and auditing standards, listing requirements and corporate governance requirements).[2] 11

(c) Discuss the need for international audit firm networks in implementing international auditing standards.[2] 11

(d) Distinguish, for example, between 'global auditing firms' and second tier firms.[2] 11

(e) Discuss the impact of globalisation on audit firms and their clients.[2] 11

(f) Explain the advantages and problems of current trends (e.g. to merge, to divest consultancy services).[2] 11

4 Social and environmental auditing

(a) Discuss the increasing importance of policies that govern the relationship of an organisation to its employees, society and the environment.[2] 17

(b) Describe the difficulties in measuring and reporting on economic, environmental and social performance and give examples of performance measures and sustainability indicators.[2] 17

(c) Explain the auditor's main considerations in respect of social and environmental matters and how they impact on entities and their financial statements (e.g. impairment of assets, provisions and contingent liabilities).[2] 17

(d) Describe substantive procedures to detect potential misstatements in respect of socio-environmental matters.[2] 17

(e) Discuss the form and content of an independent verification statement (e.g. on an environmental management system (EMS) and a report to society).[2] 17

5 Other current issues

(a) Discuss how the potential problems associated with the audit of small enterprises may be overcome.[2] 1

(b) Explain how International Standards on Auditing affect smaller firms.[2] 1

(c) Discuss the dominance of the global firms and their influence and impact on the accounting profession.[2] 1

(d) Discuss the impact of developments in public company oversight on external auditors.[2] 1

(e) Explain current developments in auditing standards including the need for new and revised standards and evaluate their impact on the conduct of audits.[3] 1

(f) Discuss other current legal, ethical, other professional and practical matters that affect accountants, auditors, their employers and the profession.[3] 7,8

The superscript numbers in square brackets indicate the intellectual depth at which the subject area could be assessed within the examination. Level 1 (knowledge and comprehension) broadly equates with the Knowledge module, Level 2 (application and analysis) with the Skills module and Level 3 (synthesis and evaluation) to the Professional level. However, lower level skills can continue to be assessed as you progress through each module and level.

The examination

Examination format

The examination is a three hour paper constructed in two sections. Questions in both sections will be almost entirely discursive. However, candidates will be expected, for example, to be able to assess materiality and calculate relevant ratios where appropriate.

Section A questions will be based on 'case study' type questions. That is not to say that they will be particularly long, rather that they will provide a setting within which a range of topics, issues and requirements can be addressed. Different types of question will be encountered in Section B and will tend to be more focused on specific topics, for example 'auditor's reports', 'quality control' and topics of ISAs which are not examinable in Paper F8 Audit and Assurance. (This does not preclude these topics from appearing in Section A.) Current issues will be examined across a number of questions.

	Number of marks
Section A	
Two compulsory questions	50–70
Section B	
Choice of two from three questions	30–50
	100

Total time allowed: 3 hours

Paper-based examination tips

Spend the first few minutes of the examination reading the paper.

Where you have a choice of questions, decide which ones you will do.

Unless you know exactly how to answer the question, spend some time **planning** your answer. Stick to the question and **tailor your answer** to what you are asked. Pay particular attention to the verbs in the question.

Spend the last five minutes reading through your answers and making any additions or corrections.

If you **get completely stuck** with a question, leave space in your answer book and return to it later.

If you do not understand what a question is asking, state your assumptions. Even if you do not answer in precisely the way the examiner hoped, you should be given some credit, if your assumptions are reasonable.

You should do everything you can to make things easy for the marker. The marker will find it easier to identify the points you have made if your answers are legible.

Essay questions: Your essay should have a clear structure. It should contain a brief introduction, a main section and a conclusion. Be concise. It is better to write a little about a lot of different points than a great deal about one or two points.

Computations: It is essential to include all your workings in your answers. Many computational questions require the use of a standard format. Be sure you know these formats thoroughly before the exam and use the layouts that you see in the answers given in this book and in model answers.

Scenario-based questions: Most questions will contain a hypothetical scenario. To write a good case answer, first identify the area in which there is a problem, outline the main principles/theories you are going to use to answer the question, and then apply the principles/theories to the case. It is vital that you relate your answer to the specific circumstances given.

Reports, memos and other documents: some questions ask you to present your answer in the form of a report or a memo or other document. So use the correct format – there could be easy marks to gain here.

Study skills and revision guidance

This section aims to give guidance on how to study for your ACCA exams and to give ideas on how to improve your existing study techniques.

Preparing to study

Set your objectives

Before starting to study decide what you want to achieve – the type of pass you wish to obtain. This will decide the level of commitment and time you need to dedicate to your studies.

Devise a study plan

Determine which times of the week you will study.

Split these times into sessions of at least one hour for study of new material. Any shorter periods could be used for revision or practice.

Put the times you plan to study onto a study plan for the weeks from now until the exam and set yourself targets for each period of study – in your sessions make sure you cover the course, course assignments and revision.

If you are studying for more than one paper at a time, try to vary your subjects as this can help you to keep interested and see subjects as part of wider knowledge.

When working through your course, compare your progress with your plan and, if necessary, re-plan your work (perhaps including extra sessions) or, if you are ahead, do some extra revision/practice questions.

Effective studying

Active reading

You are not expected to learn the text by rote, rather, you must understand what you are reading and be able to use it to pass the exam and develop good practice. A good technique to use is SQ3Rs – Survey, Question, Read, Recall, Review:

(1) **Survey the chapter** – look at the headings and read the introduction, summary and objectives, so as to get an overview of what the chapter deals with.

(2) **Question** – whilst undertaking the survey, ask yourself the questions that you hope the chapter will answer for you.

(3) **Read** through the chapter thoroughly, answering the questions and making sure you can meet the objectives. Attempt the exercises and activities in the text, and work through all the examples.

(4) **Recall** – at the end of each section and at the end of the chapter, try to recall the main ideas of the section/chapter without referring to the text. This is best done after a short break of a couple of minutes after the reading stage.

(5) **Review** – check that your recall notes are correct.

You may also find it helpful to re-read the chapter to try to see the topic(s) it deals with as a whole.

Note-taking

Taking notes is a useful way of learning, but do not simply copy out the text. The notes must:

- be in your own words
- be concise
- cover the key points
- be well-organised
- be modified as you study further chapters in this text or in related ones.

Trying to summarise a chapter without referring to the text can be a useful way of determining which areas you know and which you don't.

Three ways of taking notes:

Summarise the key points of a chapter.

Make linear notes – a list of headings, divided up with subheadings listing the key points. If you use linear notes, you can use different colours to highlight key points and keep topic areas together. Use plenty of space to make your notes easy to use.

Try a diagrammatic form – the most common of which is a mind-map. To make a mind-map, put the main heading in the centre of the paper and put a circle around it. Then draw short lines radiating from this to the main sub-headings, which again have circles around them. Then continue the process from the sub-headings to sub-sub-headings, advantages, disadvantages, etc.

Highlighting and underlining

You may find it useful to underline or highlight key points in your study text – but do be selective. You may also wish to make notes in the margins.

Revision

The best approach to revision is to revise the course as you work through it. Also try to leave four to six weeks before the exam for final revision. Make sure you cover the whole syllabus and pay special attention to those areas where your knowledge is weak. Here are some recommendations:

Read through the text and your notes again and condense your notes into key phrases. It may help to put key revision points onto index cards to look at when you have a few minutes to spare.

Review any assignments you have completed and look at where you lost marks – put more work into those areas where you were weak.

Practise exam standard questions under timed conditions. If you are short of time, list the points that you would cover in your answer and then read the model answer, but do try to complete at least a few questions under exam conditions.

Also practise producing answer plans and comparing them to the model answer.

If you are stuck on a topic find somebody (a tutor) to explain it to you.

Read good newspapers and professional journals, especially ACCA's **Student Accountant** – this can give you an advantage in the exam.

Ensure you **know the structure of the exam** – how many questions and of what type you will be expected to answer. During your revision attempt all the different styles of questions you may be asked.

Further reading

You can find further reading and technical articles under the student section of ACCA's website.

chapter

1

Regulation in a global economy

Chapter learning objectives

Upon completion of this chapter you will be able to:

- Explain the need for laws, regulations, standards and other guidance relating to audit, assurance and related services
- Outline and explain the need for the legal and professional framework including:
  - (i) the international standard-setting process
  - (ii) the authority of national and international standards
  - (iii) public oversight and principles of corporate governance
  - (iv) the role of audit committees.
- Discuss the effectiveness of the different ways in which the auditing profession and audit markets are regulated.

1 Introduction

Audit and assurance services play a vital role in maintaining confidence and stability in global financial markets and, therefore, the world economy.

Corporate failures have meant that governments have decided that the assurance industry cannot be relied upon to regulate itself. As a result mechanisms for regulation and for maintaining standards of corporate governance have been introduced.

In this chapter we will consider the reasons behind the mechanisms for regulating assurance services and how standards of corporate governance are maintained.

2 The need for assurance services

It's all about risk

A virtuous circle

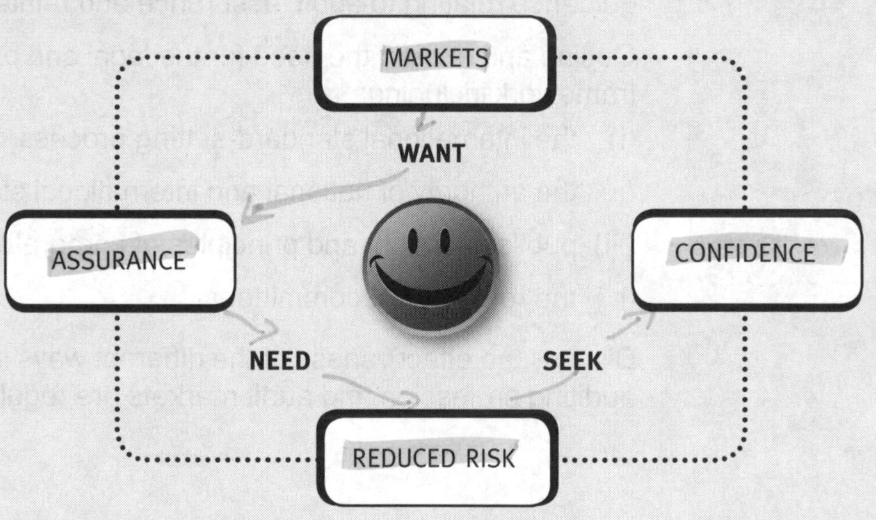

Why do clients pay for assurance services?

They do it to reduce their exposure to **RISK**.

It is imperative that decision makers within financial markets have the confidence to make informed decisions. In order to make these decisions they need information that they can trust.

It is not just shareholders that rely on this information; there are a range of other stakeholders who also rely on assurance services, such as government offices.

The nature of assurance services

Assurance professionals provide reports that give an independent opinion as to whether subject matter complies with pre-determined criteria. This enables the end user of that information to place more or less reliance on that information when making decisions.

3 The need for regulation

A vicious circle

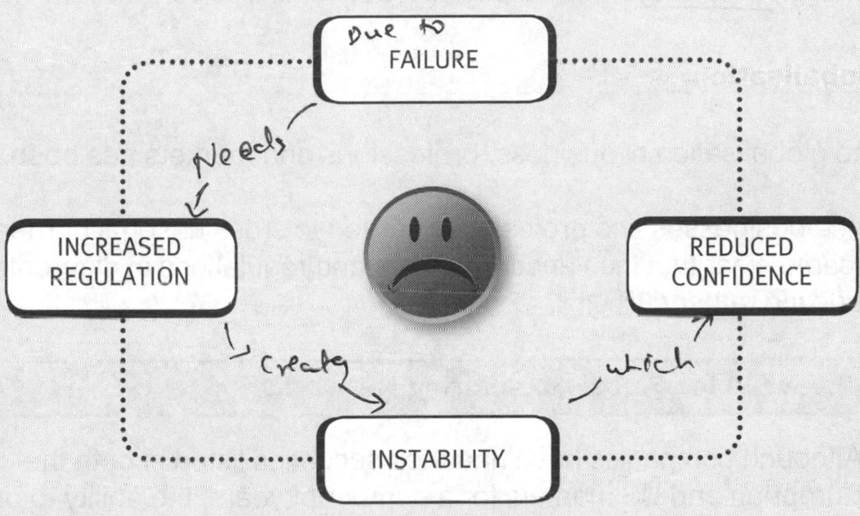

Introduction

Business failures, particularly large, high-profile businesses, disturb the virtuous circle of confidence within global financial markets.

The requirement for audited financial statements was seen as a way to reduce this risk and to protect:

- the owners of a business from unscrupulous management
- the world at large from abuse of limited liability status.

Self-regulation

Initially the system relied on self-regulation. In the 1970s the accountancy profession began to introduce standards to regulate financial reporting and shortly afterwards auditing standards were introduced.

Standards were set **by** the accounting profession **for** the accounting profession to follow.

Self-regulation seemed to make sense because:

- the accountancy organizations usually had a 'public interest' remit written into their constitutions
- they understood the business of financial reporting and auditing better than anyone.

However, two factors have led to the questioning of self-regulation as a satisfactory mechanism, which are:

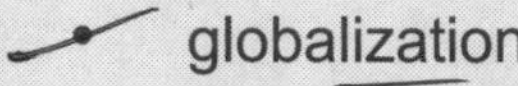

- globalization
- high-profile failures – especially, but not exclusively, Enron.

Globalisation

The globalisation of business, professions and markets has been rapid.

Once businesses and professions started to cross national borders it soon became clear that the variation of laws and regulations in different countries made life rather difficult.

The Need for Global Accounting Networks

Although companies have had their securities listed in both the European and US markets for a number of years, the ability to be based virtually anywhere in the world, and to manufacture, sell and manage businesses on a truly global basis is a more recent phenomenon. Global businesses need global professional firms to support, advise and audit them. The emergence of the 'big 4' global practices has been an accelerating process that has its origins in the 1970s. Similar globalization has happened in the banking and assurance industries and the introduction of external shareholders into the securities markets has led to, e.g. Nasdaq from the US investing in the London Stock Exchange.

IFAC

This realization led to the foundation of **IFAC** – the International Federation of Accountants in 1977.

IFAC is structured to operate through a network of boards and committees.

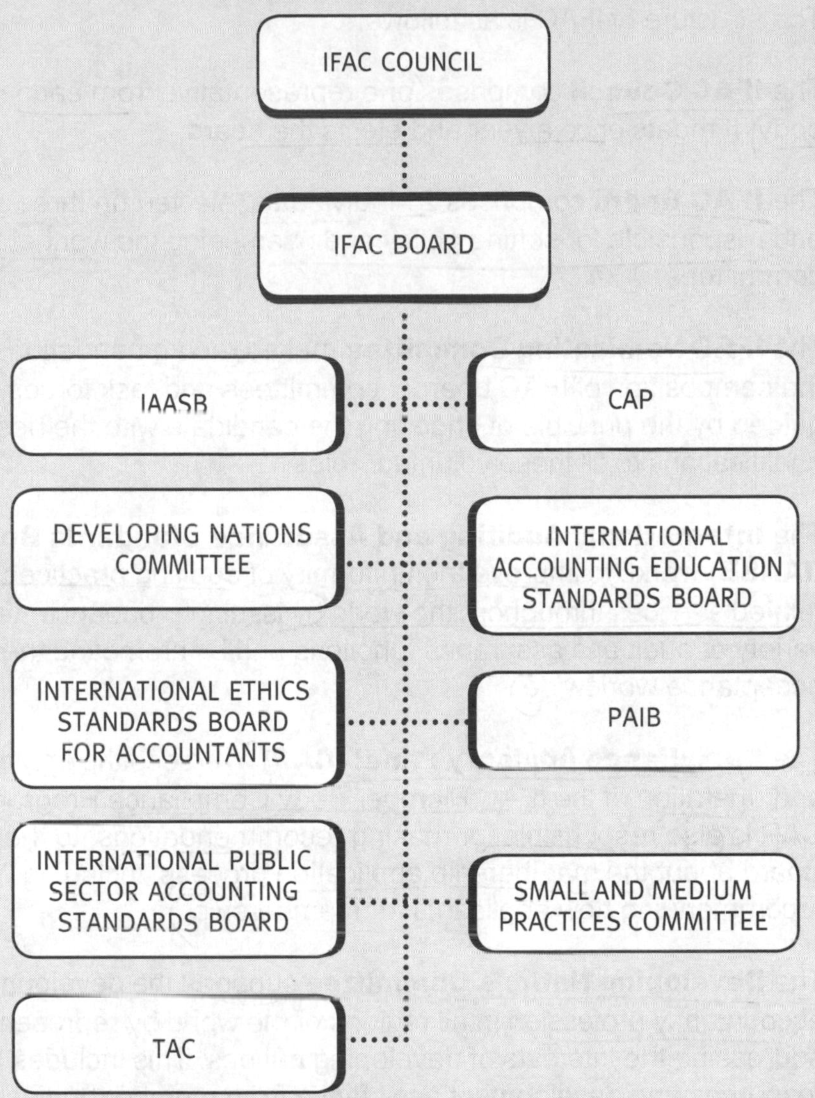

Detailed Explanation of IFAC Structure

International Federation of Accountants

The International Federation of Accountants (IFAC) is the global organization for the accountancy profession. It was formed in 1977 and is based in New York. IFAC has more than 160 member bodies of accountants (including the ACCA), representing 2.5 million accountants from 120 separate countries.

IFAC's overall mission is to serve the public interest, strengthen the worldwide accountancy profession, and contribute to the development of strong international economies by establishing and promoting adherence to high-quality professional standards.

The structure of IFAC is as follows:

The **IFAC Council** comprises one representative from each member body. It meets once a year and elects the board.

The **IFAC Board** comprises 21 individuals, elected on three-year terms and responsible for setting policy and overseeing the work of the various committees.

The **IFAC Nominating Committee** makes recommendations regarding the composition of IFAC boards, committees and task forces. It is guided by the principle of choosing the candidate with the best qualifications to fill these volunteer roles.

The **International Auditing and Assurance Standards Board (IAASB)** works to improve the uniformity of auditing practices and related services throughout the world by issuing pronouncements on a variety of audit and assurance functions and by promoting their acceptance worldwide.

The **Compliance Advisory Panel (CAP)** oversees the implementation and operation of the IFAC Member Body Compliance Program. The CAP is also responsible for making recommendations, to the IFAC Board about the membership application process, including recommending new applicants for membership.

The **Developing Nations Committee** supports the development of the accountancy profession in all regions of the world by representing and addressing the interests of developing nations. This includes seeking resources and development assistance from member bodies and other organizations on their behalf.

The **International Accounting Education Standards Board** (formerly the Education Committee) develops guidance, conducts research, and facilitates the exchange of information to ensure that accountants are adequately trained to meet their responsibilities to the public and their employers and to contribute to the worldwide harmonization of the profession. An important committee focus is assisting developing nations in the advancement of accounting education.

The **International Ethics Standards Board for Accountants** (formerly the Ethics Committee) develops guidance on professional ethics and promotes its understanding and acceptance by member bodies. Significantly, the committee continually monitors and stimulates debate on a wide range of ethical issues to ensure that its guidance is responsive to the expectations and challenges of individuals, businesses, financial institutions and others relying on accountants' work.

Professional Accountants in Business Committee (PAIB) publishes guidance, sponsors research programs – unless computer jargon, and facilitates the international exchange of ideas to develop and support financial and management accounting professionals. It also works to build public awareness, understanding and demand for the services of these professionals worldwide.

The **International Public Sector Accounting Standards Board** focuses on the accounting and financial reporting needs of national, regional and local governments, related governmental agencies, and the constituencies they serve. It addresses these needs by issuing and promoting benchmark guidance, conducting educational and research programs, and facilitating the exchange of information among accountants and those who work in the public sector or rely on their work.

The **Small and Medium Practices Committee** represents the interests of professional accountants operating in small- and medium-sized practices and other professional accountants who provide services to small- and medium-sized enterprises to international standard setters, IFAC boards and committees, and other international organizations.

The **Transnational Auditors Committee (TAC)** is the executive committee of the Forum of Firms (FoF) and a committee of IFAC. Membership in the FoF is open to all firms performing or wishing to perform transnational audits. Member firms will be expected, among other things, to conform to the FoF Quality Standards.

For your purposes you need to be clear about the existence of the following.

- IAASB (International Auditing and Assurance Standards Board) which develops and promotes ISAs and other assurance standards.
- The International Ethics Standards Board for Accountants which promotes the IFAC Code of Ethics.
- TAC (Transnational Auditors Committee) which deals with issues arising from the international dimension of audits.

IFAC took on the role of setting international standards for assurance engagements and quality control. It also developed its own code of ethics.

The trouble with IFAC

IFAC has encountered a number of difficulties in carrying out its role.

- it is financed by the accountancy profession and run by accountants;
- varying national interests; and
- the influence of a small number of large accountancy firms

Further Explanation of Troubles

- As it was set up by and continues to be financed by the accountancy profession worldwide it represents a self regulatory body. It is suggested that this is an inappropriate mechanism for regulating the audit profession.
- National interests still came into play leading to the implementation of international standards being bogged down in arguments between different national approaches.
- Its members are the professional accountancy bodies, whose authority, arguably, has been eclipsed to some extent by the power of the large professional firms.

The forum of firms

An attempt to overcome this last problem a 'Forum of Firms' was created. It was set up so that the largest accountancy practices could work alongside IFAC to develop International Standards on Assurance Engagements.

However, the demise of Andersens – a founder member of the Forum of Firms – in the wake of the Enron affair has not exactly helped the credibility of the whole process.

The Public Interest Oversight Board (PIOB)

A further development was the establishment of PIOB in 2005. PIOB has oversight of the IAASB and other public interest IFAC committees. Its members are drawn from the World Bank and the banking, insurance and securities industries with observers appointed by the EU. Clearly this represents external oversight. It is, nevertheless, voluntary.

The trouble with regulation in a global market

Going global – Regulation

The main problem is that harmonisation requires national regimes to adopt International Standards of Auditing. IFAC cannot impose them on a global scale. Many countries have adopted ISAs but they have been adapted to suit local customs/laws and as a result many differences still exist in the quality of audits worldwide.

The most recent attempt to encourage worldwide harmonisation was the Clarity Project (discussed in greater detail later on). This simplified the structures of ISAs and made them more prescriptive so that they are easier to understand and apply in practice.

And then there was Enron!

Enron is important because:

- creative accounting techniques were at the heart of the scandal;
- it was major, global company based in the US;
- its collapse had global repercussions; and
- it lead to the collapse of one of the (then) "Big 5" accounting firms.

What Happened at Enron?

Enron is not the only commercial collapse to have occurred. The UK provided a fertile source of examples during the 1980s and, in more recent years, there has been Parmalat, Hollinger and Worldcom to mention just three.

So what went wrong with Enron?

Before its bankruptcy, Enron employed approximately 22,000 and was one of the world's leading electricity, natural gas, and communications companies. In 2001 its revenue peaked at nearly $101 billion. However, much of the reported profit and position was sustained by institutionalized and systematic accounting fraud.

The scandal also caused the dissolution of Arthur Andersen, at that point one of the "Big 5" global accounting firms. The firm was found guilty of obstruction of justice for destroying documents related to the Enron audit and was forced to stop auditing public companies (although the conviction was thrown out by the US Supreme Court in 2005).

The story can be briefly summarised as follows:

- a significant portion of Enron's profits were the result of deals with special purpose entities (SPE's), which it controlled.
- many of the entities were offshore, which – in summary – allowed Enron to avoid taxes, move currency and hide overall company losses.
- Enron used an accounting technique known as marking to market (MTM), which effectively meant that Enron could recognize sales and earnings on deals way before the actual transactions crystallised.
- the huge profits reported drove up the stock price. This allowed executives (who knew about the offshore accounts and hidden losses!) to trade millions of dollars worth of Enron stock (to their own benefit).
- the share price began to fall and so the off balance sheet liabilities put pressure on the debt agreements, which eventually led to credit downgrades
- the margins were very thin and the lower credit rating increased the cost of Enron's borrowing to the point where the whole company fell into a liquidity trap
- and then … the veil was lifted and the extent of mis-reporting exposed…

What happened at Enron?

Weak ethical leadership was partly to blame. In 1987 it was discovered that several Enron traders were booking and settling falsified trades. Ken Lay, the CEO, reorganized the unit and altered its reporting structure. Rich Kinder, the COO, wanted the operation shut down. Within months the traders repeated the fraud and further losses were incurred.

However there was a deep flaw running right the way through Enron's corporate culture. Were these failures in ethical and business judgment caused by a few people at the top or was the flaw endemic within the whole business?

The fallout for the regulation of audits

The results of the financial scandals – and the public concern that followed – were:

- In the US – The Sarbanes Oxley Act (Sarbox) led to the setting up of the Public Company Accounting Oversight Board with monitoring rights over the files of the auditors of Public Interest bodies in the US and their affiliates abroad.
- In the EU – the introduction of ISAs as the only auditing standards for EU audits and the adoption of ISAs by national standard setting bodies
- In the UK this has led to the end of self-regulation of the audit profession by:
  - the national auditing standard setter – the Auditing Practices Board (APB) – being brought under the control of the Financial Reporting Council (FRC), the regulatory authority for all financial reporting matters in the UK
  - the creation and promotion of Ethical Standards for Audits
  - the establishment of the Professional Oversight Board (POB) with responsibility for oversight of the accountancy and actuarial professions
  - the establishment of the Audit Inspection Unit (AIU) to monitor the quality of the audits of public interest bodies
  - the establishment of the Accountancy Investigation and Disciplinary Board (AIDB)

In summary

- ISAs are set by an international, self-regulating body. (IAASB)
- National regulators oversee national accountancy bodies operating through Oversight Boards.
- National standard setters have adopted ISAs, which they modify for local purposes.

Providing Some Clarity

In 2004 the International Audit and Assurance Standards Board began a comprehensive overhaul of all the International Standards of Auditing (ISAs). The aim of the project was to issue a set of updated ISAs, which were easier to understand and encouraged more consistent standards of auditing across the world. The new "Clarified" ISAs became effective for audits beginning on, or after, 15 December 2009.

In order to achieve this aim the ISAs have been redrafted to make their objectives and the responsibilities of the auditor clearer. As a result all standards now adopt the following structure:

- Introduction;
- Objective;
- Definitions;
- Requirements; and
- Application and other explanatory information.

The language used in the standards is also less ambiguous, making it clear exactly what is expected of an auditor applying ISAs. In addition to redrafting the existing standards, a number of them have also been revised with the aim of improving audit practice. This means that the guidance provided has been updated to reflect current issues and developments.

In August 2009 the P7 examiner published an article entitled "The IAASB Clarity Project," which summarises the key changes from the old regime. This article can be found on the ACCA website.

IFIAR

IFIAR – a postscript

In September 2006, the national regulatory bodies from Australia, Austria, Brazil, Canada, Denmark, France, Germany, Ireland, Italy, Japan, Mexico, the Netherlands, Norway, Singapore, South Africa, Spain, Sweden, and the United Kingdom, announced the establishment of the International Forum of Independent Audit Regulators (IFIAR). PCAOB from the US was an observer, as were the bodies behind PIOB. The EU also sent observers. Its first meeting took place in Tokyo in March 2007.

It is possible, therefore, that a global regulatory authority may emerge. It is possible that it will set its own assurance standards, thereby supplanting IFAC and the ISA setting process. But then again …

4 Corporate Governance

Introduction

The chapter has so far looked at mechanisms external to the audit firm and their clients (auditing standards, company law and the regulatory framework) that aid confidence and stability in the market place. The next section introduces an internal mechanism, namely corporate governance,and how its principles are enforced.

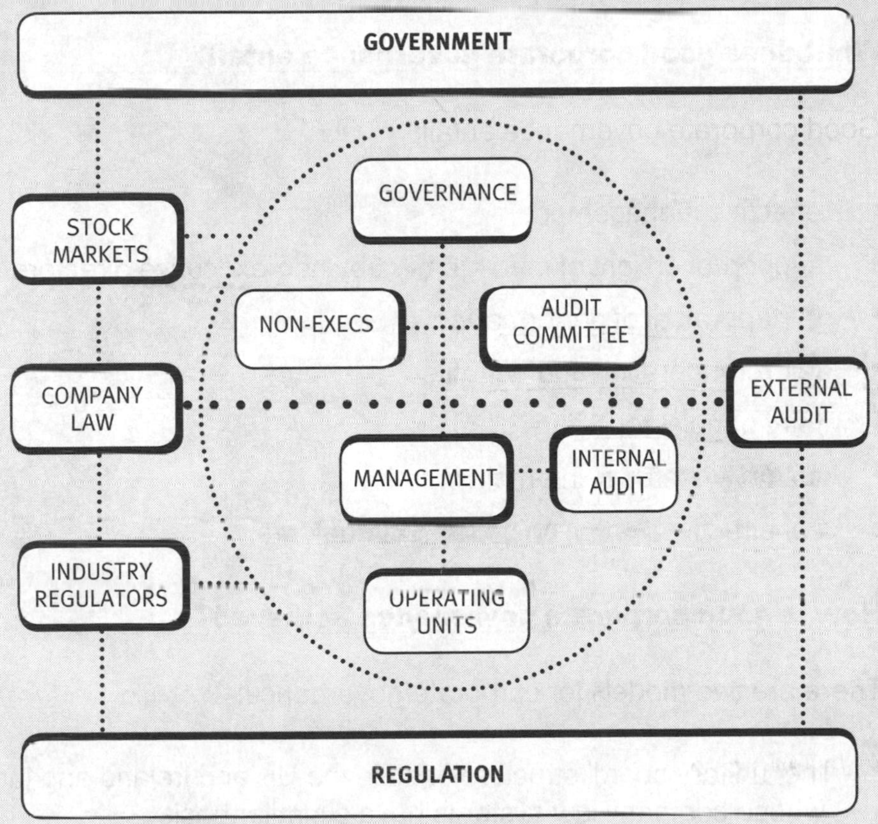

What is corporate governance?

Corporate governance is about ensuring that public companies are:

- managed effectively
- for the benefit of the company and its shareholders.

Why all the fuss?

Corporate governance pronouncements tend to happen in response to corporate scandals that arise because unscrupulous management has:

- manipulated the share price for personal gain
- disguised poor results /mismanagement
- extracted funds from the company
- raised finance fraudulently.

What does good corporate governance entail?

Good corporate governance entails:

- effective management
- support/oversight of management by non-executive directors
- fair appraisal of performance
- fair remuneration and benefits
- fair financial reporting
- sound systems of internal control
- constructive relationship with shareholders.

How is good corporate governance achieved?

There are two models for corporate governance:

- the 'unitary board' structure used in the UK and Ireland and jurisdictions whose company law systems have a similar basis
- the 'supervisory board' structure used in the US and similar jurisdictions.

Board Structures

The unitary board structure

Features of unitary board structure are:

- collective board responsibility
- no distinction in law between the responsibilities of executive and non-executive directors
- the need to distinguish between the function of executive and non-executive directors

- the need to establish board committees to monitor and act on different functions – nominating committee, remuneration committee, audit committee, etc.

The supervisory board structure, which has complete separation of powers between:

- executive management with operational responsibility for running the business – the CEO, CFO, Vice presidents, etc.
- the board, with its remuneration and audit committees, etc., which has purely an oversight role.

How corporate governance is enforced

Good corporate governance can be enforced:

- by law
- by agreement through codes of best practice or
- through a combination of the two.

In the **US**, post Enron this was achieved through the introduction of the Sarbanes Oxley Act, which, as well as dealing with the oversight of auditors (see above), also covers:

- sound systems of controls
- clear documentation of financial processes, procedures, risks, and controls
- evidence that management have evaluated the adequacy of the design and the effectiveness of operation of the procedures and controls
- evidence that the auditor has adequately evaluated the design and operation of financial controls
- evidence that the audit committee and/or disclosure committee have taken a keen interest in the effectiveness of controls
- explicit 'sign off' procedures by the chief executive and chief financial officer.

Sarbanes Oxley

Sarbanes Oxley – Overview of the act

'The primary benefit is to provide the company, its management, its board and audit committee, and its owners and other stakeholders with a reasonable basis to rely on the company's financial reporting.

The integrity of financial reporting represents the foundation upon which this country's public markets are built.'

The key characteristics of Section 302

CEO and CFO need to certify that:

- the SEC report being filed has been reviewed
- the report does not contain any untrue statements or omit any material facts
- the financial statements fairly present the financial position, results of operations and cash flows of the registrant
- they are responsible for, and have designed, established, and maintained disclosure controls and procedures as well as evaluated and reported on the effectiveness of those controls and procedures within 90 days of the report filing date
- deficiencies and material weaknesses in disclosure controls and procedures have been disclosed to the registrant's audit committee and external auditors
- significant changes in internal control affecting internal controls in the period have been reported.

The key characteristics of Section 404

With the filing of their accounts, companies are required to include an annual internal control report of management over financial reporting including:

- responsibilities for establishing and maintaining adequate internal controls and procedures
- conclusions about the effectiveness of the company's internal controls and procedures
- an attestation by the company's registered public accounting firm on management's evaluation.

This contrasts with the approach in **the UK**.

While the UK has longstanding and wide ranging laws governing the operation of companies, the main driver of good corporate governance comes from the 'Combined Code' (last updated in 2003) under which all listed companies are supposed to operate.

Its main provisions are:

- collective responsibility of the (unitary) board
- segregation of role of the Chairman and Chief Executive
- good practice for appointments to the board ensuring people with the necessary abilities are appointed
- arrangements for the development of board members
- suitable balance between executive and non-executive directors
- board members should receive complete, relevant, well presented information on a timely basis
- good practice for evaluating the performance of directors
- regular re-election of board members and planned refreshing of board membership over time
- fair remuneration through a remuneration committee
- fair financial reporting
- sound internal controls
- appropriate relationship with the external auditors
- appropriate relationship and communication with shareholders.

5 Audit committees

Objectives of audit committees

- Increasing public confidence in the credibility and objectivity of published financial information.
- Assisting directors in meeting their responsibilities in respect of financial reporting.
- Strengthening the independent position of a company's external auditor.

Membership of audit committees

- A group of independent, non-executive directors
- At least one member should have recent and relevant financial experience.
- Committee members should be independent of operational management.

The functions of an audit committee

These could include the following.

- Review of a company's internal control procedures.
- Review of the internal audit function – the audit committee providing an independent reporting channel.
- Review of the company's current accounting policies and possible changes resulting from the introduction of new accounting standards.
- Review of regular management information (for example, monthly management accounts).
- Review of the annual financial statements presented to shareholders.
- Receiving and dealing with external auditors' criticisms of management, and ensuring that recommendations of internal and external auditors have been implemented.
- Recommending nomination and remuneration of the external auditors.
- Ensuring compliance with codes of practice on corporate governance set out by stock exchanges or other similar institutions.
- Providing a reporting channel for 'whistleblowing'.

Advantages of audit committees

- They may improve the quality of management accounting, being better placed to criticize internal functions.
- They should lead to better communication between the directors, external auditors and management.
- They help to avoid conflicts arising between management and auditors.

Potential areas of difficulty for audit committees

Audit committees may lead to:

- fear that their purpose is to catch management out

- non-executive directors being over-burdened with detail
- a 'two-tier' board of directors
- additional cost in terms of, at the least, time involved.

Test your understanding 1 – 'Becher'

Becher are an independent construction company, dealing with large scale contracts throughout the UK and with some international interest in Europe, particularly in Spain. Becher have recently established an Audit Committee, the members of which are very concerned about meeting corporate governance 'best practice', particularly since they are currently looking at the possibility of obtaining a stock exchange listing.

You are an internal auditor with the company and have been asked to conduct a review of how well the company is meeting relevant corporate governance requirements.

You are required to prepare a report that addresses the following.

(a) What is meant by 'corporate governance' and why is it important that companies should comply with relevant corporate governance requirements?

(4 marks)

(b) What are the key issues for Becher to address to achieve effective corporate governance?

(5 marks)

(c) What is the role of internal audit in achieving corporate governance compliance?

(4 marks)

(d) What should the role of the Audit Committee in relation to corporate governance be?

(4 marks)

(e) List the types of regular reporting that would be useful for Becher in the context of establishing sound corporate governance.

(3 marks)

6 Chapter summary

This chapter has covered the following topics:

- the reasons for regulating the audit and assurance professions
- the difficulties facing national and international regulators in the global economy
- the difficulties facing national and international standard setting bodies
- the need for good standards of corporate governance
- how standards of corporate governance are maintained
- the function of the audit committee.

Test your understanding answers

Test your understanding 1 – 'Becher'

Report to the Audit Committee

(a) **Corporate Governance**

Corporate Governance concerns the way that a company is directed and controlled. It encompasses the following key aspects:

– The role of the Board and Audit Committee.
– Overall control and risk management framework.

Corporate Governance has become increasingly important to all organisations, particularly those with a stock exchange listing. For example, in the UK such companies are subject to the requirements of the Combined Code and the Turnbull report. Management and control is often more difficult to achieve in larger, more complex organisations. In addition, shareholders (the owners) tend to be more remote from the directors who manage the company on their behalf.

The Turnbull report for example requires that companies have an ongoing process for identifying, evaluating and managing the company's key risks. This process should comply with the Turnbull guidelines, and should be regularly reviewed by the Board. Failure by a company to comply with relevant corporate governance requirements could result in a qualification in the audit report and could damage the company's image and reputation.

(b) **Requirements of Corporate Governance**

Becher need to ensure that the following key requirements are met:

– **Evaluate risks within the organisation.** The key risks throughout the organisation need to be identified, measured and reported.
– **Consider the nature and extent of the risks regarded as acceptable.** There needs to be a clear understanding of the risk attitude of Becher.
– **Assess the chances of such risks materialising and their likely impact.**

- **Evaluate the ability of the company** to reduce incidence and impact if risks arise. This will include a review of the contingency arrangements which are in place.
- **Costs and benefits relating to operating relevant controls will need to be considered.**
- The Board and Audit Committee need to establish a **culture** in the company which is responsive to the requirements of sound corporate governance.
- **Regular reporting** should be in place to demonstrate that risks are being managed on an ongoing basis.

(c) **Role of Internal Audit**

Turnbull says that an independent and adequately resourced internal audit function should be in a position to provide the Board with much of the assurance it requires regarding the effectiveness of the system of internal control.

Internal Audit's main role is normally to evaluate risk and monitor the effectiveness of the system of internal control.

The precise role of internal audit will depend on the nature and type of organisation and what other risk type functions are in existence within the company.

Key internal audit procedures will be to:

- review the company's measures to achieve corporate governance
- ensure that the Internal Audit Department's operation is consistent with the major risks facing the organisation
- produce analysis of and opinions on the effectiveness of the organisation's control mechanisms, which should be communicated regularly to the Board and Audit Committee.

(d) **Role of the Audit Committee**

The role and importance of the Audit Committee has increased as the corporate governance requirements have been strengthened. The Audit Committee should have at least three non-executive directors who should be independent of the company in that they have no direct involvement in the day to day running of its affairs.

The Audit Committee should:

- assess the framework for complying with corporate governance guidelines within the company, including the risk assessment procedures

- review the major risks identified including their chances of occurring and their likely impact
- require regular reporting from internal and external auditors and any other review bodies, showing how the risks are being managed
- receive and review internal audit assignment reports and follow up information
- discuss and consider any concerns of directors and internal audit staff
- review annual financial statements and the results of the external auditors' examination to ensure that the auditors have performed an effective, efficient and independent audit
- receive and deal with external auditors' comments on management and ensure that recommendations of internal and external auditors have been implemented.

(e) **Types of Regular Reporting**

Types of regular reporting that could be produced for the Audit Committee include:

- listing of current major risks and up-to-date assessment of impact and likelihood
- reports on control of risks including how they are being managed
- details of any issues / concerns that have arisen since the last report
- audit reports issued and impact on corporate governance
- information on follow up on outstanding risks and findings from reports.

chapter

2

Code of ethics and conduct

Chapter learning objectives

Upon completion of this chapter you will be able to:

- explain the fundamental principles and the conceptual framework approach
- identify, evaluate and respond to threats to compliance with the fundamental principles
- discuss and evaluate the effectiveness of available safeguards
- recognize and advise on conflicts in the application of fundamental principles.

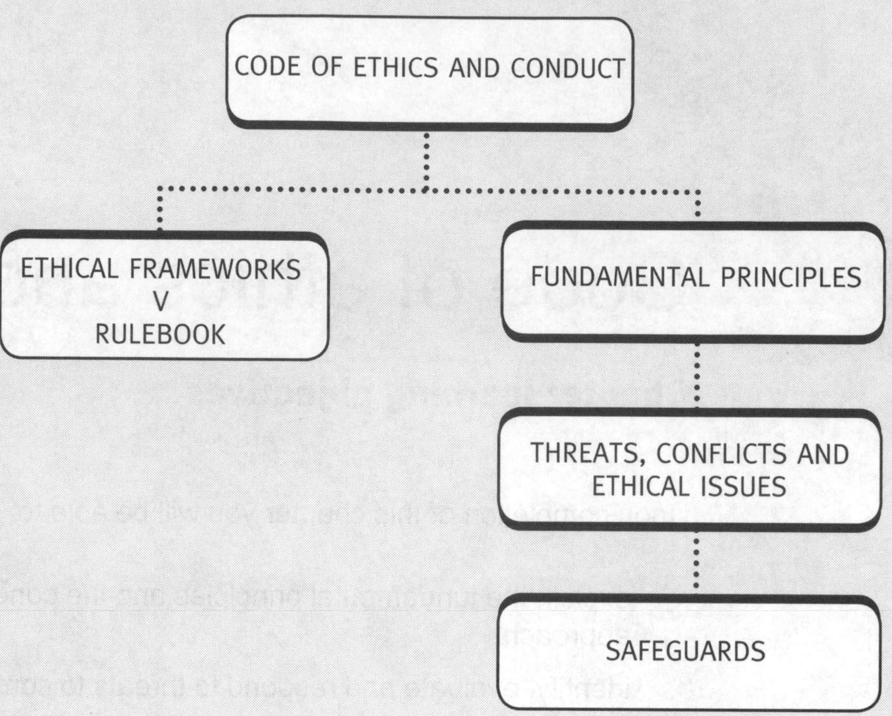

1 Framework Versus Rulebook Approach to Ethical Guidance

Ethical guidance can either be principles-based (a conceptual framework approach) or rules-based.

Advantages of a 'rulebook' approach

- Certainty.
- Clarity regarding what is not permitted.

However, it is virtually impossible for rule-based systems to be able to deal with every situation that may arise, particularly across various national boundaries and in a dynamic industry.

They can also be interpreted narrowly in order to circumvent the underlying 'spirit' or intention of the rule.

Advantages of an 'ethical framework' approach

An ethical framework approach has advantages over rule-based systems.

- A framework is more appropriate to changing circumstances in a dynamic profession.
- Principles may be applied across national boundaries, where laws may not.

- The onus is placed on the auditor to demonstrate that **all matters** are considered within the principles of the framework.
- A framework approach may include some specific 'prohibitions' or deal with specific matters.

Both IFAC and the ACCA have decided on a principles-based approach.

Sources of ethical guidance for accountants

THE IFAC CODE OF ETHICS FOR PROFESSIONAL ACCOUNTANTS ········ THE ACCA CODE OF ETHICS AND CONDUCT ········ ACCA MEMBERS AND STUDENTS

- The International Ethics Standards Board for Accountants (IESBA) operates under the auspices of the International Federation of Accountants (IFAC).
- IESBA develops the IFAC Code of Ethics for Professional Accountants, which applies to all professional accountants, whether in public practice or not.
- The IFAC Code serves as the foundation for codes of ethics developed and enforced by member bodies of IFAC.
- Any ethical guidance issued by a member body of IFAC must be at least as stringent as the IFAC Code.

The ACCA is a member body of IFAC. The ACCA's ethical guidance, based on the IFAC Code, is set out in the Code of Ethics and Conduct in Section 3 of the ACCA Rulebook for members.

The fundamental principles

All ACCA members and students are obliged to follow the fundamental principles.

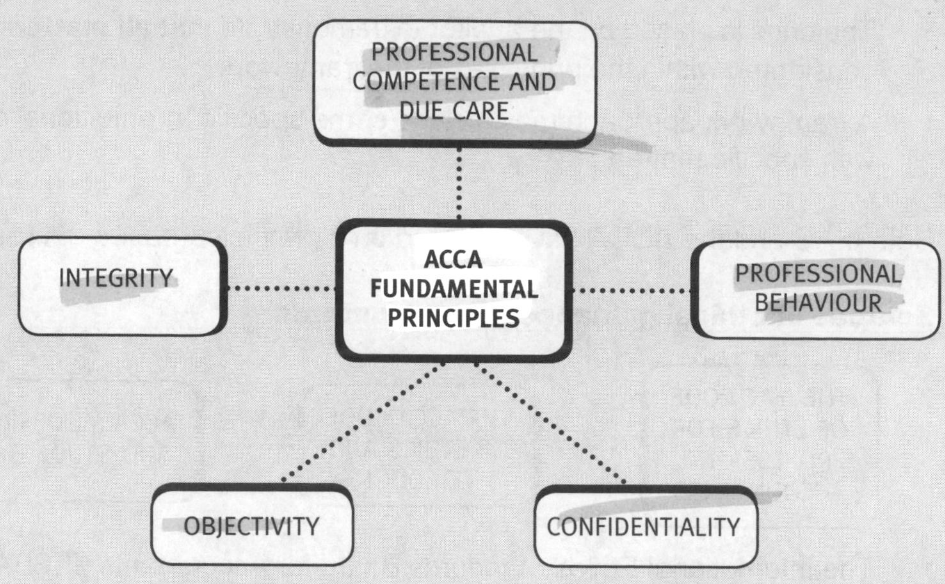

Ethics Definitions

- **Integrity:** Members should be straightforward and honest in all professional and business relationships.
- **Objectivity:** Members should not allow bias, conflicts of interest or undue influence of others to override professional or business judgments.
- **Professional competence and due care:** Members have a continuing duty to maintain professional knowledge and skill at a level required to ensure that a client or employer receives competent professional service based on current developments in practice, legislation and techniques. Members should act diligently and in accordance with applicable technical and professional standards when providing professional services.
- **Confidentiality:** Members should respect the confidentiality of information acquired as a result of professional and business relationships and should not disclose any such information to third parties without proper and specific authority or unless there is a legal or professional right or duty to disclose. Confidential information acquired as a result of professional and business relationships should not be used for the personal advantage of members or third parties.
- **Professional behaviour:** Members should comply with relevant laws and regulations and should avoid any action that discredits the profession.

2 Applying the conceptual framework approach

The threats

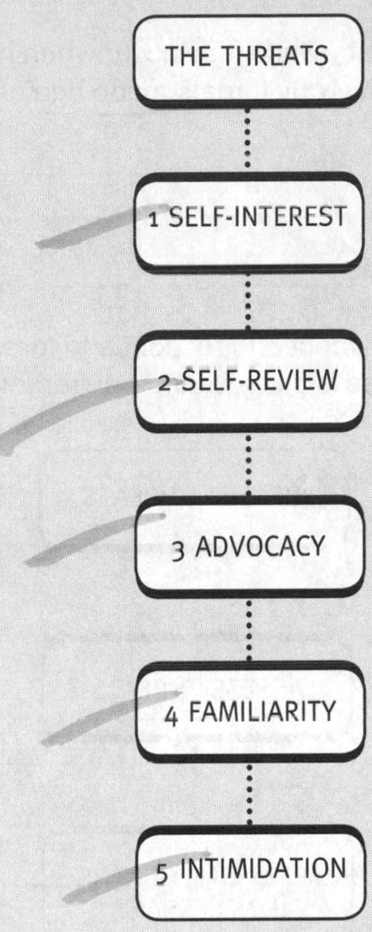

Threat Definitions

Both the IFAC Code and the ACCA Code set out the broad range of categories that the threats fall into.

(1) **Self-interest threat** (which may occur as a result of financial or other interests of members or their close family, e.g. due to financial interests in clients in the form of shares, or personal relationships, e.g. when family members are employed at a client).

(2) **Self-review threat** (which may occur when a previous judgment made by a member has to be re-evaluated by that member, for example, as would be the case if an accountant compiled a set of financial statements and then audited them).

(3) **Advocacy threat** (which may occur when members act as an advocate for – i.e. speaking on behalf of – a client by supporting management in an adversarial context, e.g. acting as a legal advocate for a client in litigation).

(4) **Familiarity threat** (which may occur when members become too sympathetic to a client's interest through a close relationship with them).

(5) **Intimidation threat** (which may occur when members are deterred from acting objectively by threats made against them, such as the threat of litigation).

Threats and safeguards

The identification, assessment and response to threats to compliance with the fundamental principles is a key exam requirement.

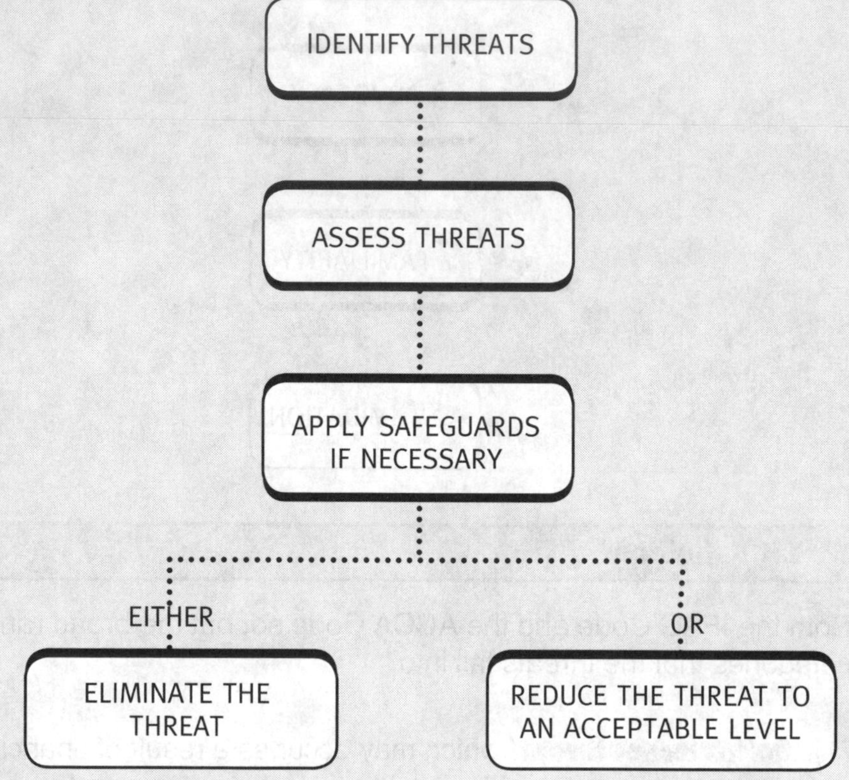

Assessing Threats

- In any given situation, an accountant may face circumstances that could prevent him from complying with the Fundamental Principles. Such circumstances are called threats.
- The scale of these threats must be assessed.
- If a threat is other than clearly insignificant, then the accountant must apply procedures (called safeguards) to either eliminate the threat or to reduce it to an acceptable level.
- A threat is acceptable when a reasonable and informed third party would probably not conclude that the accountant's compliance with the Fundamental Principles was impaired.

The ACCA Code sets out three general types of safeguard that can be put in place to guard against threats.

(1) Safeguards created by the profession, legislation or regulation.

(2) Safeguards in the work environment.

(3) Safeguards created by the individual.

Examples of safeguards per the ACCA Code

Safeguards created by the profession	**Safeguards in the work environment**	**Safeguards created by the individual**
• educational requirements for entry into the profession • continuing professional development (CPD) requirements • corporate governance requirements (e.g. the Combined Code) • professional standards (e.g. the IFAC Code of Ethics and the IAASB's ISAs)	• each employer should have a publicized ethical code of conduct and visible ethical leadership • strong internal controls • consultation with another professional accountant in areas of uncertainty	• complying with CPD requirements • keeping up to date with professional standards • maintaining contact with the ACCA

Ethics and the auditor

Threats to an auditor of not complying with the fundamental principles

An auditor is a professional accountant, so must comply with the IFAC Code and Fundamental Principles. As an ACCA member, auditors must comply with the ACCA Code and Fundamental Principles.

The principal threats must be considered during all stages of a professional engagement. In addition to the threats identified previously auditors must also be careful to avoid 'management threats.' These arise where auditors take decisions that are the responsibility of management.

Confidentiality

The rule

Members acquiring information in the course of their professional work should not disclose such information to third parties without first obtaining permission from the client, unless there is a legal right or duty to disclose, or it is in the public interest to do so.

Role of confidentiality

It is important in the auditor-client relationship that the client trusts the auditor to observe confidentiality to ensure that all information necessary for the audit is communicated or made available to the auditor.

Circumstances in which disclosure is permitted or required

The general rule is that disclosure should only be made if:

- the client's permission has been given
- the client is suspected of treason, terrorism, drug trafficking, or money laundering
- such disclosure is required to protect the member's interests
- required by law
- it is in the public interest.

Public Interest

There is no official definition of the public interest, so the auditor must use his or her judgment together with legal advice obtained. The auditor would consider:

- the materiality of the monetary values involved
- whether members of the public are likely to be involved
- the seriousness of the matter
- the likelihood of repetition of the problem
- the reasons for the client's unwillingness to make the disclosures
- relevant legislation, accounting standards and auditing standards
- legal advice obtained.

Conflicts of interest

A conflict of interest concerning objectivity or confidentiality can arise where an auditor acts for both a client company and also for a competitor company of the client.

- There is nothing improper in a firm having two or more clients whose interests may be in conflict.
- In such a case, however, the work of the firm should be so managed as to avoid the interests of one client adversely affecting those of another.
- Where the acceptance or continuance of an engagement would, even with safeguards, materially prejudice the interests of any client, the appointment should not be accepted or continued, or one of the appointments should be discontinued.

Safeguards against conflicts of interest

Reasonable steps that should be taken to minimize conflicts of interest include the following:

- the use of different partners and teams of staff for different engagements
- standing instructions and all other steps necessary to prevent the leakage of confidential information between different teams and sections within the firm

- regular review of the situation by a senior partner or compliance officer not personally involved with either client
- advising at least one or all clients to seek additional advice. This should obviously be seen as a last resort.

'Chinese Walls'

Accountancy firms can set up internal arrangements within their firms so that two groups of employees do not mix with each other and undertake not to discuss their work with members of the other group. Such arrangements are known as 'Chinese Walls', perhaps because the Great Wall of China was effective in separating China from the outside world.

Some commentators believe the term 'Chinese Walls' is culturally insensitive and have argued for its removal from business use, but for the time being it remains in common use.

3 The auditor's integrity, objectivity and independence

Areas of risk to integrity, objectivity and independence

Common examples of threats to the auditor's integrity, objectivity and independence arise from:

- personal relationships between the auditor and the client
- financial and business relationships between the auditor and the client
- undue economic dependence on an audit client
- acceptance by the auditor of goods and services or hospitality from the client
- provision of non-audit services to an audit client (key ethical issue)
- overdue fees
- litigation between the auditor and the client.

Discussion of Threats to Independence

Discussion of possible threats to integrity, objectivity and independence

Relationships

(1) **Family and other personal relationships**

A member's objectivity may be threatened (or appear to be threatened) as a consequence of entering into a professional engagement with a client managed by a family member or someone with whom the auditor has a close relationship.

Possible safeguards

- Remove the individual from the engagament team.
- Structure the engagement team so that the individual does not deal with matters that are the responsibility of the close family member.

(2) **Business relationships**

Audit firms should not enter into business relationships with clients, e.g. run a joint venture together. The self-interest threat is so great that **no safeguards can reduce the threat to an acceptable level**. Either the business relationship must be terminated, or the audit firm must resign from the audit.

(3) **Financial interests**

A member's objectivity may be threatened (or appear to be threatened) where they hold a beneficial interest in the shares, or some other form of investment, in a company upon which the practice reports.

Possible safeguards:

- Dispose of the shares
- Remove the individual from the audit team.
- Do not undertake loan or guarantee arrangements with clients (except where the loan is in the normal course of business and the transaction is at arm's length)

Staffing

(1) **Long association of audit personnel with audit clients**

Using the same senior personnel in an audit team over a long period may create a familiarity threat to objectivity.

Possible safeguards:

- rotate the senior personnel serving on the audit team;
- Additional partner reviews.

The ACCA Code states that, for the audit of listed companies, the **engagement partner should be rotated after normally no more than five years,** and should not return to the engagement for a further five years.

(2) **Employment with audit clients**

This creates a self-interest threat and a familiarity threat to objectivity. The seriousness depends on the seniority of the individual and the length of time that has passed since he or she left the audit firm. The ACCA Code states that a key audit partner should not accept a key management position with an audit client unless at least two years have elapsed since the conclusion of the audit.

(3) **Recent service with audit clients**

(i.e. someone moves from the client company to the audit firm)

There is a self-interest, self-review and a familiarity threat to objectivity, depending on the seniority of the individual and the length of time that has passed since he or she left the client company. The ACCA Code states that no-one should take part in an audit if in the past two years they have been an employee of that company.

Other relationships

Associated firms: Influences outside the practice

A firm's objectivity may be threatened or appear to be threatened as a result of pressures arising from associated practices or organizations, or from other external sources, such as bankers, solicitors, government or those introducing business.

Dependence

Undue dependence on an audit client

Objectivity may be threatened or appear to be threatened by undue (economic) dependence on any audit client or group of connected clients.

The ACCA Code specifies certain fee limits (for individual clients as a percentage of total practice income):

	Listed or public interest	Other entities
No action required	<5%	<10%
Review independence	5–10%	10–15%
Limits not to be exceeded of gross recurring fee income of the practice except in opening years of the practice	>10%	>15%

Goods and services: Hospitality

Objectivity may be threatened or appear to be threatened by acceptance of goods, services or hospitality from an audit client.

Recommendation: Goods or services should not be accepted by a practice or by anyone closely associated with it unless the value of the benefit is clearly insignificant.

Provision of non-audit services to audit clients

There are occasions where objectivity may be threatened or appear to be threatened by the provision to an audit client of services other than the audit. Such work can generate significant levels of income which may overly influence decisions made and conclusions reached during the statutory audit process.

There is no objection in principle to a practice providing additional services. However, care must be taken not to make **management decisions** and to avoid the possibility of **self-review**. Attention should also be paid to the level of fee income generated from recurring non-audit services.

Possible safeguards:

- Separate engagement teams;
- Additional partner reviews;
- Must not assist plc clients with preparation of accounts (save in emergency situations) prior to conducting the audit.

Overdue fees

The existence of significant overdue fees from an audit client or group of connected clients can be a self-interest threat or appear to be a threat to objectivity akin to that of a loan.

Suggestion: Add overdue fees to the projected fees for the current year before applying the above percentage recommendations. If significant additional work should not be undertaken until an agreement for settlement has been reached.

Actual or threatened litigation

A firm's objectivity may be threatened or appear to be threatened when it is involved in, or even threatened with, litigation in relation to a client.

Discussion: Litigation could represent a breakdown in the relationship of trust between auditor and client. This adversarial position may affect the impartiality of the auditor, and lead to a reluctance of management to disclose relevant information to the auditor.

Exam Focus

- Professional and ethical considerations are a key element of the P7 paper. The examiner commented in her article on the approach to paper P7 (30 Jan 2007) that "Ethics and professional issues are also important areas within the syllabus, likely to feature in every sitting, either in Section A or Section B."
- A question on ethics will not require you to 'dump knowledge' but to apply the rules and principles to a case study/scenario question, and apply your common sense!
- All that the framework requires is that you apply the fundamental principles to unique situations, as observed in practice.

Emerging ethical issues

Further possible measures to improve independence

The following possibilities might improve the independence of auditors still further:

- Compulsory rotation of audit firms (as already happens in some countries, e.g. Italy).
- A ban on the provision of non-audit services by auditors.
- A State Audit Board to audit all public interest companies.
- The government to appoint the auditors of all public interest companies.
- Tightening all the limits stated in the ACCA Code (e.g. no client to exceed 5% of a firm's total fee income, engagement partners to serve no more than two years, etc.).

FIXED TEST 1 – 'Aventura'

Aventura International, a listed company, manufactures and wholesales a wide variety of products including fashion clothes and audio-video equipment. The company is audited by Voest, a firm of Chartered Certified Accountants, and the audit manager is Darius Harken. The following matters have arisen during the audit of the group's financial statements for the year to 31 March 2009 which is nearing completion:

(i) During the annual physical count of fashion clothes at the company's principal warehouse, the audit staff attending the count were invited to purchase any items of clothing or equipment at 30% of their recommended retail prices.

(ii) The chief executive of Aventura International, Armando Thyolo, owns a private jet. Armando invoices the company, on a monthly basis, for that proportion of the operating costs which reflects business use. One of these invoices shows that Darius Harken was flown to Florida in September 2008 and flown back two weeks later. Neither Aventura nor Voest have any offices or associates in Florida.

(iii) Last week Armando announced his engagement to be married to his personal assistant, Kirsten Fennimore. Before joining Aventura in January 2009, Kirsten had been Voest's accountant in charge of the audit of Aventura.

Required

Identify and discuss the ethical issues raised in each of the scenarios and the responses required by the auditor in relation to these matters.

(15 marks)

Test your understanding 1 – 'Audit Partner Rotation'

In order to comply with the ethical code of conduct it is widely recognised that senior audit personnel should be removed from engagements after a certain period (between five and ten years, depending upon the status of the client and national customs). To strengthen the ethical code of conduct further, professional accountancy bodies are currently debating whether to impose mandatory "rotation" periods for senior personnel as low as every two years.

Required

(a) Discuss why audit partner rotation is important in an ethical code of conduct.

(4 marks)

(b) Identify and explain **TWO** problems a small or medium sized firm of chartered certified accountants might face if the threshold is lowered and identify a possible solution to each problem.

(4 marks)

Test your understanding 2 – Blake Seven

(a) Explain the importance of the role of confidentiality to the auditor-client relationship.

(5 marks)

(b) Your firm acts as auditor and adviser to Blake Seven and to its four directors. The company is owned 50% by Brad Capella, 25% by his wife Minerva and 10% by Janus Trebbiano. Brad is the chief executive and Janus the finance director. Janus's sister, Rosella Trebbiano, has recently resigned from the executive board, following a disagreement with the Capellas. Rosella has now formed her own company, Blakes Heaven, in competition with Blake Seven.

Rosella is currently negotiating with her former co-executives the profit-related remuneration due to her and the sale of her 15% holding of shares in Blake Seven to one or all of them.

Rosella has contacted you to find out Brad's current remuneration package since he refuses to disclose this to her.

She has also requested that your firm should continue to act as her personal adviser and become auditor and adviser to Blakes Heaven.

Required

Comment on the matters that you should consider in deciding whether or not your audit firm can comply with Rosella's requests.

(10 marks)

(Total: 15 marks)

4 Chapter summary

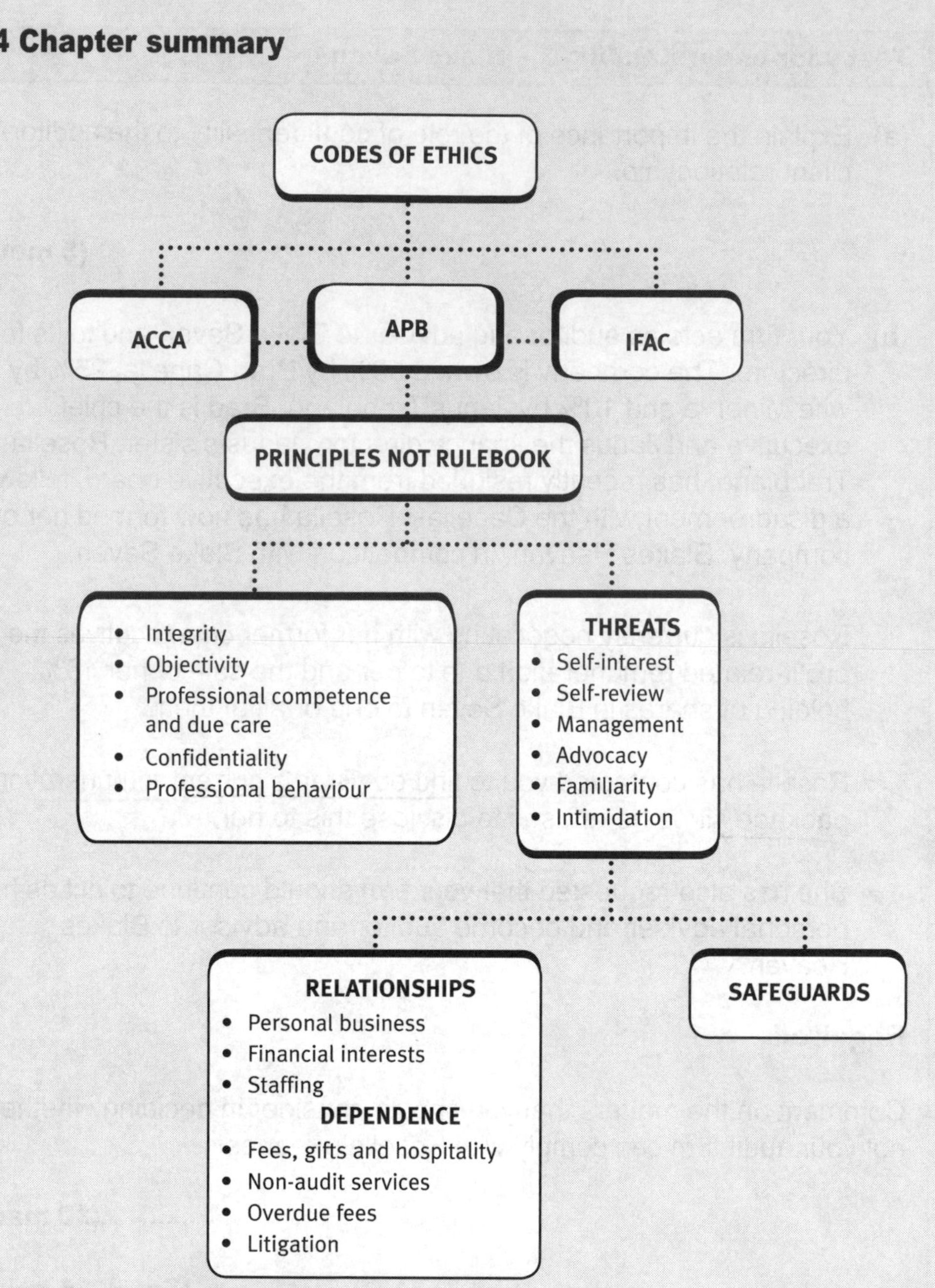

Test your understanding answers

FIXED TEST 1 – 'Aventura'

THIS IS A FIXED TEST – Please answer the question in full (long form written). Then log on to en-gage at the following address: www.en-gage.co.uk. Follow the link to 'Fixed Test 1' and answer the questions based on your homework answer.

Once you have answered the questions on en-gage a model answer will be available for your reference.

Test your understanding 1 – 'Audit Partner Rotation'

Importance of Rotation

Rotation of senior audit staff is important because it reduces the risk of **familiarity threat**. This arises when relationships develop between members of the audit team and the client that go beyond normal professional boundaries. This raises a number of concerns with regard to the professional completion of audit assignments.

Firstly, familiarity increases the risk of collusion between the director's of the client and senior audit personnel to bring about mutually beneficial ends, rather than performing the objective services required by shareholders. In the worst case scenario this could lead to fraud. Rotation of key staff reduces the likelihood of such undesirable relationships developing.

Secondly, familiarity could encourage the development of personal or business relationships between the auditor and their client. This would then create a self interest threat to objectivity, where the audit firm may benefit financially from the client. Once again rotating the partner reduces the likelihood of this occurring but also removes the partner in question away from engagements where relationships have already developed.

Finally, rotation reduces potential threats to professional competence/due care. This is due to the fact that an over-reliance on historical knowledge of a business and trust of directors can cause senior audit staff to overlook key issues. It is vital that auditors remain professionally sceptical at all times. Rotation freshens up perspectives and ideas, which should ensure consistently high quality services and professional due care.

Problems Faced by Small/Medium Sized Firms

In some legislative authorities there are limits that restrict the requirement for small companies to have a statutory audit. For example: in the UK companies with turnover less than £6.5mn and a statement of financial position total of less than £3.25mn are exempt. Therefore many small firms have few, if any, remaining audit clients. The impact on these firms will be minimal.

In many firms partners specialise in certain industries, meaning there would only be a small pool of partners to rotate between. This could be overcome by allowing partners to return to a previous client after a "cooling off" period. It could also be overcome by firms pooling their audit teams to reduce specialist departments, replacing them with staff able to adapt to a broad range of industries.

Each time a new partner takes over a client there will be a necessary "transition of knowledge." It could potentially take a significant amount of time for a partner to get to grips with the key issues and risks relating to a client that the previous partner would have been aware of. To overcome this successor partners could be identified well in advance. They could then review the audit file each year prior to taking over the client to build an awareness of the key issues. Another solution might be the creation of a "knowledge bank" by the incumbent partner that they could give to their successor.

In small and medium sized firms many clients are won over by the local reputation of a certain partner. They may feel let down by the rotation policy and this could lead to problems accepting the new engagement partner. To manage this firms could work with their clients to ensure they are fully informed about the changes. They could include the client when deciding upon the replacement partner, perhaps even conducting interviews of the possible replacement.

Test your understanding 2 – Blake Seven

(a) **The Importance of confidentiality to the auditor-client relationship**

That auditors should monitor and maintain the confidentiality and security of information is one of the mandatory competence requirements for membership of newly qualified Chartered Certified Accountants. It applies to all professional accountants.

In particular:

- confidential information is only disclosed to those entitled to receive it
- information obtained in the course of professional work is not used for purposes other than the client's benefit
- any decision to over-ride the duty of confidentiality (e.g. if required by a court order) is taken after due consideration and discussion with professional colleagues
- the duty of confidentiality continues even after an auditor-client engagement ceases
- an accountant who moves into new employment must distinguish previously gained experience from confidential information acquired from their former employment
- prospective accountants must treat any information given by existing accountants in the strictest confidence.

As well as being a fundamental principal of the Code of Ethics for Professional Accountants, confidentiality will also undoubtedly be an implied contractual term.

In order to fulfil their duties, auditors require full disclosure of all information they consider necessary. A duty of confidentiality is therefore essential to ensuring that the scope of the audit is not limited as a result of information being withheld.

(b) **Matters to consider**

Rosella has made three requests:

(1) disclosure of a former co-executive's level of remuneration

(2) continuing to act as personal adviser

(3) accepting an appointment as audit and adviser to Blakes Heaven.

(1) **Disclosure of remuneration package**

In an audit appointment, the auditor owes a duty of confidentiality to the client (i.e. the company not individual shareholders or executives). There is no legal or professional right or duty to disclose client information on an ad hoc basis merely because it is available to the auditor.

It would be a breach of the audit firm's duty of confidentiality to Blake Seven (in acting as auditor) and Brad (in acting as adviser) to disclose the information requested when clearly there is no process of law or 'public interest' involved.

The audit firm could only disclose the information to Rosella with Brad's consent. This is highly unlikely since Brad has refused to do so. Also, attempting to obtain permission from Brad is likely to result in a breach of the duty of confidence that the audit firm owes to Rosella (in their current role as adviser).

In general, the audit firm's working papers are its own property and any request for them (e.g. if Rosella requested a schedule of emoluments, etc) should be refused.

The latest audited financial statements (which are available to Rosella in her capacity as a shareholder) may disclose Brad's remuneration for the previous year (e.g. as chairman and/or highest paid executive). Rosella will need to wait for this information to be publicly available.

As a member of the company (i.e. shareholder), Rosella would also be entitled to inspect any relevant documents required to be held at Blake Seven's registered office (e.g. if Brad has a service contract with the company).

(2) **Continuing as personal adviser**

A conflict between the interests of Blake Seven (and its continuing directors) and Rosella Trebbiano (in a personal capacity) is likely to arise (e.g. over the valuation of Rosella's shareholding).

It would be inappropriate for one adviser to act for both parties in certain matters, such as negotiating a share price (in the event of subsequent disagreement) without appropriate safeguards.

Valuing Rosella's shareholding and negotiating her profit-related remuneration may appear to threaten the objectivity of the audit of Blake Seven. Rosella may try to exert influence to overstate profits (e.g. over Janus, as her brother and finance director, as well as the auditor).

However, the interests of these clients may not be materially prejudiced in all matters if:

– adequate disclosure is possible (i.e. of all relevant matters to all parties); and
– appropriate safeguards are implemented (e.g. advising one or all clients to seek additional independent advice).

In particular it may be possible to advise Rosella on personal tax matters.

(3) **Appointment as auditor**

A conflict between the interests of Rosella's new company, Blakes Heaven, and Blake Seven is likely to arise as the former has been set up in competition with the latter.

There is nothing improper in having both companies as audit clients if there are appropriate safeguards (e.g. different reporting partners and teams of staff for each audit engagement).

However, even with safeguards, the directors of Blake Seven (the Capellas in particular) may perceive that the involvement of the company's auditors with a competitor (in the capacity of auditor and adviser) could materially prejudice their interests. Also, that the new company has been set up with so similar a name suggests that Rosella may be quite aggressive in targeting Blake Seven's business.

In view of the adversarial relationship between Rosella and Blake Seven it would be prudent to include in their respective engagement letters a clause reserving the right to act for other clients subject to confidential information being kept secure.

The provision of other services (as adviser) could threaten the objectivity of the audit assignment. In particular, it would be inappropriate for the personal adviser to be the reporting partner or otherwise involved in the audit.

Conclusion

The request to disclose Brad's remuneration must be declined. However, Rosella may be directed to alternative sources of information, which may be of use (though not strictly current).

The firm may continue to act as Rosella's personal adviser subject to appropriate conditions and safeguards being put in place in respect of matters which may materially prejudice either client. For example:

- the agreement of Blake Seven (and the remaining directors)
- Rosella being advised to seek additional independent advice.

However, given the apparent acrimony between Rosella and her former associates, it seems unlikely that Blake Seven would agree to such an arrangement.

The audit appointment could only be accepted with appropriate safeguards (e.g. reporting partner and audit staff not involved in the audit of Blake Seven or the provision of other services). However, even with safeguards, if Rosella's appointments are accepted, Blake Seven may decide not to re-appoint the firm in future.

chapter

3

Professional appointments

Chapter learning objectives

Upon completion of this chapter you will be able to:

- explain the matters to be considered and the procedures that an audit firm/professional accountant should carry out before accepting a specified new client/engagement including:
  - client acceptance
  - engagement acceptance
  - agreeing the terms of engagement
- explain the key issues that underlie the agreement of the scope and terms of an engagement with a client
- outline the procedures for the transfer of books, papers and information following a new appointment.

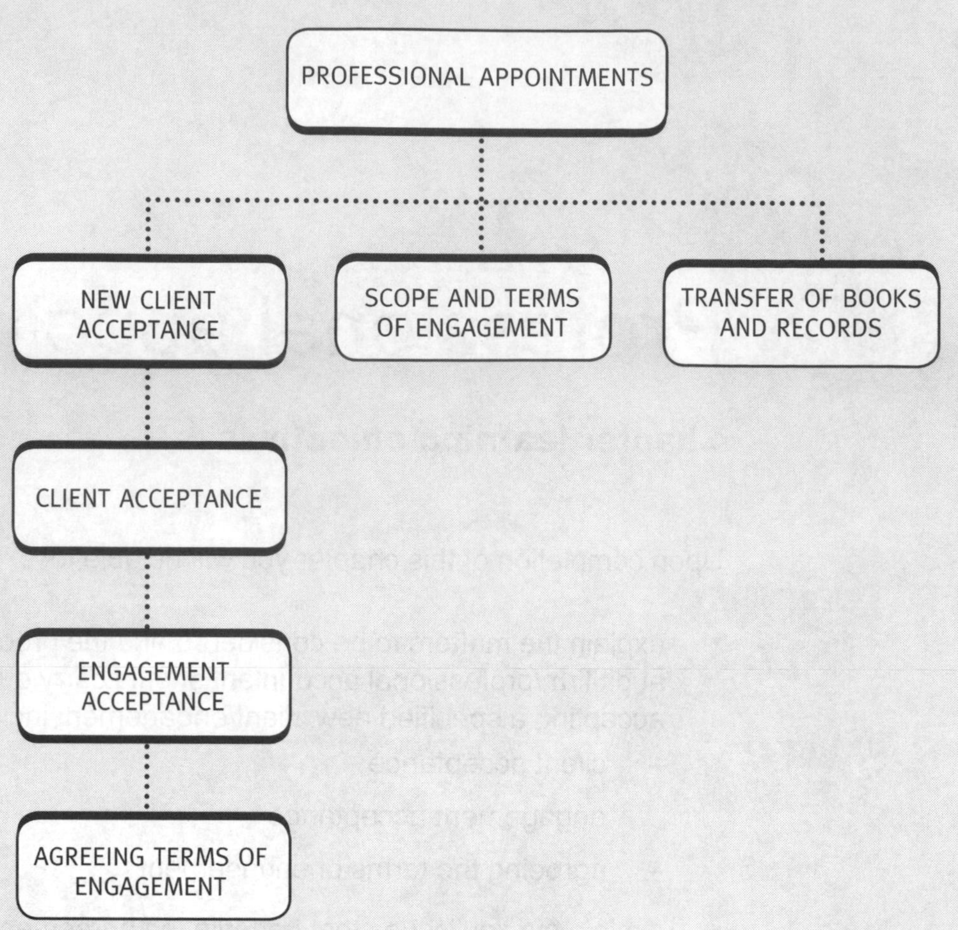

1 Accepting a new client or engagement

ISA 210 *Agreeing the Terms of Audit Engagements* and the Code of Ethics and Conduct provide guidance to the professional accountant when accepting new work.

According to ISA 210 before accepting (or continuing with) an engagement the auditor must establish whether the preconditions for an audit are present and that there is a common understanding between the auditor and management and, where appropriate, those charged with governance.

The preconditions for an audit are:

- That an acceptable financial reporting framework is to be applied to the preparation of the financial statements;
- That management understands and acknowledges its responsibilities for preparing the financial statements and providing the auditor with access to all relevant information and explanations.

If the client imposes a limitation on the scope of the auditor's work to the extent that the auditor believes it likely that a disclaimer of opinion will ultimately be issued then the auditor shall not accept the engagement, unless required to do so by law.

In addition, before accepting any engagement, the accountant should consider whether acceptance would create any threats to compliance with the fundamental ethical principles.

As in all circumstances, if the threats are other than clearly insignificant, then the accountant must apply appropriate safeguards to manage those threats. If the threat is considered so great that no safeguard would effectively reduce the risk then the engagement should be declined.

It is of particular importance to modern accountancy firms to consider whether they have the competence to perform engagements. Given the proliferation of services offered and the reduction in traditional audit services (due to the imposition of audit thresholds) many accountants may feel pressurised into offering unfamiliar services to keep up with competitors.

2 Changes in professional appointments

The following procedures are necessary before accepting a new client. (It is assumed that the organization previously had an auditor. The same principles apply in respect of changes in appointments for all recurring professional work.)

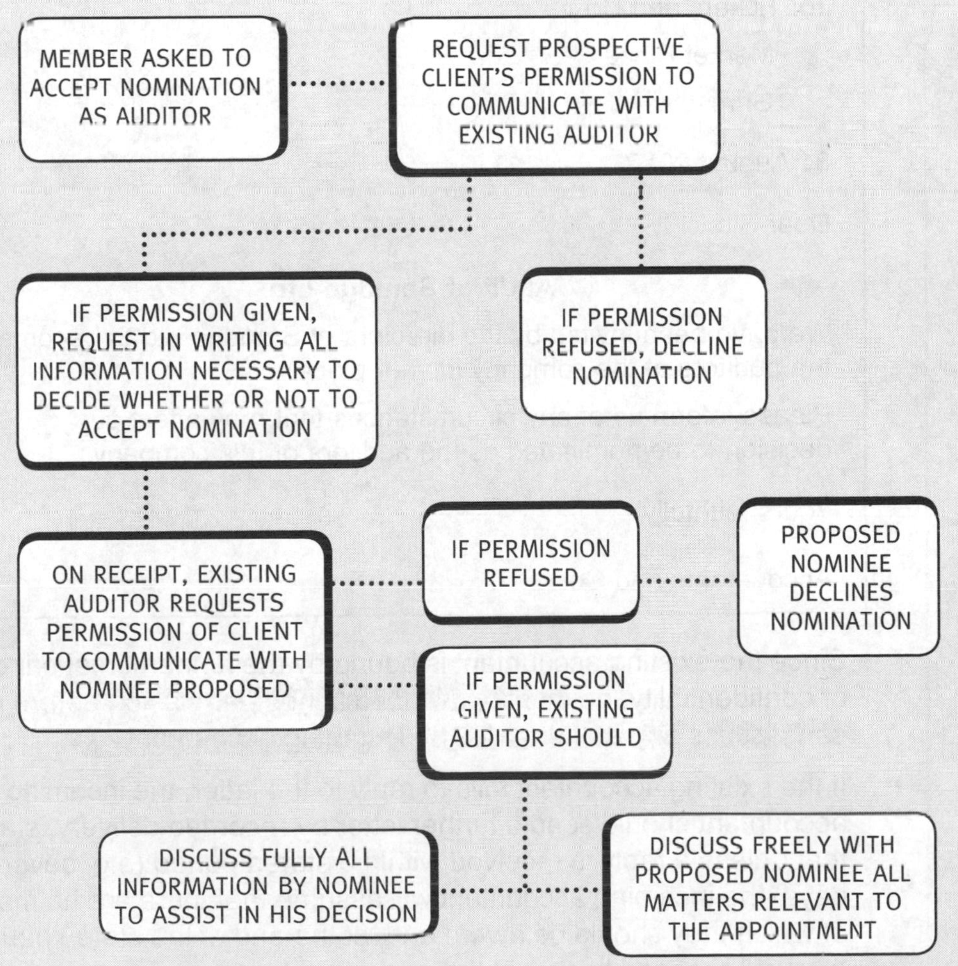

The etiquette letter

Accountants who are considering replacing an existing accountant should contact the existing accountant to determine whether there are any reasons that would preclude the accountant from taking on this engagement. The purpose of this professional etiquette letter is twofold:

- as a matter of professional courtesy to the existing accountant
- to enable the accountant to decide if there are any issues due to which, on ethical grounds, the accountant would not want to accept the appointment.

Example Etiquette Letter

(Note that the client's permission must be obtained before sending this letter.)

Accountants and Co.
14 The Crescent
Grimsby

To: Tickers and Co.
Market Place
Grimsby

31 August 20X7

Dear Sirs

Audit of Smudge Ltd

We have been invited by the directors of Smudge Ltd to become the auditors of the company in your place.

Please inform us of any circumstances that may affect our decision to be nominated as the auditors of this company.

Yours faithfully

Accountants and Co.

- Since the existing accountant is bound by the fundamental principle of confidentiality, he must obtain the client's permission before he can discuss any matters with the incoming accountant.
- If the existing accountant fails to reply to the letter, the incoming accountant should send a further letter by recorded delivery, stating that unless a reply is received within a stated period (e.g. seven days) the incoming accountant will assume that there are no matters of which they should be aware and, at the end of the stated period, they will proceed to accept the appointment.

- Any information supplied by the existing accountant should be considered carefully before the incoming accountant decides to accept or reject the appointment. All such information should be treated in confidence.
- The fact that there are unpaid fees owed to the existing accountant does not necessarily mean that the incoming accountant should refuse the appointment.

Additional professional work

- Accountants may be asked to undertake work that is complementary or additional to the work of existing accountants, who are not being replaced.
- Before accepting such work, the accountant should communicate with the existing accountants to inform them of the general nature of the work being done.

Appointment as auditor

Where an accountant is being appointed as the new auditor of a company, the accountant should confirm that:

- the outgoing auditor has vacated office in a correct manner
- the new auditor has been properly appointed as the incoming auditor.

3 Agreeing the terms of engagement

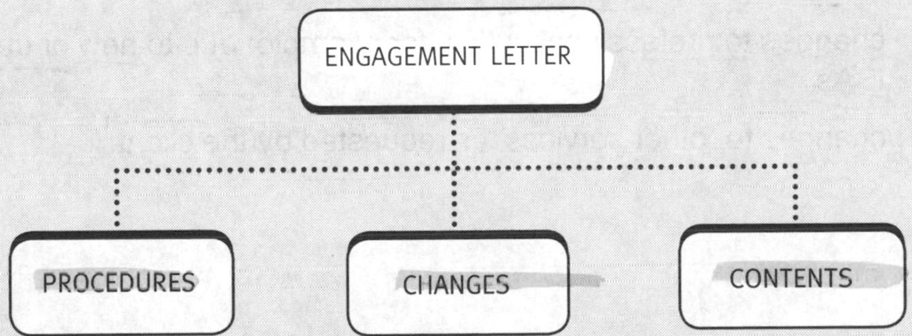

ISA 210 states that the auditor shall agree the terms of the audit engagement with management or those charged with governance, as appropriate. The terms are recorded in a written audit engagement letter and should include:

- The objective and scope of the audit of the financial statements;
- The responsibilities of the auditor;
- The responsibilities of management;
- Identification of the applicable financial reporting framework for the preparation of the financial statements; and
- Reference to the expected form and content of any reports to be issued by the auditor.

The content of the engagement letter should be agreed with the client before any engagement related work commences. The client's acknowledgement of the terms of the letter should be formally documented in the form of a director's signature.

Changes to the engagement letter

The engagement letter specifies the nature of the contract between the audit firm and the client. The auditor should issue a new engagement letter if the scope or context of the assignment changes after initial appointment.

Reasons for changes would include:

- changes to statutory duties due to new legislation
- changes to professional duties, for example: due to new or updated ISAs
- changes to 'other services' as requested by the client

Engagement Letter Contents in Detail

The items noted above should all be included in an engagement letter. However the wider form and content of engagement letters may vary depending upon the nature of the client and the audit being conducted. In addition it may make reference to:

- Applicable regulations, legislation, ISAs and ethical pronouncements;
- The form of any other communications as a result of the engagement;
- The inherent limitations of audit procedures;
- Arrangements regarding the planning and performance of the audit;
- The expectation that management will provide written representations;
- The agreement of management to make available to the auditor draft financial statements and any accompanying information in time to allow the auditor to complete the audit in accordance with the timetable;
- The agreement of management to make available to the auditor facts pertinent to the preparation of the financial statements, which management may become aware of during the period from the date of the auditor's report to the date the financial statements are issued; The basis upon which fees are computed and billed;
- A request for management to acknowledge receipt of the engagement letter and to agree to the terms of engagement outlined therein;
- Arrangements concerning the involvement of other auditors and experts (where relevant);
- Arrangements concerning the involvement of internal auditors (where relevant);
- Any restriction on the auditor's liability, when such possibility exists; and
- Any obligations to provide audit working papers to other parties.

Example Engagement Letter

Accountants and Co.
14 The Crescent
Grimsby

To: The Directors
Smudge Ltd
High Street
Grimsby

20 September 20X7

Dear Sirs

Audit of Smudge Ltd

The purpose of this letter is to set out the basis on which we are to act as the auditors of Smudge Ltd and the respective areas of responsibility of the directors and of ourselves.

Responsibilities of directors and auditors

XXXX

Scope of the audit

XXXX

Other services

XXXX

Fees

XXXX

Applicable law

XXXX

Agreement of terms

Once it has been agreed, this letter will remain effective, from one audit appointment to another, until it is replaced. We shall be

Audit of components of a group

- Where the auditor of a parent company is also the auditor of a subsidiary, branch or division of the group, the audit firm must decide whether to issue a single engagement letter covering all the components, or a separate letter to each component.
- If the audit firm sends one letter relating to the group as a whole, it is recommended that the firm should identify in the letter the components of the group for which the firm is being appointed as auditor.

4 Transfer of books, papers and information

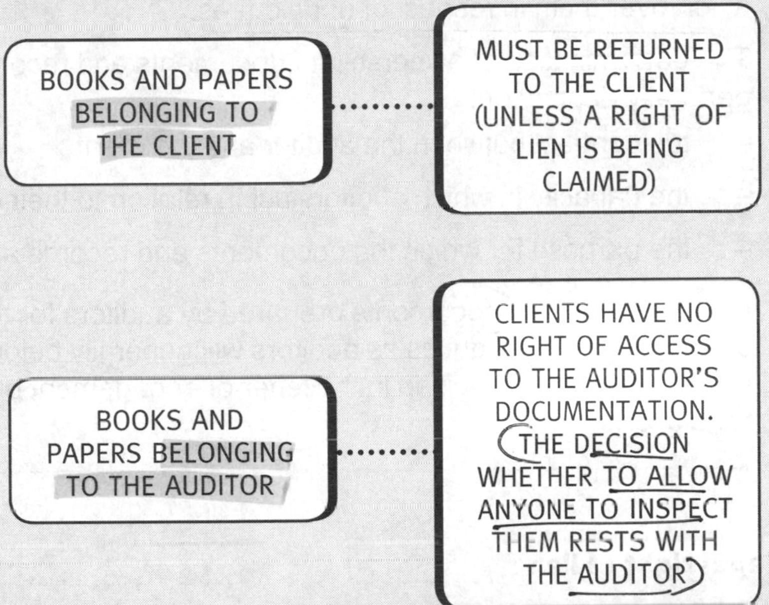

The ACCA Code of Ethics and Conduct gives guidance to the professional accountant (based on the IFAC Code of Ethics) on the outgoing accountant's duty to transfer books, papers and relevant information.

Transfer of books and papers

Books and papers comprise the client's materials as well as the audit documentation (incuding those stored electronically)

What are they and who should have them?

i.e. the working papers prepared by or for the auditor in connection with the performance of the audit. 'Books and papers' does not refer only to paper documents; it includes all data sources stored on paper, film, electronic media and other media.

- On ceasing to hold office, the former accountant should ensure that all books and papers belonging to the former client that are in his possession are properly transferred, except where they are claiming a lien over them in respect of unpaid fees.
- The determination of ownership of documents and records will generally depend on:
  - the contract between the auditor and the client
  - the capacity in which auditors act in relation to their client
  - the purpose for which the documents and records are created.
- Broadly speaking, documents prepared by auditors for the purpose of carrying out their duties as auditors will generally belong to them unless otherwise specified in the letter of engagement or national regulations

The legal right of lien

A **lien** is a creditor's right to retain possession of the debtor's property until the debtor pays what he owes to the creditor.

Implementing the right to a lien

- A general lien is a lien over property that can be retained until payment of all amounts that the debtor owes the creditor, however they arose. General liens are rare.
- A particular lien is a lien over property that can be retained until the debtor pays the creditor a particular debt in respect of that property.
- If an accountant has performed work on documents belonging to his client but has not yet been paid the agreed fee for the work, then he has a particular lien over those documents.
- For a particular lien to be valid the following circumstances must apply:

(1) the documents or records retained must be the property of the client who owes the money

(2) work must have been done on the documents or records and a fee note rendered before the member can exercise a particular lien

(3) the documents or records must be in the member's possession by proper means and

(4) fees for which the lien is exercised must relate to the retained documents or records.

Note: In most countries a lien cannot be exercised over the statutory books of companies, since they have to be available for public inspection, and for directors' use.

Transfer of information

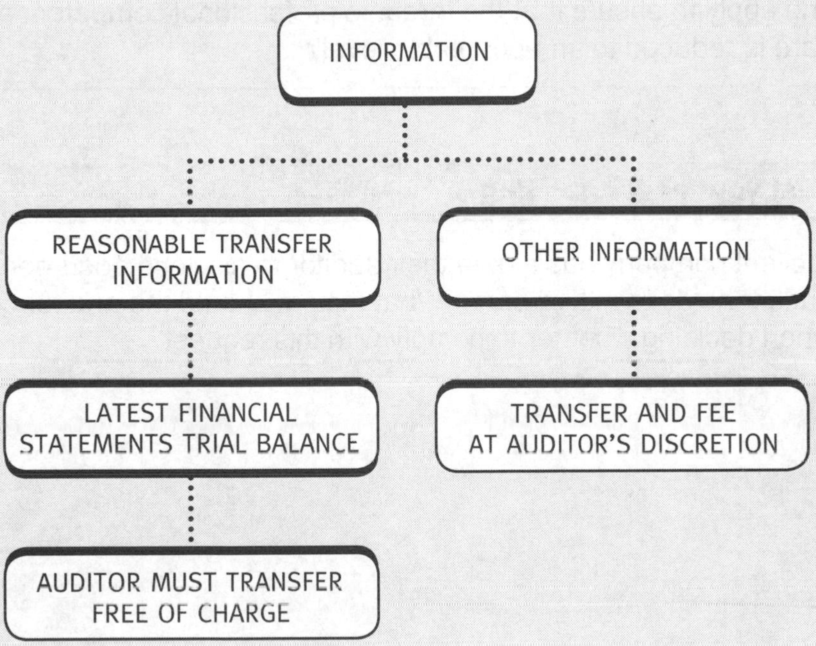

- The former accountant should promptly provide the incoming accountant with all reasonable transfer information that they request, free of charge.
- This 'reasonable transfer information' comprises a copy of the latest set of accounts and a detailed trial balance (list of balances) that agrees with these accounts.
- This information must be provided, even where there are unpaid fees.
- Any information in addition to this 'reasonable transfer information' is provided at the discretion of the former accountants who may charge a fee to whoever is requesting it.

Test your understanding 1

AB Accountants has been invited to become the auditors of XY Ltd, a company with a poor reputation since several senior managers were convicted of corruption recently. The company is adamant that it has now changed its culture, and is hoping that AB Accountants will become its auditors as part of this new ethical outlook.

Identify possible safeguards AB Accountants might consider using.

Test your understanding 2

An accountant has been invited to carry out an engagement for a client, but she has only limited experience in this area. What safeguards could she apply to ensure that the threat to professional competence and due care is reduced to an acceptable level?

Test your understanding 3

A client company has asked their auditor to disclose documents the auditor holds to a third party. What factors should the auditor consider when deciding whether to comply with this request?

5 Chapter summary

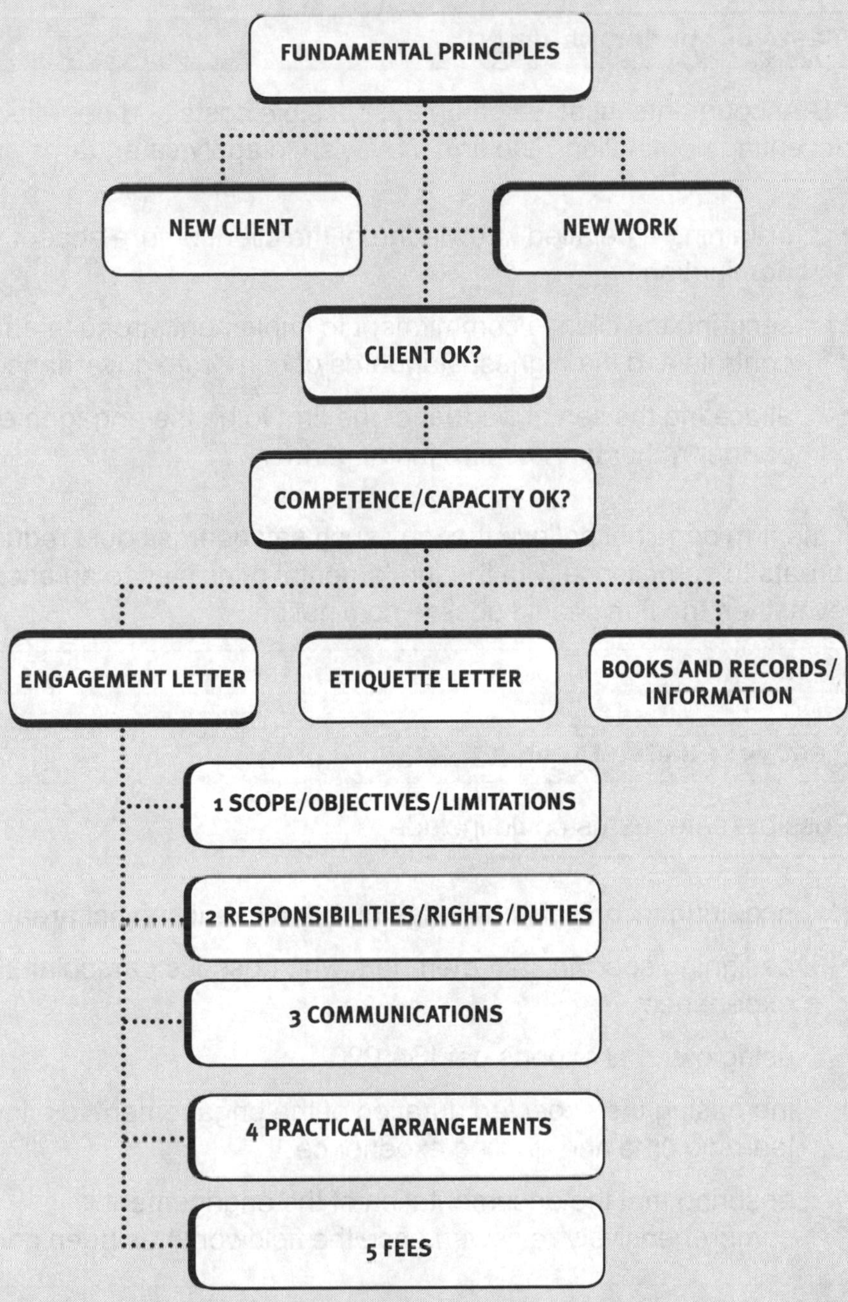

Test your understanding answers

Test your understanding 1

AB Accountants must weigh up the possible costs and benefits of accepting nomination. The firm may wish to apply safeguards such as:

- obtaining a detailed knowledge of the client before accepting nomination
- securing the client's commitment to implement strong internal controls and the highest standards of corporate governance
- allocating the senior partner of the firm to be the engagement partner rather than a more junior partner.

If the firm does not believe that any such safeguards could reduce the threats to compliance with the fundamental principles to an acceptable level, then the firm should decline nomination.

Test your understanding 2

Possible safeguards could include:

- acquiring technical knowledge of the relevant subject area
- assigning specific staff members who possess particular skills and experience
- using external experts per ISA 620
- increasing the expected duration of the engagement to allow for learning time and gaining experience
- ensuring that the documentation of the engagement is comprehensively reviewed once the fieldwork has been completed.

Test your understanding 3

It depends who owns the documents whose disclosure is being requested. If they belong to the client company, then the auditor should comply with the request unless there are unpaid fees concerning work performed on the documents and the auditor is exercising a right of lien. If the documents belong to the auditor, then there is no obligation to comply with the request. The auditor can choose to comply if they wish to.

chapter

4

Quality control

Chapter learning objectives

Upon completion of this chapter you will be able to:

- explain the principles and purpose of quality control of audit and other assurance engagements.
- describe the elements of a system of quality control relevant to a given firm.
- select and justify quality control procedures that are applicable to a given audit engagement .
- assess whether an engagement has been performed in accordance with professional standards and whether reports issued are appropriate in the circumstances.

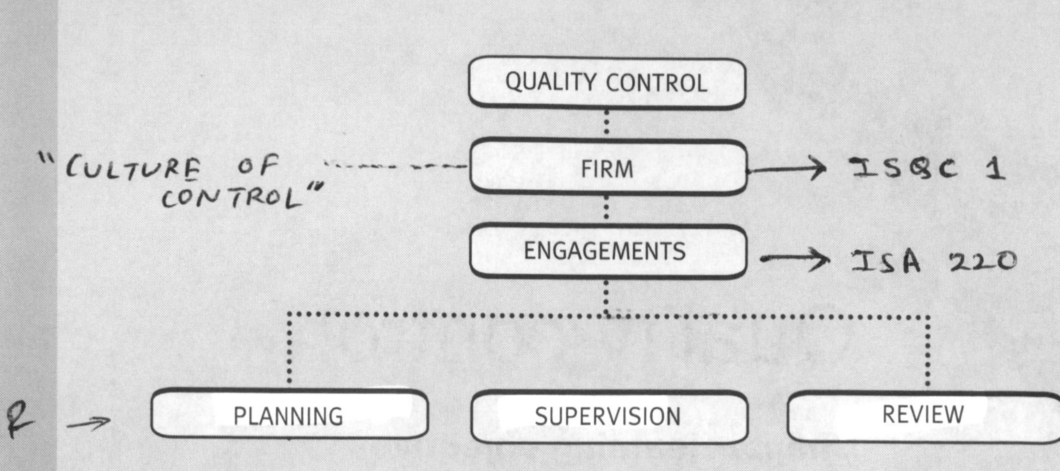

1 The purpose of quality control procedures for assurance engagements

We saw in Chapter 1 that the purpose of assurance services is to boost confidence by reducing investors' risk and how this led to a need for regulation.

As part of this process firms need to have policies and procedures to ensure that the quality of their work is satisfactory.

Otherwise:

- in the short term there may be individual audit failures, leading to professional negligence claims
- in the long term public confidence in the assurance process as a whole will be diminished.

Quality control issues impact at two levels

- The firm as a whole.
- Individual engagements.

2 Quality control standards

There are two standards that set out the responsibilities of auditors regarding quality control:

- **ISQC 1** Quality Control for Firms that Perform Audits and Reviews of Financial Statements, and Other Assurance and Related Services Engagements. (Any Practicing A/cing Firm)
- **ISA 220** – Quality Control for an Audit of Financial Statements.

ISQC 1 sets out an accountancy firm's responsibilities with regard to their systems of quality control for audits, reviews and other assurance engagements. Those quality control systems should include policies designed to ensure that the firm and its personnel comply with applicable professional standards and regulatory requirements and that reports issued are appropriate. The system should also include procedures necessary to implement those policies and monitor compliance with them.

ISA 220, by contrast, establishes the responsibilities of the auditor (mainly the engagement partner and engagement quality reviewer) regarding their quality control procedures during audits. It states that within the context of the firm's system of quality control, the engagement team have a responsibility to implement quality control procedures applicable to the audit engagement.

3 Quality control and the firm

ISQC1 identifies six building blocks of a firm's system of quality control:

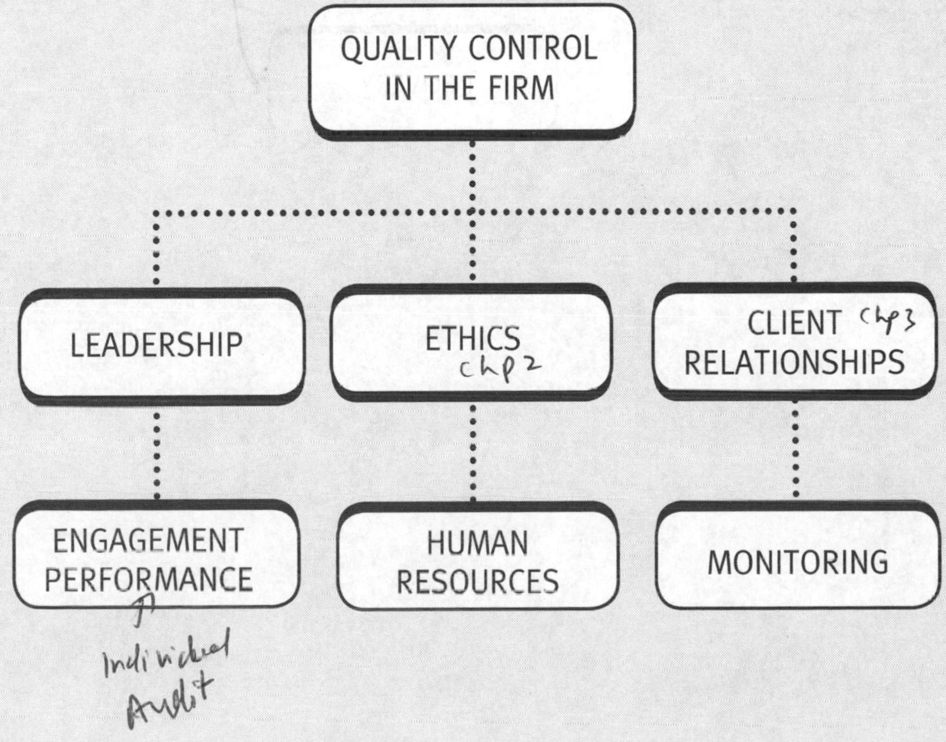

Ethical requirements and the arrangements for the acceptance and continuance of client relationships and specific engagements are dealt with in chapters 2 and 3 respectively. In this chapter we will focus on the remaining four 'building blocks'.

4 Leadership issues

The underlying message is simple – firms must:

- perform work that complies with professional standards and regulatory and legal requirements; and
- issue reports that are appropriate in the circumstances.

To achieve this firms must establish policies and procedures to promote an internal culture that recognises the importance of quality in performing engagements. This requires the firm's management team (i.e. managing partners) to assume ultimate responsibility for the system of quality control.

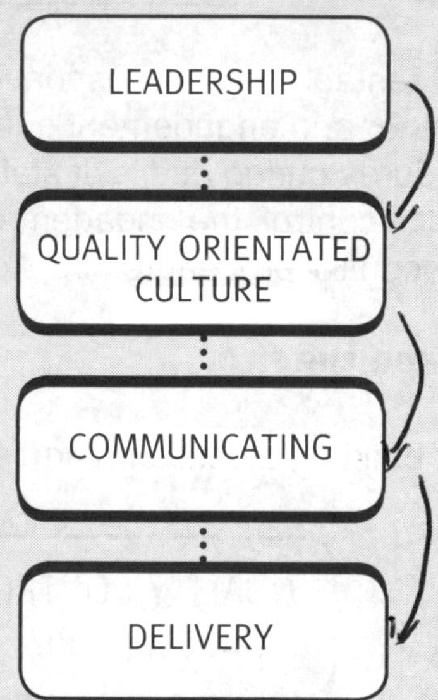

Communicating the Message

The promotion of quality depends on clear, consistent and frequent actions and messages from all levels of the firm's management that emphasis the firm's quality control policies and procedures. This can be achieved via:

- training seminars
- meetings
- formal or informal dialogue
- mission statements
- newsletters
- briefing memoranda
- training materials
- partner and staff appraisals.

Really meaning it

At the heart of this part of the standard are some clear and quite tough messages:

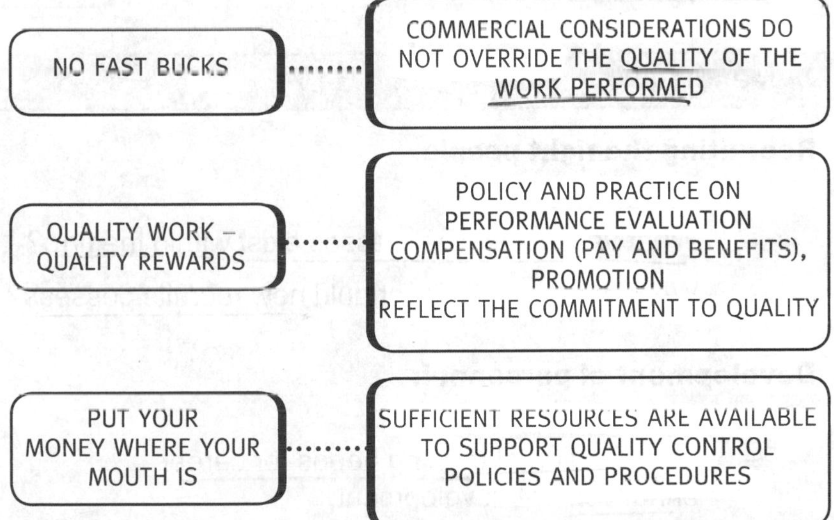

You should not use the expressions on the left in your exam answers, but hopefully they sum up what the standard setters had in mind.

5 Human resources issues

The standard sets out a comprehensive – albeit brief – guide to the HR function. It stresses that if a firm wants quality flowing through all levels of staff it must go through the steps outlined below.

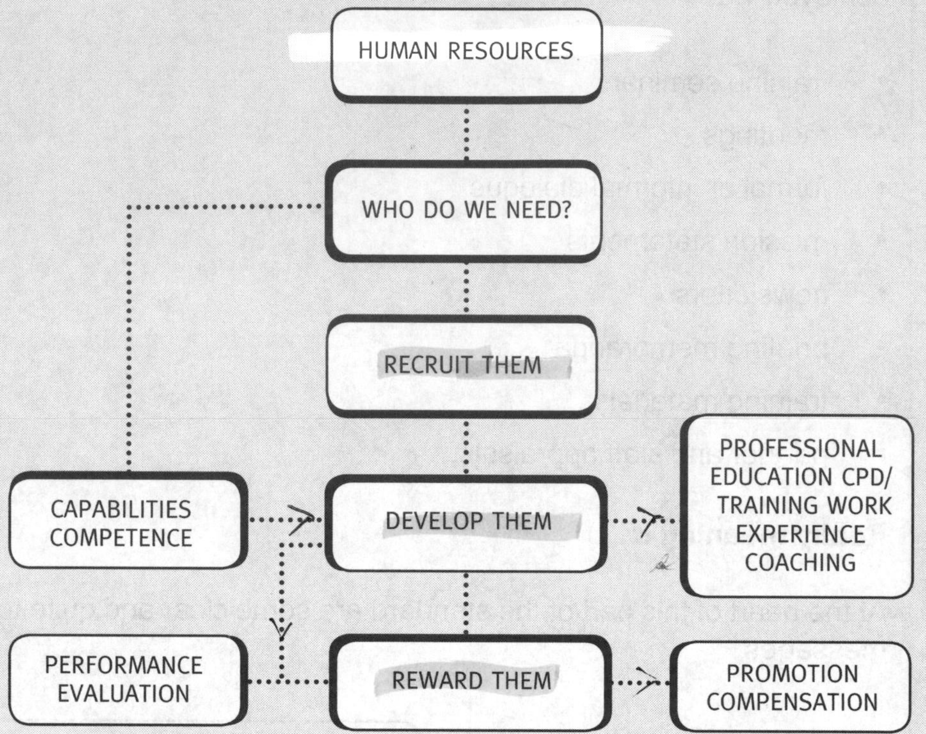

Human Resource Management

Recruiting the right people:

- What vacancies/weaknesses exist within the firm?
- What entry level skills should new recruits possess?

Development of personnel:

- Identification of training needs for career enhancement/development;
- Appraisal and performance evaluation;
- Development of capabilities and competences through education, training and professional development.

Reward systems:

– Appraisal and performance evaluation;
– Career development opportunities/promotion;
– Appropriate remuneration/compensation.

6 Quality control at engagement level

ISQC 1 identifies three areas of policy and procedure relevant to the performance of an engagement:

- Matters relevant to promoting consistency in the quality of engagements;
- Supervision responsibilities; and
- Review responsibilities.

Specific elements of audit engagement performance, namely planning and review, are covered in later chapters. Here we focus on the broad principles that firms should consider when designing quality control systems.

7 Consistency in the Quality of Engagement Performance

Firms promote consistency through their policies and procedures. This is often accomplished through written manuals, software tools and standardised documentation. Particular matters that can be addressed include:

- How engagement teams are briefed to obtain an understanding of the engagement and their objectives;
- Processes for complying with engagement standards;
- Processes of engagement supervision, training and coaching;
- Methods of reviewing work, judgements and reports issued;
- Documentation of work performed and the timing and extent of reviews; and
- Processes to keep policies and procedures current.

0208 426 6860

The Role of Planning

People

- Do they have the necessary levels of training for this engagement?
- Do they have sufficient knowledge of the client?
- Do they have sufficient experience of this type of engagement?
- Have they been briefed?

NB Remember that **ISA 315** has a requirement for the audit team to discuss the known risks with the client and for the discussion to be documented.

The work

ISA 330 stresses that audit procedures must be targeted at assessed risks. At the planning phase those risks must be identified so that appropriate, targeted procedures can be performed during fieldwork.

Consultation

ISQC1 and ISA 220 both contain the requirement for appropriate consultation on difficult or contentious matters. Clearly, as far as possible, possible areas requiring consultation (both internally and externally) should be organized in advance to facilitate timely – and cost effective – completion of the engagement.

Reviews

All reviews should be timetabled in advance to enable timely completion. This includes identifying the need to perform second partner and 'hot' reviews.

Independence

The independence and objectivity of the firm is crucial to the credibility of any assurance engagement. If that independence is perceived to be flawed, however technically skilled the work may be, the quality of the work may still be called into question. It is vital that all independence issues are discussed and relevant safeguards adopted before any fieldwork is performed.

8 The role of supervision in quality control

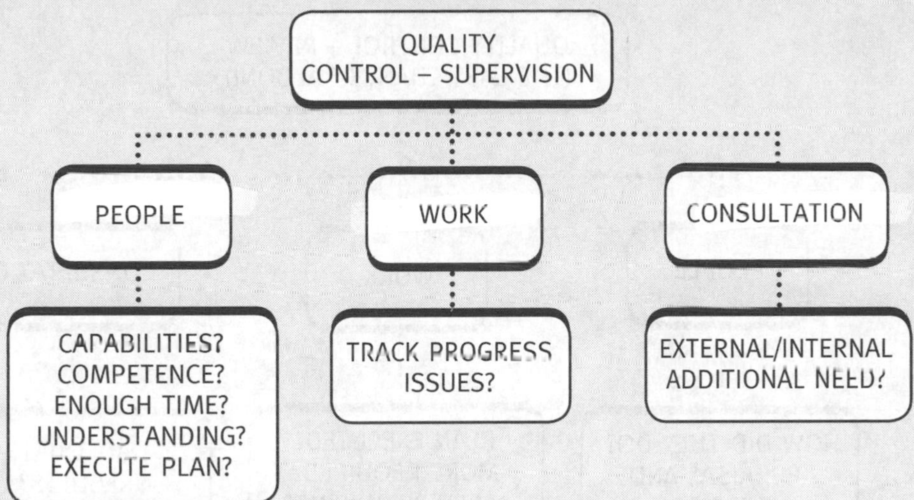

Good quality supervision

Supervisor should consider:

- whether the right decisions were made at the planning stage
- whether the staff conducting the work have the knowledge and experience to be able to execute the plan whether unforeseen circumstances have arisen in the course of the engagement
- whether progress is satisfactory
- whether unforeseen risks have arisen
- whether there is a need for consultation over and above anything foreseen in the original plan.

The delegation problem

The hardest thing about supervision is knowing how tight or loose control should be.

- Supervise too closely and you risk demotivating staff or even causing disruption.
- Supervise too loosely and things could go badly wrong before you are aware of it.

9 The role of review in quality control

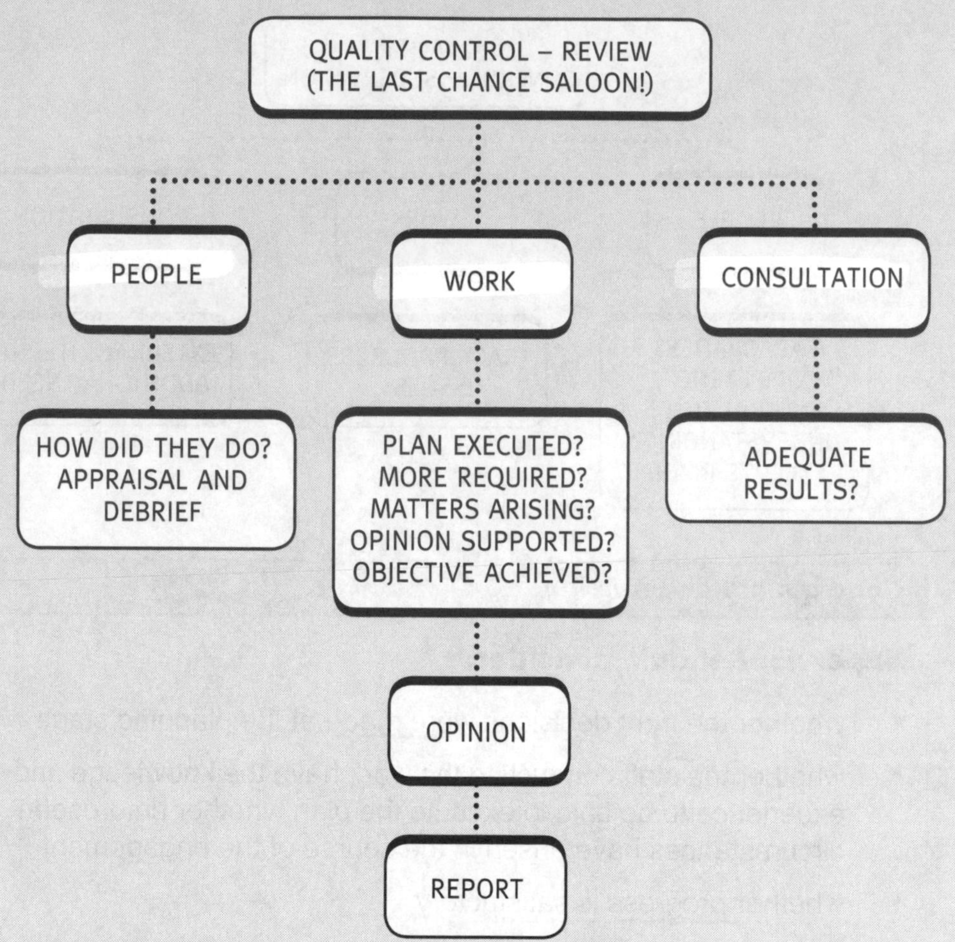

Good quality review

The role of review is to consider whether:

- Work has been performed in accordance with identified standards;
- Significant matters have been raised for further consideration;
- Appropriate consultations have taken place and been documented;
- There is a need to revise the nature, timing and extent of procedures;
- The work performed supports the conclusions reached and is appropriately documented;
- The evidence obtained is sufficient and appropriate to support the report; and
- The objectives of the engagement procedures have been achieved.

The broader role

Because the review phase is the final link in the chain, it plays a wider part in the firm's quality control procedures than simply ensuring that an individual engagement has been completed satisfactorily.

- Lessons learned about failures at the planning stage can be communicated so that similar mistakes are not made elsewhere in the firm.
- Staff appraisals, conducted promptly after an engagement, are an immensely powerful tool in quality control for the firm as a whole. If good work is praised and rewarded and poor work constructively criticised and plans made for improvement, there can be a lasting effect on the quality of the firm's work.

10 Engagement Quality Control Reviews

Firms should establish policies and procedures for performing engagement quality ("hot") reviews for all listed clients and for other engagements, as appropriate.

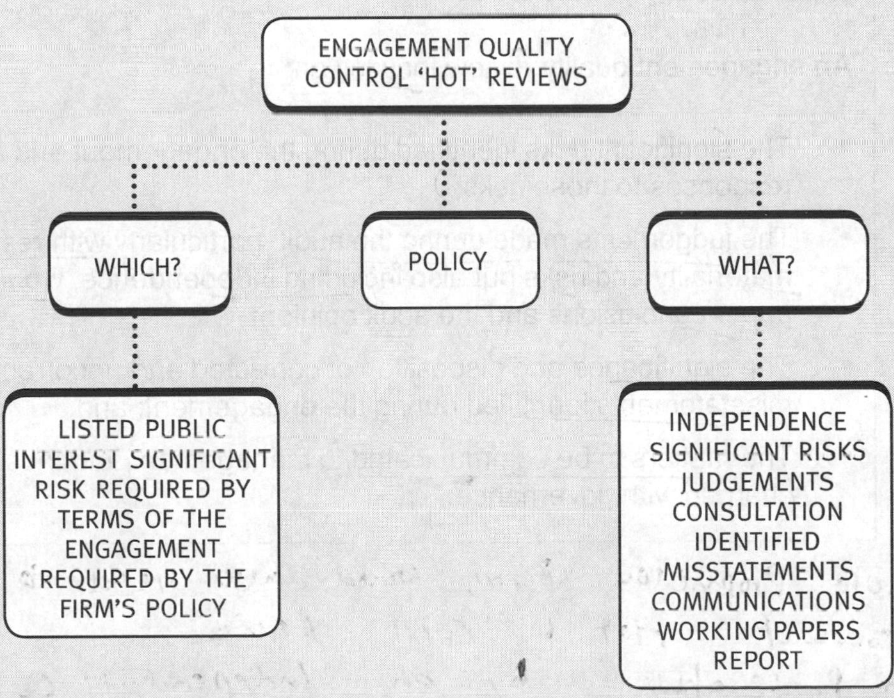

What is a 'hot' review not?

Purpose

The purpose of the 'Engagement quality' or 'hot' review is to enhance the quality of assurance work by subjecting engagements to an independent review by a suitably qualified reviewer. The reviewer is usually a partner, possibly a senior manager, independent of the engagement team. The review is conducted before the firm's report is issued.

Which files?

All listed company engagements must be included according to ISQC1 and ISA 220.

Other files dictated by the firm's policy, which should include those that are deemed to be of public interest or where there are particular risks, should also be reviewed.

It is normally expected that some engagements from each partner's portfolio would be reviewed.

What is being considered?

An engagement quality review focuses on:

- The significant risks identified during the engagement and the responses to those risks;
- The judgements made during the audit, particularly with respect to materiality and risks but also including independence, working paper conclusions and the audit opinion;
- The significance and disposition of corrected and uncorrected misstatements identified during the engagement; and
- The matters to be communicated to management and those charged with governance.

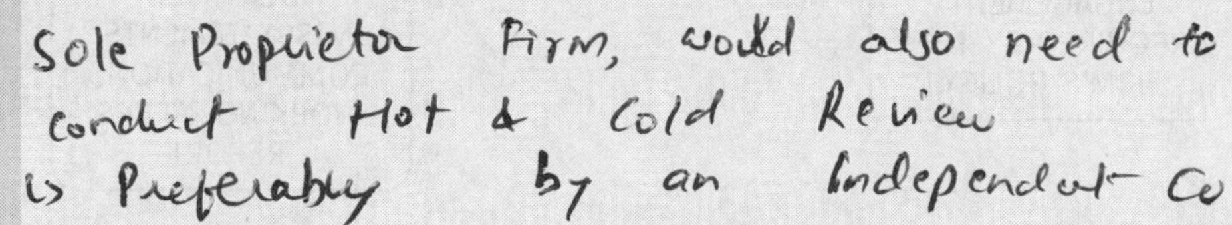

11 Cold reviews

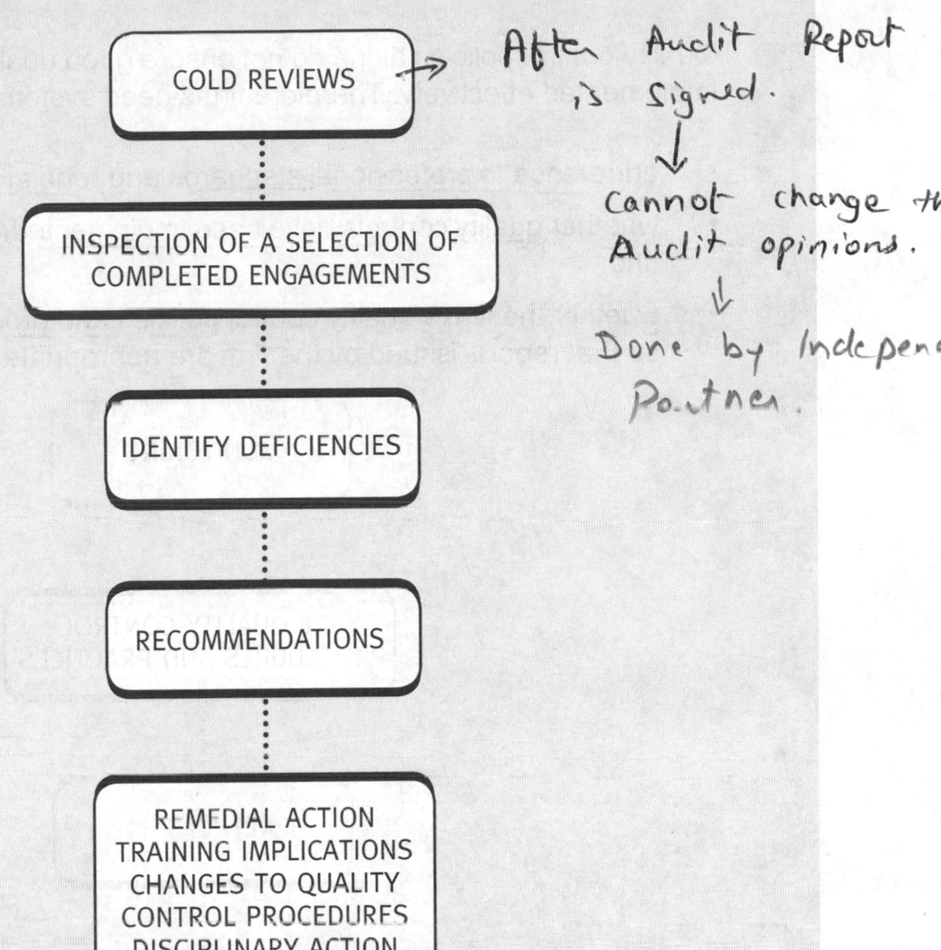

What is a 'cold' review?

Purpose

Cold reviews form a part of the firm's quality monitoring process.

They are designed to identify deficiencies within the firm's practices and procedures.

Outcomes

The outcomes from the process will be recommendations for:

- improvements to the firm's procedures
- identification of training needs
- in some circumstances, disciplinary action.

12 Monitoring

Quality control policies alone do not ensure good quality work. They must be implemented effectively. Therefore firms need systems to evaluate:

- adherence to professional standards and regulatory/legal requirements;
- whether quality controls have been implemented on a day-to-day basis; and
- whether the firm's quality control policies and procedures are effective so that reports issued by the firm are appropriate in the circumstances.

MONITORING

ARE QUALITY CONTROL PROCEDURES AND PRACTICES

RELEVANT?

ADEQUATE?

OPERATING EFFECTIVELY?

COMPLIED WITH IN PRACTICE?

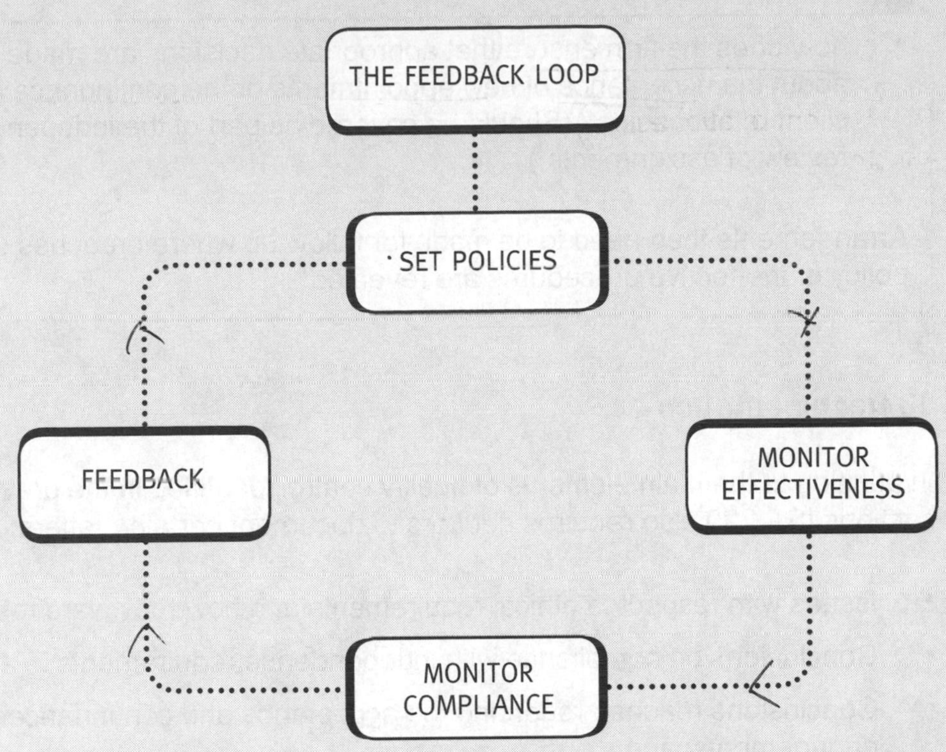

Good quality monitoring

The redrafted version of ISQC 1 requires that monitoring is performed on an ongoing, cyclical basis, including an inspection of at least one completed engagement for each engagement partner. The responsibility for this monitoring process should be assigned to a partner and those performing the inspections should not have had any involvement in the engagements under review.

The monitoring process goes beyond the simple enforcement of policies and procedures. It has to consider:

- how does the firm respond to new developments in professional standard and regulatory and legal requirements?
- how does the firm ensure compliance with, e.g. independence rules, by all its partners and staff? (Usually achieved through the use of independence or 'fit and proper' forms, which will need checking for completeness)
- how does the firm ensure that all partners and staff comply with continuing professional development requirements? (Often achieved by controlling course bookings centrally, or by the maintenance of training logs.)

- how does the firm ensure that appropriate decisions are made about the acceptance of new appointments or the continuance of client relationships? (Should be covered as part of the independent review of assignments.)

Arrangements then need to be made for follow up where breaches of policy or ineffective procedures are revealed.

13 Documentation

In addition to the main elements of quality control identified in the previous sections ISA 220 also requires auditors to document certain matters:

- Issues with respect to ethical requirements and how they were resolved;
- Conclusions on compliance with independence requirements;
- Conclusions reached regarding the acceptance and continuance of engagements; and
- The nature, scope and conclusions resulting from consultations undertaken during the course of the audit.

During completion of the audit the engagement quality reviewer has to document:

- The procedures required by the firm's engagement quality review procedures;
- That the engagement quality review has been completed (on or before the date of the auditor's report); and
- That the reviewer is not aware of any unresolved matters that would cause the reviewer to believe that the significant judgements of the team were not appropriate.

Test your understanding 1 – 'Cello'

You are a senior manager with Flute and Co. and are a member of the team conducting cold reviews this year. In your review of Cello Ltd, a subsidiary of a listed overseas parent, which imports and distributes office furniture, usually manufactured by other group companies. The company is large enough to require a statutory audit, but is still not a particularly large company.

In the course of your review you notice the following.

- Minutes of the planning meeting are on file but were not signed by the partner.
- The company has a December 31 year end. Fieldwork was completed by February 15 and the financial statements together with the audit report were signed on April 15. The subsequent events checklist was completed on February 15.
- The company has very little headroom in its overdraft and apparently no other borrowing facilities.
- There is a letter of support on file from the holding company dated April 15.
- Materiality is calculated at $60,000, which is in line with the firm's recommended procedures.
- Non-current assets consist of office furniture, office equipment and racking and forklifts for the rented warehouse. Net book value is $250,000 and additions in the year were $40,000. Copy invoices for all the additions are on file but you find it difficult to see precisely what work was done and the working papers other than the pre-printed audit programme and lead schedule were neither initialled nor dated.
- The receivables circularization was successful except for one non-reply for $40,000.

Required

- What conclusions are you able to draw about the quality of the audit of Cello Ltd?
- What recommendations would you make to the firm's audit quality committee?

Test Your Understanding 2 – 'Agnesal'

(a) 'The objective of the auditor is to implement quality control procedures at the engagement level that provide the auditor with reasonable assurance that:

– The audit complies with professional standards and applicable legal and regulatory requirements; and

– The auditor's report issued is appropriate in the circumstances.'

(**ISA 220** *Quality Control for an Audit of Financial Statements*)

Required

Describe the nature and explain the purpose of quality control procedures appropriate to the individual audit.

(7 marks)

(b) You are the manager responsible for the quality of the audits of new clients of Signet, a firm of Chartered Certified Accountants. You are visiting the audit team at the head office of Agnesal, a limited liability company. The audit team comprises Artur Bois (audit supervisor), Carla Davini (audit senior) and Errol Flyte and Gavin Holst (trainees). The company provides food hygiene services which include the evaluation of risks of contamination, carrying out bacteriological tests and providing advice on health regulations and waste disposal.

Agnesal's principal customers include food processing companies, wholesale fresh food markets (meat, fish and dairy products) and bottling plants. The draft accounts for the year ended 31 March 2007 show turnover $19.8 million (2006 $13.8 million) and total assets $6.1 million (2006 $4.2 million).

You have summarised the findings of your visit and review of the audit working papers relating to the audit of the financial statements for the year to 31 March 2007 as follows:

(i) Against the analytical procedures section of the audit planning checklist, Carla has written 'not applicable – new client'. The audit planning checklist has not been signed off as having been reviewed by Artur.

(ii) Artur is currently assigned to three other jobs and is working from Signet's office. He last visited Agnesal's office when the final audit commenced two weeks ago. In the meantime Carla has completed the audit of non-current fixed assets (including property and service equipment) which amount to $1.1 million as at 31 March 2007 (2006 $1.1 million).

(iii) Errol has just finished sending out requests for confirmation of trade receivable balances as at 31 March 2007 when trade receivables amounted to $3.5 million (2006 $1.6 million).

(iv) Agnesal's purchase clerk, Jules Java, keeps $2,500 cash to meet sundry expenses. The audit program shows that counting it is 'outstanding'. Carla has explained that when Gavin was sent to count it he reported back, two hours later, that he had not done it because it had not been convenient for Jules. Gavin had, instead, been explaining to Errol how to extract samples using value-weighted selection. Although Jules had later announced that he was ready to have his cash counted, Carla decided to postpone it until later in the audit. This is not documented in the audit working papers.

(v) Errol has been assigned to the audit of inventory (comprising consumable supplies) which amounts to $150,000 (2000 $90,000). Signet was not appointed as auditor until after the year-end physical count. Errol has therefore carried out tests of controls over purchases and issues to confirm the 'roll-back' of a sample of current quantities to quantities as at the year-end count.

(vi) Agnesal has drafted its first 'Report to Society' which contains health, safety and environmental performance data for the year to 31 March 2007. Carla has filed it with the comment that it is 'to be dealt with when all other information for inclusion in the company's annual report is available'.

Required

Identify and comment on the implications of these findings for Signet's quality control policies and procedures.

(18 marks)

(Total: 25 marks)

14 Chapter summary

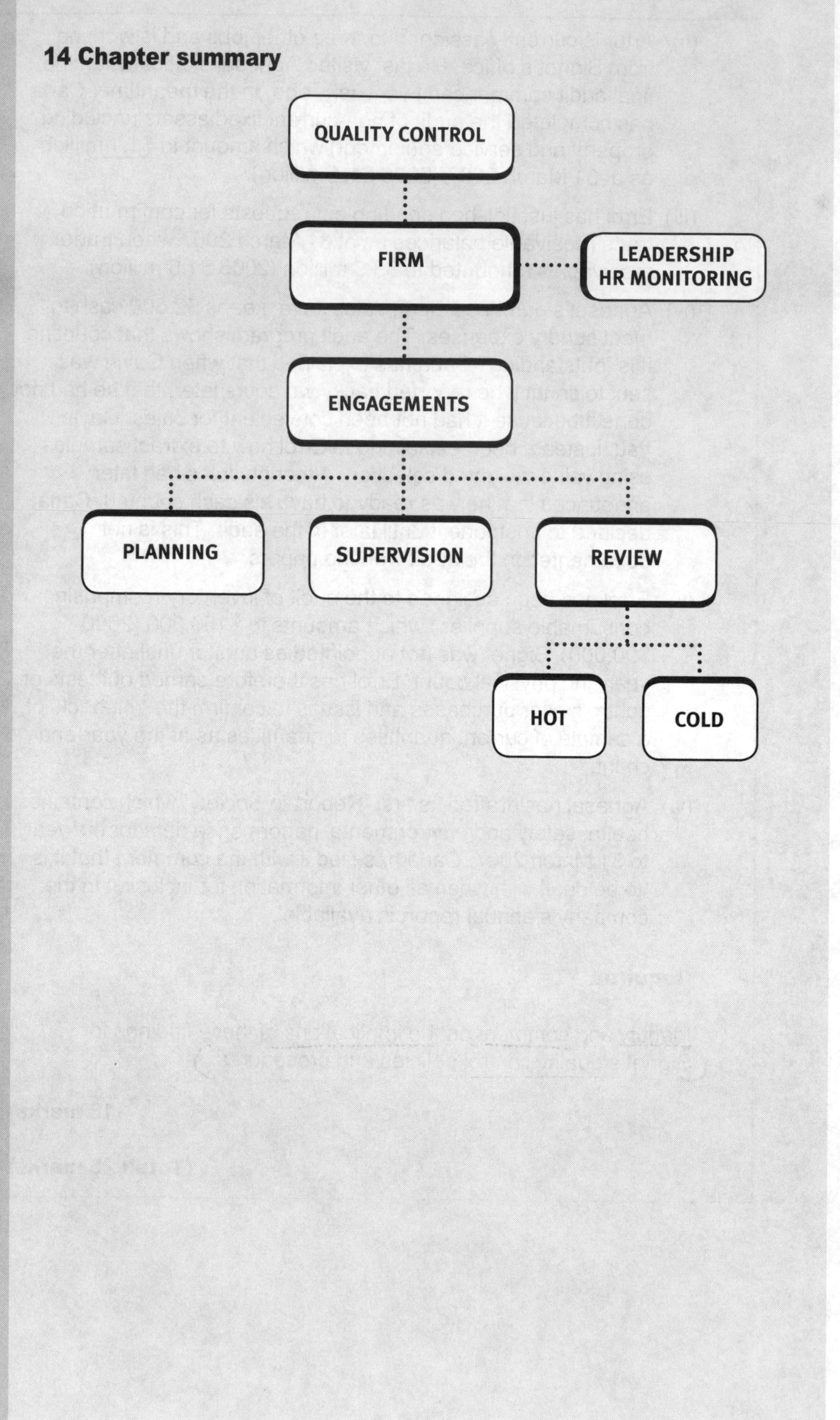

Test your understanding answers

Test your understanding 1 – 'Cello'

Planning meeting

The planning should be documented fully and approved by the partner before the start of fieldwork. It is possible that evidence of this approval is to be found elsewhere on the file, but it would have been better if the partner had signed off the meeting minutes as soon as they were available.

Going concern and subsequent events

- The subsequent events review should be updated to the date of signing the audit report. The review should arguably be more rigorous and comprehensively documented because of the lack of financial facilities and the raised risk of going concern issues.
- It may be that the letter of comfort from the holding company is sufficient to eliminate this risk, but this should be made clear on the file, and the checklist still needs updating.
- The fact that the parent is listed overseas does not, of itself, mean that the comfort letter is valid evidence that Cello Ltd is a going concern and there may be an increased level of risk, because of the parent's listed status.

Non-current assets

- Non-current assets might be considered low risk, but the total is material even if the current year's additions may not be in themselves.
- This section of the file demonstrates a lack of clarity in the approach to the audit and the firm's basic procedures for initialling and dating working papers have not been observed, albeit in what may be a relatively low-risk area.

Receivables

- The uncleared item may not be material as such, but it may well be in excess of the tolerable error threshold.
- The item should have been followed up and other evidence obtained and, if this was impossible, the potential mis-statement should have been calculated in theoretical terms to see if the mis-statement in the financial statements as a whole might have been material.

Conclusions/recommendations

- There is a risk that the audit report (on the assumption that an unmodified opinion was given) might have been wrong because of the going concern and debtor questions.
- Laid down audit procedures need to be followed for the planning meeting, subsequent events review, non-current assets working papers and receivables sample.
- Training implications need to be considered.

Test Your Understanding 2 – 'Agnesal'

The first part of this question requires knowledge of standard quality control procedures and policies that should be incorporated in to each audit undertaken. Knowledge of the requirements under ISA 220 and ISQC 1 is required here.

(a) **QC procedures**

Quality controls are the policies and procedures adopted by a firm to provide reasonable assurance that all audits done by a firm are being carried out in accordance with the objective and general principles governing an audit.

Individual audit level

Work delegated to assistants should be directed, supervised and reviewed to ensure the audit is conducted in compliance with ISAs.

Assistants should be professionally competent to perform the work delegated to them with due care.

Direction (i.e. informing assistants about their responsibilities and the nature, timing and extent of audit procedures they are to perform) may be communicated through:

- briefing meetings and on-the-job oral instruction
- the overall audit plan and audit programs
- audit manuals and checklists
- time budgets.

Supervisory responsibilities include monitoring the progress of the audit to ensure that assistants are competent, understand their task and are carrying them out as directed. Supervisors must also address accounting and auditing issues arising during the audit (e.g. by modifying the overall audit plan and audit program).

The work of assistants must be reviewed to assess whether:

- it is in accordance with the audit program
- it is adequately documented
- significant matters have been resolved
- objectives have been achieved
- conclusions are appropriate (i.e. consistent with results).

Documentation which needs to be reviewed on a timely basis includes:

- the overall audit plan (including risk assessments)
- the audit program (and modification thereto)
- results from tests of control/substantive procedures and conclusions drawn
- financial statements, proposed audit adjustments and the proposed audit opinion.

An independent review (i.e. by personnel not otherwise involved in the audit), to assess the quality of the audit (before the issue of an audit report) should be undertaken for listed and other public interest or high risk audit clients.

Additional point

Quality control procedures reduce the risk of litigation claims (thereby reducing PII costs).

(b) **Implications of findings for QC policies and procedures**

Key answer tips

'Planning an answer' means, as a minimum, deciding how marks are likely to be allocated and structuring the answer accordingly. In general, the more a question is broken down into parts, the less time needs to be spent on 'formal' writing out of an answer plan. In this question there are 18 marks for addressing six matters, i.e. just 3 marks of answer for each. However, there are also 'pervasive' issues which can be brought out as overall conclusions on QC policies and procedures at the level of the audit firm. It is a higher skill to recognise causes and effects or other links between the findings.

(i) **Analytical procedures**

Applying analytical procedures at the planning stage, to assist in understanding the business and in identifying areas of potential risk, is an auditing standard and therefore mandatory. Analytical procedures should have been performed (e.g. comparing the draft accounts to 31 March 2007 with prior year financial statements).

Audit staff may have insufficient knowledge of the highly specialised service industry in which this new client operates to assess risks. In particular, Agnesal may be exposed to risks resulting in unrecorded liabilities (both actual and contingent) if claims are made against the company in respect of outbreaks of contamination (e.g. CJD, BSE, foot and mouth, listeria, etc).

The audit has been inadequately planned and audit work has commenced before the audit plan has been reviewed by the audit supervisor. The audit may not be carried out effectively and efficiently.

(ii) **Supervisor's assignments**

The senior has performed work on non-current assets which is a less material (18% of total assets) audit area than trade receivables (57% of total assets) which has been assigned to an audit trainee. Non-current assets also appear to be a lower risk audit area than trade receivables because the carrying amount of non-current assets is comparable with the prior year ($1.1m at both year ends), whereas trade receivables have more than doubled (from $1.6m to $3.5m). This corroborates the implications of (i).

The audit is being inadequately supervised as work has been delegated inappropriately. It appears that the firm does not have sufficient audit staff with relevant competencies to meet its supervisory needs.

(iii) **Direct confirmation**

It is usual for direct confirmation of trade receivables to be obtained where trade receivables are material and it is reasonable to expect customers to respond. However, it is already more than two months after the balance sheet date and, although trade receivables are clearly material (57% of total assets), an alternative approach may be more efficient (and cost effective). For example, monitoring of after-date cash will provide evidence about the collectability of trade receivables (as well as corroborate their existence).

This may be a further consequence of the audit having been inadequately planned.

Alternatively, monitoring of the audit may be inadequate. For example, if the audit trainee did not understand the alternative approach but mechanically followed circularisation procedures.

Depending on the reporting deadline, there may still be time to perform a circularisation. However, consideration should be given to circularising the most recent month end balances (i.e. November) rather than the year end balances (which customers may be unable or reluctant to confirm retrospectively).

(iv) **Cash count**

Although $2,500 is very immaterial, the client's management may well expect the auditor to count it, albeit routinely, to confirm that it has not been misappropriated.

Monitoring of the trainee may have been inadequate. For example, Gavin may not have understood the need to count the cash immediately the request was made of the client. However, the behaviour of Gavin also needs to be investigated in that he failed to report back to the audit senior on a timely basis and allowed himself to be unsupervised.

The trainees do not appear to have been given appropriate direction. Gavin may not be sufficiently competent to be explaining sample selection methods to another trainee.

Although it is not practical to document every matter, details should have been recorded to support Carla's decision to change the timing of a planned procedure. (Carla's decision appears justified as it is inappropriate to perform a cash count when the client is 'ready' for it.) Also, if some irregularity is discovered by the client at a later date (e.g. if Jules is found to be 'borrowing' the cash), documentation must support why this was not detected sooner by the auditor.

(v) **Inventory**

Inventory is almost as immaterial as the cash in (4) from an auditing perspective, being less than 2.5% of total assets (2006 2.1%). Although it therefore seems appropriate that a trainee should be auditing it, the audit approach appears highly inefficient. Such in-depth testing (of controls and details) on a immaterial area provides further evidence that the audit has been inadequately planned.

Again, it may be due to a lack of monitoring of a mechanical approach being adopted by a trainee.

This also demonstrates a lack of knowledge and understanding about Agnesal's business – the company has no inventory-in-trade, only consumables used in the supply of service.

(vi) **'Report to society'**

The audit senior appears to have assumed that this is 'other information' to be included in a document containing audited financial statements (the annual report). 'To be dealt with' presumably means 'to be read' with a view to identifying significant misstatements or inconsistencies. However, Agnesal may be intending to publish it as an entirely separate report and require an assurance service (other than audit) such as an independent verification statement on performance standards.

As the preceding analysis casts doubts on Signet's ability to deliver a quality audit to Agnesal, it seems highly unlikely that Signet has the resources and expertise necessary to provide such assurance services.

QC policies procedures at audit firm level/Conclusions

That the audit is not being conducted in accordance with ISAs (e.g. ISA 315 Identifying and Assessing the Risks of Material Misstatement Through Understanding the Entity and Its Environment and ISA 520 Analytical Procedures) means that Signet's quality control policies and procedures are not established and/or not being communicated to personnel.

That audit work is being assigned to personnel with insufficient technical training and proficiency indicates weaknesses in procedures for hiring and/or training of personnel.

That there is insufficient direction, supervision and review of work at all levels to provide reasonable assurance that audit work is of an acceptable standard suggests a lack of resources.

Procedures for acceptance of clients appear to be inadequate as the audit is being conducted so inefficiently (e.g. procedures are inappropriate and/or not cost-effective). In deciding whether or not to accept the audit of Agnesal, Signet should have considered whether it had the ability to serve the client properly. The partner responsible for accepting the engagement does not appear to have evaluated the firm's (lack of) knowledge of the industry.

chapter

5

Advertising, publicity, obtaining professional work and fees

Chapter learning objectives

Upon completion of this chapter you will be able to:

- explain the need for guidance in these areas.
- recognize situations in which specified advertisements are acceptable.
- discuss the restrictions on practice descriptions, the use of the ACCA logo and the names of practicing firms.
- discuss the extent to which reference to fees may be made in promotional material.
- explain the determinants of fee-setting and justify the bases on which fees and commissions may and may not be charged for services.
- discuss the ethical and other professional problems involved in establishing and negotiating fees for a specified assignment.

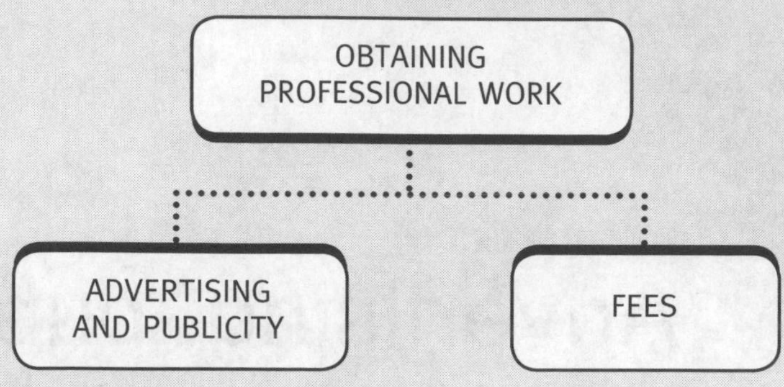

1 Advertising and publicity

Advertising

The ACCA Rules of Professional Conduct state that it is perfectly acceptable in principle for ACCA members to advertise their services, but there is a general proviso that the advertising must not reflect adversely on:

- the member
- the ACCA or
- the accountancy profession as a whole.

The aim of adverts should be 'To inform, rather than impress'.

ACCA Rules

The rules state that advertisements and promotional material should not:

- bring ACCA into disrepute or bring discredit to the member, firm or the accountancy profession
- discredit the services offered by others whether by claiming superiority for the member's own services or otherwise
- be misleading, either directly or by implication
- fall short of the requirements of any relevant national Advertising Standards Authority's Code of Advertising Practice, notably as to legality, decency, clarity, honesty, and truthfulness.

Publicity

Publicity is the management of the public's perception of a subject.

Guidance on advertising and publicity is required to make sure that ACCA members comply with the fundamental principle of 'professional behaviour' at all times. This requires compliance with relevant laws and regulations (such as the Advertising Standards Authority's Code) and also the avoidance of any action that discredits the profession.

Example Advertisement

Antoine Smith ACCA is drafting an advertisement to appear in a local business directory. His assistant has suggested the following.

Mr Smith will not be willing to use this draft advertisement, since:

> Antoine Smith ACCA
> Tel: 020 72341234
> I am the only competent accountant in this town. Ring me if you want advice on how to reduce your tax liability, probably even to zero. Disabled clients are not welcome since my office is up a flight of stairs

(1) it discredits the other accountants in the area and thus brings the profession into disrepute

(2) it is misleading to suggest that tax liabilities can routinely be reduced to zero

(3) the reference to disabled people is offensive and may be contrary to disabled rights legislation.

In fact only the name and telephone number are acceptable from the assistant's suggested advertisement!

Test your understanding 1

Possible advertisement

Comment on whether the following advertisement acceptable?

Deidre Jones ACCA
www.djonesacca.co.uk
Advice for small businesses
Friendly and professional service
Business start-up specialist
'The best and friendliest service in this town'

2 Restrictions on practice names and descriptions

There are restrictions on practice names and descriptions and the use of the ACCA logo, which all members should be aware of.

Members' descriptions

- Members of the ACCA are entitled to call themselves Chartered Certified Accountants or just Certified Accountants, and may use the letters ACCA (as members) or FCCA (if they are fellows).
- These descriptions may not be used in the registered names of companies. For example you may not set up a company called John Smith Certified Accountant Ltd.

Practice descriptions

- An accountancy firm may describe itself as a 'firm of Chartered Certified Accountants', or a 'firm of Certified Accountants', or an 'ACCA practice' provided that:
  - at least half of the partners (or directors) are ACCA members, and
  - these partners (or directors) control at least 51% of the voting rights under the firm's partnership agreement (or constitution).

- On its professional stationery, a firm in which all the partners are ACCA members may use the description 'Members of the Association of Chartered Certified Accountants'.
- In the case of a mixed firm (e.g. some partners are ACCA members and others are members of other Chartered Accountancy bodies), the firm should not use the description 'Certified Accountants and Chartered Accountants' or similar, since this could be misleading.
- Instead they may print the following statement on their stationery: 'The partners of this firm are members of either the Association of Chartered Certified Accountants or (e.g.) the Institute of Chartered Accountants in England and Wales'.

Use of the ACCA logo

- A firm that has at least one ACCA member as a partner (or director) may use the ACCA logo (also called the ACCA 'mark') on its professional stationery and on its website.
- The ACCA logo should be separate from the logo of the firm.
- The positioning, size and colour of the ACCA logo should be chosen so that it is clearly recognizable.
- The logo can be downloaded by members from the ACCA website in electronic format.

Names of practicing firms

Generally, members may practice under whatever name they want, but:

- a practice name should be consistent with the dignity of the profession
- a practice name should not be misleading (e.g. a firm could not trade as 'PQ International Accountants' if all its offices were in one country)
- a practice name should not run the risk of being confused with the name of another firm
- a sole practitioner should not add 'and partners' to the name under which he practices.

3 Fees

The need for guidance

The setting of fees is a sensitive subject, so the ACCA Rules of Professional Conduct contain a number of important provisions, to :

- Minimize the possibility of a dispute between a member and his clients.
- Ensure that the member behaves at all times in accordance with the fundamental principles.

References to fees in promotional material

- Where reference is made in promotional material to fees, the basis on which those fees are calculated, hourly or other charging rates, etc. should be clearly stated.
- Members may make comparisons in such material between their fees and the fees of other accounting practices, whether members or not, provided that any such comparison does not give a misleading impression, and does comply with relevant codes of conduct.
- Promotional material that is based on the offer of percentage discounts on existing fees is permitted but must not detract from the professional image of the firm and the profession as a whole.
- Members may offer a free consultation to potential clients, at which levels of fees will be discussed.

Determinants for fee-setting

- The general principle is that members are entitled to charge a fair and reasonable fee for their services. This amount will be:
  - the fee considered appropriate for the work undertaken
  - the fee in accordance with the basis agreed with the client
  - the fee by reference to custom in certain specialized areas.
- Members will usually consider the following matters in setting a fee:
  - the seniority of the persons necessarily engaged on the work
  - the time spent by each person
  - the degree of risk and responsibility that the work entails
  - the urgency of the work to the client
  - the importance of the work to the client
  - the overhead expenses of the firm.
- The fee charged should include the recovery of any expenses properly incurred by the audit staff in the course of the engagement.
- The general basis on which fees are normally computed should be communicated to clients or potential clients in the letter of engagement, in order to reduce the risk of misunderstandings.

Bases on which fees and commissions may be charged

Hourly rates

The basis used by most accountancy practices is to set an hourly rate for each grade of staff and to invoice the client for the number of hours involved in the assignment.

Introductions

Members may, in return for the introduction of a client, pay a referral fee to a third party. The payment of such a fee may create a self-interest threat, therefore safeguards should be established to eliminate the threat or reduce it to an acceptable level (usually by disclosing any such arrangements to the client).

Contingency fees

A **contingency fee** is an arrangement made at the outset of an engagement under which a pre-determined amount or percentage is payable to the accountant upon the happening of a specified event, or the achievement of a particular outcome.

The ACCA's position is that **fees should not be charged on a percentage, contingency or similar basis**, save where that course of action is generally accepted practice for certain specialized work or as specifically permitted by the Rules of Professional Conduct.

Illustration

AB accountants employs the following staff.

	Charge-out rate
Mr B, Partner	$90 per hour
Mr C, Partner	$90 per hour
Miss D, Manager	$75 per hour
Mr F, Assistant	$40 per hour
Mr G, Assistant	$40 per hour

The audit of X Ltd has taken 14 hours of Mr B's time, 105 hours of Miss D's time, 140 hours of Mr F's time and 150 hours of Mr G's time. Travelling expenses of $600 have been incurred by the audit team.

The audit fee that will be charged to X Ltd will be:

	$
Mr B's time (14 hours @ $90)	1,260
Miss D's time (105 hours @ $75)	7,875
Mr F's time (140 hours @ $40)	5,600
Mr G's time (150 hours @ $40)	6,000
Travelling expenses	600
Total audit fee to be invoiced	21,335

4 The ethical problems involved in setting fees

In establishing and negotiation fees for a specific assignment, members may come across ethical and other professional problems.

Fee quotations

When negotiating fees for a particular assignment members may quote whatever fee is believed to be appropriate. The fact that one accountant has quoted a fee lower than another is not in itself unethical. However, if a fee quoted is so low that it becomes difficult to perform the engagement in accordance with applicable professional standards for that price, then an ethical threat to professional competence and due care may be created.

Safeguards may be applied to eliminate this threat or to reduce it to an acceptable level, for example:

- making it clear to the client which services are covered by the quoted fees and the basis on which fees are to be charged, and
- assigning appropriate time and staff to the engagement.

If a member is investigated following allegations of unsatisfactory work, an inappropriate fee quote may be taken into account during the disciplinary process.

Explanations should always be given to clients when a fee is for extra work, is different from previous years, or is in excess of quotation, estimate or tender.

Test your understanding 2

Ethical aspects of auditing

The provision of audit services to clients (as opposed to other assurance services or non-assurance services) brings with it specific ethical issues in relation to fees. What do you believe are the appropriate responses to the following ethical problems?

(1) The assignment of audit staff to a low audit fee engagement.

(2) The acceptability of contingency fees.

(3) Overdue fees from the previous audit.

Test your understanding 3 – 'Hawk'

You are a training manager in Hawk Associates, a firm of Chartered Certified Accountants. The firm has suffered a reduction in fee income due to increasing restrictions on the provision of non-audit services to audit clients. The following proposals for obtaining professional work are to be discussed at a forthcoming in-house seminar:

(a) 'Cold calling' (i.e. approaching directly to seek new business) the chief executive officers of local businesses and offering them free second opinions.

(5 marks)

(b) Placing an advertisement in a national accountancy magazine that includes the following:

'If you have an asset on which a large chargeable gain is expected to arise when you dispose of it, you should be interested in the best tax planning advice. However your gains might arise, there are techniques you can apply. Hawk Associates can ensure that you consider all the alternative fact presentations so that you minimise the amount of tax you might have to pay. No tax saving – no fee!'

(6 marks)

(c) Displaying business cards alongside those of local tradesmen and service providers in supermarkets and libraries. The cards would read:

'Hawk ACCA Associates
For PROFESSIONAL Accountancy, Audit,
Business Consultancy and Taxation Services
Competitive rates. Money back guarantees.'

(4 marks)

Required

Comment on the suitability of each of the above proposals in terms of the ethical and other professional issues that they raise.

(Total: 15 marks)

5 Chapter summary

OBTAINING PROFESSIONAL WORK

Professional guidance is needed on obtaining professional work in order to ensure that ACCA members apply the Fundamental Principles of the ACCA Code of Ethics in their daily conduct

ADVERTISING AND PUBLICITY

Material must not:

- Bring disrepute to the ACCA
- Discredit the services offered by others
- Be misleading
- Fall short of any advertising codes

FEES

Fees should be:

- Fair and reasonable
- Based on factors such as staff seniority, time spent, urgency of the work, etc.
- Contingency fees should be avoided except where customary (e.g. in merger and acquisition work)

TENDERING FOR ENGAGEMENTS

See next chapter

Test your understanding answers

Test your understanding 1

No. Deidre Jones is entitled to inform the public of her special skills (e.g. advice for small businesses, business start-ups, etc.) but claiming that she offers the best service in the area again discredits the services offered by other accountants. The 'smiley' symbols are not consistent with an image of professionalism and should be replaced. Finally, she should state a business telephone number or physical address in the advertisement, not just a web address.

Nowhere in the advertisement does Deidre Jones state that she is an accountant (although obviously the ACCA designation states this for those who know what it means). If this advertisement is to be included in a directory of accountants, there is no need to include this point. However, if the advertisement is to go in a general publication, it is probably best to clearly state the fact that Deidre Jones is a certified accountant or chartered certified accountant (as well as including the ACCA designation after her name).

Test your understanding 2

(1) Every audit must have assigned to it sufficient staff and sufficient time to carry out the audit properly, regardless of the audit fee to be charged. There are no circumstances in which a low audit fee can justify any lack of appropriate resource or time taken to perform a proper audit in compliance with auditing and ethical standards.

(2) No audit can be carried out on a contingency fee basis. The threat to objectivity from such an arrangement would be too great.

(3) Arrangements to pay such overdue fees must be agreed with the client before an auditor can accept appointment as auditor for the following period. If the amounts overdue are significant, the engagement partner should consider whether the firm can continue as auditors, or whether it is necessary to resign.

Test your understanding 3 – 'Hawk'

A good working knowledge of the professional codes is required here and an ability to apply them. However, it should be helpful to identify issues which common sense would indicate do not sit comfortably with a professional approach (that must be independent where assurance is given)

(a) **'Cold calling'**

Tutorial note: Recognising that there are three issues to address (i.e. 'cold calling', 'free' and 'second opinions') is likely to earn more marks than focusing on just one.

- Until relatively recently 'cold calling' has been largely prohibited throughout the profession (and still is in some countries e.g. Hong Kong). Therefore the 'direct' approach may not be suitable.
- Where 'cold-calling' restrictions have been relaxed it may still only be permitted for existing business clients (i.e. to offer them additional services), the direct approach to non-business clients being prohibited. This inhibits competition.
- Although the practice may be viewed as 'a bit grubby and commercial' it is now generally regarded as an accepted modern business practice. Along with other professional bodies, ACCA removed its prohibition on 'cold calling' in 2002.
- Whilst Hawk is permitted to 'cold call', the fundamental ethical principles must be adhered to. Whilst solicitation which is decent, honest and truthful may be acceptable, cold calling which amounts to harassment is not.
- Offering a service for 'free' is not prohibited provided that the client is not misled about future levels of fees.
- There are strict ethical codes regarding 'second opinions' (on accounting treatments). Practitioners are advised NOT to provide second opinions, when requested, without following a procedure of contacting the incumbent auditor/accountant. Therefore to be offering second opinions clearly goes against ethical guidelines – as the practice is to be discouraged.

(b) **Tax planning**

- Advertising is generally allowed subject to the observance of the fundamental principles of ethical codes (e.g. IFAC's Code of Ethics for Professional Accountants, ACCA's Code of Ethics and Conduct).

- Although direct advertising (i.e. on television, radio, cinema) is prohibited in many jurisdictions (e.g. Hong Kong), an advertisement in a national accountancy magazine is generally permitted.
- Where advertising is permitted, the minimum requirements are that it be decent, honest, truthful and in good taste. These criteria may not be met in this proposal as:
  - expectations of favourable results (lower tax liabilities) may be unjustifiable (or created deceptively);
  - 'techniques you can apply' may imply an ability to influence taxation authorities;
  - 'the best' is likely to be a self-laudatory statement and not based on verifiable facts;
  - 'the best' may also be making an unjustifiable comparison with other professional accountants in public practice;
  - 'the best tax planning advice' may be an unjustifiable claim of expertise or specialism in the field of tax.
- 'Can ensure …' and the assertion of 'all' may not be supportable claims, therefore the advertisement is not honest in these respects.
- There is a 'fine line' between tax avoidance and tax evasion and 'techniques you can apply' and 'alternative fact presentations' may lean toward the latter and so not be in keeping with the integrity of the profession.
- The assertion of being able to 'minimise the amount of tax' may expose Hawk Associates to litigation. The engagement risk associated with taking on this work would be high and so should carry commensurately high fees.
- The 'no tax saving – no fee' offer does not compensate for the risk associated with undertaking the work advertised.
- Contingency fees, whereby no fee will be charged unless a specific result is obtained, are prohibited by IFAC (unless otherwise permitted by statute of member body).

(c) **Business cards**

- Business cards may be considered a form of stationery and should be of an acceptable professional standard and comply with legal and member body requirements concerning names of partners, principals, professional descriptions, designatory letters, etc.
- Whilst placing such an advertisement where a target audience might reasonably be expected to exist (e.g. in an Institute of Directors or Business Men's Club), displaying it alongside 'local tradesmen' may appear to belittle the status of professional accountants.
- An advertisement the size of a business card would be sufficient to provide a name and contact details and in this respect is suitable. However, the danger of giving a misleading impression is pronounced when there is such limited space for information.
- However, the tone of the advertisement may discredit the ACCA name. It is also unsuitable that it seeks to take unfair advantage of the ACCA name. Although the ACCA mark can be used by Hawk Associates on letterheads and stationery (for example) it cannot be used in any way which confuses it with the firm.
- The emphasis on 'professional' may be unsuitable as it could suggest that there are other than professional accounting, audit (etc) services to be had.
- Offering a range of non-audit services in the same sentence as 'audit' may mislead interested persons picking up the card into thinking that Hawk can provide them together. This conflicts with the fact that Hawk is restricted in providing non-audit services to audit clients.
- There is no basis for asserting 'competitive rates'.
- It is unlikely that any professional would offer 'money back'. In the event of dispute (e.g. over fees), the matter would be taken to arbitration (with their member body) if a satisfactory arrangement could not be reached with the client.
- A tradesman may guarantee the quality of his work – and that it can be made good in the event that the customer is not satisfied. However, an auditor cannot guarantee a particular outcome for the work undertaken (e.g. reported profit or tax payable). Most certainly an auditor cannot guarantee the truth and fairness of the financial statements in giving an audit opinion.

chapter

6

Tendering

Chapter learning objectives

Upon completion of this chapter you will be able to:

- discuss the reasons why entities change their auditors/professional accountants
- recognize and explain the matters to be considered when a firm is invited to submit a proposal or fee quote for an audit or other professional engagement
- identify the information required for a fee proposal
- prepare the content of an engagement proposal document
- discuss and appraise the criteria that might be used to evaluate tenders received from audit firms in a given situation
- discuss reasons why audit fees may be lowered from the previous year's fees
- explain 'lowballing' and discuss whether or not it impairs independence.

1 Changing auditors/professional accountants

Why change auditors?

Companies may change their auditors or other professional accountants for a number of reasons, with the impetus for change coming either from the company or from the audit firm.

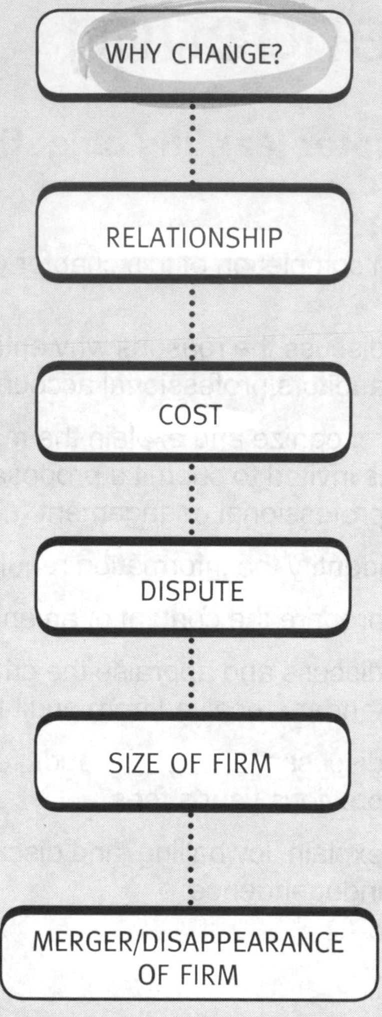

Why change auditor?

Reasons why a company may wish to change their auditors include:

- a change in the relationship between auditor and client;
- an attempt to reduce costs;
- a dispute between the company and the incumbent firm, maybe over financial reporting practices;
- the company might seek a larger audit firm who can offer a wider range of services;
- the audit firm may have ceased trading.

Why step down?

Audit firm may not seek re-appointment for many reasons. Examples include:

- independence issues
- doubts regarding the integrity of the company's management
- strategic decision making, such as: concentrating in other markets.

EU research into reasons for changing auditor

The EU has carried out research on the reasons why companies in practice have changed their auditors. The results were as follows.

Reason	Percentage of responses (%)
Company policy of regular rotation of audit firm	24
Appointment of a group auditor	16
Audit fees of incumbent auditor are too high	8
Dissatisfaction with quality of incumbent's work	4
Differences of opinion regarding financial statements	4
Insufficient advisory suggestions from incumbent	4
Other/not specified	40
	100

The prominence of rotation reflects the special case of Italy where there is a statutory requirement to rotate audit firms. The situation of a parent company imposing a group auditor is relevant across Europe and often arises when a company is sold to a new group.

Test your understanding 1

Who chooses a company's auditors?

2 Matters to be considered when a firm is invited to tender

Tendering is the process of quoting a fee for work before the work is carried out.

Tendering and changes in the market
As a consequence of being required to tender for audits, audit firms have found that fees have been substantially reduced. This has (in theory) resulted in certain changes in the accountancy market: • mergers of audit practices to become more efficient. The 'Big 4' firms (PwC, Deloittes, Ernst & Young and KPMG) now dominate audit provision throughout the world • adoption of risk-based auditing techniques so that fewer hours of auditing are needed to reach the same standard of audit conclusion • acceptance that audit fees might fall in amount, but a hope that money can be made by carrying out lucrative non-audit work for the client (e.g. consultancy, tax planning, recruitment services, etc.).

When invited to tender, a firm must decide whether it wishes to take part in the tendering process. The following should be considered:

Ethical issues	Legal issues	Commercial issues
• Is the firm independent? • Will the quoted audit fee exceed accepted ethical fee limits? • Does the firm have the necessary resources to complete the engagement with competence and due care?	• Is the firm is eligible under company law to be appointed, e.g. are any partners of the firm also employees of the company?	• Are the firm's resources available to complete the engagement on time? • Need for external experts? • Do the expected rewards outweigh the perceived costs/risks? • How much was the prior year audit fee? • Is the potential client profitable and growing? • What additional services could be sold?

In addition to the risk associated with any new client the specific risks of being involved with the tender include:

- wasted time – if the audit tender is not accepted
- setting an uncommercially low fee in order to win the contract
- making unrealistic claims or promises in order to win the contract

3 The engagement proposal document

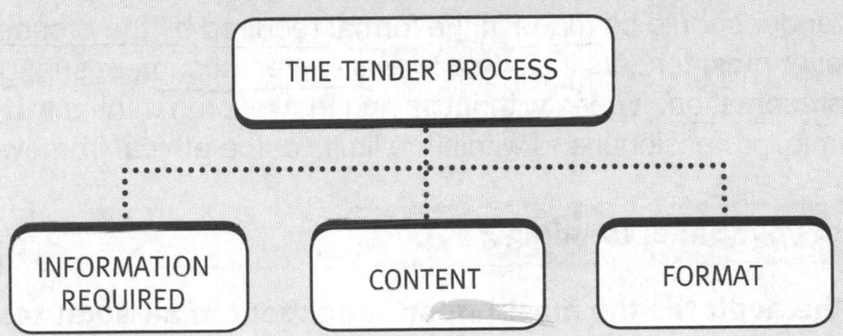

The preparation of an engagement proposal document is an important step in obtaining new work.

Information required for the proposal

Prior to drafting any proposals an audit firm should consider the following:

- precisely what does the potential client expect from its auditors?
- what timetable does the client expect: an interim audit followed by a final audit, or a longer final audit after the year end?
- by what date are the audited financial statements required?
- what are the company's future plans, e.g. public flotation, expansion, contraction, concentration on certain markets?
- are there any perceived problems with the potential client's current auditors?

The content of the proposal

The content of the proposal should include:

- the fee and how it has been calculated
- the nature, purpose and legal requirements of an audit (clients are often not clear about this)
- an assessment of the requirements of the client

- an outline of how the audit firm proposes to satisfy those requirements
- the assumptions made, e.g. on geographical coverage, deadlines, work done by client, availability of information, etc.
- the proposed approach to the audit or audit methodology
- an outline of the firm and its personnel
- the ability of the firm to offer other services.

The format of the proposal

The tender should be made in the format required by the prospective client. However most tenders include a formal written document supported by an oral presentation. It goes without saying that all presentations should be dynamic, professional and within the limits of the ethical framework.

Test your understanding 2

Is the audit fee the most important aspect of an audit tender? Is the audit always awarded to the firm that bids the lowest fee?

4 The evaluation of tenders received

Criteria used to evaluate tenders received

After each of the prospective firms of auditors has made its presentation, the company must make its choice. Relevant criteria are likely to include:

- clarity
- relevance
- professionalism
- personal/standardized
- timeliness of delivery
- originality
- range of other services
- ability to deliver
- reputation.

Ali

Perception of audit value

A report prepared in 2006 for the UK government, identified the three most important criteria in the perception of the value of an audit:

- technical competence in carrying out the audit
- value-added services provided on top of the audit itself
- using the good reputation of the audit firm to enhance the reputation of the company.

The 'Big 4' audit firms are seen in the market as offering these criteria, as well as having greater capacity and international coverage to deliver the audit itself. Thus there is an 'IBM effect' in auditing. No-one gets fired for choosing IBM computers, and no-one gets fired for choosing a 'Big 4' firm of auditors.

Test your understanding 3

How can small and mid-tier audit firms win the audits of large companies if those companies don't even invite them to tender for the audit?

5 Benefits and drawbacks of the tendering process

The benefits and drawbacks to the process of tendering and possible practice of constantly changing auditors include the following:

Benefits

- More efficient auditing.
- A tendency by companies to boost their internal audit departments so as to reduce external audit costs.
- Companies have also tended to simplify their group structures to reduce audit costs (among other reasons).

Drawbacks

- Greater market concentration, which has in fact reduced market choice.
- Loss of long-term relationships with auditors.
- A slight loss of perceived independence. The audit firms would deny this.

You decide

- Greater emphasis by audit firms on other services they can sell the client (auditing could be a loss leader).
- Lowballing – the tendency for audit firms to tender below cost with the objective of getting the audit and hoping to raise the fee later, and to get lucrative non-audit work to compensate for the low audit fee. Surveys have found no correlation between lowballing (predatory pricing) and negligent auditing.

Exam hint

Almost everything on this list is double edged – greater concentration may be interpreted as an increase in expertise or as a reduction in choice.

In the exam you may be required to express the arguments clearly and to have a grasp of both sides of the argument. You may even be required to form a conclusion based upon your interpretation of the argument.

6 The pressure to cut audit fees

The lowering of audit fees from year to year

During 2002 to 2006 audit fees charged to large European companies were high, due to a combination of the transition to IFRSs and the regulatory burden of complying with the US Sarbanes-Oxley Act. Finance directors now hope that audit fees in future can be reduced year by year, due to:

- stability in accounting standards (the IASB intend to make no major amendments to IASs/IFRSs during the next two years, to give standards a chance to 'bed in')
- improved internal controls in companies should enable more systems-based and less substantive auditing
- an ongoing learning curve effect as audit firms build up cumulative audit knowledge about their clients.

Lowballing

Lowballing is the setting of a low price at the start of an arrangement in order to secure the business, with the intent later to raise the price.

Impact of 'lowballing'

- In the sphere of auditing, firms are accused of lowballing when they tender a low price for audit work in the hope that, once they are appointed as auditors, they will be given lucrative non-audit work by the company.
- Some commentators have argued that a self-interest threat to independence arises to an audit firm that has won an audit contract after lowballing the tender. It is argued that the firm is unable to act objectively since they are motivated to please the directors so that they will be awarded contracts for non-audit services.
- There is no evidence that lowballing produces negligent audits. The regulatory system and the keenness of audit firms to maintain their good reputation should ensure that a quality job is always done, regardless of the fee charged.
- The fear of litigation, fear of loss of reputation, fear of investigation by the ACCA, and independence of spirit should be enough to safeguard the independence of auditors.

Test your understanding 4 – 'Azure'

Azure sells inclusive tours (i.e. international flights, hotel accommodation and meals) to two million customers. All hotels are independently owned and operated. The company employs 5,000 people and uses 11 leased aircraft. Azure has a representative office at each of 13 holiday locations. Your firm has been invited to tender for the audit of Azure for the year ending 31 December 2007. As the prospective audit engagement manager, you have been asked to identify the principal audit risks and other planning issues, including audit strategy, to be presented as part of your firm's written submission. The invitation to tender indicates that written submissions will be used as a means of shortlisting for the presentation stage.

Required:

Suggest and comment on appropriate selection criteria which should be used by Azure in its evaluation of submissions received.

(10 marks)

7 Chapter summary

TENDERING

WHY CHANGE AUDITORS

THE 'BEAUTY CONTEST'

THE PROPOSAL

SETTING THE FEE

LOWBALLING

INFORMATION

CONTENT
- Fee
- What is an audit?
- Client's needs and firm's response
- Assumptions
- Approach
- Who we are
- Other services

FORMAT

Test your understanding answers

Test your understanding 1

In short – the shareholders.

Best practice on corporate governance recommends that an audit committee recommends to the board the appointment and removal of the external auditor, which is then put to the shareholders for their approval in general meeting.

Test your understanding 2

No to both questions. All other things being equal, a lower fee would make a tender more attractive. However, in practice all other things are not equal. A company is looking today for far more than simply an audit report at the end of the audit. The company expects the auditor to offer value-adding suggestions and to be a partner in the business, at the same time as remaining independent – a difficult combination!

Test your understanding 3

This is a real problem. In countries like the UK, the audit market is becoming increasingly concentrated. Every FTSE 100 company is audited by 'Big 4' audit firms. The 99% of audit fees in the FTSE 350 are paid to the 'Big 4'. As the market has become more concentrated, the level of audit fees has risen, as economic theory would suggest.

Small and mid-tier firms find it difficult to enter the market for auditing large companies. Less than 10% of FTSE 350 companies surveyed said that they would consider using a mid-tier firm. Even if they are invited to tender, the costs of assembling a credible bid are high, so there is a real risk of high wasted costs if the bid is unsuccessful.

Until mid-tier firms can acquire a credible reputation among large company finance directors and audit committees, and can establish a co-ordinated international presence, this situation is unlikely to change.

Test your understanding 4 – 'Azure'

Appropriate selection criteria

Tutorial notes: The marking scheme indicates that full marks could be obtained by identifying and briefly commenting on 10 criteria or identifying and providing a more detailed commentary on just four criteria – or anything in between. This answer is indicative of the comments that could be made, it is not prescriptive.

Audit firm

'Background information' provided by the audit firms invited to tender is likely to include:

- organisation structure (e.g. into specialised departments for audit, tax, etc)
- its size (e.g. in terms of staffing levels)
- locations of offices (including overseas locations relevant to Azure)
- affiliated firms (if any)
- its relevant client portfolio (as an indicator of the firm's relevant experience and reputation in the travel/holiday/leisure industry).

Azure may be particularly interested in the reputation of the audit firm (i.e. how highly it is regarded). For example, Azure may be seeking to improve its 'standing'/image (e.g. with its bankers or other finance providers) by association with a distinguished audit firm name.

First impressions

Whether the submission deadline for responses was met (on a timely basis or at the last minute) – as evidence of speed of delivery (e.g. in meeting the audit reporting deadlines).

The quality of the submission (e.g. whether it is complete, well-presented, factually correct, etc) – as evidence of the likely quality of audit work.

Understanding the business

Azure will expect the submissions to demonstrate the experience of each of the audit firms in the travel/holiday/leisure industry (e.g. as evidenced by its relevant client portfolio). An appreciation of significant economic and legal issues in any of the countries in which Azure offers holidays would also be relevant.

Azure may rank, in particular, the audit firms' understanding of Azure's business (how it works) and its objectives (future aspirations) – which must be evident in the submissions.

The audit team

Factors to consider when Azure is assessing the calibre of each of the proposed audit teams may include:

- its size (staffing levels) and mix (between grades of staff)
- its organisation (e.g. between subordinates/managers and audit/tax etc) and coordination (e.g. with clear communication channels and lines of reporting)
- the relevant experience of key individuals (audit engagement partner and managers)
- the level of partner input
- access to relevant specialists both within the firm and external consultants (e.g. in IT).

Services

The services of greatest interest to Azure are likely to be international tax and IT (in addition to audit). However, legal matters (e.g. relating to contracts and franchises or licences) may also be relevant. Azure is most likely to be looking for a firm with the capability to deliver the range and quality of services relevant to their immediate and future needs (for the benefits of 'one-stop shopping' such as economies of scale).

Azure may be seeking an audit firm with a proactive approach and the ability to add value to its business. For example, there may be tax or other benefits to be obtained by changing the status and/or registration of representative offices (e.g. from overseas branches to local companies or vice versa).

Audit approach

In having requested, as part of the submission, 'principal audit risks ... other planning issues ... audit strategy', Azure will expect the firms to have demonstrated, for example:

- a high level of planning
- an understanding of audit issues (and how these issues will be reported to Azure)
- an audit methodology offering a cost effective approach.

Tax

Submissions will be expected to show an understanding of tax issues (e.g. in relation to overseas operations) and proactivity in providing practical, cost-effective solutions.

Chemistry

Although personal rapport and the audit firm's enthusiasm for a working relationship with Azure will be more apparent at the presentation stage, Azure will make some assessment about 'chemistry' before then. Azure will be asking 'Do they understand our business issues?' and if, for example, Azure met with any of the firms before the submission 'Does the submission show that they listened to us?'.

Fees

Azure will expect competitive fees/value for money/constructive business advice.

A fee breakdown (e.g. split between grades of staff and/or audit and tax compliance work) will probably have been requested to facilitate comparison between the firms.

Azure may be suspicious of (have reservations about) an audit fee proposed by a tenderer if it is significantly lower ('lowballing'?) or higher than others.

Other criteria

Whilst there is no suggestion that Azure is seeking 'malleable' (i.e. acquiescent) auditors, Azure is unlikely to invite to the presentation stage any firm whose submission shows a lack of empathy for the organisation's business objectives, risk management policies, etc.

Tutorial note: Whilst 'nepotism' may be a factor considered in the selection of auditors or advisors, it is not one that should be used in the 'evaluation of submissions received'.

chapter

7

Money Laundering

Chapter learning objectives

Upon completion of this chapter you will be able to:

- define 'money laundering'
- explain the scope of criminal offences of money laundering
- explain the need for ethical guidance in this area
- explain the importance of customer due diligence (CDD)
- describe, with reasons, the basic elements of an anti-money laundering program

1 Definition of money laundering

Money laundering is the process by which criminals attempt to conceal the true origin and ownership of the proceeds generated by illegal means, allowing them to maintain control over the proceeds and, ultimately, providing a legitimate cover for their sources of income.

Examples

Consider the following scenarios.

- Whilst preparing or auditing accounts you realize that a client has incorrectly reclaimed value added tax (or other national recoverable taxes) on the purchase of a motorcar. You point this out to the client and propose an adjustment to the financial statements to provide for the additional tax that is due. You also advise the client that he must rectify this with the tax authorities. However, the client tells you that he has just had an inspection by the tax authorities that did not reveal the error. The client tells you he wants to just forget it.
- Another client issues an invoice to a customer for $800. At the end of the month the accounts department issues a statement showing the invoice as being outstanding. The next day a check for $800 arrives attached to a copy of the invoice. A month later another check for $800 arrives attached to a copy of the statement – the customer mistakenly pays twice.

  In carrying out the audit work some six months later you ask the client about the $800 credit balance. The sole shareholder/director comments that he tells his accounts department to ignore negative balances when they issue statements to customers. If the customer orders from them again they will use the $800 against the cost of the goods. Otherwise he will leave the balance on the account for a year or so and then write it off.

  Errors and mistakes of the type illustrated above may not constitute criminal conduct, provided that they are corrected. However, in all the cases there appears to be an intention to gain a permanent benefit from another's mistake or to avoid a legal liability. In the UK, for example, this is criminal conduct. As such, each of these cases would result in the accountant knowing or suspecting that a client is involved in money laundering.

2 International efforts to combat money laundering

The Financial Action Task Force (FATF) is an international body that promotes policies globally to combat money laundering and terrorist financing. In 1990 FATF issued recommendations to combat the misuse of financial systems to launder drug money.

The recommendations included:

- making money laundering a criminal offence
- measures to be taken by businesses and professions to prevent money laundering, including:
  - customer due diligence and record-keeping
  - reporting of suspicious transactions to an appropriate authority
- international co-operation including extradition of suspects.

These recommendations have become the benchmark against which a country's rules are assessed.

FATF Recommendations

FATF focuses on three principal areas:

- setting standards aimed at combating money laundering and terrorist financing
- evaluating the degree to which countries have implemented measures that meet those standards, and
- identifying and studying money laundering and terrorist financing techniques.

In 1990, FATF drew up a document entitled "The Forty Recommendations" as an initiative to combat the misuse of financial systems to launder drug money. These recommendations (including the ones noted above) were endorsed by over 130 countries worldwide and now form the benchmark against which national anti-money laundering systems are assessed. Although different countries have moved forward in different ways.

The UK has adopted the recommendations of FATF.

The Republic of Ireland has similar legislation to the UK, with all reports of suspected money laundering to be made to the Garda Bureau of Fraud Investigation.

The USA has a number of similar Acts:

- the Bank Secrecy Act 1970: this requires all cash deposits, withdrawals and transfers above $10,000 to be reported to the Inland Revenue Service
- the Money Laundering Control Act 1986
- the Uniting and Strengthening America by Providing Appropriate Tools Required to Intercept and Obstruct Terrorism (USA PATRIOT) Act 2001: this requires all financial institutions to establish an anti-money laundering program, including the development of internal policies and the designation of a compliance officer.

3 Examples of Legislation

Introduction

Different countries have moved forward in different ways with the implementation of the FATF recommendations. The main legislation and requirements below relate to the money laundering regulatory regime as it stands in the UK. The principles, however, are appropriate on an international basis.

UK Legislative Background

Following the 1993 Criminal Justice Act, four further laws have tightened up the regulations in the UK:

- Terrorism Act 2000
- Proceeds of Crime Act 2002 (POCA)
- Money Laundering Regulations 2007 (the Regulations)
- Serious Organized Crime Police Act (SOCPA) 2005

In 2003 the ACCA issued Technical Fact Sheet 94 'Anti-money Laundering (Proceeds of Crime and Terrorism)' giving guidance to accountants in this area.

Money Laundering Offences

Under the UK's Proceeds of Crime Act 2002 the following are all criminal activities:

- Concealing or disguising criminal property, or removing it from the UK.
- Acquiring, using or having possession of criminal property.
- Tipping off.

The Money Laundering Regulations 2007 impose certain obligations on financial services businesses, which are designed to assist in detecting money laundering and preventing the financial services organisations being used for money laundering purposes. These obligations are:

- To put in place internal controls and policies to ensure compliance with the legislation;
- To appoint a Money Laundering Reporting Officer (MLRO);
- To establish/enhance record keeping systems for:
  - all transactions;
  - the verification of clients' identities;
- To establish internal reporting procedures; and
- To educate and train all staff in the main requirements of the legislation.

Criminal property and criminal conduct

Criminal property is property that has arisen from criminal conduct. Examples include:

Property acquired by theft;

The proceeds of tax evasion

Bribery or corruption

Saved costs arising from a criminal failure to comply with a regulatory requirement

Tipping off

Tipping-off, by word or action, or by failure to speak or act, is also a criminal offence. Accountants must guard against:

- carrying out any action that may tip-off suspected money launderers that they are under investigation, or
- otherwise prejudicing an investigation.

Money Laundering Offences

Money laundering includes:

- an attempt or conspiracy or incitement to commit such an offence;
- aiding, abetting, counseling or procuring the commission of such an offence; or
- an act which would constitute any of these offences if done in the UK.

Failure to Report Offences

Other offences under POCA include:

- failure by an individual in the regulated sector to inform the Serious Organised Crime Agency (SOCA), a Financial Intelligence Unit (FIU)) or the business's Money Laundering Reporting Officer (MLRO), as soon as practicable, of knowledge or suspicion (or reasonable grounds for knowing or suspecting) that another person is engaged in money laundering
- failure by MLROs in the regulated sector to make the required report to SOCA as soon as practicable if an internal report leads them to know or suspect that a person is engaged in money laundering.

Tipping Off and Other Offences

The offence of tipping-off occurs when the MLRO, or any individual makes a disclosure which is likely to prejudice any investigation which might be conducted following a report, if they know or suspect that such a report (including an internal one) has been made. It is a defence if the person did not know or suspect that the disclosure was likely to prejudice the investigation.

Measures Imposed on Financial Institutions

Some of the recommendations of FATF cover measures to be taken by financial institutions, non-financial businesses and professions to prevent money laundering and the financing of terrorist activities. These measures include:

- Customer Due Diligence.
- Record Keeping.
- Reporting of suspicious transactions and compliance to the Financial Intelligence Unit (FIU).

In the UK, for example, some of these measures are covered by the Money Laundering Regulations 2007.

Relevant Businesses

The recommendations of the FATF apply not only to accountants but to other business as well.

In the UK these are defined by the MLR 2007 and in broad terms the "relevant businesses" subject to the requirements of are:

- businesses in regulated investment activities
- banking and bureau de change activities
- estate agencies
- tax advisors
- insolvency practitioners
- accountants and auditors
- providers of legal services
- businesses involved in the formation, operation or management of trusts and companies
- casino operators
- dealers in goods (if a transaction involves accepting a total cash payment of 15,000 euro or more).

4 Client identification procedures

Accountants are required to establish that new clients are who they claim to be by requesting the potential client provides satisfactory evidence of identity. This is often referred to as 'Client Due Diligence.'

This must be performed as soon as is reasonably practicable after contact is first made between the two parties. Where satisfactory evidence of identity is not obtained by the accountant, the business relationship or one-off transaction must not proceed any further.

Detailed Procedures

Basic identification procedures include:

- For individuals: inspection of evidence to establish the full name and permanent address of the client, e.g. a driving licence or a passport (both of which include a photograph) and a recent utility bill to confirm the address.
- For businesses: inspection of evidence including: the certificate of incorporation; lists of registered members and directors; certificate of registered address.
- For trusts: inspection of evidence to establish and confirm: the nature and purpose of the trust; its original source of funding; and the identities of the trustees, controllers and beneficiaries.

Copies of the evidence inspected must be maintained for a period of five years after the relationship with the client has ended.

5 General staff training procedures

Every person in the conduct of relevant business must take appropriate measures to ensure that relevant employees are:

- made aware of the provisions of the relevant anti-money laundering regulations, and are
- given training in how to recognize and deal with transactions which may be related to money laundering.

This is because businesses and their employees must:

- comply with the requirements of regulations; and
- establish procedures of internal control and communication as may be appropriate for the purposes of forestalling and preventing money laundering.

6 General reporting procedures

The FATF recommend reporting procedures. In the UK these are codified in the MLR 2007 that are typical of procedures adopted internationally.

In the UK, the MLR 2007 establishes that a relevant business must maintain reporting procedures which require that:

- a person in the organization is nominated to receive disclosures under this regulation ("the nominated officer")
- anyone in the organization, to whom information comes in the course of the relevant business as a result of which he suspects that a person is engaged in money laundering, must disclose it to the nominated officer

- where a disclosure is made to the nominated officer, the officer must consider it in the light of any relevant information which is available to the organization and determine whether it gives rise to suspicion, and

- where the nominated officer does so determine the information must be disclosed to a person authorized for the purposes of these Regulations by the Director General of the SOCA.

Client Privilege

'Client privilege' in the context of reporting requirements

Accountants working in practice must report knowledge or suspicions of money laundering (whether involving a client or another party)

- to a Financial Intelligence Unit (FIU), which in the UK is SOCA, or
- in accordance with their employer's anti-money laundering procedures.

General defences against charges are that:

- a report has been made to:
  - SOCA or
  - to the employer's Money Laundering Reporting Officer (MLRO, an officer nominated by each business to receive such reports)
- it was intended to make a report but there was a reasonable excuse for not having done so, e.g. a fear of physical violence in reprisal
- the property was acquired for adequate consideration in good faith.

Legal privilege may provide a legal advisor with a defence to a charge of failing to report suspicions of money laundering. It applies where a lawyer receives information in privileged circumstances that is not communicated with the intention of furthering a criminal purpose. Accountants could only claim this defence if they were also professionally legally qualified.

7 Making a Report

The recommendations of the FATF include measures to be taken by businesses and professions to prevent money laundering, including reporting of suspicious transactions to an appropriate authority

As an example of typical national reporting requirements, in the UK these are covered by the Money Laundering Regulations.

The MLRO and reporting

- The MLRO should be an individual of suitable seniority and experience. Alternative arrangements must be made when the MLRO is unavailable (on holiday, sick, jury service, etc).
- The MLRO receives and assesses money laundering reports from colleagues, and passes on valid suspicions to SOCA on a standard form that identifies:
  (1) the suspect's name, address, date of birth and nationality
  (2) any identification or references seen
  (3) the nature of the activities giving rise to suspicion
  (4) any other information that may be relevant.
- Sole practitioners with no employees or associates are exempt from the requirement to appoint an MLRO, since clearly they would be reporting to themselves.
- Necessary record keeping includes a full audit trail of transactions for at least the last five years. The ACCA Rules of Professional Conduct also apply.

8 Potentially suspicious transactions

Characteristics

There is no formal definition of "suspicious". A suspicious transaction will often be inconsistent with the client's known or usual legitimate activities.

Examples of potentially suspicious transactions:

- Unusually large cash deposits;
- Frequent exchanges of cash into other currencies; and
- Overseas business arrangements with no clear business purpose.

REMEMBER! It is a criminal offence not to report knowledge or suspicion of money laundering.

'De Minimis' Concessions

Note that in the UK the obligation to report does not depend on the amount involved or the seriousness of the offence. There are no de minimis concessions.

9 The elements of an anti-money laundering program

Auditors, in carrying out their review of a client's adherence to the money laundering regulations, should ensure that the following basic elements exist in the client's anti-money laundering program:

- dedicated resources
- written policies and procedures
- comprehensive coverage
- timely escalation and resolution of matters
- explicit management support
- sufficient training and education
- regular review/audit of the program.

10 The need for ethical guidance on money laundering

ACCA provides guidance in its Code of Ethics and Conduct in the area of money laundering.

- This is needed because there is a clear conflict between:

  (1) the accountant's professional duty of confidentiality in relation to his client's business, and

  (2) the duty to report suspicions of money laundering to the appropriate authorities as required by law.

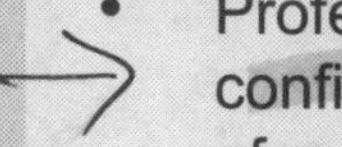

- Professional accountants are not in breach of their professional duty of confidentiality if they report in good faith their knowledge or suspicions of money laundering to the appropriate authority.
- Disclosure in bad faith or without reasonable grounds would possibly lead to the accountant being sued for breach of confidence.
- Auditor's duty of confidentiality will not be breached if they report, in good faith, any money laundering knowledge or suspicions to the appropriate authority. Statutory protection also applies where reports are made in good faith.

11 Money Laundering – Summary

MONEY LAUNDERING

FINANCIAL ACTION TASK FORCE ON MONEY LAUNDERING (FATF)

Legislation

(UK example)

Criminal Justice Act 1993

Terrorism Act 2000

Proceeds of Crime Act 2002

Money Laundering Regulations 2007

Offences

- Money laundering
- Tipping off
- Not setting up procedures
- Not complying with procedures

Relevant businesses

- Including accountants

Ethical guidance

- Conflict with confidentiality

Duties

Client identification

- Know your client
- Client due diligence

Appointing an MLRO

- With specified responsibilities

Staff training

- For all relevant personnel

Reporting

- Internal to MLRO
- External to FIU

Basics of a client system

To enable auditors to review client anti money laundering procedures.

chapter

8

Professional Responsibilities and Liabilities

Chapter learning objectives

Upon completion of this chapter you will be able to:

- discuss the responsibillties of both management and accountants with regard to laws and regulations and how this affects engagement planning and completion
- define 'fraud' and 'error' and discuss the responsibilities of both management and auditors towards fraud and error
- discuss the course of action that should be taken when fraud and/or error are identified
- discuss liability in the context of assurance engagements and the impact on professional practice management.

1 Laws and Regulations

Guidance regarding responsibility to consider laws and regulations in an audit of financial statements is provided in **ISA 250** Consideration of Laws and Regulations in an Audit of Financial Statements.

Responsibilities are considered from the perspective of both auditors and management.

Responsibilities of Management

ISA 250 clearly states that it is the responsibility of management, with the oversight of those charged with governance, to ensure that the entity's operations are conducted in accordance with relevant laws and regulations, particularly those that determine the reported amounts and disclosures in the financial statements.

Preventing and Detecting Non-Compliance

In order to help prevent and detect non-compliance, management can implement the following policies and procedures:

- Monitoring legal requirements applicable to the company and ensuring that operating procedures are designed to meet these requirements;
- Instituting and operating appropriate systems of internal control;
- Developing, publicising and following a code of conduct;
- Ensuring employees are properly trained and understand the code of conduct;
- Monitoring compliance with the code of conduct and acting appropriately to discipline employees who fail to comply with it;
- Engaging legal advisors to assist in monitoring legal requirements; and
- Maintaining a register of significant laws and regulations with which the entity has to comply.

In larger entities, these policies and procedures may be supplemented by assigning appropriate responsibilities to:

- An internal audit function;
- An audit committee; and/or
- A compliance function.

Responsibilities of the Auditor

The auditor is responsible for obtaining reasonable assurance that the financial statements. taken as a whole, are free from material misstatement, whether caused by fraud or error (ISA 200). Therefore, in conducting an audit of financial statements the auditor must take into account the applicable legal and regulatory framework.

More specifically the auditor must obtain sufficient, appropriate evidence regarding compliance with those laws and regulations generally recognised to have a direct effect on the determination of material amounts and disclosures in the financial statements.

To help meet this objective they must perform specified audit procedures to help identify instances of non-compliance that may have a material impact on the financial statements. If non-compliance is identified (or suspected) the auditor must then respond appropriately.

Further discussion of auditor responsibility

IFAC recognises that the auditors have a role in relation to non-compliance with laws and regulations. Auditors plan, perform and evaluate their audit work with the aim of providing reasonable, though not absolute, assurance of detecting any material misstatement in the financial statements which arises from non-compliance with laws or regulations.

However, auditors cannot be expected to be experts in all the many different laws and regulations where non-compliance might have such an effect. There is also an unavoidable risk that some material misstatements may not be detected due to the inherent limitations in auditing.

2 The auditors' considerations and procedures

Non-compliance with laws and regulations may have a fundamental effect on:

- the operations of the entity (and its ability to continue as a going concern); and
- disclosures in the financial statements (most notably provisions and contingencies).

The auditors should perform procedures to help identify instances of non-compliance with those laws and regulations by:

- **obtaining a general understanding** of the legal and regulatory framework applicable to the entity and the industry, and of how the entity is complying with that framework
- **inspecting correspondence** with relevant licensing or regulatory authorities
- **enquiring of the management and those charged with governance** as to whether the entity is in compliance with such laws and regulations
- **remaining alert** to the possibility that other audit procedures applied may bring instances of non-compliance to the auditor's attention
-  **obtaining written confirmation** from the directors that they have disclosed to the auditors all those events of which they are aware which involve possible non-compliance, together with the actual or contingent consequences which may arise from such non-compliance.

How to Obtain a General Understanding

ISA 250 provides some guidelines to assist auditors when obtaining an understanding of their clients' legal and regulatory environments. The standard provides the following examples:

- Using the auditor's existing understanding of the industry;
- Updating the auditor's understanding of laws and regulations that directly determine reported amounts and disclosures in the financial statements;
- Enquiry of management as to other laws and regulations that may be expected to have a fundamental effect on the operations of the entity;
- Enquiry of management concerning the entity's policies and procedures regarding compliance;
- Enquiry of management regarding the policies or procedures adopted for identifying, evaluating and accounting for litigation claims.

(ISA 250, A7)

Indications of situations where non-compliance may have

The appendix to ISA 250 sets out examples of the types of information or situations that may come to the attention of the auditor and may indicate non-compliance with laws or regulations.

These include:

- investigation by government department
- payment of fines or penalties
- loans or payments for unspecified services to consultants, related parties, employees or government employees
- sales commissions or agents' fees that appear excessive in relation to those normally paid by the entity or in its industry
- unusual payments in cash
- unusual transactions with companies registered in tax havens
- an accounting system that fails to provide adequate audit trail or sufficient evidence (either by design or by accident)
- transactions that are unauthorised
- improperly recorded transactions
- comment in the media.

3 Audit procedures when non-compliance is discovered

When the auditors become aware of information concerning a possible instance of **non-compliance** with laws or regulations, they should:

- understand the **nature of the act**
- understand the **circumstances** in which it has occurred
- obtain sufficient other information to **evaluate** the possible effect on the financial statements
- **document** their findings
- **report** their findings to an appropriate level of management (subject to any requirement to report directly to a third party)

Written representations

Written representations should be obtained to the effect that management has disclosed to the auditor all known actual or possible non-compliance with laws and regulations whose effect should be considered in the preparation of financial statements. The discovery of non-compliance again may require the auditor to reconsider his risk analysis and the reliability of management representations.

4 Reporting non-compliance

The auditor should report non-compliance to management. However, in certain circumstances they should consider reporting directly to shareholders or third parties (perhaps in cases of fraud or money laundering?)

Where the auditors conclude that suspected non-compliance with laws or regulation has a material effect on the financial statements and they disagree with the accounting treatment or with the extent, or the lack, of any disclosure in the financial statements they should consider a modified audit opinion.

Reporting non-compliance to third parties

Confidentiality is an implied term of the auditors' contract. The duty of confidentiality, however, is not absolute. In certain exceptional circumstances auditors are not bound by the duty of confidentiality and have the right to report matters to a proper authority in the public interest. Auditors need to weigh the public interest in maintaining confidential client relationships against the public interest in disclosure to a proper authority. Determination of where the balance of public interest lies requires careful consideration. Auditors whose suspicions have been aroused need to use their professional judgement to determine whether their misgivings justify them in carrying the matter further or are too insubstantial to deserve report.

The auditor may need to seek legal advice before deciding on a course of action.

5 Engagement withdrawal

The auditor may decide that the situation is so serious that it needs to withdraw from the engagement (i.e. resign as auditor).

From the perspective of financial reporting, the auditor can issue a disclaimer or an adverse or qualified opinion on the accounts. However, there may have been a breakdown of trust between the auditor and management, or the auditor may have doubts about the competence of management that could lead to the auditor considering resignation. The auditor should take legal advice before embarking on this course of action.

6 Laws and Regulations – Summary

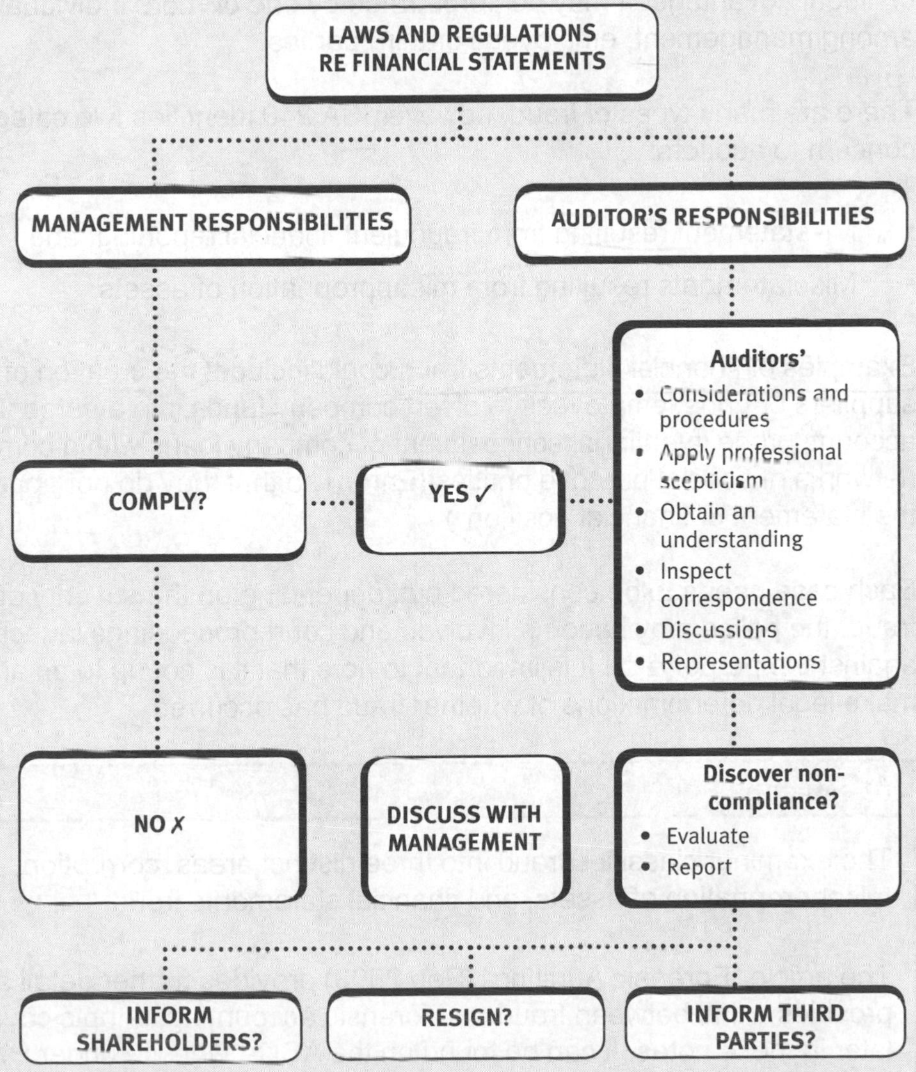

7 Fraud and error

Definitions

In **ISA 240** the Auditor's Responsibilities Relating to Fraud in an Audit of Financial Statements, it states that "misstatements in the financial statements can arise from fraud or error. The distinguishing factor between fraud and error is whether the underlying action that results in the misstatement of the financial statements is intentional or unintentional."

Fraud

Fraud is an intentional act involving the use of deception to obtain an unjust or illegal advantage. It may be perpetrated by one or more individuals among management, employees or third parties.

There are many types of fraud, however ISA 240 identifies two categories of concern to auditors:

- Misstatement resulting from fraudulent financial reporting; and
- Misstatements resulting from misappropriation of assets.

Examples of financial statements fraud could include the creation of dummy suppliers or ghost employees to divert company funds into a personal bank account; or the intentional concealment of company loans within complex networks of special purpose entities (Enron) so that they do not appear on the statement of financial position.

Each case needs to be considered but, depending on the severity of the fraud, the police may become involved and court proceedings launched against the perpetrator. It is important to note that it is not up to an auditor to make legal determinations of whether fraud has occurred.

Article Focus

The examiner classifies fraud into three distinct areas: corruption, misappropriation of assets, and financial statements fraud.

The article "Forensic Auditing" (Sep 2008) provides further detail and provides a link between fraud and forensic accounting, a topic covered later in these notes. It can be found on the ACCA website under P7 resources.

Case Study: Kingston Cotton Mill

Re Kingston Cotton Mill (1896)

The Kingston Cotton Mill case emphasised that the reader of an audit report should have a realistic viewpoint of what the auditor's role should actually be.

'An auditor is not bound to be a detective or to approach his work with suspicion or with a foregone conclusion that there is something wrong. He is a watch-dog, but not a bloodhound.'

As the remainder of this section will explore, the attitude towards auditors and fraud has changed somewhat over the last 115 years. Auditors do have a recognised responsibility for considering fraud when conducting an audit of financial statements, even if it is not a primary one.

Error

Errors can be defined as an unintentional misstatement in financial statements, including the omission of amounts or disclosures, such as the following:

- A mistake in gathering and processing data from which financial statements are prepared;
- An incorrect accounting estimate arising from oversight or a misinterpretation of facts; or
- A mistake in the application of accounting principles relating to measurement, recognition, classification, presentation or disclosure."

Errors are normally corrected by clients when they are identified. If a material error has been identified but has not been corrected, it may effect the ultimate audit opinion (see chapter 14 for further explanations).

8 Responsibilities for fraud and error

ISA 240 explains that the "primary responsibility" for the prevention and detection of fraud rests with both those charged with governance of an entity and with management.

However, auditors are required to provide reasonable assurance that the financial statements are free from material misstatement, whether caused by fraud or error. In order to meet this responsibility auditors must plan, perform and review audits in light of the risk of misstatement due to fraud.

Of fundamental importance to this is the concept of professional scepticism. This means that auditors should always remain aware of the possibility that fraud could take place. They must always consider the potential for management override of controls and recognise the fact that audit procedures that are effective for detecting error may not be effective for detecting fraud.

ISA 240 also recognises the inherent limitations of an audit and that there is an unavoidable risk that some material misstatements may not be detected, even though the audit is properly planned and performed in accordance with ISAs. This risk is greater in relation to misstatement due to fraud, rather than error, because of the potentially sophisticated nature of organised criminal schemes.

Management vs. Auditor

Management should:

- place a strong emphasis on fraud prevention and error reduction
- reduce opportunities for fraud to take place
- ensure the likelihood of detection and punishment for fraud is sufficient to act as a deterrent
- ensure controls are in place to provide reasonable assurance that errors will be identified
- foster, communicate and demonstrate a culture of honesty & ethical behaviour
- consider potential for override of controls or manipulation of financial reporting
- implement and operate adequate accounting and internal control systems.

Auditors

- ISA 315 requires a discussion amongst the engagement team regarding the susceptibility of the client's financial statements to material misstatement due to fraud.
- The auditor shall than perform risk assessment procedures to obtain an understanding of the client and its environment. According to ISA 315 this should include the following procedures:
  - Enquiry of management regarding their assessment of fraud risk, the procedures they conduct and whether they are aware of any actual or suspected instances of fraud;

– Enquiry of the internal audit function to establish if they are aware of any actual or suspected instances of fraud;

– Enquiry of those charged with governance with regard to how they exercise oversight of management processes for identifying the risk of fraud and whether they are aware of any actual or suspected fraud; and

– Consideration of relationships identified during analytical procedures.

- In response, in accordance with ISA 330, the auditor shall determine overall responses to address the risks of material misstatement due to fraud at the financial statements level. This includes: the design of further audit procedures; the allocation of – and supervision of – team members to particular procedures; evaluation of accounting policies; and incorporation of an element of unpredictability in the selection of the nature, timing and extent of audit procedures

(ISA 240, P.29)

Absolute Assurance – Never!

An auditor **cannot obtain absolute assurance** over the accuracy of the financial statements because of such factors as:

- the use of judgement
- the use of testing
- the inherent limitations of internal control, and
- the fact that much of the audit evidence available to the auditor is persuasive rather than conclusive in nature.

9 Investigations of possible misstatements

When an actual or potential misstatement is identified by an auditor, a number of matters must be considered, and procedures carried out, to determine the impact (if any) on the audit.

- The nature of the event and the circumstances in which it has occurred should be understood.
- Sufficient information should be gathered to allow evaluation of the possible effect on the financial statements.

- If the auditors believe that the indicated fraud or error could have a material effect on the financial statements, they should perform appropriate modified or additional procedures.
- ISA 240 requires that where a fraud is identified or information indicating that one may exist the auditor should communicate the matter to the appropriate level of management.

Implications for the audit

Modified or additional procedures

Procedures will depend on the nature of the fraud indicated, the likelihood of its occurrence and the likely effect on the financial statements. Auditors cannot assume that frauds are isolated. Where such additional procedures do not dispel the suspicion of fraud or error, the auditor should discuss the matter with management and consider whether it has been properly reflected in the financial statements.

Implications for the audit

Auditors should consider the effect of the fraud or error on their preliminary risk assessment and on the reliability of management representations. This is particularly important where senior management is involved.

Discuss with management

Regardless of the materiality of the actual or suspected fraud or error, the auditor will need to communicate factual findings with management and those charged with governance in order to:

(i) keep them informed and to ensure that they understand the position correctly

(ii) discover what action they have taken or intend to take to rectify the position, e.g. management may consider amending the system of internal control in order to reduce or eliminate the risk of such irregularities in the future

(iii) evaluate the likelihood that the irregularity has recurred or will recur

(iv) discover what, if any, legal advice has been taken.

Management Override

Management is uniquely placed to commit fraud due to their access to and ability to manipulate accounting records and financial statements. This is due to the fact that many controls rely on the effective operation of management and management can abuse their power to override those controls.

All the famous, high profile (and most economically damaging) cases, such as Enron and Maxwell, include some form of managerial fraud.

Although the risk of management varies it is always present and auditors must always consider this possibility when planning, performing and evaluating their audit.

In response auditors should design and perform procedures to:

- Test the appropriateness of journal entries in the general ledger and adjustments made in the preparation of the financial statements. These procedures include:
  - Enquiring of those involved in financial reporting about unusual activity relating to adjustments;
  - Selecting journal entries and adjustments made at the end of the reporting period; and
  - Considering the need to test journal entries throughout the period.
- The auditor should also consider the accounting estimates made by management and the possibility of bias or direct manipulation affecting their judgement. In performing this review auditors shall:
  - Evaluate the reasonableness of judgements and whether they indicate any bias on behalf of management; and
  - Perform a retrospective review of management judgements reflected in the prior year.
- If there are any significant transactions that are outside the normal course of business, or appear unusual, the auditor should consider whether this suggests an increased risk of fraudulent financial reporting.

10 Fraud, error and the role of auditors

The action taken by auditors to report an event varies in relation to its nature and the gravity of its consequences.

Reporting to management

If the auditor has identified a fraud, or obtained evidence that indicates one may have occurred, the auditor should communicate this on a timely basis to an appropriate level of management.

If the auditor suspects either management, employees with a significant role in internal control or others where the fraud results in a material misstatement, then the auditor should communicate the matter to those charged with governance.

The requirement to report such matters also stems from ISA 260, which requires the auditor to communicate matters of governance interest in a timely fashion. If the matter is significant it should be reported in writing.

If the auditor has doubts about the integrity of those charged with governance then the most appropriate course of action would be to obtain legal counsel before any reports are made.

Reporting to shareholders

If the matter leads to a material misstatement or an inability to obtain sufficient appropriate evidence then the auditor must consider the impact upon the nature and wording of their audit report. If matters are significant the auditor may choose to speak directly to the shareholders at the AGM, however, if the matter relates to fraud the auditor would obtain legal advice first.

Reporting to third parties

- Where the auditor believes that a suspected fraud should be reported to an appropriate authority in the public interest, he should notify the directors in writing of his view and, if the entity does not voluntarily do so, should report it himself.
- Where the suspected fraud casts doubt on the integrity of the directors, the auditor should make a report direct to the proper authority in the public interest without delay and without informing the directors in advance.

Test your understanding 1

You are the auditor of a chain of restaurants. You have noticed a newspaper report that guests at a wedding have fallen ill after eating at one of your client's restaurants.

What impact should this report have on your considerations of compliance with laws and regulations and what audit procedures would you perform?

Test your understanding 2

For the following, state whether you think they are examples of fraud or error.

(a) The finance director accounted for $10 million of sales in the financial year being reported on, despite knowing that the goods involved will not be delivered until Q2 of the next financial year.

(b) An order for $10 million was received and processed as sales in the last month of the financial year being reported on. It was believed that the goods would be delivered prior to the year end but, due to delivery problems, they were not dispatched until half way through Q1 of the next financial year.

Test your understanding 3

The directors of Jubilee Ltd have asked your firm to produce a much more detailed report at the end of the audit than usual, listing down all the deficiencies in the internal control system. They are unhappy that during the course of the year discounts had been given to customers who did not qualify for them, as a result of the non-application of an internal control process. They have expressed dissatisfaction with your audit firm as this control deficiency was not reported to them by your firm.

Draft points to include in your reply to Jubilee Ltd.

Test your understanding 4

You are the auditor of Promise Co. The Finance Director has asked for a meeting with you. She recently discovered that the purchase ledger manager has diverted company funds into his own bank account. The Finance Director has identified funds of $50,000 to date as being diverted and wants and explanation as to why you did not highlight this issue during the course of your recently completed audit. The profit for the year was $17.5m. Prepare a set of briefing notes to assist you in your meeting with the Finance Director.

11 Fraud and Error – Summary

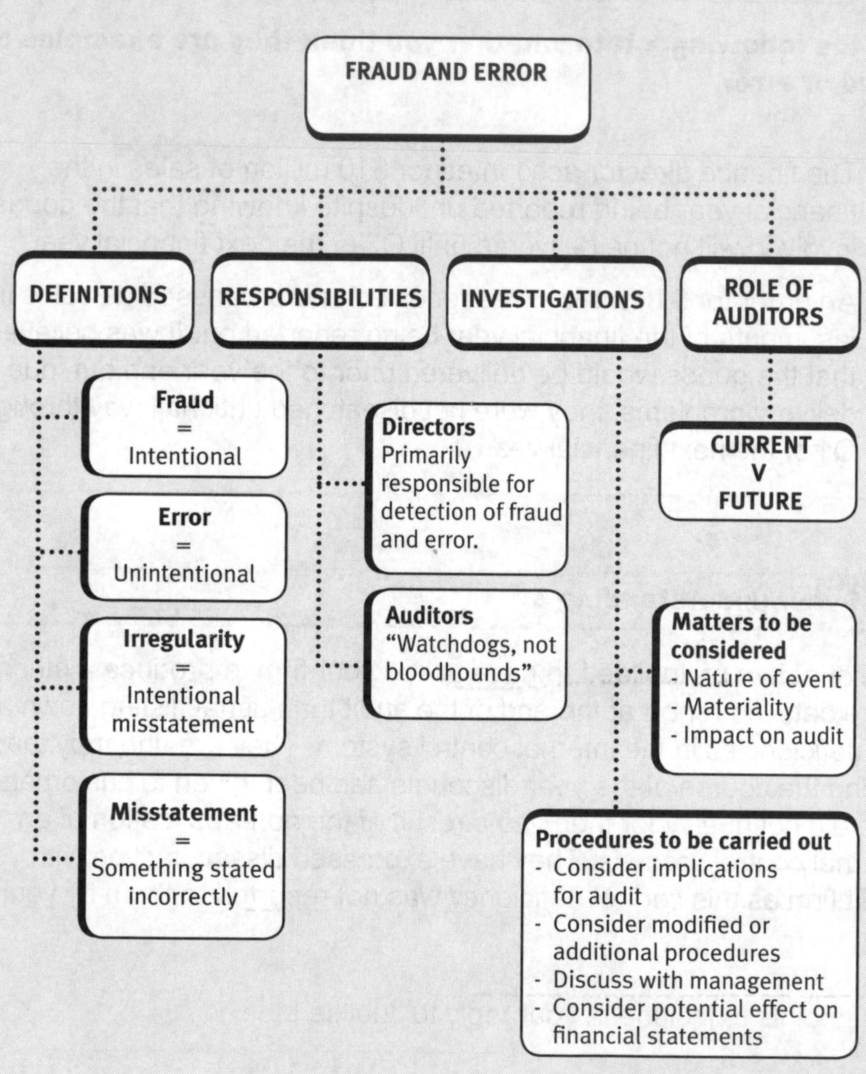

12 Legal liability

The circumstances in which auditors may have legal liability

Typically, the auditor has a statutory duty to report to the members on whether:

- the financial statements are free from material misstatement;
- the financial statements have been properly prepared in accordance with relevant national legal frameworks (e.g. in the UK - the Companies Act); and
- the Directors' Report is consistent with the financial statements

Such duties impose liabilities if things go wrong. Auditors' liability can be categorised under the following headings:

- civil or criminal liability arising under legislation
- liability under common law arising from negligence

Criminal vs. Civil

Civil liability

Auditors may be liable in the following circumstances.

- To third parties suffering loss as a result of relying on a negligently prepared audit report – see below.
- Under insolvency legislation to creditors – auditors must be careful not to be implicated in causing losses to creditors alongside directors.
- Under tax legislation – particularly where the auditor is aware of tax frauds perpetrated by his client.
- Under financial services legislation to investors.
- Under stock exchange legislation and/or rules.

The only possible penalty for a civil offence is payment of damages.

Criminal liability

Insolvency, tax and financial services legislation may involve both criminal and civil liability. Penalties for criminal liability may include imprisonment.

Criminal liability can arise in the following circumstances.

- Accepting an appointment as auditor when ineligible to do so, or continuing in office after becoming ineligible.
- Instances of fraud, such as:
  - misappropriation of assets
  - obtaining financial advantage by deception
  - falsifying accounting records or documents
  - publishing misleading statements intended to deceive members or creditors.
- 'Insider dealing' under securities legislation. This is the misuse of 'unpublished price sensitive information'. Auditors are in a privileged position to obtain price sensitive information such as forthcoming mergers and take-overs or sudden changes in profits.
- Financial services legislation, provides criminal sanctions for auditors and others (principally directors) who knowingly or recklessly make false statements in connection with the issue of securities (principally via the prospectus).

The remedy for a criminal offence can be the payment of a fine, imprisonment, or both.

In addition to the various civil and criminal liabilities the professional bodies that regulate accountants and auditors have various sanctions, such as:.

- warnings, fines, reprimands, severe reprimands and exclusion from membership for misconduct by members
- Conviction of a criminal offence involving financial misconduct is normally sufficient to warrant exclusion from membership of a reputable professional body.

Liability to the client and liability to third parties

Liability in contract

- Liability to the client arises from contract law. The company has a contract with the auditor and hence can sue the auditor for breach of contract if the auditor simply fails to deliver , or delivers a negligently prepared, audit report.
- When carrying out his duties the auditor must exercise care and skill. The degree of care and skill to be shown, in particular in relation to the depth of his investigation and the types of check to be made, is shown by judicial precedent.
- In the ACCA's Rules of Professional Conduct the fundamental principles in respect of professional competence and due care state that:
- 'Members have a continuing duty to maintain professional knowledge and skill at a level required to ensure that a client or employer receives competent professional service based on current developments in practice, legislation and techniques. Members should act diligently and in accordance with applicable technical and professional standards when providing professional services.'
- Generally if auditors can show that they have complied with generally accepted auditing standards, they will not have been negligent.

Liability in tort

A third party (i.e. a person who has no contractual relationship with the auditor) may sue the auditor for 'damages', i.e. a financial award.

In the tort of negligence, the plaintiff (i.e. the third party) must prove that:

- the defendant (i.e. the auditor) owes a duty of care; and
- the defendant has breached the appropriate standard of care as discussed above (i.e. has been negligent); and
- the plaintiff has suffered loss as a direct result of the defendant's breach.

On the whole litigation is not concerned whether the auditor has in fact been negligent but whether a duty of care is owed in the first place. If no duty is owed, it cannot be breached.

Case Study: Lloyd Cheyham v Littlejohn de Paula

Lloyd Cheyham v Littlejohn de Paula (1985)

Littlejohn de Paula successfully defended themselves against a negligence claim in this case by showing:

- that they had followed the standard expected of the normal auditor, i.e. the standard in Accounting Standards and Auditing Standards
- that their working papers were good enough to show consideration of the problems raised by the plaintiff and reasonable decisions made after consideration
- that the plaintiff had not made all the reasonable enquiries one could expect when, in this case, purchasing a company. For example a review of the business was not undertaken upon investigating the purchase but only after purchase
- the judge, therefore, held that far too much reliance was placed on the accounts by the plaintiff and he awarded costs against the plaintiff to the defendant.

13 Negligence

The critical matter in most negligence scenarios is whether a duty of care is owed in the first place.

When is a duty of care owed?

A duty of care exists when there is a special relationship between the parties, i.e. where the auditors knew, or ought to have known, that the audited accounts would be made available to, and would be relied upon by, a particular person (or class of person).

The injured party must therefore prove:

- that the auditor knew, or should have known, that the injured party was likely to rely on the financial statements
- that the injured party has sufficient 'proximity', i.e. belongs to a class likely to rely on the financial statements
- that the injured party did in fact so rely, and
- that the injured party would have acted differently if the financial statements had shown a different picture.

Case Study: ADT Ltd v BDO Binder Hamlyn

ADT Ltd v BDO Binder Hamlyn (1995)

BH were the joint auditors of the Britannia Security Systems Group. Before the 1989 audit was finished, ADT were considering bidding for Britannia, so an ADT representative met the BH audit partner and asked him to confirm that the audited accounts gave a true and fair view and that he had learnt nothing subsequently which cast doubt on the accounts. The partner said that BH stood by the accounts and there was nothing else that ADT should be told. ADT then bought Britannia for $105m, but it was found to be worth only $40m.

It was held that BH owed ADT a duty of care when the partner made his statements, and the accounts had been negligently audited, so ADT were awarded $65m plus interest. The shortfall in BH's insurance cover was $34m; the partners were therefore individually liable for that amount.

BH appealed, and ADT agreed an out-of-court settlement.

Has the auditor exercised due professional care?

The term due professional care cannot be explained in precise terms. There is no absolute standard. The following points are relevant in determining what is a reasonable standard of care:

- applying the most up-to-date accounting and auditing standards.
- adhering to all standards of ethical behaviour laid down by the relevant professional bodies.
- being aware of the terms and conditions of appointment as set out in the letter of engagement and as implied by law.
- employing competent staff who are adequately trained and supervised in carrying out instructions.

Has the injured party suffered a loss?

This is normally provable as a matter of fact. For example, if X relies on the audited financial statements of Company A and pays $5m to buy the company, but it soon becomes clear that the company is worth only $1m, then a loss of $4m has been incurred.

Case Study: Caparo

The Caparo case (Caparo Industries v Dickman and others (1984))

Caparo Industries took over Fidelity plc in 1984 and alleged that it increased its shareholding on the basis of Fidelity's accounts, audited by Touche Ross. Caparo sued Touche Ross for alleged negligence in the audit, claiming that the stated $1.3m profit for the year to 31 March 1984 should have been reported as a loss of $460,000.

It was held in this case that the auditors owed no duty of care in carrying out the audit to individual shareholders or to members of the public who relied on the accounts in deciding to buy shares in the company.

The House of Lords looked at the purpose of statutory accounts. They concluded that such accounts, on which the auditor must report, are published with the principal purpose of providing shareholders as a class with information relevant to exercising their proprietary interests in the company. They are not published to assist individuals (whether existing shareholders or not) to speculate with a view to profits.

Case Study: Bannerman

The Bannerman case (Royal Bank of Scotland (RBS) v Bannerman Johnstone Maclay (2002))

RBS provided overdraft facilities to APC Limited and Bannerman were APC's auditors. The relevant facility letters between RBS and APC contained a clause requiring APC to send RBS, each year, a copy of the annual audited financial statements.

In 1998 APC was put into receivership with approximately $13.25m owing to RBS. RBS claimed that, due to a fraud, APC's financial statements for the previous years had misstated the financial position of APC and Bannerman had been negligent in not detecting the fraud. RBS contended that it had continued to provide the overdraft facilities in reliance on Bannerman's unqualified opinions.

Bannerman applied to the court for an order striking out the claim on the grounds that, even if all the facts alleged by RBS were true, the claim could not succeed in law because Bannerman owed no duty of care to RBS.

The judge held that the facts pleaded by RBS were sufficient in law to give rise to a duty of care and so the case could proceed to trial. The judge held that, although there was no direct contact between Bannerman and RBS, knowledge gained by Bannerman in the course of their ordinary audit work was sufficient, in the absence of any disclaimer, to create a duty of care owed by Bannerman to RBS. In order to consider APC's ability to continue as a going concern, Bannerman would have reviewed the facilities letters and so would have become aware that the audited financial statements would be provided to RBS for the purpose of RBS making lending decisions. Having acquired this knowledge, Bannerman could have disclaimed liability to RBS but did not do so. The absence of such a disclaimer was an important circumstance supporting the finding of a duty of care.

14 Restricting auditors' liability

Ways in which liability may be restricted

Audit firms may take the following steps to minimise their exposure to negligence claims:

- screening potential audit clients to accept only clients where the risk can be managed
- using a letter of engagement as per ISA 210 in order to establish the respective responsibilities and duties of directors and auditors
- carrying out high quality audit work
- using clauses to disclaim liability to third parties
- taking out professional indemnity insurance (PII)
- attempting to regulate the use of documents and restrict their use to their specific, intended purpose
- obtaining specialist legal advice where appropriate.

Disclaimer Statements

Reaction to the Bannerman decision – disclaimer statements

In the Bannerman case the judge commented that, if the auditors had inserted a disclaimer statement in their audit report, then they would have had no legal liability to RBS who was suing them.

Following this case, the ICAEW recommended additional wording to be routinely included in all audit reports by ICAEW members, on the lines of:

> 'This report is made solely to the company's members as a body. Our audit work has been carried out so that we might state to the company's members those matters we are required to state to them in an audit report and for no other purpose. We do not accept responsibility to anyone other than the company and the company's members as a body, for our audit work or for the opinions we have formed.'

The ACCA's view (in Technical Factsheet 84) is that standard disclaimer clauses should be discouraged since they could have the effect of devaluing the audit report. Disclaimers of responsibility should be made in appropriate, defined circumstances (e.g., where the auditor knows that a bank may rely on a company's financial statements) but the ACCA does not believe that, where an audit is properly carried out, such clauses are always necessary to protect auditors' interests.

In practice, the difference of opinion between the ICAEW and the ACCA may not be so great. If an ACCA auditor is not aware that a bank is going to place reliance on an audit report (so no disclaimer is given), then it seems likely under Caparo or Bannerman that no duty of care would be owed to the bank in any event.

The impact of limiting audit liability

Some commentators have argued that limiting audit liability is contrary to the public interest, since auditors will be less motivated to do a first class job if they know that they won't have to pay for their mistakes.

Other commentators say that this ignores the professional nature of the audit discipline. People choose to be audit partners because they want to do a high quality job for themselves and for society.

Possible Methods of Limiting Audit Liability

(a) **A financial cap on liability**

This could be a fixed amount (as in Germany) or a multiple of the audit fee. A possible adverse effect of the latter would be to either reduce the quality of work done, or to reduce the fee, as the lower the fee, the lower the liability.

(b) **Incorporating audit firms as limited liability partnerships (now permitted in the UK under the Limited Liability Partnerships Act 2000).**

(c) **Permitting auditors to agree the limits of their liability with their clients**

In the UK such agreements were illegal until the Companies Act 2006, which now permits 'liability limitation agreements' between auditors and companies, subject to shareholders' approval. The Act does not specify what sort of limit can be agreed, so a fixed cap, or a multiple of fees, or any other type will all now be possible once this section of the Act has been implemented.

(d) **Modification of the 'joint and several liability' principle**

Auditors are jointly and severally liable with directors where negligence claims are made, either under legislation, or under case law. This means that directors and auditors are held responsible together for the issue of negligently prepared and audited financial statements. If, say, the auditors and directors share the blame for falsifying records (i.e. the auditors did not detect it), the auditor may bear all of the costs if the directors have no resources to pay. The objective is to protect the plaintiff and maximise their chances of recovery of losses. The effect in practice is to load all of the costs onto auditors who have to be insured!

An associated problem is the fact that all partners and directors are responsible for the misconduct of other partners and directors in audit firms, regardless of whether they were directly involved in a particular audit. In the US - and now the UK - this problem is partly dealt with by limited liability partnerships.

(e) **Compulsory insurance for directors – for the reasons noted in above.**

Professional indemnity insurance

One of the obligations of practising as a professional accountant is to ensure that, if an accountant's negligence has caused loss to a client, the accountant has an insurance policy to ensure that he can pay any damages awarded.

- **Professional indemnity insurance (PII)** is insurance taken out by an accountant against claims made by clients and third parties arising from work that the accountant has carried out.
- **Fidelity guarantee insurance (FGI)** is insurance taken out by an accountant against any liability arising through acts of fraud or dishonesty by any partner or employee in respect of money or goods held in trust by the accountancy firm.

If an accountant did not have PII, it is possible that a successful claim could be made against him in excess of his personal resources, so that the claimant could not be paid.

Settlements out of Court

On occasions legal cases may be settled out of court due to negotiation between the plaintiff and the dependent.

Benefits

- Cost saving (i.e. lower fees);
- Time saving;
- Less risk of damage to reputation.

Drawbacks

- Does not address the importance of the practitioner's legal responsibilities; and
- May be due to pressure from insurers, who are willing to risk a court settlement; and
- Insurance premiums may still rise.

Test your understanding 5

A recent industry commentator has written: "In respect of the many recent corporate collapses, the auditor is often seen as the easy scapegoat. Not least because of their professional indemnity insurance. This damages the reputation of the profession and over time can only lead to reduction in the number and quality of skilled audit practioners, and a consequential increase in costs to their clients. Legislation has to be changed, in order to protect the auditor and the future of the profession, to allow auditors to agree a contractual cap on their liability for statutory audits."

Set out what you believe are the arguments for and against allowing auditors to agree on a contractual cap as describe above.

15 The expectation gap

The **expectation gap** is the gap between what the public believe that auditors do (or ought to do) and what they actually do.

This expectation gap can be categorised into:

- a **standards gap** – where the public believe auditing standards to be different from what they actually are.
- a **performance gap** – where auditors operate below current standards.
- a **liability gap** – where the public do not understand to whom the auditor is legally responsible.

Expectations gap – examples

Typical manifestations of the expectation gap are:

- the public believe that auditors are responsible for preventing and detecting fraud and error, while auditors maintain that they need only have a reasonable expectation of detecting material fraud and error.
- the public believe that they can sue the auditors if companies fail, while auditors maintain that it is the directors' responsibility to run their business as a going concern, and following Caparo it is not the auditor's function to protect individual shareholders if they make a poor investment decision.

Bridging the gap

Recent developments include:

- educating the public to reduce the standards gap e.g. the 'long-form' audit report now specifically states the auditor's responsibilities, detail that was not included in the shorter wording used previously
- improving the quality of audits to reduce the performance gap.
- possible changes in auditors' liability.

Test your understanding 6 – 'Lambley'

The partner in charge of your audit firm has asked your advice on frauds which have been detected in recent audits.

(a) The audited financial statements of Lambley Trading were approved by the shareholders at the AGM on 3 June 20X2. On 7 June 20X2 the managing director of Lambley Trading discovered a petty cash fraud by the cashier. Investigation of this fraud has revealed that it has been carried out over a period of a year. It involved the cashier making out, signing and claiming petty cash expenses which were charged to motor expenses. No receipts were attached to the petty cash vouchers. The managing director signs all cheques for reimbursing the petty cash float. Lambley Trading has sales of about $2 million and the profit before tax is about $150,000. The cashier has prepared the draft financial statements for audit.

The partner in charge of the audit decided that no audit work should be carried out on petty cash. He considered that petty cash expenditure was small, so the risk of a material error or fraud was small.

You are required to:

(i) briefly state the auditor's responsibilities for detecting fraud and error in financial statements

(ii) consider whether your firm is negligent if the fraud amounted to $5,000

(iii) consider whether your firm is negligent if the fraud amounted to $20,000.

(9 marks)

(b) The audit of directors' remuneration at Colwick Enterprises, a limited company, has confirmed that the managing director's salary is $450,000, and that he is the highest paid director. However, a junior member of the audit team asked you to look at some purchase invoices paid by the company. Your investigations have revealed that the managing director has had work amounting to $200,000 carried out on his home, which has been paid by Colwick Enterprises. The managing director has authorised payment of these invoices and there is no record of authorisation of this work in the board minutes. The managing director has refused to include the $200,000 in his remuneration for the year, and to change the financial statements. If you insist on qualifying your audit report on this matter, the managing director says he will get a new firm to audit the current year's financial statements. The company's profit before tax for the year is $91 million.

Assuming the managing director refuses to amend the financial statements, **you are required to:**

(i) consider whether the undisclosed remuneration is a material item in the financial statements

(ii) describe the matters you will consider and the action you will take:

- to avoid being replaced as auditor; and
- if you are replaced as auditor

assuming the managing director owns 60% of the issued shares of Colwick Enterprises.

(iii) describe the matters you will consider and the action you will take to avoid being replaced as auditor, assuming Colwick Enterprises is a listed company with an audit committee, and the managing director owns less than 1% of the issued shares.

(11 marks)

(Total: 20 marks)

Exam Style Question: Ethical, Professional and Legal Issues

Study note: this question is typical of the current P7 exam. It is one of the 'core' topics identified in the 'Examiner's Approach to Paper P7' article (January 2007). Therefore a question of this nature (or similar case style presentation) should be expected in each sitting of P7.

Twilight Plc

You are a senior audit manager at Obrey & Taylor, a firm of chartered certified accountants. You have recently been assigned to a long standing audit client, Twilight Plc, after the previous senior manager on the job resigned. You are currently planning the final audit for the year ended 31 March 2007. During you preliminary reviews and investigations you identify the following matters:

(1) Twilight acquired a competitor company, Sunset Ltd, in the previous financial year. However, the merger has not progressed as planned and, as such, Twilight have issued a profit warning. It has emerged that some of Sunset's long term contracts have ended in losses, rather than the profits initially expected. As a result is appears that profits in prior years were overstated. Your firm's corporate finance department carried out the due diligence investigation of Sunset on behalf of Twilight prior to completion of the acquisition.

(6 marks)

(2) One of the seniors assigned to assist with the audit of Twilight appeared to be unduly upset by the news of the profit warning. Upon further investigation you have discovered that the senior in question was given shares in Twilight some years ago by his late grandfather.

(4 marks)

(3) During discussions with one of the audit juniors from the prior year you discover that during the previous years' audit a significant unexplained investment in an East Asian company was identified. According to the junior the FD declared that "it was nothing to concern them" and that the previous senior manager was satisfied with this response so took no further action.

(5 marks)

Required:

(a) Comment upon the legal, professional and ethical issues raised by the above matters for the year end audit and for your firm as a whole.

The breakdown of marks for the discussion of each sub-section is shown above.

(15 marks)

(b) Identify and discuss THREE areas of quality control that could be strengthened by Obrey & Taylor to help avoid a reoccurrence of the incident noted in (3) above.

(9 marks)

16 Legal Liability – Summary

AN AUDITOR MAY HAVE A CIVIL OR CRIMINAL LIABILITY ARISING FROM LEGISLATION, OR A LIABILITY UNDER COMMON LAW ARISING FROM NEGLIGENCE.

IN THE TORT OF NEGLIGENCE, THE PLAINTIFF MUST PROVE:

- the auditor owes them a duty of care
- the auditor has breached this duty
- the plaintiff has suffered loss as a direct result.

KEY LEGAL CASES INCLUDE CAPARO AND BANNERMAN. THE BANNERMAN CASE EMPHASISES THE ADVANTAGES OF INCLUDING DISCLAIMER STATEMENTS IN THE AUDIT REPORT IN RELEVANT CIRCUMSTANCES.

THE BEST WAY TO AVOID PAYING OUT MONEY FOR NEGLIGENCE CLAIMS IS TO CARRY OUT HIGH QUALITY AUDITS IN THE FIRST PLACE.

HISTORICALLY THERE HAS BEEN AN EXPECTATION GAP BETWEEN WHAT THE PUBLIC BELIEVE AUDITORS DO, AND WHAT THEY ACTUALLY DO. THE PROFESSION IS TRYING TO EDUCATE THE PUBLIC, IN ORDER TO CLOSE THE GAP.

Test your understanding answers

Test your understanding 1

The auditor should consider whether any laws or regulations have been broken (for example laws and regulations over health and safety, food hygiene, product use by dates etc.).

Procedures include:

- obtaining a general understanding of the relevant legal and regulatory framework
- talking to the directors and other appropriate management (perhaps at the local level) to assess compliance or not
- examining relevant documentation, for example correspondence with the local authority and hygiene inspectors
- evaluating the financial impact of the non-compliance (for example, possible penalties, the cost of compensation claims, the cost of remedial action, the impact on the value of the brand name)
- obtain management representations re full disclosure of non-compliance and its impact
- consult experts in the area if considered necessary.

Test your understanding 2

(a) Fraud: intentional misstatement in the financial statements

(b) Error: unintentional misstatement. An adjustment should be made to the financial statements to remedy this, otherwise it will become and irregularity.

Test your understanding 3

Auditors must determine the most effective approach to each area of the financial statements. This may involve testing of the internal controls or substantive procedures, or a combination of the two.

Where the auditors choose to test the internal control systems of the company, they must design their work so as to have a reasonable expectation of detecting any weaknesses which would be likely to result in a material misstatement in the financial statements.

The area of discounts may have been one which did not involve testing of the internal controls as analytical procedures are likely to be effective.

Even if the controls in this area were tested, if the discounts given to customers were recorded accurately in the financial statements then no material error is likely to result. This would again make detection less likely. Jubilee must be reminded that the control weaknesses report issued at the conclusion of the audit is simply a by-product of the audit function and is not intended to be a comprehensive list of all possible weaknesses.

Should Jubilee Ltd require a more comprehensive review, then this could be undertaken as a separate assurance assignment.

Test your understanding 4

Notes for meeting with Finance Director

- Engagement letter:
  - Refer to any specific points regarding work in this area
  - Refer to section on auditors and directors responsibilities
  - Client signed engagement letter
- Responsibility for detection of fraud primarily responsibility of management
- Implementation of internal control system is responsibility of management
- Auditors role is to obtain *reasonable assurance* that financial statements are free from *material error*
- Amounts in question not material
- Ascertain how FD discovered fraud
- Ascertain how amounts of diverted funds were quantified
- Discuss whether there might be further unidentified sums

Test your understanding 5

For

- Avoid firms exiting from the statutory audit market and thus maintaining choice and competition
- Management of costs for both audit firms and their clients
- Clearly quantifies the extent of auditors liability – clear to the public
- Reduces risk of auditors being used as scapegoats and hence:
- Ensures that directors bear their extent of liability

Against

- Auditors may not feel as accountable or be seen to be as accountable
- Auditors who carry out their work with due professional skill and care should not fear unlimited liability
- May reduce the perceived value of an audit if risk to auditors is reduced
- Extent of cap may be a difficult and contentious issue to agree with the client
- Shareholders, or other parties to whom the auditors owe a duty of care may find themselves inadequately protected
- Level of cap would have to be agreed with directors who may be tempted to agree to a lower cap in order to save on fees – this may not afford shareholders sufficient protection

Test your understanding 6 – 'Lambley'

There are three main aspects of auditing examined in this question – the role of and potential liability of the auditor in connection with the detection and prevention of fraud, the concept of materiality and the position of the auditor when threatened with dismissal and replacement.

Note that in questions involving materiality, the usual assumption is that, as regards the effect on profit and/or assets and liabilities, a difference of less than 5% is not material, a difference of more than 10% is material, and differences between these limits may be material depending on the circumstances.

(a) **Lambley Trading**

(i) ISA 240 The Auditor's Responsibility to Consider Fraud in an Audit of Financial Statements says that auditors should design their audit procedures so as to have a reasonable expectation of detecting material fraud and error in the financial statements. So, an auditor is probably liable (in negligence) if he fails to detect material fraud and error. However, the auditor may not be liable if the fraud is difficult to detect (i.e. the fraud had been concealed and it is unreasonable to expect the auditor to have detected the fraud).

For immaterial fraud and error, a claim for negligence against the auditor for not detecting immaterial fraud or error would be unsuccessful (except in the circumstances described in the next section). An auditor may be negligent if he:

– finds an immaterial fraud while carrying out his normal procedures and does not report it to the company's management (but he may not be negligent if the evidence to support a suspected fraud is weak)

– carries out audit procedures on immaterial items, of which the company's management is aware, and these procedures are not carried out satisfactorily, so failing to detect an immaterial fraud. For instance, there may be a teeming and lading fraud, and the auditor may check receipts from sales are correctly recorded in the cash book and sales ledger, but fail to check that the cash from these sales is banked promptly.

– carries out audit procedures on immaterial items at the specific request of the company's management, and the auditor failed to detect an immaterial fraud due to negligent work. The management would have a good case to claim damages for negligence against the auditor.

(ii) The fraud of $5,000 is 3.3% of the company's profit before tax, so it is immaterial. As the auditor has carried out no work in this area, and is not responsible for detecting immaterial fraud, it is probable that he is not negligent. It could be argued that the other audit procedures should have detected an apparent irregularity, such as analytical review. This might have indicated an increase in motor expenses compared with the previous year and budget, or the auditor could have looked at petty cash expenditure, which would show an increase compared with the previous year.

It could also be argued that the auditor should have looked at the absolute level of petty cash expenditure in order to decide whether to carry out work on the petty cash system. However, these arguments against the auditor are relatively weak, and it is unlikely that a claim for negligence would be successful. However, not detecting the fraud is likely to lead to a deterioration of the client's confidence in the auditor.

(iii) The fraud of $20,000 is 13.3% of the company's profit before tax, so it is material. It appears that the auditor is negligent in not carrying out any audit work on petty cash, as he/she has contravened the advice given in ISA 240.

ISA 240 says the auditor should design audit procedures so as to have a reasonable expectation of detecting material fraud or error, so as he/she performed no work on petty cash there is no chance of him/her detecting the fraud. As a minimum, the auditor should have looked at the level of petty cash expenditure, comparing it with the previous year and the budget. This should have highlighted the increase in expenditure and led to the auditor carrying out further investigations. As this is a petty cash fraud, it could be difficult to detect, but the cashier writing out and signing the petty cash vouchers, with no receipt attached, should have led the auditor to suspect the fraud.

It could be argued that the company has some responsibility for allowing the fraud to take place, as there was a serious weakness in the system of internal control (i.e. the cashier recorded and made petty cash payments, and appeared to be able to authorise petty cash vouchers). So, some employee (e.g. the managing director) should have checked the cashier's work. Also, the managing director would have signed cheques which reimburse the petty cash, and he should have been aware that these had increased and investigated the reasons for the increase.

(b) **Colwick Enterprises**

(i) In terms of profit before tax, the sum of $200,000 is immaterial. Normally a material item, in terms of profit before tax is an error which exceeds either 5% of the profit before tax (i.e. $4.55m) or 10% of the profit before tax (i.e. $9.1m), so $200,000 is very small. However, in terms of the director's remuneration, the $200,000 is 44% of the managing director's annual salary of $450,000. Directors' remuneration is a very important item in financial statements, both as far as legal requirements are concerned, and to the readers of accounts. For example, recent press reports and public interest in the remuneration of directors of public companies in the UK (particularly the privatised utilities) has confirmed the importance of this figure in financial statements. The company is proposing that the financial statements should show only 69% of the managing director's remuneration, so the understatement is very material.

(ii) If the managing director refused to change the financial statements, I would have to qualify my audit report and state his total emoluments are $650,000. However, it seems probable that he will try to dismiss me as auditor before I am able to give an audit report on the financial statements. In order to change the auditor, he must:

- find another auditor who is prepared to replace me as auditor and
- call a general meeting to vote on the change of auditor and
- notify the shareholders, the new auditor, and myself, as retiring auditor.

I may have the right to make representations to the shareholders, which can either be sent to the shareholders before the meeting, and/or I can make the representations at the meeting when it is proposed that I am replaced.

Although these representations are likely to have little effect on the change of auditor (as the managing director owns 60% of the shares, and only a 50% vote is required to change the auditor), it would alert the other shareholders to the action of the managing director and concealment of information.

As a further point, provided the new auditors are a member of the ACCA or one of the recognised bodies, the ethical rules require the new auditor to write to me asking if there are any matters I ought to bring to their attention to enable them to decide whether or not they are prepared to accept the audit appointment. I will reply to their letter, saying that the managing director has had $200,000 of benefits-in-kind, which he refuses to allow to be disclosed in the financial statements. I have explained to the managing director that I would have to qualify my audit report if these emoluments are not disclosed, and this is the reason why he is proposing that I should be replaced as auditor. If the proposed new auditors have the expected amount of integrity, they should discuss this point with the managing director, and point out that they will have to qualify their audit report if the benefits of $200,000 are not included in his remuneration in the financial statements.

If the new auditors take over the appointment and give an unqualified report, I will take legal advice. The action I could take would include:

- disclosing information about the director's remuneration to the new auditor's professional body, and the fact that the audit report has not been qualified
- notifying the authorities of the alleged understatement of the managing director's remuneration
- disclosing the benefit to the tax authorities (as it may not have been subject to income tax)
- disclosing the benefit to the police.

(iii) If the managing director owned less than 1% of the issued shares, my position as auditor would be much stronger than in the situation in part (ii) above. If the managing director refused to increase his remuneration in the draft accounts, I would explain that I would have to contact the audit committee. If he still refused to change the remuneration, I would contact the chairman of the audit committee and arrange a meeting with its members. I would explain that I would have to qualify my audit report, unless the remuneration was increased to $650,000. Also, it is likely that either the company or the managing director is committing an offence by not disclosing this benefit to the tax authorities. It seems probable that this meeting will decide to incorporate the benefit in the financial statements.

However if the audit committee believes the financial statements should not be changed, I will have to insist on qualifying my audit report. If, at this stage, the directors decide to replace me as auditor, they will have to convene a general meeting for this purpose. I may be able to make representations in writing to the shareholders, and/or make those representations at the general meeting.

As Colwick Enterprises is a listed company, this information is likely to be picked up by the press and financial institutions, and result in adverse publicity for the company. In addition, it will make shareholders suspicious of the honesty of the managing director and the other directors.

It seems probable that the directors would realise the problems of adverse publicity if they try to replace me as auditor, and this will prevent them from proposing the change of auditor. So, it seems probable that the other directors will insist that the full remuneration of the managing director should be shown in the financial statements.

Exam Style Question: Ethical, Professional and Legal Issues

*Study note: as indicated in the 'Examiner's Approach to Paper P7' article (January 2007) the majority of marks will be awarded for application of knowledge to the scenario. Regurgitation of rote-learned facts will **not** score well in P7. Therefore, in your answer keep referring to the situations, companies and individuals described in the question.*

It is also important to answer the question set! Too many candidates focus solely on ethical issues and therefore restrict the pool of marks they can access. Therefore, breakdown each sub question into its basic components and structure your plan and answer around those components. The use of headings (as shown below) is an effective (and neat) way of doing this.

Twilight Plc

(a) **Professional, Legal and Ethical Issues**

(1) **Profit Warning**

Ethical Issues

There may be a 'self review' threat. In the prior year our firm performed both the due diligence on Sunset and the audit of Sunset's results in the context of the group accounts. It could be argued that the audit may have been carried out without necessary due care due to the procedures performed previously on the due diligence, which in hindsight appear may have been inadequate.

An 'advocacy threat' may arise in any possible legal dispute. Obrey & Taylor would attempt to defend their due diligence work to avoid penalty, which may be seen as an attempt to defend the decision of Twilight to purchase Sunset.

It is possible that either (or both) the due diligence or the audit were carried out without due professional competence. The assessment of profitability of long term contracts is a high risk area due to its subjectivity and, as such, should have been thoroughly investigated.

Legal Issues

The firm may have been negligent in undertaking its due diligence review of long term contracts. It is possible that, under the terms of the due diligence, Obrey & Taylor may be liable for damages. It will be important to assess the extent of potential damages and to whom they are liable (i.e. the company? The shareholders? The providers of finance?

Professional Issues

The profit warning increases the audit risk. More work may need to be performed on this year's audit, particularly with regard to the assessment of profitability of long term contracts. As a result we may need additional staff, staff with greater experience and additional time. This may impact the budget for the audit and, ultimately, the assessment of fees.

Given that a non-audit engagement was offered separate teams and separate partners should have been used. It is important to maintain these barriers so that no future audit staff belonged to the due diligence team.

A thorough review of the audit work performed should be conducted to ensure the quality of the conclusions made. Given the potential seriousness of the situation a second partner review should be conducted.

The extent of any possible negligence claims needs to be assessed. If the likelihood is high the solicitors of the firm should be contacted for advice.

(2) **Shares**

Ethical Issues

There is a 'self interest' threat for the audit senior, who directly benefits from the profits declared in Twilight's financial statements. As a result the senior might overlook adjustments to the profit identified during the audit.

Despite the audit seniors apparent lack of understanding of the situation they are still not independent of the client and are in breach of IFAC's (and therefore ACCA's) "Code of Ethics."

Professional Issues

The audit senior should be removed from the audit. Any work he or she has already conducted should be subject to an immediate review to assess whether it has been carried out with relevant due care.

The senior may be re-admitted to the audit team in the future if the shares are sold. If the senior refuses to sell the shares then at the least they must be segregated from any engagement related to Twilight.

The reason for the senior not declaring their shareholding should be reviewed. If the senior knew of the restrictions from holding shares in clients then they have acted without due care and should be punished accordingly.

However, if the senior was not aware of such restrictions it suggests that the firm's internal training and communications have not operated effectively. In this instance internal procedures should be updated.

In the more immediate term a communication should be sent to all staff disclosing the client companies that employee must not invest in. They should also communicate the disciplinary procedure for failing to adhere.

(3) **Foreign Transaction**

Legal Issues

The explanation for the "significant, unexplained overseas investment" was not sufficient to justify it. The previous manager should have gone to greater lengths to identify the nature of the transaction and should have documented any such investigation.

The investment appears to be suspicious and, according to the Money Laundering Regulations 2007, all suspicions should be communicated to the firm's Money Laundering Reporting Officer.

Failure to do so is a criminal offence by the firm and by the individuals involved.

Ethical Issues

The previous audit manager and the audit junior have both acted without due professional care. Both should be aware of the money laundering regulations and the procedures for reporting suspicious activity. As a consequence the firm could have acted negligently.

Professional Issues

Firstly, the new senior manager must report this suspicious activity to the MLRO. Once this has been performed the manager's responsibility has been discharged. It is then up to the MLRO to investigate further and, if they feel the suspicion is justified, to report this to the Serious Organised Crime Agency.

The behaviour of the outgoing manager and the junior should be reviewed. If they were both appropriately trained and were therefore aware of their responsibilities, the junior should be reminded of their duty and disciplined.

If, however, the firm's internal training and communication of money laundering reporting channels were not adequate then the firm is again in breach of the Money Laundering Regulations 2007. In this instance the firm should review its internal training procedures and, if necessary, update them and communicate them to all staff.

(b) **Quality Control**

Leadership

Good quality, in terms of ethically sound behaviour and professional due care, should be spread throughout the firm in a top down approach. The partners of the firm should ensure quality in everything they do and all their communications. It is up to the partners to stress the importance of money laundering and to communicate the importance to all staff.

Partners should also try and identify possible money laundering risks at the planning and review stage. In this instance, a significant, unexplained transaction has been "swept under the carpet." The partner should ensure appropriate planning has been conducted to identify and address such risks and should also have conducted sufficient reviews to identify issues important to the final audit opinion.

Human Resources

As well as recruiting the right staff at the right time it is also HR's function to ensure that staff are adequately trained and informed of important changes/developments in financial reporting standards/laws.

All new staff entering the firm should be made aware of the money laundering regulations requirements. They should also have been informed of their responsibilities if they have any suspicions. Finally they should be told who to report to and how to make a report.

The same is true for any senior members of staff who joined the firm prior to the money laundering regulations in 2007. HR should identify such individuals and ensure they are adequately briefed, perhaps in the form of internal CPD.

Monitoring

The firm should have a monitoring system in place to identify whether internal procedures and controls are effective. If any deficiencies are identified then procedures can be updated and changes communicated to all staff.

With regard to money laundering one method might be to make all staff sign a form stating that they understand their responsibilities with regard to money laundering and that they know what to do if they have any suspicions.

chapter

9

The audit of historical financial information – methodology and approach

Chapter learning objectives

Upon completion of this chapter you will be able to:

- describe the key features of the following audit methodologies
  - risk-based auditing
  - 'top down' approach
  - systems audit
  - balance sheet approach
  - transaction cycle approach
  - directional testing
- justify an appropriate approach to a given assignment and recognise when an approach is unsuitable.

1 The impact of ISAs

The risk-based approach to auditing

The adoption of International Standards of Auditing was an important junction in the evolution of audit methodology. Certain standards included direct reference to the need for auditors to consider and reduce their exposure to audit risk.

This overwhelming principle is laid out in **ISA 200** *Overall Objectives of the Independent Auditor and the Conduct of an Audit in Accordance with International Standards on Auditing*. It lists the objectives of an audit, including: the need for the auditor to express an opinion on the truth and fairness of the financial statements; the need to carry out the audit in accordance with ISAs; and the need for professional scepticism, etc.

It also introduces the concept of audit risk:

'Reasonable assurance is a high level of assurance. It is obtained when the auditor has obtained sufficient appropriate evidence to reduce audit risk to an acceptably low level.'

In other words, for an audit to be conducted in accordance with ISAs, the auditor **must** use a risk-based approach.

ISAs 315 and 330

These two ISAs are vitally important!

ISA 315 *Identifying and Assessing the Risks of Material Misstatement through Understanding the Entity and Its Environment* clearly prescribes the responsibility of the auditor for adopting a risk based approach:

"The objective of the auditor is to identify and assess the risks of material misstatement, whether due to fraud or error, at the financial statement and assertion levels, through understanding the entity and its environment, including the entity's internal control, thereby providing a basis for designing and implementing responses to the assessed risks of material misstatement."

In a nutshell: an assessment of risk must take place at the planning phase of an audit to assist with the design of further audit procedures.

ISA 330 *the Auditor's Response to Assessed Risks* further develops the concept by stating that:

"The objective of the auditor is to obtain sufficient appropriate audit evidence regarding the assessed risks of material misstatement, through designing and implementing appropriate responses to those risks."

The ISA's are clear: auditors should assess the risk of misstatement at the planning phase and design audit tests to respond to that risk assessment. Failure to comply with these requirements (or failure to document that these processes have been followed) could constitute professional negligence.

2 Risk-based auditing

The audit risk theory

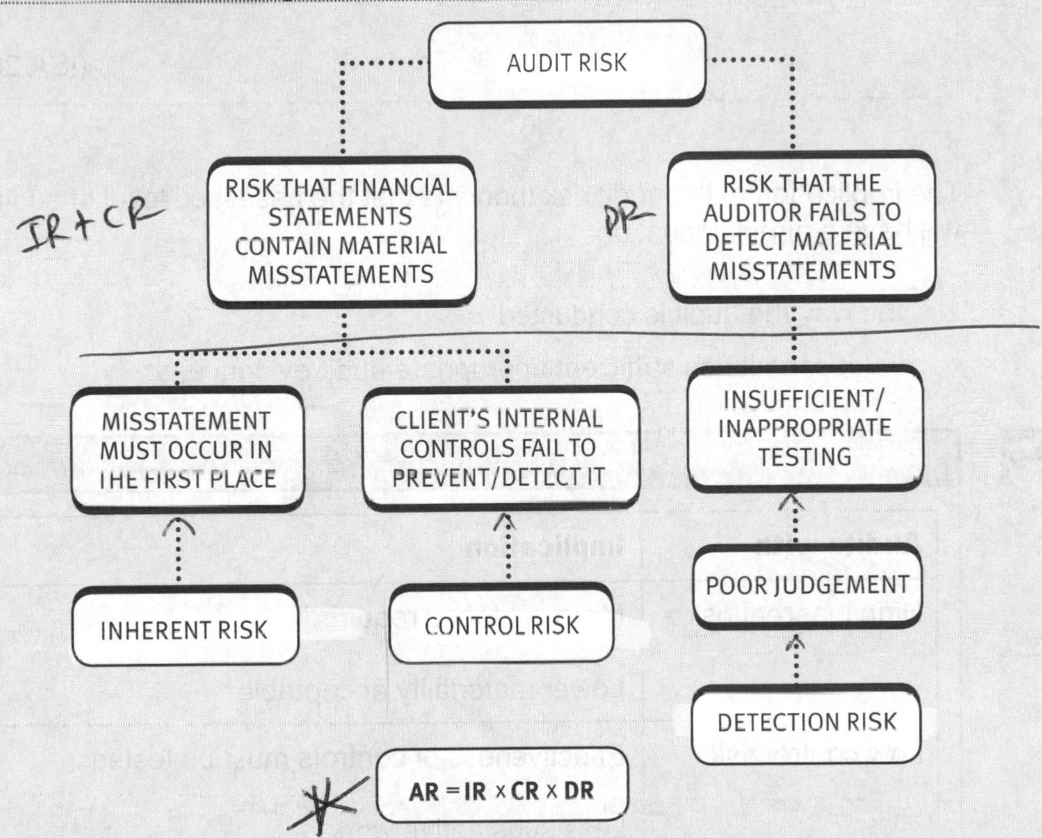

Audit risk is effectively the risk that the auditor expresses an inappropriate audit opinion when the financial statements are materially misstated. It can be further analysed as the risk of material misstatement and the risk of failing to detect said misstatement. The risk of material misstatement can be broken down into inherent and control risk.

This has lead to the commonly known formula:

Audit Risk = Inherent Risk x Control Risk x Detection Risk.

Risk definitions

'Inherent risk' is the susceptibility of an assertion about a class of transaction, account balance or disclosure to a misstatement that could be material, before consideration of any related controls (i.e. that it occurs in the first place).

'Control risk' is the risk that a misstatement that could occur (as above) will not be prevented, or detected and corrected, on a timely basis by the entity's internal control.

'Detection risk' is the risk that the procedures performed by the auditor to reduce audit risk to an acceptably low level will not detect a misstatement that exists that could be material.

(ISA 200)

The implication of the audit risk theory is that the assessed level of audit risk will have a direct impact on:

- the way the audit is conducted
- what constitutes sufficient appropriate audit evidence.

Illustration 1 – Risk-based auditing

Remember

Audits with	**Implication**
High inherent risk	More evidence required Lower materiality acceptable
Low control risk	Effectiveness of controls must be tested Less substantive work
High control risk	Less (or no) reliance on controls More substantive work
High detection risk	Should the firm be undertaking the audit at all? Need for independent review

The assessment of audit risk

When assessing the different components of risk, auditors should consider the following:

Inherent risk

- financing issues – exceeding facilities, borrowing covenants, etc.
- the sector in which the client operates – market volatility, mature or declining market, rapid technological change
- the regulatory environment – the need to comply with the regulatory regime of, e.g. the financial services, or food sectors
- pressure from external interest in the financial statements – regulated clients, clients with significant external shareholdings, clients with sensitive borrowing limits
- dominance of the CEO
- pressure to meet targets because of external expectations management bonus schemes, etc

Control risk

- the design of systems
- the training of staff
- the segregation of duties
- physical security measures

Detection risk

- appropriately tailored audit programs
- experience of the audit team
- safeguards against familiarity and self-review threats
- arrangements for independent review.

3 Other methodology considerations raised by the syllabus

Introduction

The syllabus specifically mentions:

- the 'top down' approach;
- systems audit;
- balance sheet approach;
- transaction cycle approach; and
- directional testing.

It should be noted that the risk based approach is embedded in ISA's and is therefore mandatory. The methods above may only be used in conjunction with a risk based methodology.

Top down approach

The theory is relatively simple.

- Assess the business risks that the client is facing (high level review)
- Consider how these might be reflected in the financial statements?
- Focus the audit effort on those areas subject to increased risk of misstatement (detailed level review).

The 'top down' approach affects procedures as follows:

- Controls are assessed at a high level. The focus is on the control environment rather than on detailed control procedures.
- Analytical procedures are used extensively because they enable the auditor to gain an understanding of the client's business.
- Tests of details are reduced by focussing primarily on those risk areas identified by tests of controls and analytical procedures. The need for these procedures will never be eliminated completely.

Systems Audit

Under this approach the auditors satisfies themselves that the client's system was operating effectively during the period in question, thus ensuring that financial data captured by the accounting system was complete and accurate. Based upon the assessment of the accounting system the auditor may reduce or increase substantive testing during the final audit.

Balance Sheet Approach

Under this approach the auditors satisfies themselves, through substantive testing, that the figures in the closing Statement of Financial Position (SFP) are reasonable. If the SFP was audited on the same basis last year, and satisfactory work was carried out on any new capital raised and dividends paid, it follows that the profit or loss for the period must also be satisfactory.

The Logic of the Balance Sheet Approach

Under the balance sheet approach, work is heavily focused on assessing year-end valuations. The tendency when using this approach is to perform limited analytical review on the income statement. This can lead to material misstatement of the income statement, particularly if issues of presentation are not fully considered.

Transaction Cycle Approach

The transaction cycle approach recognizes that different aspects of the financial statements are linked, so that, for example:

- Sales are linked to inventory despatches, accounts receivables, and cash receipts.

- Purchases are linked to receipts of inventory, accounts payable, and cash payments.

It is therefore possible to structure testing procedures so that items are traced through their cycle, enabling conclusions to be drawn about the completeness and accuracy of the sales or purchases cycle. This is closely linked to systems testing, which tends to focus on the sales, purchases and payroll recording cycles.

Directional testing

Directional testing is a method of testing for specific errors. For example:

- a review of sales invoices may be undertaken to identify the **overvaluation** of inventory, which should be valued at the lower of cost and NRV;
- a review of goods received prior to the year-end (through inspection of goods received notes) might be conducted to test possible **undervaluation** of inventory (i.e. unrecorded purchases).

It is likely that a detailed audit programme would contain a series of directional tests aimed at testing both over and undervaluation of items (including possible omissions).

- Directional testing also means that balances are tested directly by reference to the key risk to which they are exposed.
  - Assets – much more likely that these will be overstated rather than understated, e.g. receivables are often overstated due to over-optimistic judgments concerning recoverability of debts.
  - Liabilities – normally understated through oversight, e.g. the directors may fail to accrue for certain expenses incurred in the period.

4 Chapter summary

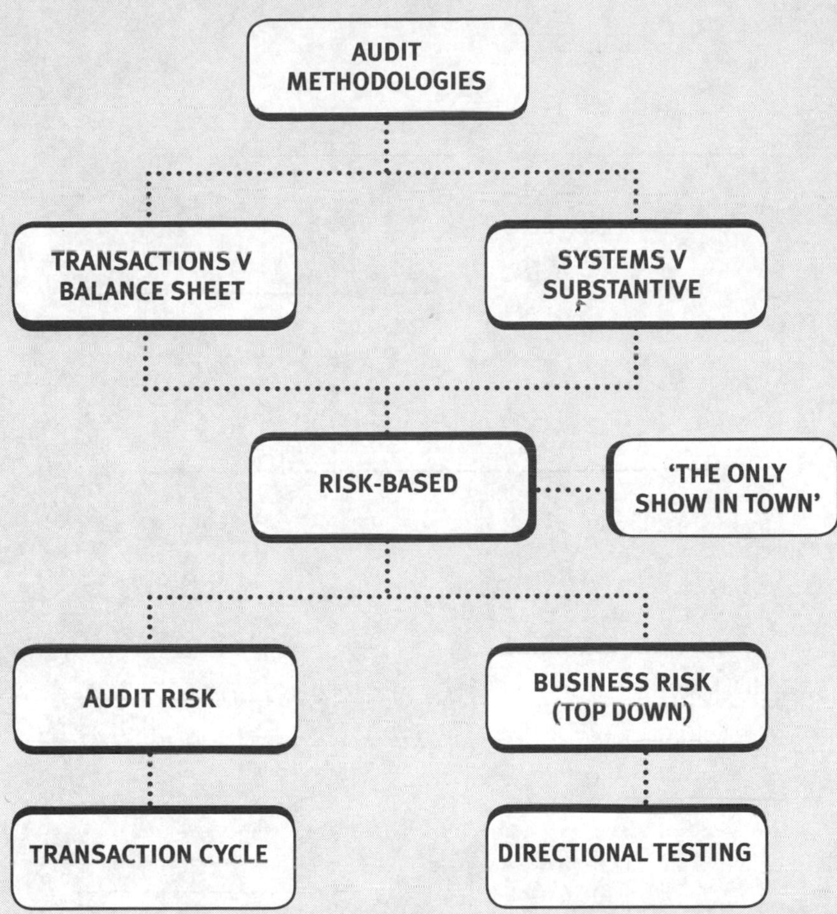

chapter

10

Planning, materiality and assessing the risk of misstatement

Chapter learning objectives

Upon completion of this chapter you will be able to:

- specify the matters that should be considered in planning a given assignment;
- define, explain and apply the concept of materiality;
- explain and apply the concept of audit risk – including its various components – to given situations;
- explain how and why the assessments of risks and materiality affect the nature, timing and extent of auditing procedures;

- Martin Jones - Article. (Pg 27)
- Massaging the figures - (Pg 35)
  ↳ Imp

1 Planning considerations

Planning entails developing an overall strategy and a detailed plan for the expected nature, timing and extent of the audit.

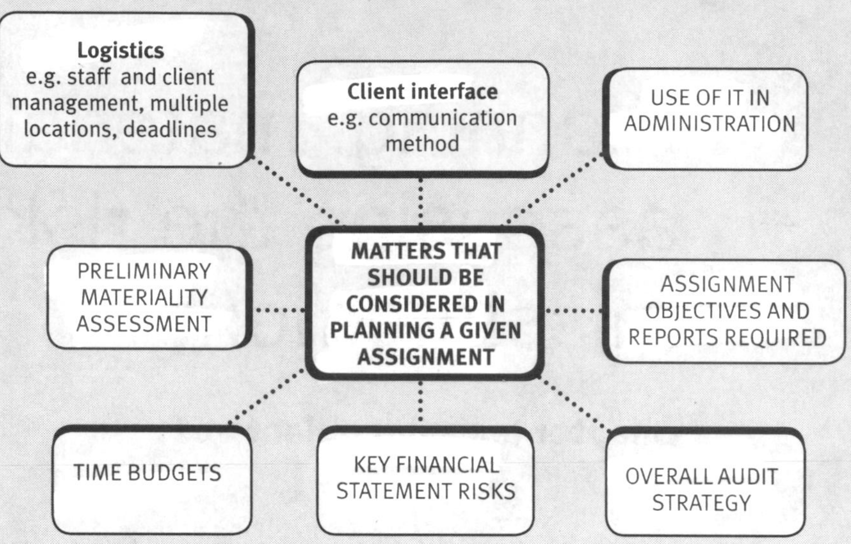

The purpose of planning is to:

- Help the auditor devote appropriate attention to important areas of the audit;
- Help the auditor identify and resolve potential problems on a timely basis;
- Help the auditor properly organise and manage the audit engagement so that it is performed in an effective and efficient manner;
- Assist in the selection of engagement team members with appropriate competencies and the assignment of work to them;
- Facilitate the direction and supervision of engagement teams and the review of their work; and
- Assist, where applicable, in the coordination of work done by auditors of components (see chapter 11) and experts.

Administrative Issues

Logistics

This describes matching staff availability to client requirements. Considerations Include:

- number and grade of audit staff to be allocated.
- use of other offices/partner firms to cover multiple/overseas locations
- timing of significant phases in the preparation of the financial statements
- deadlines and specific dates to be met including attendance at inventory counts.

Administrative tasks/IT

- time sheets
- maintenance of the fees ledger
- staff planning
- collection and payment of expenses
- staff appraisals

Time budgets

- At the planning stage, a budget should be prepared allocating the time of each member (or grade) of the audit team.
- This budget should be used to control the time spent on that audit and any major variation (time both under and over-spent) should be investigated by the manager.

Objectives/Reports

When preparing the audit plan, the auditor must continually bear in mind the overall objectives of the assignment - usually the issue of an audit report, in accordance with IASs and national legislation.

Client Interface

- Client communications is important throughout the audit process.
- A single point of contact should be assigned through which all significant communications are made.
- At the planning stage the key contact should:
  - meet the senior management of the client to identify problem areas
  - ensure that timing of work, client staff availability, specific information requests, scope of work and anticipated completion dates are discussed and agreed with the client.

2 The audit strategy and plan

The auditor should establish an overall strategy for the audit. This addresses such matters as:

- Which resources to deploy for specific audit areas;
- The amount of resources to deploy;
- When resources are deployed; and
- How those resources are managed, directed and supervised.

In establishing the strategy **ISA 300** *Planning an Audit of Financial Statements* states that the auditor shall:

- Identify the characteristics of the engagement that define its scope;
- Ascertain the reporting objectives of the engagement;
- Consider the factors that are significant in directing the engagement team's efforts;
- Consider the results of preliminary engagement activities; and
- Ascertain the nature, timing and extent of resources necessary to perform the engagement.

Once the strategy has been established the auditor should develop an audit plan. This is more detailed than the strategy and includes a description of:

- The nature, timing and extent of planned risk assessment procedures;
- The nature timing and extent of further audit procedures;
- The nature, timing and extent of direction and supervision of engagement team members and the review of their work; and
- Other planned audit procedures required to comply with ISA's.

Both the strategy and the plan must be formally documented in the audit working papers.

3 Materiality

As stated in ISA 200, the objective of an audit is to express an opinion whether the financial statements are prepared, in all material respects, in accordance with an applicable financial reporting framework. It is therefore of vital importance for auditors to apply the concept of materiality in the planning and performance of the audit.

Various frameworks discuss materiality in slightly different terms. However, a generally accepted definition of materiality in the context of an audit is as follows:

"Misstatements, including omissions, are considered to be material if they, individually or in aggregate, could reasonably be expected to influence the economic decisions of users taken on the basis of the financial statements."

Unfortunately many practitioners have, in the past, applied materiality in a purely mechanical, numerical fashion. Whilst numerical guidelines are an accepted method for identifying a starting point in the consideration of materiality, arbitrary pre-conceived thresholds do not meet the above definition.

ISA 320 *Materiality in Planning and Performing an Audit* has recognised this weakness and therefore requires that auditors use **judgement** when determining what constitutes a material matter. In order to achieve this they must consider the circumstances surrounding the business and its shareholders. This demands a consideration of the common financial information needs of the users as a group.

Once established the concept of materiality is applied by the auditor in both the planning and performance of the audit and then in the evaluation of the effect of identified misstatements, particularly uncorrected ones.

Calculation

ISA 320 recognises, and permits, the use of benchmark calculations of materiality. However, it must be stressed, that these should be used in the initial assessment of materiality. The auditor must then use judgement to modify materiality so that it is relevant to the unique circumstances of the client.

A traditional calculation basis is as follows:

	Value	**Comments**
Pre-tax profit	5 – 10%	Users usually interested in profitability of the company.
Turnover	½ – 1%	Materiality relates to the size of the business, which can be measured in terms of revenue
Total assets	1 – 2%	Size can also be measured in terms of the asset base

When deciding on an appropriate benchmark the auditor must consider:

- The elements of the financial statements;
- Whether particular items tend to be the focus of the users;
- The nature of the entity, its life cycle and its environment;
- The ownership and financing structure; and
- The relative volatility of the benchmark.

Performance Materiality

Once materiality has been derived this does not act as a threshold for the performance of the entire audit in such a way that any uncorrected misstatement below the threshold will always be evaluated as immaterial. The circumstances surrounding some misstatements may cause the auditor to evaluate them even if they are below the threshold.

For this reason auditors must also consider what is known as 'performance materiality.'

This is an amount, established by the auditor, set below the materiality to be used when designing the nature, timing and extent of further procedures. The aim is to reduce the risk that misstatements in aggregate exceed materiality for the financial statements as a whole.

Performance materiality also considers the significance of individual classes of transaction, account balances or disclosures to the users of accounts.

4 Risk assessment

According to **ISA 315** auditors are required to identify and assess the risks of material misstatement through understanding the client entity and its environment and through understanding the internal control environment.

In order to fulfil this objective they are required to perform – although they are not limited to – the following procedures:

- Enquiries of management;
- Analytical procedures; and
- Observation and inspection.

Analytical procedures are used to highlight critical audit areas requiring attention during the audit. Effectively the auditor compares current draft balances with prior year reported balances, forecasts and/or industry averages to confirm expectations regarding performance or identify unexpected trends that require further investigation (for further description see chapter 12).

The Entity and Its Environment

Auditors should obtain an understanding of:

- Relevant industry, regulatory and other external factors;
- The nature of entity, including:
  - Its operations;
  - Its ownership and governance structures;
  - The types of investment the entity makes; and
  - The way the entity is structured and financed.
- The entity's selection and application of accounting policies;
- The entity's objectives and strategies, and those related business risks that may result in material misstatement; and
- The measurement and review of the entity's financial performance.

The Entity's Internal Control

Most controls relevant to the audit are likely to relate to financial reporting, although others may also have an impact. It is a matter of judgement whether an auditor ultimately considers a control to be relevant to the audit or not.

The components of internal control include:

- The control environment;
- The entity's risk assessment process;
- The information system relevant to financial reporting;
- The control activities; and
- The monitoring system.

The auditor must evaluate the design of the controls to determine whether they have been implemented during the financial reporting period and whether they are effective at preventing and detecting potentially material fraud and error.

5 Business Risk

A business risk is one resulting from "significant events, conditions, circumstances, actions or inactions that could adversely affect an entity's ability to achieve its objectives and execute its strategies" (ISA 315). It is vital that auditors consider the impact of these risks on inherent risk, i.e. the susceptibility of classes of transaction, accounts balances or disclosure to material misstatement.

For example; operating in a technologically fast paced market is a business risk because failure to innovate and develop new products could leave businesses with obsolete, undesirable inventories that they cannot sell. The consequence of this is that the net realisable value of inventory may fall below cost, requiring a write-down of inventory balances. Failure to recognise this could lead to an overstatement of inventory in the financial statements.

Examples of Business Risks

In examinations you must be able to identify business risks from scenarios and indicate what impact they will have on the planning of the audit.

These risks are often categorised as being 'external' or 'internal' risks.

Typical 'external risks'	Typical 'internal risks'
changing legislation	employees
changing interest rates (N.B. Highly geared companies)	failure to modernise products, processes, labour relations, marketing
changing exchange rates	excessive reliance on a dominant CEO
public opinion, attitudes, fashions	cash flow difficulties
price wars initiated by competitors	rapidly increasing gearing
import competition	inappropriate acquisitions
untried technologies and ideas	overtrading
political factors	
natural hazards	fraud
	excessive reliance on one or few products, customers, suppliers
	computer systems failures

Implications

Business risks have implications at all stages of an audit assignment, but are of particular interest at the planning stage.

- Understanding of business risks promotes greater knowledge of the business
- Identification of risks provides focus for the audit
- Identification of business risk aids understanding of directors' motives

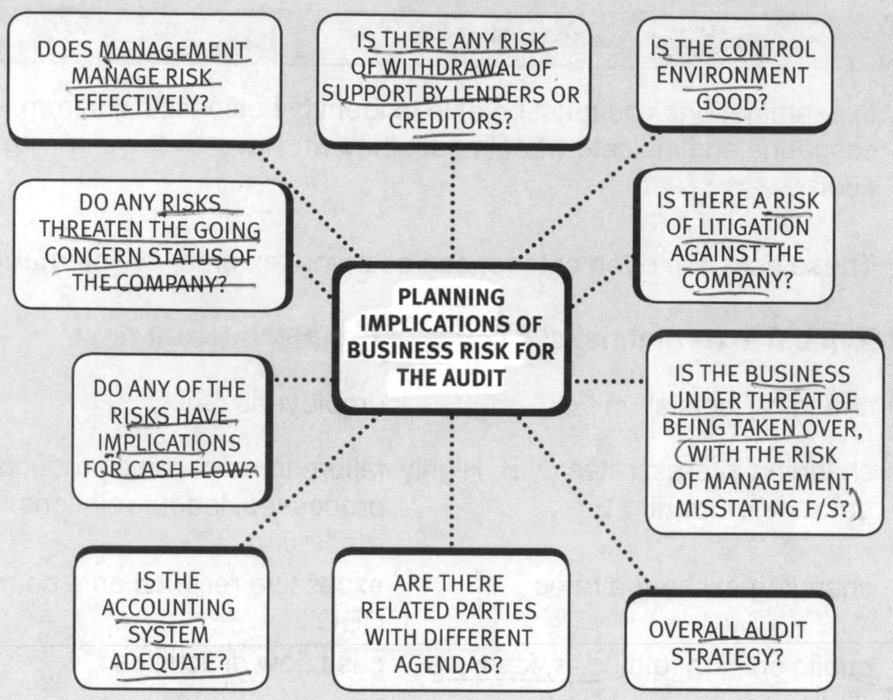

Test your understanding 1

(1) Kingston Co operates in the computer games industry, developing new games for sale in retail stores

(2) Portmore Co is currently waiting for confirmation from their bank that their overdraft facility will be extended. The bank have requested a copy of the audited financial statements as soon as they are available

(3) Montego Co has recently begun selling their products into overseas markets

(4) Lucea Co, a manufacturer, has negotiated a contract with a new supplier for all its raw materials

Required

For each of the scenarios below identify the business risks and state what, if any, impact this might have on your assessment of financial statement risk for the planning of a year-end audit.

6 Factors influencing the assessment of risk

As part of the risk assessment process auditors have to consider the significance of the identified risks, including:

- Whether the risk is one of fraud;
- Whether it is related to recent economic, accounting or other developments that require specific attention;
- The complexity of the related transactions;
- Whether it involves related parties;
- The degree of subjectivity involved in measuring financial information; and
- Whether it involves transactions outside the normal course of business.

If the auditor determines that a significant risk exists they must then obtain the necessary understanding of how the entity controls that risk. Only then can the auditor determine an appropriate response in terms of further audit procedures.

7 Response to risk assessment

The main purpose of performing risk assessment is to guide the auditor in the designing and performance of further audit procedures to obtain sufficient appropriate audit evidence. It assists in a number of ways:

By identifying those areas where special audit consideration may be necessary, for example where related party transactions are involved or a particular balance is subject to increased risk of error. The audit of these items can be assigned to a member of the audit team with the necessary experience to reduce audit risk to an acceptable level;

By identifying those areas where it may be necessary to consult an external expert;

By developing expectations that may be used when performing analytical procedures; and

By allowing the auditor to modify the level of substantive testing required in certain areas of the audit, thus avoiding over or under auditing. Where risks are assessed as high, detection risk must be minimised by the audit procedures performed, as illustrated below:

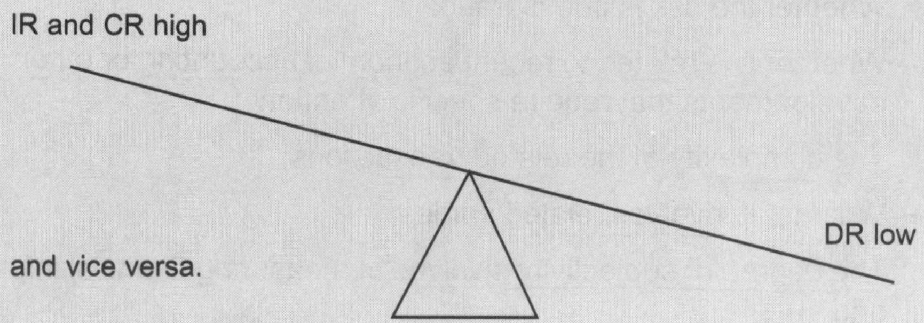

Current Issues – Going Concern

During times of economic hardship, particularly during recession, there is always an increase in the number of failed businesses. This does not just include small businesses, even significant institutions fail, for example; Lehman Brothers, a large Wall Street investment bank, filing for chapter 11 bankruptcy protection in September 2008.

During such times auditors must be aware that there is a heightened risk that companies may not be going concerns and that the basis of preparing the financial statements and the nature of disclosures relating to uncertainty must be closely scrutinised.

Recently the IAASB produce a practice alert "Audit Considerations in Respect of Going Concern in the Current Economic Environment." In response the P7 examiner produced an article entitled "Going Concern" (Feb 2010). This must therefore be considered an important issue.

The nature of the auditor's responsibilities are considered in more detail in chapter 13 "Completion." However, it should be noted that consideration of going concern risks should be incorporated into all aspects of planning, performing and reviewing audit procedures.

8 Audit procedures

Audit procedures should be designed to reduce the level of audit risk to an acceptable level. When designing those tests auditors must consider both the assessment of risk and materiality.

	High Risk/Material	Low Risk/Immaterial
Nature of procedures	Detailed substantive testing	Analytical review
Extent of procedures	Significant sample size	Reduced sample size

The timing of procedures depends on the nature of the tests being performed. Controls testing should ideally be performed during an interim audit so that the results can be used in the assessment of control risk. The bulk of the detailed, substantive work takes place after the year-end. The length of time that passes between the year-end and the audit greatly affects the quality of the information available, particularly with regard to provisions and other estimates.

9 Computer systems

Testing of computerised accounting systems should be adequately considered at the planning phase of an audit. Testing needs to be performed to ensure that the system operates effectively and that adequate controls are in place to prevent and detect fraud and error.

It may be appropriate to use Computer Assisted Audit Techniques (CAATs) to obtain the required information and evidence.

However, complex IT systems may provide certain barriers that need to be overcome before adequate evidence can be gathered to support an assessment of control risk:

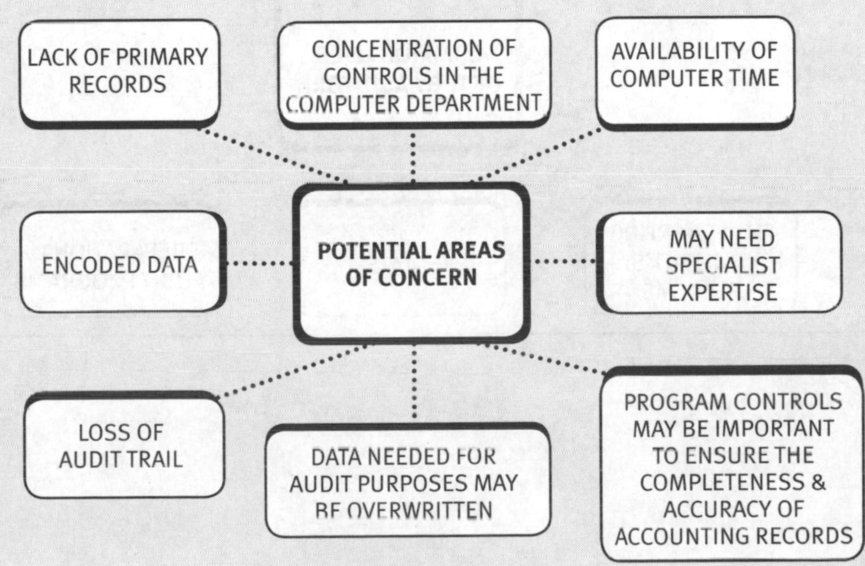

Advantages of IT

- There are also advantages where clients have computerised accounting records.
  - Availability of high quality, timely reports.
  - Ability to quickly drill down into individual balances.
  - Single location of information reduces need to involve many different parties.
  - Audit trail may be more logical and simple to follow.

IT and the Auditor

Automation and rapid IT developments are affecting all aspects of life and the auditing profession is no exception.

- The laptop computer and the Internet have been utilised to assist in auditing.
- Whilst the essential process of the audit is the same the computerised techniques and software available to the auditor have developed significantly.
- There are many useful software packages available to the auditor.
- Audit time can be reduced with the appropriate use of IT.

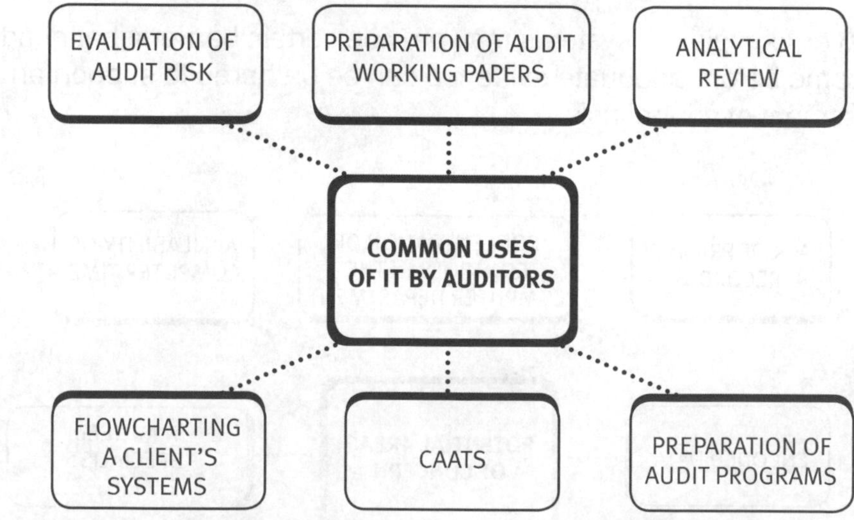

- There are many benefits in automating audit procedures, however, automation also brings problems.
  - Increased automation (added to the need for firms to be competitive) may reduce the level of trained and experienced staff used on the audit thereby increasing the risk of errors not being detected.
  - Significant levels of controls are required over IT systems.

Control	**Explanation**
Security of information	Information should be kept secure from unauthorised access by the use of appropriate passwords, encryption and physical security such as keeping hardware locked.
Back-up of information	Information should be protected from accidental loss or corruption by maintaining adequate back-ups.
Adequacy of documentation	There is a risk that inadequate documentation will be maintained where computer based auditing is carried out – controls are required to ensure sufficient appropriate audit evidence is obtained and maintained.
Testing of programmes	Especially important where using programmes which impact on client systems – untested software can cause BIG problems and should be avoided.

Article Focus

The P7 examiner, Lisa Weaver, has produced a two part article that discusses how she believes well prepared candidates should approach the reading, planning and writing of planning style questions.

The articles, entitled "How to Tackle Audit and Assurance Case Study Questions" (part 1 and 2) (Aug and Sep 2007) can be found on the ACCA website.

Test your understanding 2 – 'Ivor'

You are the audit senior in a firm of accountants. One of the partners has given you some financial information for a client, Ivor Ltd, whose final audit is due to take place in a month's time. The partner has asked you to conduct an analytical review of the management accounts in comparison to the prior year's financial statements.

	31.12.2007 (Management Accounts)		31.12.2006 (Audited Financial Statements)	
	$000	$000	$000	$000
Income statement				
Turnover		13,095		10,160
Sales discounts		(525)		(200)
		12,570		9,960
Cost of sales				
Opening inventory	1,200		1,085	
Purchases	10,150		7,830	
Purchase discounts	(154)		(112)	
Closing inventory	(1,640)		(1,200)	
		(9,556)		(7,603)
Gross profit		3,014		2,357
Distribution costs		(762)		(498)

Admin expenses				
Wages and salaries	1,275		960	
Directors' salaries	125		115	
Depreciation:				
Land & buildings	18		40	
Plant & machinery	42		49	
Amortisation	26		25	
Rent	35		12	
Rates	5		4	
Gas and electricity	5		2	
Profit on disposal	(510)		(75)	
Bad Debts	8		7	
Insurance	16		15	
Cleaning	2		1	
Miscellaneous	15		10	
		(1,062)		(1,165)
Net profit before tax		1,190		694
Statement of financial position				
Non current assets				
Tangible assets (note 1)		1,073		2,130
Intangible assets (note 2)		54		75
Current assets		1,127		2,205
Inventory	1,640		1,200	
Trade receivables (note 3)	2,204		1,353	
Other receivables	46		42	
Cash	104		–	
		3,994		2,595
		5,121		4,800

Equity and liabilities			
Ordinary share capital		1,700	1,000
Retained earnings		1,894	1,004
		3,594	2,004
Non current liabilities			
Bank loan		500	1,000
Current liabilities			
Overdrafts	–		129
Trade payables	703		1,479
Other payables	32		20
Tax payable	292		168
		1,027	1,796
		5,121	4,800

Note 1	**Land & buildings**	**Plant & machinery**	**Total**
	$000	$000	$000
Cost			
B/fwd at 1 Jan 2007	2,000	750	2,750
Disposals	(1,100)	–	(1,100)
C/fwd at 31Dec 2007	900	750	1,650
Depn			
B/fwd at 1 Jan 2007	200	420	620
Disposals	(110)	–	(110)
Charge	18	49	67
C/fwd at 31 Dec 2007	108	469	577
NBV			
At 31 Dec 2007	792	281	1,073
At 31 Dec 2006	1,800	330	2,130

Buildings are depreciated over 50 years on a straight line basis.

Plant and machinery are depreciated at 15% using the reducing balance method.

Note 2

Development costs

	Total
	$
Cost	
B/fwd at 1 Jan 2007	125
Additions	5
C/fwd at 31 Dec 2007	130
Amortisation	
B/fwd at 1 Jan 2007	50
Charge	26
C/fwd at 31 Dec 2007	76
NBV	
At 31 Dec 2007	54
At 31 Dec 2006	75

Development costs are being depreciated over five years using the straight line method.

Note 3

	31.12.2007	31.12.2006
	$000	$000
Trade receivables	2,274	1,423
Provision for doubtful debt	(70)	(70)
	2,204	1,353

Required

Prepare an internal report for the partner that identifies and explains the audit risks discovered during your analytical review of the financial information that should be taken into consideration when planning the final audit of Ivor Ltd.

Note: calculations for materiality are not required.

One professional mark is available.

(12 marks)

FIXED TEST 2 –'Engine'

Engine Ltd

You are the audit senior in a firm of accountants. You are assisting with the planning for the year end audit of one of your main clients, Engine Limited. The senior manager has asked you to perform an analytical review of the financial statements that she can use to brief the engagement partner of the key audit risks.

	30.06.2009 (Draft)		30.06.2008 (Audited)	
	$m	$m	$m	$m
Income statement				
Turnover		128		107
Cost of sales				
Opening inventory	9		6	
Purchases	87		74	
Closing inventory	(14)		(9)	
		(82)		71
Gross profit		46		36
Distribution costs		(11)		(9)
Admin expenses (note 1)		(20)		(18)
Net profit before tax		15		9
Statement of financial position				
Non current assets				
Tangible assets (note 2)			77	67
Intangible assets (note 3)			17	13
			94	80

Current assets				
Inventory (note 4)	14		9	
Trade receivables	17		13	
Cash	3		3	
		34		25
Total assets		128		105
Equity and liabilities				
Ordinary share capital		20		20
Revaluation reserve		38		30
Retained earnings		30		25
		88		75
Non current liabilities				
Bank loan		13		11
Current liabilities				
Trade payables	17		13	
Other payables	5		3	
Tax payable	5		3	
		27		19
		128		105

Note 1

Included within Operating Profits are the following items:

	30.06.2009	30.06.2008
	$m	$m
Wages and salaries	7	7
Directors' salaries	2	2
Depreciation	3	3
Amortisation	4	3

Note 2

	Land & buildings	Plant & machinery	Total
	$m	$m	$m
Cost			
B/fwd at 1 July 2008	70	30	100
Additions	–	5	5
Revaluations	8	–	8
C/fwd at 30 June 2009	78	35	113
Depn			
B/fwd at 1 July 2008	10	23	33
Charge	1	2	3
C/fwd at 30 June 2009	11	25	36
NBV			
At 30 June 2009	67	10	77
At 30 June 2008	60	7	67

The revaluation relates solely to a piece of land.

Plant and machinery are depreciated at 25% using the reducing balance method.

Note 3

Development costs	**Total**
	$
Cost	
B/fwd at 1 July 2008	16
Additions	8
C/fwd at 30 June 2009	24
Amortisation	
B/fwd at 1 July 2008	3
Charge	4
C/fwd at 30 June 2009	7

NBV

At 30 June 2009	17
At 30 June 2008	13

During the year significant research and development has taken place with regard.

To a new product, for which commercial production has now commenced.

Note 4

	30.06.2009	**30.06.2008**
	$m	$m
Inventory	3	2
Raw materials	1	1
WIP	11	7
Finished goods	(1)	(1)
Provision for slow moving stock	14	9

Required

Prepare a memo for your manager that identifies and explains the key audit risks discovered during your analytical review of the financial statements. Your review should briefly discuss the possible implications for the final audit.

Note: *calculations for materiality are not required.*

One professional mark is available.

(12 marks)

Test your understanding 3

Your firm has recently been appointed as the auditor of Holifex Co. The company provides and erects scaffolding on building sites and other industrial locations.

Your client, Stoke Co, has recently expanded its operations overseas. This is Stoke's first venture outside of its home country, where it has operated as a single entity. The venture has been set up by acquiring an entity overseas which is run and operated by its own, recently appointed, management team.

Chantry Co has been your client for many years. In recent years it has experienced rapid growth as its range of bottled water products has become more 'fashionable'. In order to cope with this level of growth, Chantry has introduced a new accounting system and transferred the data from their current software.

Westbourne Co is a major building and construction company focussing mostly on large projects such as the construction of major sporting and entertainment venues. Contracts are usually won through a tender process with construction work on successful tenders taking many years. During the year Westbourne has found itself in dispute with one of its major customers who claim that the concert venue Westbourne has constructed does not meet the specifications per the original contract. As a result the customer is withholding the final completion payment representing 30% of the contract value.

Required

Identify and explain the financial statements risks to assist with the planning for each of the engagements above.

10 Chapter Summary

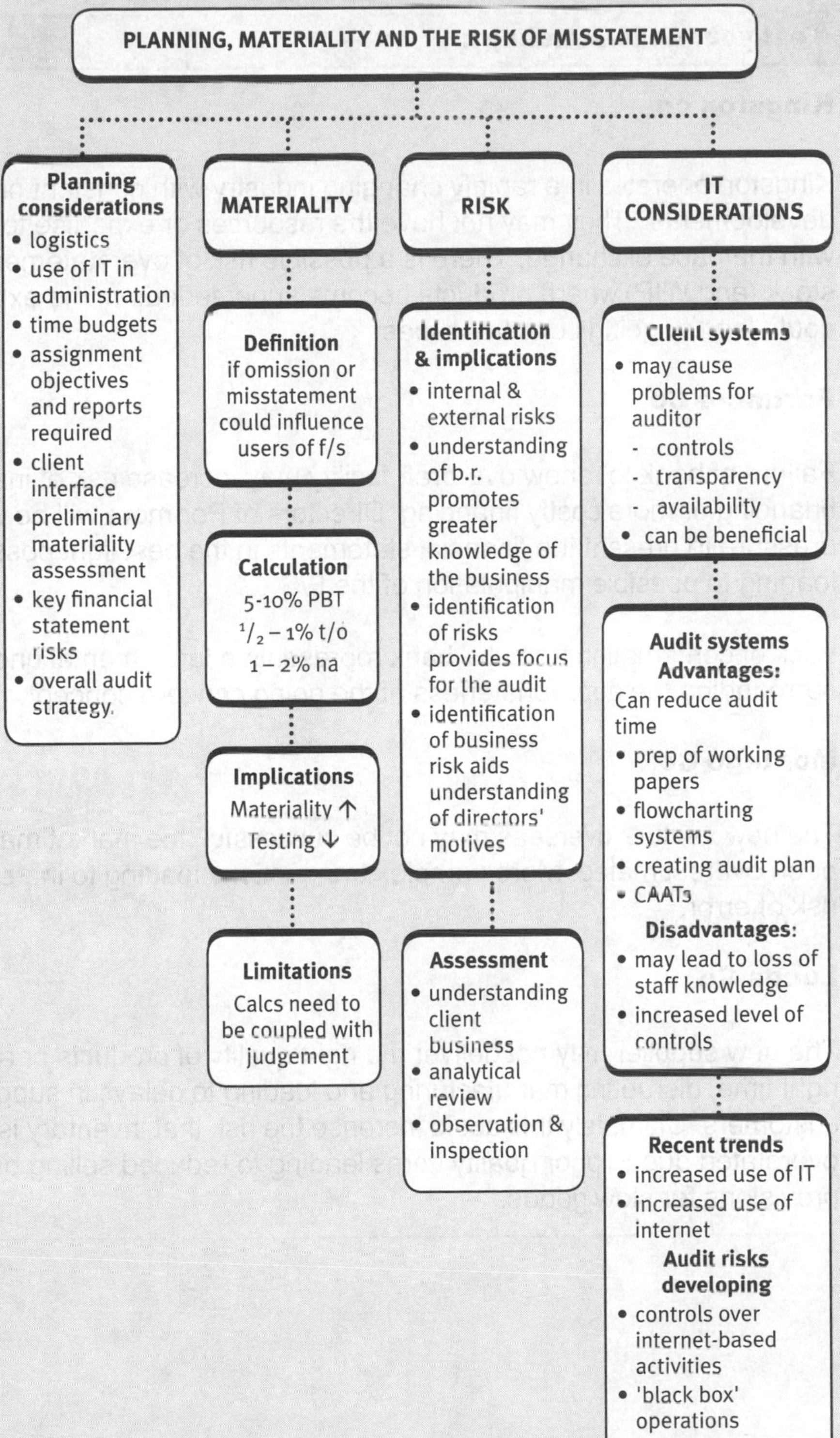

Test your understanding answers

Test your understanding 1

Kingston co

Kingston operates in a rapidly changing industry with constant product developments. They may not have the resources or expertise to keep up with the pace of change. There is a possible risk of overstatement of stock (and WIP) where products become superseded. In the extreme could lead to going concern issues

Portmore Co

Failure of bank to renew overdraft facility may increase risk of insufficient financing or more costly financing. Directors of Portmore will be under pressure to present the financial statements in the best light possible leading to possible manipulation of the F/S.

Lack of confirmation from the bank represents a fundamental uncertainty surrounding the appropriateness of the going concern concept.

Montego Co

The new venture overseas may not be successful; the market may have been overestimated. More complex transactions leading to increased risk of error.

Lucea Co

The new supplier may not deliver the right quality of products or at the right time, disrupting manufacturing and leading to delays in supplying customers. Ultimately this could increase the risk that inventory is overstated due to poor quality items leading to reduced selling prices or provisions for slow goods.

Test your understanding 2 – 'Ivor'

To: M.R. Partner
From: A.N. Accountant
Date: 24 March 2008
Subject: Analytical review of Ivor Ltd to assist the planning of the year end audit.

As requested, please find a summary of the key audit risks of Ivor Ltd identified during the analytical review of the management accounts for the year ended 31 December 2007 and the audited financial statements for the prior year in preparation of next week's planning meeting.

Turnover

Turnover has increased by 29% during the year to 31 December 2007. This significant increase suggests a risk that turnover – and certain related balances – could be overstated.

The increase in turnover has been partly fuelled by offering greater discounts, totalling 4% of turnover in 2007 as opposed to 2% in the prior year. This could imply an increased risk that closing inventory is overvalued. Inventory should be valued at the lower of cost and net realisable value in accordance with SSAP 9/IAS 2. The discounts offered must be taken into account when determining the net realisable value. Some products may be used as loss leaders in a drive to tempt new customers.

It also appears that extended credit terms have been offered due to the lengthening of the receivables collection period from an average 49 days in 2006 to an average 61 days in 2007.

The overall increase in credit sales, coupled with the greater credit period increases the risk of non collection of receivables. However, the bad debt provision has not been adjusted from the previous balance of $70,000, which represented 5% of total receivables in 2006 but only 3% of receivables in 2007. This suggests that the bad debt provision is understated and the trade receivables balance overstated. It also suggests that bad debt expenses in the income statement are understated.

The significant increase also suggests that we should pay close attention to the cut-off procedures adopted by the client and our testing of this process. There is no evidence to suggest that cut-off has been incorrectly performed but such a rapid increase in turnover may have put a strain on the company's sales recording system. It is therefore imperative to assess whether there has been any impact on the efficiency of the internal control system.

Distribution Costs

These have increased by over 53% during the financial year. It is difficult to identify the cause of this fluctuation without further information. However it is likely that Ivor Ltd has tried to increase their customer base in different geographical locations. Assuming all invoices are made in dollars, this should not greatly affect our assessment of audit risk.

Gas and Electricity Costs

These have increased by 250% during the financial year. I would have expected such costs to rise directly in comparison with production levels; however this does not appear to be the case. There is a risk that these costs are therefore overstated.

It is unlikely that these balances are material to the financial statements, however enquiries should be made of management during the final audit to identify why the costs have risen so sharply.

Depreciation Costs

The income statement shows depreciation charges of $42k in 2007 and $49k in 2006 for plant and machinery. However, the reconciling note clearly shows that the depreciation charge for plant and machinery in 2007 is $49k. It appears that depreciation charges have been understated by $7k in the income statement. At 0.6% of profits this is clearly immaterial. However, it should still be reported to management/those charged with governance in a comprehensive list of unadjusted audit differences.

Sale of Buildings

During the year buildings [they have been depreciated!] with a net book value of $990,000 have been sold for $1,500,000. At the same time the company's rental expenses have increased by 190%. There is no indication elsewhere in the income statement that the company has moved premises, such as removal costs, and it is unlikely that the company would be able to increase production so much having sold half of their buildings. It is therefore likely that the company has entered into a sale and leaseback arrangement.

There are no finance lease liabilities on the statement of financial position, hence it appears the lease is being treated as an operating lease. This presents the risk that the lease may have been misclassified and that non-current assets and finance lease liabilities are both understated on the statement of financial position. This would also have the knock on effect that depreciation charges are understated in the income statement. This could be as much as $33,000 per annum, which is the disposal proceeds of the building of $1.5mn depreciated over the remaining useful life of 45 years.

Going Concern

During the year there appears to have been an improvement in the liquidity of the company, with the current and quick ratios improving from 1.4 and 0.8 in 2006 to 3.9 and 2.3 in 2007 respectively.

However, it should be noted that during the year Ivor Ltd has raised a significant amount of cash from the disposal of buildings and the issuing of new shares. In total $2.2mn has been raised ($1.5mn disposal + $700k share issue) and it appears as though this has been used to pay off significant external debts, most notably the bank loan and trade payables. The result is a healthier statement of financial position.

It should be noted, though, that there is very little residual cash left over and the company appears to be having difficulty generating trading cash balances. Inventory days have increased slightly from 58 to 63 days and, crucially, receivable days have increased from 49 days to 61 days. The increase in the operating cycle could be caused by offering extended credit in an attempt to woo new customers. However, the inability to generate cash balances could indicate problems ahead, particularly if the company is unable to meet loan or lease repayments. A failure to pay trade payables could also lead to a loss of supplier goodwill and have implications for future trade relationships.

Given the nature of the sale and leaseback, and the attempt to keep this debt off the statement of financial position, caution should be used assessing managements' basis of preparing the accounts. If the business is no longer a going concern then the break up basis should be used.

Conclusion

The company has experienced a significant growth in turnover. However, this could come at the expense of greater bad debt risk and slower cash collection. This means the valuation of receivables and associated provisions is crucial. The use of a sale and leaseback mechanism also means the audit of non current assets and leases is a high risk area. Finally, despite a healthy statement of financial position, it appears that Ivor has cash flow problems and this means care needs to be used identifying the appropriate going concern status.

Appendix: Analytical Review

Annual Movements

Turnover	2,935/10,160 x 100	28.9%
Purchases	2,320/7,830 x 100	29.6%
Distribution Costs	264/498 x 100	53%
Wages/Salaries	315/960 x 100	32.8%
Directors' Salaries	10/115 x 100	8.7%
Depreciation	(29)/89 x 100	(32.6%)
Amortisation	1/25 x 100	4%
Rent	23/12 x 100	191.7%
Rates	1/4 x 100	25%
Gas/Electricity	5/2 x 100	250%
Insurance	1/15 x 100	6.7%
Cleaning	1/2 x 100	50%
Miscellaneous	5/10 x 100	50%

Ratio Analysis

	2007		2006	
Gross Margin	3,014/13,095 x 100	23%	2,357/10,160 x 100	23.2%
Operating Margin	1,190/13,095 x 100	9.1%	694/10,160 x 100	6.8%
ROCE	1,190/4,094 x 100	29.1%	694/3,004 x 100	23.1%
Asset Turnover	13,095/4,094	3.2	10,160/3,004	3.4
Current	3,994/1,027	3.9:1	2,595/1,796	1.4:1
Quick	2,354/1,027	2.3:1	1,395/1,796	0.8:1
Inventory Days	1,640/9,556 x 365	62.6	1,200/7,603 x 365	57.6
Receivable Days	2,204/13,095 x 365	61.4	1,353/10,160 x 365	48.6
Payable Days	703/10,150 x 365	25.3	1,479/7,830 x 365	68.9

FIXED TEST 2 –'Engine'

THIS IS A FIXED TEST – Please answer the question in full (long form written). Then log on to en-gage at the following address: www.en-gage.co.uk. Follow the link to 'Fixed Test 2' and answer the questions based on your homework answer.

Once you have answered the questions on en-gage a model answer will be available for your reference.

Test your understanding 3

Holifex Co

There is a risk that provisions are understated or that contingencies are undisclosed. Holifex operates in an industry where health and safety is paramount; any breaches in regulations may lead to fines.

There is a further risk of understating provisions and a more serious risk to the going concern assumption because Holifex could be exposed to potential claims by injured parties if they have been negligent in erecting scaffolding.

There is a possible overstatement of non-current assets. These are dispersed across many different locations. To this end controls over the storage and valuation of the assets could potentially be diluted.

There is also a risk that turnover is overstated due to cut off error. Use of scaffolding by customers is likely to span the year end in some instances.

Stoke Co

Lack of experience of recording this type of acquisition increases the risk of error both in recording and measuring transactions.

The new entity will require consolidation into the group accounts. There is a risk that this has not been performed correctly. The overseas operation will require translation prior to consolidation. There is a risk that incorrect rates have been used to translate the balance sheet and income statement.

The overseas entity is operated by its own management team. This increases control risk, as these may not be in line with group controls. This exposes the company to both prevention and detection risk.

Chantry Co

The period of rapid growth could indicate the possibility of increased control risk due to systems and procedures not been able to cope with the expansion.

An external business risk is the 'fashionable' demand of the product. Such items are prone to rapid changes in demand as social attitudes change. As a result the company must not rely solely on this product for future prosperity and ultimately this could affect the going concern assumption.

There is a risk of understatement of provisions/undisclosed liabilities. The bottled water industry has to comply with health and safety regulations and failure to comply could lead to fines and penalties.

Another inherent risk could be that staff may not be familiar/adequately trained re new accounting system, which increases the risk of human error.

Data has been transferred from old accounting system. There is a risk that the transfer was not performed correctly or that the information is in some way incompatible. Either way there is a risk that errors occurred on transfer.

Westbourne Co

Long term contracts in building and construction could present the risk that turnover is overstated and that related balances (WIP, receivables, payables) are also misstated.

The possible over reliance on few customers given size of contracts poses a constant going concern threat if tenders are unsuccessful and new clients are not found. This threat has been heightened by the dispute and the possible negative PR consequences.

The disputed receivable increases the risk that receivables are overstated and provisions (for doubtful debt) are understated.

The dispute also impacts cash flow, which is likely to be significant at 30% of the contract value. The shortfall in cash could lead to problems meeting debt requirements, particularly is liquidity is also an issue. Once again this could threaten going concern.

chapter

11

Group and transnational audits

Chapter learning objectives

Upon completion of this chapter you will be able to:

- recognise the matters to be considered before accepting appointment as auditor to a group;
- compare and contrast the organisation and planning of group audits with those of joint audits;
- recognise the specific audit problems encountered in group audits and describe audit procedures designed in response;
- identify and describe the matters to be considered and the procedures to be performed when using the work of other auditors;
- explain the implications of group accounting for the auditor's report on the financial statements; and
- discuss the impact of the trend toward globalisation and transnational audit

→ March 2008, "Group Audit Issues objectives & Responsibility" by L.W.
↳ ISA 600 Requirements.

1 Revision of Consolidations

At a basic level consolidating a set of group accounts involves taking a number of sets of individual company financial statements and adding them all together to form one combined set. Due to various complications, such as companies using different currencies and intergroup trading, a number of adjustments have to be made before the consolidated set of accounts can be finalised. This is illustrated in the diagram below:

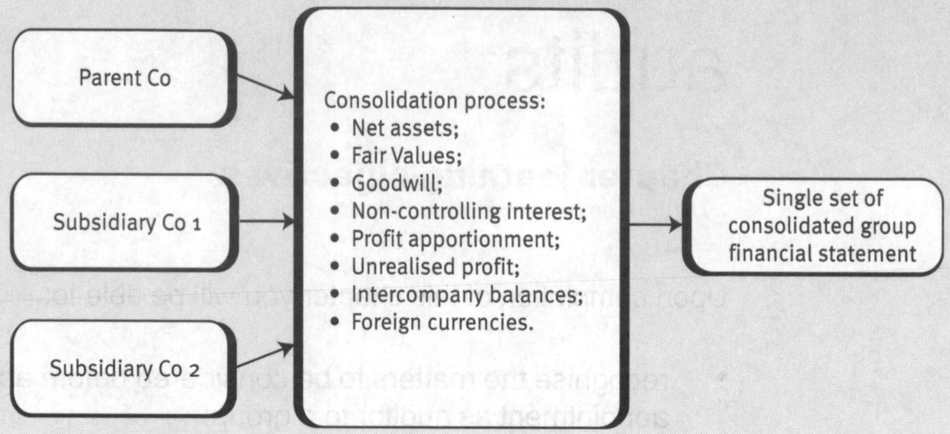

The impact on the auditing process

Before any group considerations can be made the individual company's financial statements have to be prepared and subjected to audit. In the diagram above this includes Parent Co, Subsidiary Co 1 and Subsidiary Co 2. It is the responsibility of individual company directors/management to prepare their accounts. These may be audited by the group auditor or another firm of auditors.

Once this process is complete the individual sets of accounts are combined and adjusted to create a single set of consolidated financial statements. This process is the responsibility of the group's directors. Once the consolidated accounts have been prepared the group auditor performs an audit of the consolidated financial statements.

As the group is a summary of the trading results and positions of the various components of the group (and is itself not a trading entity) the group auditor does not need to audit the group accounts in the same way. They rely upon the audited figures of the individual accounts to confirm the majority of balances and then they audit the consolidation process/adjustments.

2 Group audits – specific considerations

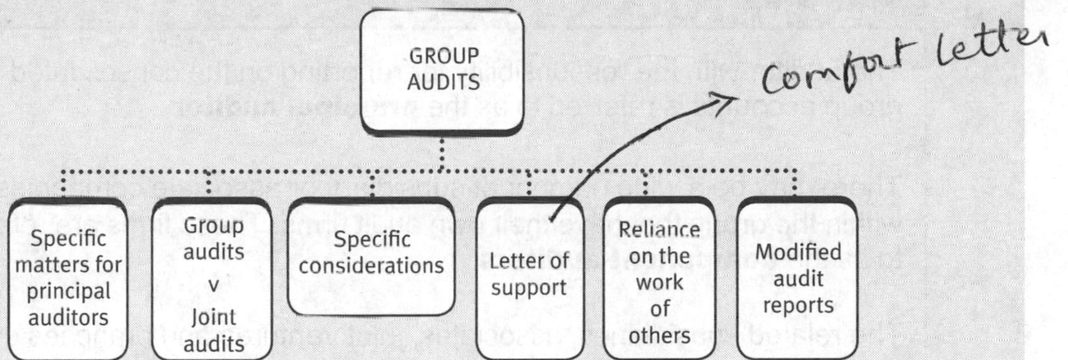

Most of the principles of auditing a group are the same as the audit of a single company and, of course, all the ISA's are still relevant to a group audit. There are, however, some specific considerations relevant to the audit of a group, as listed below:

- Group financial statements require numerous, and potentially complicated, consolidation adjustments;
- Specific accounting standards relating to group accounts must be complied with;
- The components of the group (i.e. the subsidiaries) may be audited by firms other than the principal group auditor; and
- The organisation and planning of a group audit may be significantly more complex than for a single company.

The objectives of an auditor with regard to these matters are identified in **ISA 600** *Special Considerations – Audits of Group Financial Statements (Including the Work of Component Auditors)* as follows:

- To determine whether to act as the auditor of the group financial statements; and
- If acting as the auditor of the group financial statements:
  - To communicate clearly with the component auditors about the scope and timing of their work on financial information related to components and their findings; and
  - To obtain sufficient appropriate evidence regarding the financial information of the components and the consolidation process to express an opinion on whether the group financial statements are prepared, in all material respects, in accordance with the applicable financial reporting framework.

Key Terms

The auditor with the responsibility for reporting on the consolidated group accounts is referred to as the **principal auditor**.

There may be a wide number of subsidiary or associate companies within the group that have their own audit firms. These firms are referred to as the **component auditors**.

The related subsidiaries, associates, joint ventures and branches etc of the group are referred to as **components**.

3 Acceptance as Principal Auditor

In addition to the normal acceptance considerations of ISA's 210 and 220 (discussed in chapters 3 and 4), guidance regarding whether to accept nomination as principal auditor is contained in ISA 600. It encourages firms to consider whether their own participation is sufficient to enable them to take the role of principal auditor. To assist the decision they must consider:

- Whether sufficient appropriate audit evidence can reasonably be expected to be obtained in relation to the consolidation process and the financial information of the components of the group;
- Where component auditors are involved the engagement partner shall evaluate whether the group engagement team will be able to be involved in the work of the component auditors;

If the engagement partner concludes that it will not be possible to obtain sufficient appropriate evidence due to restrictions imposed by group management and that the possible effect of this will result in a disclaimer of opinion then they shall not accept the engagement. If it is a continuing engagement, the auditor should withdraw from the engagement, where possible under applicable laws and regulations.

Don't forget ethics!!

Don't forget that in addition to these specific acceptance considerations the auditor must also consider the ethical and professional issues covered in chapters 1 to 7!

4 Overall Audit Strategy and Plan

The group auditor is responsible for establishing an overall group audit strategy and plan (in accordance with ISA 300). The group engagement partner is ultimately responsible for reviewing and approving this.

In order to fulfil this objective the group auditor has to obtain an understanding of:

- the group;
- its components and their environments;
- group-wide controls; and
- the consolidation process.

This understanding has to be sufficient to confirm or revise the initial identification of components that are likely to be significant and assess the risk of material misstatement of the group financial statements.

Examples of Matters to be Understood

In order to perform their risk assessment thoroughly the group auditor must obtain a wide ranging understanding of matters relevant to the unique circumstances of the group and its components. Whilst the list below is not exhaustive, it provides a range of common examples to be considered specific to the circumstances of a group:

- Group-wide controls:
  - Regularity of meetings between group and component management;
  - Monitoring process of components operations and financial results;
  - Group management's risk assessment process;
  - Monitoring, controlling, reconciling and elimination of intra-group transactions;
  - Centralisation of IT systems;
  - Activities of internal audit;
  - Consistency of policies across the group; and
  - Group wide codes of conduct and fraud prevention.

- Consolidation process:
  - The extent to which component management understand the consolidation process;
  - The process for identifying and accounting for components;
  - The process for identifying reportable segments;
  - The process for identifying related party transactions;
  - How changes to accounting policies are managed;
  - The procedures for dealing with differing year-ends;
  - The procedures for dealing with differing accounting policies;
  - Group's process for ensuring complete, accurate and timely financial reporting;
  - The process for translating foreign components;
  - How IT is used in the consolidation;
  - Procedures for reporting subsequent events;
  - The preparation and authorisation of consolidation adjustments;
  - Frequency, nature and size of transactions between components; and
  - Steps taken to arrive at fair values.

5 Relying on Component Auditors

Principal auditors cannot simply rely on the work of other auditors. The principal may have assessed audit risk and designed their own procedures in accordance with ISA's but they have no guarantee that other auditors have been as prudent. In fact the other auditors may not even follow International Standards of Auditing.

Therefore the principal should obtain and understanding of:

- Whether the component auditor understands and will comply with the code of ethics;
- The professional competence of the component auditor;
- Whether the group auditor will be able to be involved in the work of the component auditor; and
- Whether the component auditor operates in a regulatory environment that actively oversees auditors.

If the group auditor has serious concerns about any of the above issues then they shall obtain sufficient appropriate evidence relating to the financial information of the component, without requesting that the component auditor performs any work.

6 Planning the Group Audit

Materiality

The group auditor is responsible for establishing materiality and performance materiality for the group financial statements as a whole. In addition the group auditor should establish materiality for the components where they are to be audited by other auditors.

As well as establishing materiality, the group auditor should define a threshold above which misstatements cannot be regarded as clearly trivial.

Risk Assessment

The group audit team has to determine the type of work to be performed on the financial information of the components, whether performed by the group team or another auditor.

If, however, the audit of a significant component is to be performed by another auditor then the group auditor shall be involved in the component's risk assessment. This includes, as a minimum:

- Discussing with the component auditor or management those components of the business that are significant to the group;
- Discussing with the component auditor the susceptibility of the component to material misstatement; and
- Reviewing the component auditor's documentation of identified risks of material misstatement.

If significant risks of material misstatement of the group accounts have been identified in a component that is audited by another auditor then the group auditor shall evaluate the appropriateness of the further audit procedures performed in response to this assessment.

If the component is not considered significant then the group auditor shall simply perform analytical procedures at group level.

Further Implications of Materiality

In order to reduce the risk of material misstatement in the group financial statements, materiality for the components should be set at an amount below materiality for the group as a whole.

If the component is considered to be financially significant to the group, then it shall be audited using component materiality. If, however, it is considered to be significant because it is likely to pose risks of material misstatement to the group due to its nature or circumstances, one or more of the following should be performed:

- An audit using component materiality;
- An audit of one or more classes of transaction, account balances or disclosures relating to the risk of misstatement of the group financial statements; and/or
- Specific audit procedures relating to the risk of material misstatement of the group financial statements.

Risk Indicators

The following examples, whilst not exhaustive, cover a wide range of conditions or events that could indicate an increased risk of material misstatement of the group financial statements:

- A complex group structure;
- Frequent acquisitions, disposals and/or reorganisations;
- Poor corporate governance systems;
- Non-existent or ineffective group-wide controls;
- Components operating under foreign jurisdictions that may be subject to unusual government intervention;
- High risk business activities of components;
- Unusual related party transactions;
- Prior occurrences of intra-group balances that did not reconcile;
- The existence of complex transactions that are accounted for in more than one component;
- Differing application of accounting policies;
- Differing financial year-ends;
- Prior occurrences of unauthorised or incomplete consolidation adjustments;
- Aggressive tax planning; and
- Frequent changes of auditor.

Communication with Component Auditors

The group auditor is responsible for communicating with the auditors of the components on a timely basis. Communication shall include;

- The work to be performed by the component and the use made of this;
- The form and content of the communications made by the component auditor to the group auditor;

- A request that the component auditor co-operates with the group team;
- The ethical requirements relevant to the group audit;
- Component materiality and the threshold for triviality;
- Identified significant risks of material misstatement of the group financial statements; and
- A list of identified related parties.

As part of the communication process the group auditor should also request that the component auditor communicates matters that are relevant to the group audit on a timely basis. Such matters include:

- Compliance with ethical standards;
- Compliance with audit instructions;
- Identification of financial information upon which the component auditor is reporting;
- Instances of non-compliance with laws and regulations;
- Uncorrected misstatements;
- Indications of management bias;
- Significant deficiencies in internal control;
- Other significant matters to be communicated to those charged with governance;
- Any other matters relevant to the group audit; and
- The component auditor's overall conclusion.

Further Communications

As well as the matters identified above, the group auditor should also communicate further matters in a letter of instruction. This is likely to include

- Matters relevant to the planning of the component audit:
  - the timetable for completion;
  - dates of planned visits by the group auditor;
  - a list of key contacts;
  - work to be performed on intra-group balances;
  - guidance on other statutory reporting responsibilities;
  - instructions for subsequent events review.

- Matters relevant to the conduct of component auditor work:
  - The findings of the group auditors tests of controls on common systems;
  - The findings of internal audit relevant to the component;
  - A request for timely communication of evidence that contradicts evidence used in the group risk assessment;
  - A request for written representations on component management's compliance with the applicable financial reporting framework;
  - Matters to be documented by the component auditor.
- Other information:
  - A request that the following be reported in a timely fashion:
    - Significant accounting, financial reporting and auditing matters, including accounting estimates and related judgements;
    - Matters relating to the going concern status of the component;
    - Matters relating to litigation and claims;
    - Significant deficiencies in internal control and information that indicates the existence of fraud
  - A request that the group auditor be notified of any unusual events as early as possible.

7 Review

The group auditor has to review the communications from the component auditors. If any significant matters have arisen they should then engage in a discussion with the component auditor or group management, as appropriate. If necessary the group auditor should then also review other relevant parts of the component auditor's working papers.

If the group auditor is not satisfied with the sufficiency or appropriateness of the component auditor's work they are responsible for determining what additional procedures are required. If it is not feasible for the component auditor to perform this then the group auditor must perform the procedures.

When all procedures on the components have been completed the group engagement partner must consider whether the aggregate effect of any uncorrected misstatements will have a material impact on the group financial statements.

8 Auditing the Consolidated Accounts

For many groups the consolidation process will be complicated. There are also significant areas where adjustments and estimations are required. The principal needs to plan to perform sufficient procedures on the consolidation to minimise the risk of material misstatement. These include:

- Ensuring the correct figures are transferred from the component proforma accounts to the consolidation;
- Evaluating the classification of the component (i.e. subsidiary, associate, joint venture etc);
- Reviewing disclosures for related party transactions;
- Reviewing the policies and year-ends applied by the components and any consequent adjustments;
- Reviewing the calculation of specific consolidation adjustments, such as:
  - Fair values;
  - Goodwill and consequent impairment;
  - Non controlling interest;
  - Intercompany trading balances;
  - Provisions for unrealised profit;
  - Foreign component retranslation.

Significantly, these adjustments do not pass through the usual transaction processing systems and, for that reason, may not be subject to the same internal controls as other transactions. Therefore to evaluate the appropriateness, completeness and accuracy of the adjustments the group auditor may:

- Evaluate whether the adjustments appropriately reflect the events and transactions underlying them;
- Determine whether adjustments have been correctly calculated, processed and authorised;
- Determine whether adjustments are supported by sufficient appropriate documentation; and
- Check the reconciliation and elimination of intra-group balances and transactions.

Exam Focus – Standards

In an article entitled "Group Audit Issues: Objectives and Responsibilities" (March 2008) Lisa Weaver, the examiner, advises candidates that they must be 'very familiar' with the financial reporting standards relevant to consolidations. These are:

- IFRS 3, Business Combinations;
- IAS 28, Investments in Associates;
- IAS 31, Interests in Joint Ventures;
- IAS 32, Financial Instruments: Presentation; and
- IAS 39, Financial Instruments: Recognition and Measurement.

In addition to the stated financial reporting standards students would be well advised to consider International Standards of Auditing 540 and 550, which cover accounting estimates, fair value measurements and related party disclosures respectively. In a more recent article entitled, "The Importance of Financial Reporting Standards to Auditors" (October 2008) Lisa indicates that these standards, all of which are relevant to the consolidation process, are highly examinable.

9 Letters of support

In certain circumstances, a letter of support from the directors of a group may be required.

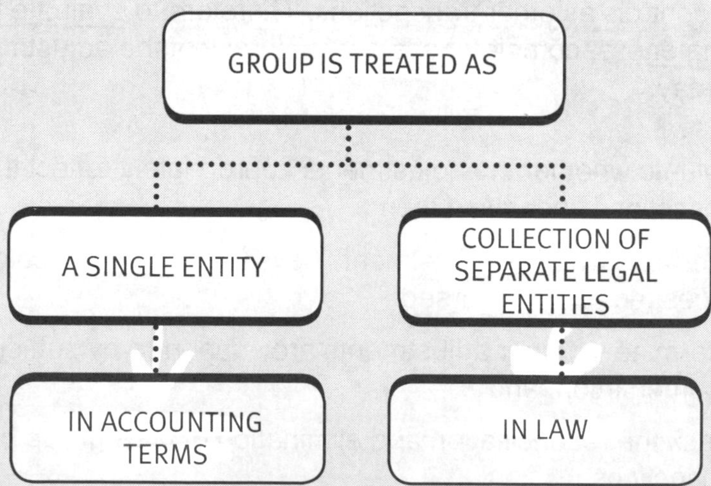

A situation may arise where a subsidiary may not be a going concern. If so, the subsidiaries accounts, which are consequently consolidated into the group accounts, should be prepared on a break up basis.

However, the group may offer support to the subsidiary to enable it to continue trading in the foreseeable future. If this is the case the directors must give the principal auditor formal documentation, usually called a 'comfort' or 'support' letter. This confirms their intention to support the ailing subsidiary.

The auditor will normally accept such as a letter as valid audit evidence of the going concern basis for the subsidiary's financial statements. However, the principal auditor should not take this at face value. They should consider the position of the group to help identify whether it has the resources to fulfil its promise of support.

10 Modified audit reports

Where one or more of the subsidiaries has a modified audit report (regardless of who audited the subsidiary) the principal auditor must consider the impact of the issue on the group financial statements, according to group materiality levels, as follows:

- If the matter is not material in a group context then they may be ignored.
- If the matter is material to both the component and the group then the modification should be carried through to the group audit report.
- Note that a disclaimer of opinion in a subsidiary, given because the component auditor has not been able to gather sufficient appropriate audit evidence, may be altered to an 'except for' opinion in the group context.

11 Joint Audit

What is a joint audit?

This is when two audit firms are appointed to provide and audit opinion on a set of financial statements. They will work together planning the audit, gathering evidence, reviewing the work and providing the opinion.

Benefits

- retention of subsidiary auditor (and therefore their cumulative audit knowledge and experience) following acquisition;
- Availability of a wider range of resources (particularly important across national boundaries);
- Possible efficiency improvements.

Disadvantages

- Cultural clashes;
- Difficulty setting a joint approach – too many cooks!
- Both firms will need to be paid a fee.

Recent Trends

Joint auditing allows small and medium sized entities to continue to be involved in an audit once their client has been acquired or merged with another organisation. Given recent trends in globalisation the alternative would likely be the replacement of the existing auditor with a larger firm.

Given the nature of the current economy and the level of acquisition activity this could significantly reduce the pool of business for small and medium sized accountancy practices. Joint audit is therefore considered to be an important tool in combating the increased power of the 'Big 4' and the more significant medium tier firms.

12 What are 'transnational audits'?

Transnational audit means an audit of financial statements which may be relied upon outside the audited entity's home jurisdiction.

Reliance on these audits might be for purposes of significant lending, investment or regulatory decisions.

The differences between a 'normal' audit, conducted within the boundaries of one set of legal and regulatory requirements, and a transnational audit are largely due to variations in:

- Auditing standards;
- Regulation and oversight of auditors;
- Financial reporting standards; and
- Corporate governance requirements.

Auditors must be aware of the different regimes that apply to the audit of a transnational entity because they will be bound by the varying laws and regulations. Given the globalisation of businesses and stock markets this is an increasingly significant concern for many firms of auditors.

Specific Differences with Transnational Audit

Auditing Standards

Despite the prevalence of International Standards of Auditing, many countries use modified versions and many continue to use local standards of auditing. As a result, in a group audit with components from a wide range of geographical backgrounds, it is possible that the audits of the components will be performed according to different standards. This could lead to inconsistency and poor quality for the group audit as a whole.

Regulation and Oversight of Auditors

As well as differing audit standards there are many different ways that the auditing profession is regulated. This can also affect the quality of the audit of components from different regimes, which will also lead to inconsistency in the quality of a group audit.

Financial Reporting Standards

Within a multinational group it is likely that adjustments will be required due to the application of differing financial reporting standards. These standards will be reflected in the component financial statements but, upon consolidation, must be adjusted to reflect the parents accounting policies. These can lead to some very technically difficult consolidation adjustments, which will likely increase the risk of material misstatement significantly.

Corporate Governance Requirements

In some countries there are very strict corporate governance requirements that not only affect the directors of the company but their auditor. Often the auditor is required to perform, and report on, procedures supplementary to the normal audit.

In other countries the corporate governance requirements, particularly with regard to internal controls, are much more relaxed. However, this also affects the audit because this could indicate that internal controls may be less effective than those of a component that operates in a highly regulated environment.

The Transnational Audit Committee

Transnational Audit Committee

The International Federation of Accountants (IFAC) has a committee with specific responsibilities for transnational audits: the Transnational Audit Committee (TAC).

ROLE OF THE TAC

- Identifying audit practice issues. When the issues suggest changes in auditing or assurance standards may be required, recommend to the appropriate IFAC standard-setting boards that the issue be reviewed.
- Proposing members to the IFAC Regulatory Liaison Group and identifying qualified candidates to serve on IFAC standard-setting boards.
- Proposing members to the IFAC Regulatory Liaison Group and identifying qualified candidates to serve on IFAC standard-setting boards.
- Acting as a formal conduit for interaction among transnational firms and international regulators and financial institutions with regard to audit quality, systems of quality control, and transparency of international networks.

13 The impact of globalisation

Globalisation is the movement toward the whole world being the market from which resources are used and to which products are sold. Factories, shops and service organisations in many countries are likely to be foreign-owned or controlled. Goods, services, capital, and people are also more likely to move across national borders.

The problem with global businesses is that they operate in widely different legal and ethical systems. As a result audit firms have to have the resources and expertise to operate in a diverse geographical market and have to know how to audit highly regulated modern businesses. As a result it is likely that only the larger audit firms can acquire the global expertise to handle such audits.

Advantages	Disadvantages
• Wide ranging expertise • Global facilities • Can invest in expensive systems and necessary IT to meet needs of international clients	• Lack of competition and choice, particularly for large companies

The concentration of the audit market into a few very large firms has come about because of globalisation. The larger firms found that amalgamations amongst the audit firms were the way forward loading to a more concentrated audit market. Affiliation is used by the larger accounting firms to develop an internationally recognised brand name, whereas co-operation is used by the mid-tier firms who join international co-operatives of firms who send each other business, but retain their own trading name in their home countries.

Current Trends

Current trends still lean towards mergers:

- of firms in the countries where the profession is more highly developed, for example USA and many European countries, and
- between firms in the more developed arenas with practices in less developed locations.

In the mid-tier sector, the fastest way for firms to grow and achieve dominance in the sector is to merge with other similar sized companies.

Due to the debate about audit firms offering other services, and the impact this may have on auditor independence, the trend may be for audit firms to divest themselves of consultancy services.

- The SEC in the USA has drawn up stricter rules on auditor independence which put pressure on large audit firms to sell off their other services, particularly their consultancy divisions.
- As a result, by the end of 2002 each of the Big Four had separated their consultancy divisions from their audit practices, either by sale or by demerger.

The auditing profession is organised much as any other business sector, with a small number of very large, global organisations, a significant number of mid-sized practices, and many smaller firms and sole practitioners.

The dawn of International Standards of Auditing (and accounting/ financial reporting) have helped to align the objectives and procedures of auditors across the globe. The aim is to ensure the quality of audits world-wide.

Test your understanding 1

You are an audit manager in Nailah & Co, a firm of Chartered Certified Accountants. One of your audit clients Chione Co provides satellite broadcasting services in a rapidly growing market. During the current accounting period Chione made the following acquisitions:

(1) Chione purchased Nubia Co, a competitor group of companies. Significant revenue, cost and capital expenditure synergies are expected as the operations of Chione and Nubia are being combined into one group of companies.

(2) Chione purchased Maahes Co, a large cable communications provider in India, where your firm has no representation. The financial statements of Maahes for the year end will continue to be audited by a local firm of Chartered Certified Accountants.

Required

Explain what effect the acquisitions will have on the planning of the audit of the consolidated financial statements of Chione Co for the current accounting period.

Test your understanding 2

Bellatrix is a carpet manufacturer and an audit client of your firm. Bellatrix has identified a company in the same business, Scorpio, as a target for acquisition in the current year.

As audit manager to Bellatrix and its subsidiaries for the year ended 31 December 2006, you have been asked to examine Scorpio's management accounts and budget forecasts. The chief executive of Bellatrix, Sirius Deneb, believes that despite its current cash flow difficulties, Scorpio's current trading performance is satisfactory and future prospects are good. The chief executive of Scorpio is Ursula Minor.

The findings of your examination are as follows:

Budget forecasts for Scorpio, for the current accounting year to 31 December 2006 and for the following year, reflect a rising profit trend.

Scorpio's results for the first half year to 30 June 2006 reflect $800,000 profit from the sale of a warehouse that had been carried in the books at historical cost. There are plans to sell two similar properties later in the year and outsource warehousing.

About 10% of Scorpio's sales are to Andromeda, a limited liability company. Two members of the management board of Scorpio hold minority interests in Andromeda. Selling prices negotiated between Scorpio and Andromeda appear to be on an arm's length basis.

Scorpio's management accounts for the six months to 30 June 2006 have been used to support an application to the bank for an additional loan facility to refurbish the executive and administration offices. These management accounts show inventory and trade receivables' balances that exceed the figures in the accounting records by $150,000. This excess has also been reflected in the first half year's profit. Upon enquiry, you have established that allowances, to reduce inventory and trade receivables' to estimated realizable values, have been reduced to assist with the loan application.

Although there has been a recent downturn in trading, Ursula Minor has stated that she is very confident that the negotiations with the bank will be successful as Scorpio has met its budgeted profit for the first six months. Ursula believes that increased demand for carpets and rugs in the winter months will enable results to exceed budget.

Required

(a) Identify and comment on the implications of your findings for Bellatrix's plan to proceed with the acquisition of Scorpio.

(10 marks)

(b) Explain what impact the acquisition will have on the conduct of your audit of Bellatrix and its subsidiaries for the year to 31 December 2006.

(15 marks)

(Total: 25 marks)

14 Chapter Summary

GROUP AUDITS

Specific matters for principal auditors

- Materiality of portion audited by them.
- Knowledge of portion audited by them.
- Extra work required on components audited by others.
- Risk in component audited by others.

Specific considerations

- correct classification of investments
- differing accounting policies and frameworks
- fair values on acquisition
- intangibles
- taxation
- goodwill on consolidation
- intra-group balances, transactions and profits
- related parties
- share options
- post balance sheet events
- entities in developing countries.

Reliance on the work of others

- professional competence of other auditors?
- a/c policies uniform?
- sufficient information to form opinion?
- other auditors covered all material matters and work can be relied on?
- effect of qualifications?
- materiality of amounts involved?

Group audits

- 1 firm appointed as the principal auditor,
- take full responsibility for f/s
- decide how and when work will be performed

v

Joint audits

- ›1 principal auditor
- responsibility is shared jointly
- cooperation is required to divide and plan the work.

Letter of support

- Issued by directors of parent co. where subsid ceases to be going concern
- Auditors accept as evidence of g.c. and audit report not modified

Modified audit reports

Ignore unless material to the group.

Test your understanding answers

Test your understanding 1

Group structure

The new group structure must be ascertained to identify the entities that should be consolidated into the group financial statements of Chione for the year end.

It will also be imperative to identify the locations of the new subsidiaries and the scale of their operations. This will help to identify the number of team members and the locations they have to visit. This could impact upon the budget for the engagement and, ultimately, on the fee charged.

Materiality assessment

Preliminary materiality will be much higher, in monetary terms, than in the prior year. The materiality of each subsidiary should be assessed, in terms of the enlarged group as at the planning stage. This will identify, for example:

- those entities requiring an audit visit by the principal auditor; and
- those for which analytical procedures may suffice.

If either acquisition is particularly material to the group, Nailah may plan (provisionally) to visit Maahes's auditors to discuss any problems shown to arise in their audit work summary (see group instructions below).

Goodwill arising

The audit plan should draw attention to the need to audit the amount of goodwill arising on the acquisitions and management's impairment test at the balance sheet date.

The assets and liabilities of Nubia and Maahes, at fair value to the group, will be combined on a line-by-line basis and any goodwill arising recognised.

Significant non-current assets such as properties are likely to have been independently valued prior to the acquisition. It may be appropriate to plan to place reliance on the work of quantity surveyors or other property valuers.

Group (related party) transactions and balances

A list of all the companies in the group (including any associated companies) should be included in group audit instructions to ensure that intra-group transactions and balances (and any unrealised profits and losses on transactions with associated companies) are identified for elimination on consolidation.

It should be confirmed at the planning stage that inter-company transactions are identified as such in the accounting systems of all Chione companies and that inter-company balances are regularly reconciled.

Analytical procedures

Having brought in the operations of a group of companies (Nubia) with similar activities may extend the scope of analytical procedures available. This could have the effect of increasing audit efficiency.

Other auditors

Other auditors will include:

- any affiliates of Nailah in any of the countries in which Chione (as combined with Nubia) operates; and
- unrelated auditors (including those of Maahes).

Nailah will plan to use the work of Maahes's auditors who are Chartered Certified Accountants. Their competence and independence should be assessed (e.g. through information obtained from a questionnaire and evidence of their work).

A letter of introduction should be sent to the unrelated auditors, with Chione's permission, as soon as possible (if not already done) requesting their co-operation in providing specified information within a given timescale.

Group instructions will need to be sent to affiliated and unrelated auditors containing:

- proforma statements;
- a list of group and associated companies;
- a statement of group accounting policies (see below);

- the timetable for the preparation of the group accounts (see below);
- a request for copies of management letters;
- an audit work summary questionnaire or checklist;
- contact details (of senior members of Nailah's audit team).

Accounting policies (Nubia & Maahes)

Whilst it is likely that Nubia has the same accounting policies as Chione (because, as a competitor, it operates in the same jurisdictions) Maahes may have material accounting policies which do not comply with the rest of the group. Nailah may request that Maahes's auditors calculate the effect of any non-compliance with a group accounting policy for adjustment on consolidation.

Timetable

The timetable for the preparation of Chione's consolidated financial statements should be agreed with management as soon as possible. Key dates should be planned for:

- agreement of inter-company balances and transactions;
- submission of proforma statements to Nailah;
- completion of the consolidation package;
- tax review of group accounts;
- completion of audit fieldwork by other auditors ;
- subsequent events review;
- final clearance on accounts of subsidiaries;
- Nailah's final clearance of consolidated financial statements.

Test your understanding 2

(a) **Implications of findings**

$800,000 profit on sale of property

Although the profit on sale of the property arises from ordinary activities, it needs to be separately identified (IAS 1) so that Scorpio's current trading performance can be assessed (by Bellatrix and the bank). It should be excluded from any trading results that are being extrapolated to provide figures for profit forecasts. To include it would result in a distortion of sustainable profits.

Scorpio's properties are being valued at historical cost in its financial statements (IAS 16). Bellatrix should obtain an independent valuation of the properties before finalising a purchase price for the acquisition of Scorpio.

The property sale could have been made to realise cash and so mitigate current cash flow difficulties. The proposed sale of two more properties and outsourcing of warehousing may further improve the cash flow situation in the short-term. However, outsourcing warehousing could place a further burden on cash flow if an agreement is entered into and no buyer can subsequently be found for the properties.

Scorpio's management is seeking (or negotiating with) a suitable organization to provide warehousing. However, one of the synergies to be obtained from acquiring Scorpio may be utilising Bellatrix's spare warehousing capacity. Bellatrix should therefore obtain warranties and indemnities in the purchase contract in respect of any contingent liabilities that could arise. For example, penalties may be incurred if an agreement to outsource warehousing is entered into and subsequently cancelled.

Sales to Andromeda

The two members of the management board of Scorpio will be related parties (IAS 24) if they are key management personnel (i.e. having authority and responsibility for planning, directing and controlling the activities of Scorpio).

Andromeda will be a related party if the management board members have the ability (acting individually or in concert) to exercise influence over Andromeda's financial and operating policy decisions. This seems likely, as 10% of Scorpio's sales constitutes material intercompany transactions. (Control of Andromeda is not an issue as the two members have only a minority interest.)

Sales to Andromeda appear to be related party transactions which should have been disclosed in Scorpio's financial statements for the year to 31 December 2006.

Although prices appear to be on an arm's length basis, the transactions may not be at arm's length if other trading terms (e.g. delivery or payment terms) are more or less favourable than transactions with unrelated parties. If credit terms are not 'normal commercial' these sales could be contributing to Scorpio's current cash flow difficulties.

The sales to Andromeda are material to Scorpio and may be lost after the acquisition (e.g. if the two minority shareholders do not continue to hold positions on the management board of Scorpio). A proportional (i.e. 10%) reduction in gross profit would also be expected (assuming margins on sales to Andromeda are not dissimilar to those on other sales).

Bank loan application

The $150,000 discrepancy between the current asset values per the management accounts and the balances per the accounting records appears to be an irregularity that could constitute a fraud against the bank. It casts serious doubts on the integrity of Scorpio's management. Revising the accounting estimates for allowances against asset values downwards is clearly inappropriate as it is most likely that they should be increased (as stock levels increase with falling demand and customers are more likely to be bad and doubtful).

Refurbishing the offices is unlikely to constitute essential expenditure when the company is experiencing cash flow difficulties. Also it is possible that refurbishment may not be required when Bellatrix acquires Scorpio because the functions of the executive and administration offices may be relocated elsewhere within the Bellatrix group of companies.

Although current trading performance is clearly below budget (after deducting the profit on disposal and reinstating the provisions against stock and debtors), the loan finance is not being sought for a purpose that would increase the company's revenue-earning opportunities. This may cast doubts on the business acumen of Scorpio's management. It is possible that the loan finance would not be forthcoming if the bank were aware of Scorpio's true position.

Bellatrix should seek to have the negotiations with the bank suspended until after the acquisition, when the need for loan finance can be reassessed. Bellatrix should obtain guarantees from Scorpio's executives in the event that they pursue the loan application (which may possibly create charges over Scorpio's assets).

Budget forecast

The profit estimates made by the management of Scorpio appear to be unduly optimistic because the first six month's budget has only been 'met' by the inclusion, in the reported results of:

- a non-sustainable profit on disposal of a warehouse;
- unwarranted reversals of provisions against asset values.

Perhaps it is more likely that the forecast 'rising profit trend' will be achieved (and the annual budget exceeded) through profits arising on the disposals of two more properties rather than increased demand.

Budgeted profits should therefore be disregarded in the determination of the purchase price.

Tutorial note: It is a higher skill to recognise, when planning an answer, that it is not always suitable to address the items in the scenario in the order in which they are presented. For example, in this Q, there is not a lot to be said about the budget forecasts until the other findings have been interpreted.

(b) **Impact of acquisition on audit**

Tutorial notes:

(1) The acquisition will be completed before 31 December 2006 (see 1st para 'acquisition in current year').

(2) Accounting year ends will be coterminous ('first half year to 30 June 2006') – to assume otherwise would be a fabrication.

(3) You will be appointed as auditor to Scorpio ('as audit manager to Bellatrix and its subsidiaries').

(4) The acquisition method will be used to consolidate Scorpio as, under IFRS 3, this is the only permitted accounting treatment.

(5) 'Conduct of your audit' must not be confined to the 'audit testing' phase but consider, within the scope of the given scenario, the whole audit process.

Practice management

It is possible that audit objectivity may appear to have suffered impairment (e.g. due to a closer relationship between Bellatrix's management and the audit team having developed during the acquisition assignment). A second partner review may therefore be required as an appropriate safeguard.

Bellatrix's individual company accounts

The acquisition will constitute an addition, at cost, to Investments in subsidiaries in Bellatrix's own financial statements. The purchase consideration paid (or contingently payable) should also be disclosed.

The cost of acquisition should be verified to the sale agreement. Cash consideration must be agreed to entries in the cash book and bank statements. Company minutes and entries in the share register will evidence consideration in shares.

Bellatrix's consolidated accounts

Balance sheet

Scorpio's assets and liabilities, at fair value to the group, will be combined on a line-by-line basis and any goodwill arising recognised.

The fair value of such assets as the properties (assuming that they have not yet been sold) may be material to the consolidated balance sheet. Assuming that the properties were independently valued prior to the acquisition, it will be appropriate to seek to place reliance on the work of the expert valuer.

The calculation of the amount attributed to goodwill must be agreed to be the excess of the cost of the acquisition over the aggregate fair values of the identifiable assets and liabilities existing at the date of acquisition.

The period over which this goodwill is to be amortised must be reviewed for reasonableness. If an amortisation method other than the straight-line approach has been adopted, Bellatrix's management must be able to offer persuasive evidence (which must be subject to audit scrutiny) that it is appropriate.

Income statement

As Scorpio is going to have been acquired quite late on in the year (certainly the second half of the year) it is possible that its post-acquisition results are not material to the consolidated income statement.

Unless accounting adjustments are required (e.g. to bring any accounting policies of Scorpio into line with Bellatrix) the addition of one more subsidiary into the consolidation working papers is unlikely to have an appreciable impact on the amount of work involved.

Other subsidiaries

The materiality of other subsidiaries, in the group context, should be reassessed in terms of the enlarged group. The existence of another company (Scorpio) in the same business within the group may extend the scope of analytical procedures available.

This could have the effect of increasing audit efficiency.

Scorpio's financial statements

Planning

Much of the collection of background information associated with planning the conduct of a new audit assignment will have already been obtained as a result of the pre-acquisition work.

Materiality assessment

Material matters requiring attention will include:

– sales to Andromeda
– property valuations
– inventory valuations (raw materials, WIP and finished carpets)
– trade receivables balances
– liabilities (including bank loans).

The management accounts for the six months to 30 June should provide information sufficient to make an initial evaluation of materiality. However, as the reliability of certain management information is in doubt, this should be reassessed before detailed work commences.

The materiality of these items should also be assessed in the context of monetary amounts in the consolidated financial statements.

Risk assessment

Specific areas of audit risk have already been identified, thereby reducing the time required to assess the risk of misstatement at the planning stage. In particular:

– inherent risk is high due to Scorpio's management overstating profit (even if the management board has since been replaced);
– inventory may be overstated/allowances understated due to inventory having increased (due to a fall in demand);

– trade receivables may be overstated/allowances for bad and doubtful debts understated due to Scorpio's management having 'massaged' these figures to achieve their profit estimates.

Ascertaining the systems and internal controls

Some systems review work may have already been undertaken (e.g. when considering the source of information used in the preparation of Scorpio budgetary information).

The relevance of Scorpio's current accounting systems and internal controls will depend on Bellatrix's plans for change. For example, a Bellatrix office may account for Scorpio's transactions. If significant changes are proposed it may be more appropriate to adopt a substantive approach to the first audit of Scorpio.

Audit evidence

Some audit evidence should have been obtained for the assignment file (e.g. concerning the sales to Andromeda and the sale of property). This should be copied/referenced to the audit working papers to ensure that work is not unnecessarily reperformed.

As Scorpio is in the same business as Bellatrix, ratio analysis and other substantive analytical procedures should provide a more cost-effective approach to obtaining audit evidence than tests of detail.

Review

The relationship between the two members of Scorpio's management board and Andromeda after the date of acquisition must be established and the extent of transactions between them, if any. (For example, these minority shareholders of Andromeda may no longer hold board positions and/or sales to Andromeda may have ceased.)

The proportion of sales should be disclosed (e.g. 10%) along with factual information concerning the pricing policy. Audit tests must verify, for example, that price is determined based on a published price list.

chapter

12

Evidence

Chapter learning objectives

Upon completion of this chapter you will be able to:

- evaluate the appropriateness and sufficiency of different sources of audit evidence and how it may be obtained
- specify audit procedures to obtain sufficient audit evidence from identified sources
- demonstrate the use of written management representations as a source of audit evidence
- recognise when it is justifiable to place reliance on the work of an expert
- assess the appropriateness of the work of internal auditors and the extent to which reliance can be placed on it.

— Articles

- Nov/Dec - 08 "The Imp of Fin. Reporting Std's" To Auditors. (Pg 41)
- Jan, 07 "Audit Evidence" by Richardson -- ISA 500.

1 The Risk Based Approach Revised

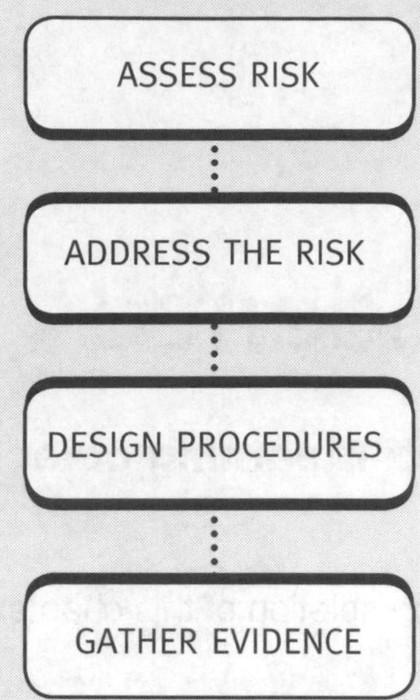

It's all about risk

Remember: the fundamental principles laid down in ISA's 315 and 330 for gathering audit evidence are:

- audit procedures are designed in response to the assessment of risk at the planning stage;
- evidence gathered must be sufficient and appropriate enough to reduce assessed risk to an acceptable level.

The risk assessment loop

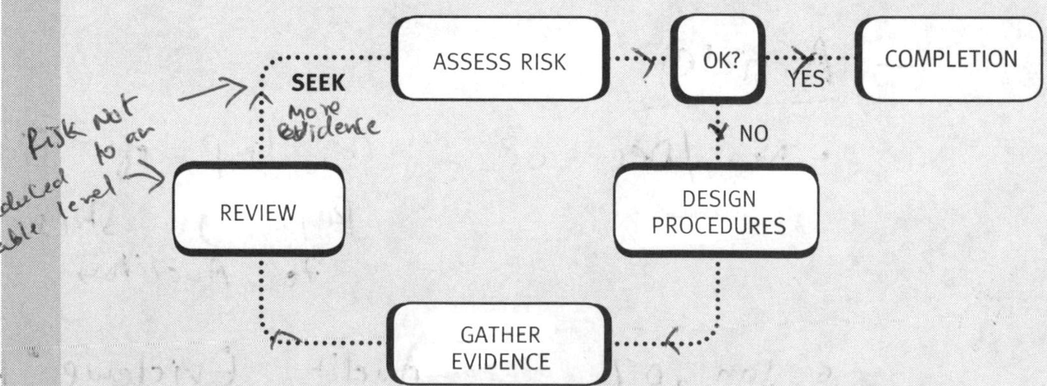

If, at the review stage, the senior audit staff deem that the risk of misstatement has not been reduced to an acceptable level, more evidence will be required.

Exam Focus

Part A of the exam, consists of case study type questions that will most likely require you to decide what pieces of evidence should be gathered to address a particular risk. For example: in question 1 "Island Co" on the December 2007 paper, students were requested to suggest tests they would perform in respect of a warranty provision.

More recently Lisa Weaver, the examiner, suggested that she would begin testing more complicated areas of the syllabus (See the article entitled "The Importance of Financial Reporting Standards to Auditors," October 2008). True to her word she followed this up in December 2008 with a question (Bluebell) regarding audit procedures to be performed in respect of:

(i) the **measurement** of share based expenses; and

(ii) the **recoverability** of deferred tax assets.

Note: the question was specific to measurement and recoverability. Responses tailored to the presentation of share based expenses and the valuation of deferred tax assets, for example, were irrelevant and did not score.

Part A is compulsory. Therefore a well prepared student must be able to suggest audit procedures.

It is also possible that in section B students may be asked to identify the evidence they would expect to see with regard to certain technical areas of financial reporting as part of a review of working files. See the self study questions accompanying this chapter as a guide.

2 Getting the right evidence

The guidance according to **ISA 500** *Audit Evidence* is simple:

"The objective of the auditor is to design and perform audit procedures in such a way as to enable the auditor to obtain sufficient appropriate evidence to be able to draw reasonable conclusions on which to base the auditor's opinion."

It then goes on to explain that the quality of audit evidence is vital and that not all forms of evidence are equally reliable:

- Independent, externally generated evidence is better than evidence generated internally by the client;
- Effective controls imposed by the entity, generally improve the reliability of evidence;
- Evidence obtained directly by the auditor is more reliable than evidence obtained indirectly or by inference;
- It is better to get written, documentary evidence rather than verbal confirmations; and
- Original documents provide more reliable evidence than photocopies or facsimiles.

Audit procedures for Obtaining Evidence

The auditor obtains evidence to draw conclusions on which to base the audit opinion. This is achieved by performing procedures to:

- Obtain an understanding of the entity and its environment, including internal control, to assess the risks of material misstatement;
- Test the operating effectiveness of controls in preventing, detecting and correcting material misstatements; and
- Detect material misstatements.

The methods of obtaining evidence for use in an audit are:

- Inspection of records, documents or physical assets;
- Observation of processes and procedures, e.g. inventory counts;
- External confirmation obtained in the form of a direct written response to the auditor from a third party;
- Recalculation to confirm the numerical accuracy of documents or records;
- Reperformance by the auditor of procedures or controls;
- Analytical procedures; and
- Enquiry of knowledgeable parties.

Financial Statements Assertions

For an audit test to be relevant it must fulfil the objective of the procedure. The objectives are usually to confirm one, or more, financial statements assertions made by management when preparing the class of transaction, accounting balance or disclosure. The assertions are:

For classes of transaction:

- Occurrence – transactions and events that have been recorded actually occurred and relate to the entity;
- Completeness – all transactions and events that should have been recorded have been recorded;
- Accuracy – amounts have been recorded appropriately;
- Cutoff – transactions and events have been recorded in the correct period; and
- Classification – transactions and events have been recorded in the correct accounts.

For accounting balances:

- Existence – assets, liabilities and equity interests exist;
- Rights and obligations – the entity controls rights to assets and liabilities are the obligation of the entity;
- Completeness – all assets, liabilities and equity interests that should have been recorded have been recorded; and
- Valuation and allocation – assets, liabilities and equity interests are included in the financial statements at appropriate amounts.

For presentation and disclosures:

- Occurrence and rights and obligations – disclosed events and transactions have occurred and pertain to the entity;
- Completeness – all disclosures that should have been recorded have been recorded;
- Classification and understandability – financial information is appropriately presented and described, and disclosures are clearly expressed; and
- Accuracy and valuation – financial and other information are disclosed fairly and at appropriate amounts.

(ISA 315)

3 Analytical procedures

The term 'analytical procedure' means the evaluation of financial information through the analysis of plausible relationships among both financial and non-financial data. This is defined in **ISA 520** *Analytical Procedures*

The purpose is to identify trends and/or relationships that are inconsistent with other relevant information or the auditor's understanding of the business. The purpose of this is to identify risk areas and guide the design of further audit procedures that are aimed at detecting and quantifying material misstatement.

Analytical procedures are used at varying stages throughout the audit:

- As part of risk assessment, in accordance with ISA 315 (see chapter 10);
- As part of substantive audit procedures, in accordance with ISA's 500 and 520; and
- As part of the review of audit procedures, towards the end of the audit, in accordance with ISA 520.

Substantive analytical procedures

The use of analytical procedures as substantive evidence is generally more applicable where:

- there are large volumes of transactions
- relationships exist amongst the data and are believed to be predictable over time.

Their suitability as substantive procedures depends, to a large extent, on the auditor's risk assessment of specific assertions and the reliability of the underlying data used for comparison. It is likely that if an assertion is considered to be high risk then other tests of detail are likely to be performed. Likewise if the data is considered unreliable then further analysis of it will be futile.

If analytical procedures identify fluctuations or relationships that are inconsistent with the auditor's knowledge of the business then the auditor should investigate those peculiarities through:

- Enquiry of management; and
- Other procedures, as deemed necessary, for example: when management's response is considered inadequate.

External Confirmations

External confirmations are written responses received from third parties directly by the auditor to help them obtain sufficient appropriate evidence. Examples include: receivables circularisations and bank letters.

As these form external, written evidence they are considered to be reliable sources of evidence. However, in accordance with ISA 505 *External Confirmations* auditors should maintain control over this process to ensure that the evidence sought remains reliable. To do this they should:

- Determine the information to be confirmed;
- Select the appropriate third party;
- Design the confirmation requests and instructions to return directly to the auditor; and
- Send the requests, including a follow up when no response is received.

If management refuses to allow the auditor to send such requests the auditor should consider whether this is reasonable or not in the circumstances. This may affect the auditor's fraud risk assessment and reliance upon written management representations.

If the auditor concludes that management's request is unreasonable and they cannot obtain sufficient appropriate evidence by another means the matter should be communicated to those charged with governance in accordance with ISA 260.

Sampling

It is understood that auditors can rarely, if ever, test ever transaction, balance and disclosure relevant to a set of financial statements. ISA 530 *Audit Sampling* states that auditors should select appropriate samples for testing that provide a reasonable basis to draw conclusions about the population from which the sample is selected.

When selecting samples auditors should consider the following concepts:

- Materiality and performance materiality (see chapter 10);
- Sampling risk: the risk that the conclusions reached based upon testing the sample would be different than the conclusions reached applying the same procedures to the whole population;

- The nature (and risk) of the population being testes, including the number of items within the population, there size relative to the total of the population and the coverage required to reduce audit risk to an acceptable level;
- The need to project, or extrapolate, the results of misstatements identified in the sample to the whole population.

When choosing a sampling method there are two broad approaches:

- Statistical sampling, where items in the population are selected randomly so that probability theory may be used to evaluate the results (through extrapolation to the whole population); and
- Non-statistical, which is a method that does not meet the characteristics of statistical. This is usually employed when the auditor uses judgement to select sample items (e.g. focussing on high value, or known high risk items). Extrapolation cannot be used when bias has been introduced into the sample because the sample is no longer representative of the whole population.

Specific sampling methods include:

- Random: through use of random selectors/number tables;
- Systematic: number of items divided by a specific testing interval (e.g. every 50th balance to be tested). The starting point should be determined haphazardly/randomly;
- Monetary unit: value weighted selection so that conclusions are permitted in monetary amounts;
- Haphazard: no structured technique but avoids bias (not appropriate for statistical analysis); and
- Block: selection of contiguous items (i.e. sequential) (rarely appropriate for statistical analysis)

4 Written representations — Corroborative Evidence

The value of written (management) representations

According to **ISA 580** *Written Representations* the auditor should obtain 'appropriate' written representations from management:

- That they have fulfilled their responsibilities for the preparation of the financial statements;
- That they have provided the auditor with all relevant information;
- That all transactions have been recorded and reflected in the financial statements;

- To support other audit evidence (relevant to the financial statements or specific assertions if deemed necessary by the auditor) and
- As required by specific ISA's.

However, as a form of evidence representations are low down in the order of reliability because they are internally produced.

ISA 580 clearly states that on their own, written representations "do not provide sufficient appropriate evidence about any of the matters with which they deal."

Therefore the auditor cannot delegate responsibility for gathering evidence to management. Moreover, auditors should only use written management representations on matters material to the financial statements when other sufficient appropriate evidence cannot reasonably be expected to be obtained.

If, having received the representations considered necessary to gather sufficient appropriate evidence, the auditor concludes that there is sufficient doubt about the integrity of management to the extent that the representations are unreliable, then the auditor shall disclaim an opinion in accordance with ISA 705.

Other Written Representations

The typical subjects of other representations include:

- Whether the selection and application of accounting policies are appropriate;
- Whether the following matters have been measured, presented and disclosed in accordance with the relevant financial reporting framework:
  - Plans or intentions that may affect the carrying value or classification of assets and liabilities;
  - Liabilities, both contingent and actual;
  - Title to, or control over, assets; and
  - Aspects of laws, regulations and contractual agreements that may affect the financial statements, including non-compliance.
- That the directors have communicated all deficiencies in internal control to the auditor;
- Specific assertions about classes of transactions, accounts balances and disclosures requiring management judgement; and
- That management has considered the effect of uncorrected misstatements and considers them to be immaterial.

Exam Focus

The limitations of management representations

Quite simply, they do not represent independent evidence, and the auditor is not able to absolve himself from his responsibilities, by obtaining representations.

Students should be careful not to suggest management representations as appropriate evidence for all areas of testing. The examiner has suggested this is a common concern amongst weaker students who do not appreciate the nature of 'appropriate' evidence and that it detracts from the quality of an answer.

5 Relying on the work of others

RELYING ON THE WORK OF OTHERS

NO DELEGATION OF RESPONSIBILITY	**We need:** • Sufficient • Appropriate audit evidence
CONSIDERATIONS	COMPETENCE INDEPENDENCE OBJECTIVITY
REFERENCE IN AUDIT REPORT?	NO!

Relying on the work of an auditor's expert

Occasionally, when the auditor lacks the required technical knowledge to gather sufficient appropriate evidence to form an opinion, they may have to rely on the work of an expert. Examples of such circumstances include:

- The valuation of complex financial instruments, land and buildings, works of art, jewellery and intangible assets;
- Actuarial calculations associated with insurance contracts or employee benefit plans;

- The estimation of oil and gas reserves;
- The interpretation of contracts, laws and regulations; and
- The analysis of complex or unusual tax compliance issues.

ISA 620 *Using the Work of an Auditor's Expert* suggests that, whilst this is acceptable, auditor still needs to obtain sufficient appropriate evidence that such work is adequate for the purposes of the audit.

To fulfil this responsibility the auditor must evaluate whether the expert has the necessary competence, capability and objectivity for the purpose of the audit procedures required. The auditor also needs to obtain an understanding of the field of expertise of the expert to:

- Determine the nature, scope and objectives of the expert's work for audit purposes; and
- Evaluate the adequacy of that work for audit purposes.

Once the auditor has considered the above issues they must then agree the following matters in writing with the expert:

- The nature, scope and objectives of the expert's work;
- The roles and responsibilities of the auditor and the expert;
- The nature, timing and extent of communication between the two parties; and
- The need for the expert to observe confidentiality

Once the expert's work is complete the auditor must scrutinise it and evaluate whether it is appropriate for audit purposes. In particular, the auditor should consider:

- The reasonableness of the findings and their consistency with other evidence;
- The significant assumptions made; and
- The use and accuracy of source data.

The competence, capability and objectivity of the expert

Information regarding the competence, capability and objectivity on an expert may come from a variety of sources, including:

- Personal experience of working with the expert;
- Discussions with the expert;
- Discussions with other auditors;
- Knowledge of the expert's qualifications, memberships of professional bodies and licences;
- Published papers or books written by the expert; and
- The audit firms quality control procedures.

Assessing the objectivity of the expert is particularly difficult, as they may not be bound by a similar code of ethics as the auditor and, as such, may be unaware of the ethical requirements and threats with which auditors are familiar. It may therefore be relevant to:

- Make enquiries of the client about known interests or relationships with the chosen expert;
- Discuss applicable safeguards with the expert;
- Discuss financial, business and personal interests in the client with the expert; and
- Obtain written representation from the expert.

The auditor's responsibilities

Auditors cannot devolve responsibility for forming an audit opinion, or for reaching conclusions with regard to specific assertions, onto an expert. The auditor has to use their professional judgment whether the evidence produced by the expert is sufficient and appropriate to support the audit opinion.

Finally, the auditor should not make reference to the use of an expert in their audit report unless it is required to aid the understanding of a modification to the audit opinion. In such circumstances the auditor shall indicate that the reference to the expert does not diminish the auditor's responsibility for the opinion.

Relying on internal audit

Internal audit forms a part of a client's system of internal control. As a result it may reduce control risk. The auditor will take this into consideration when planning audit procedures.

The auditor should also determine whether, and to what extent, it is appropriate to use the work of internal audit and, if so, if it is adequate for the purposes of the external audit.

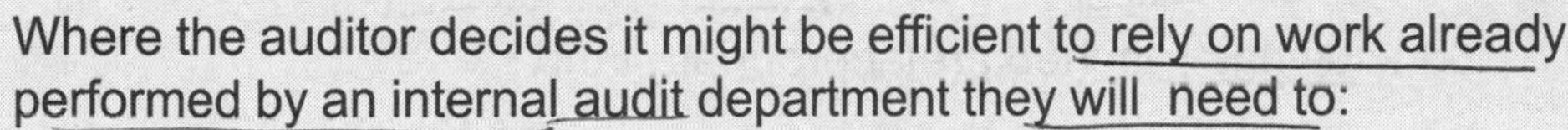

Where the auditor decides it might be efficient to rely on work already performed by an internal audit department they will need to:

- carry out an assessment of the internal audit function;
- evaluate and perform audit procedures on the piece of internal audit work to determine its adequacy for external audit purposes.

As with the use of an auditor's expert, the auditor cannot devolve responsibility for the audit opinion onto an internal audit department.

Assessment of Internal Audit

Preliminary assessment of internal audit function.

According to **ISA 610** *Using the Work of Internal Auditors*, in determining whether to work of the internal auditor is likely to be adequate the external auditor should evaluate:

- The objectivity of the internal audit function;
- The technical competence of the internal auditors;
- Whether work is likely to be carried out with due professional care; and
- Whether there is likely to be effective communication between the external and internal audit teams.

Evaluating the Work of Internal Audit:

To determine the adequacy of internal audit work the external auditor shall evaluate whether:

- The work been performed by staff with adequate technical training and proficiency;
- The work was properly supervised, reviewed and documented;
- Adequate evidence been obtained;
- Conclusions reached are appropriate; and
- Any exceptional or unusual matters have been properly resolved.

CAATs

A brief word about CAATs

CAATs are the means by which the auditor uses IT to carry out tasks that could, in theory be carried out manually.

The major advantages are:

- computers are good at testing calculations
- computers can handle high volumes of calculations and do not get bored, careless, or distracted, so will continue to produce accurate results long after their human counterparts have lapsed from peak efficiency
- computers can perform sorting and filtering operations on high volumes of transactions that would be impossible manually.

It therefore follows that, in the exam (and in practice), CAATs should be considered whenever:

- there are high volumes of transactions to be dealt with
- the process concerns calculating, sorting or filtering
- the information to be tested is itself held on a computer.

The practical problems with CAATs are:

- they involve programming and therefore need to be tested to ensure they actually achieve the objective
- lead times tend to be long and the planning has to be carried out well in advance – not just three or four weeks before the start of fieldwork, but perhaps a whole year in advance
- they tend to be expensive in terms of development time and therefore cost, although, once operational, they can process high volumes of data very fast. The scale of the audit (and its fee) therefore has to make it possible to recover these costs, although not necessarily in a single year.

6 When the evidence conflicts

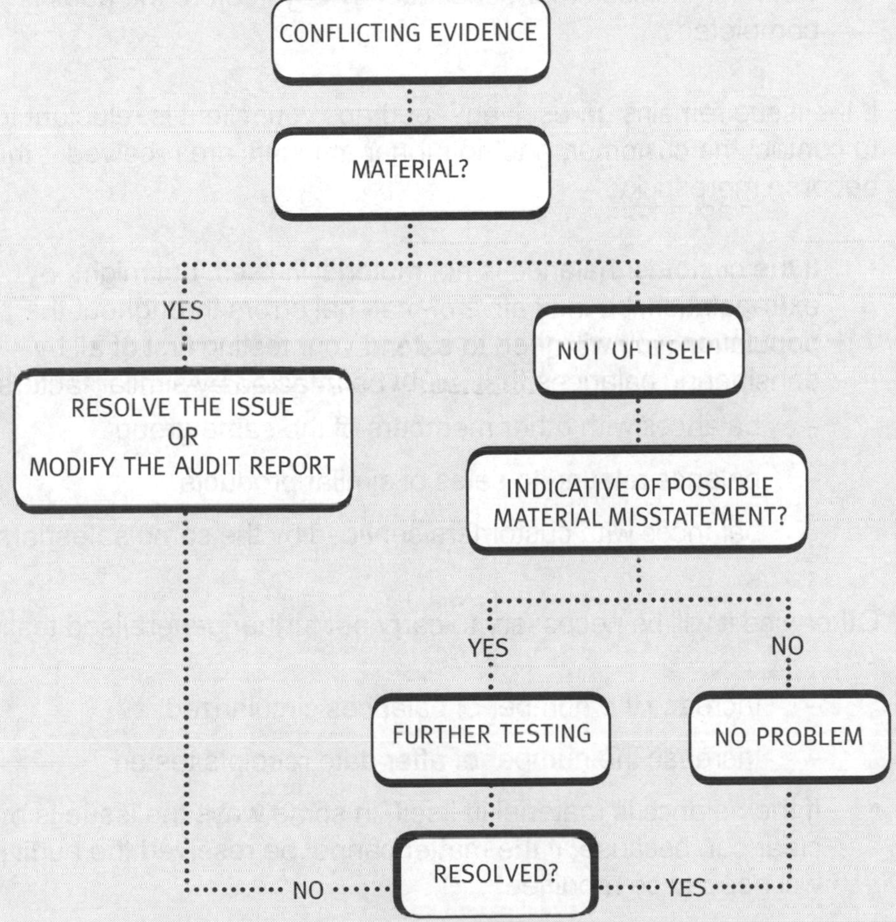

Usually evidence from different sources will complement each other:

Illustration

Your review of the receivables ageing reveals that amounts due from Sousaphone Ltd are overdue. You speak to your client's financial controller who says although the debt is overdue, Sousaphone is a long standing customer and relations with them are good. He is confident that they will pay eventually.

As auditor you should consider:

- Are the amounts involved material?
- Does it indicate a weakness in credit control?
- If so, could this indicate problems with other accounts which might together add up to a material amount?
- Whether you can contact the customer to find out what is going on?
- Whether the customer subsequently pays before the audit is completed?

If the issue remains unresolved – perhaps your client is reluctant for you to contact the customer, and no further amounts are received – things become more tricky.

- If the customer balance is not material in itself, but might, by extrapolation, be indicative of material errors throughout the population, you will need to extend your testing first of all by considering balances that might be affected by similar factors:
  - balances with other members of the same group
  - balance relating to sales of similar products
  - balances with customers serviced by the same salesperson.

Otherwise it will be necessary to carry out further generalised testing.

  - Increase the number of balances circularized.
  - Increase the number of after date receipts tested.
- If the balance is material in itself, in some ways the issue is more clear cut, because, if the matter cannot be resolved the audit report will need to be modified.

7 Documentation

The need for documentation

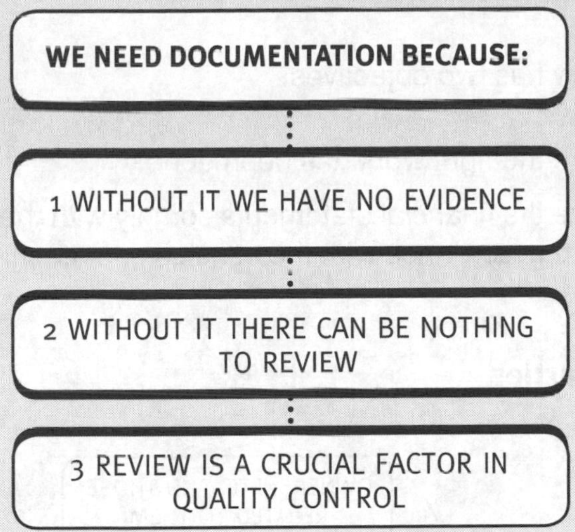

ISA 230 *Audit Documentation* deals specifically with audit documentation and requires:

- timely preparation of audit documentation necessary to provide a sufficient and appropriate record of the basis for the auditor's report, and evidence that the audit was carried out in accordance with ISAs and applicable legal and regulatory requirements
- audit documentation sufficient to enable an experienced auditor, having no previous connection with the audit, to understand the audit work performed, the results and audit evidence obtained, and the significant matters identified and conclusions reached thereon.

8 The need for review

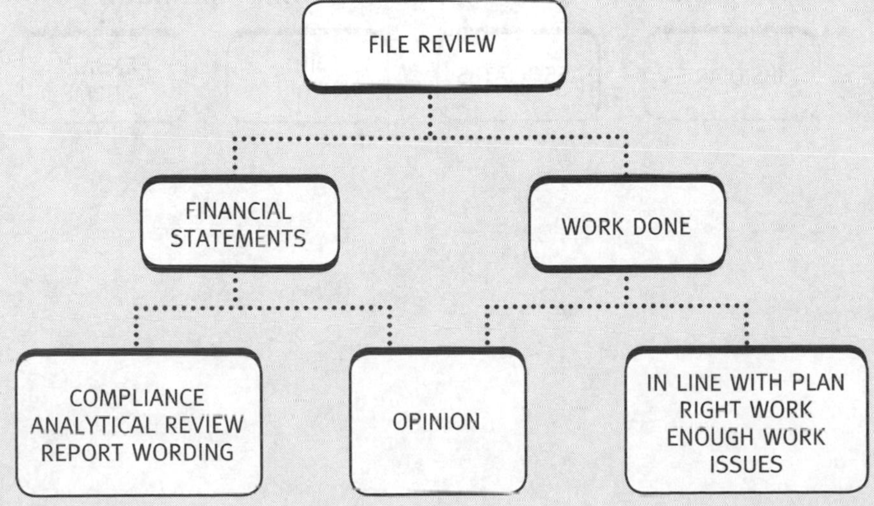

Working papers are reviewed:

- to ensure that sufficient appropriate evidence has been gathered to support the audit opinion.

The file review has two objectives.

- To ensure the right work has been done.
- To ensure the financial statements comply with the regulatory framework and are in accordance with the conclusions reached in the working papers.

9 Related parties

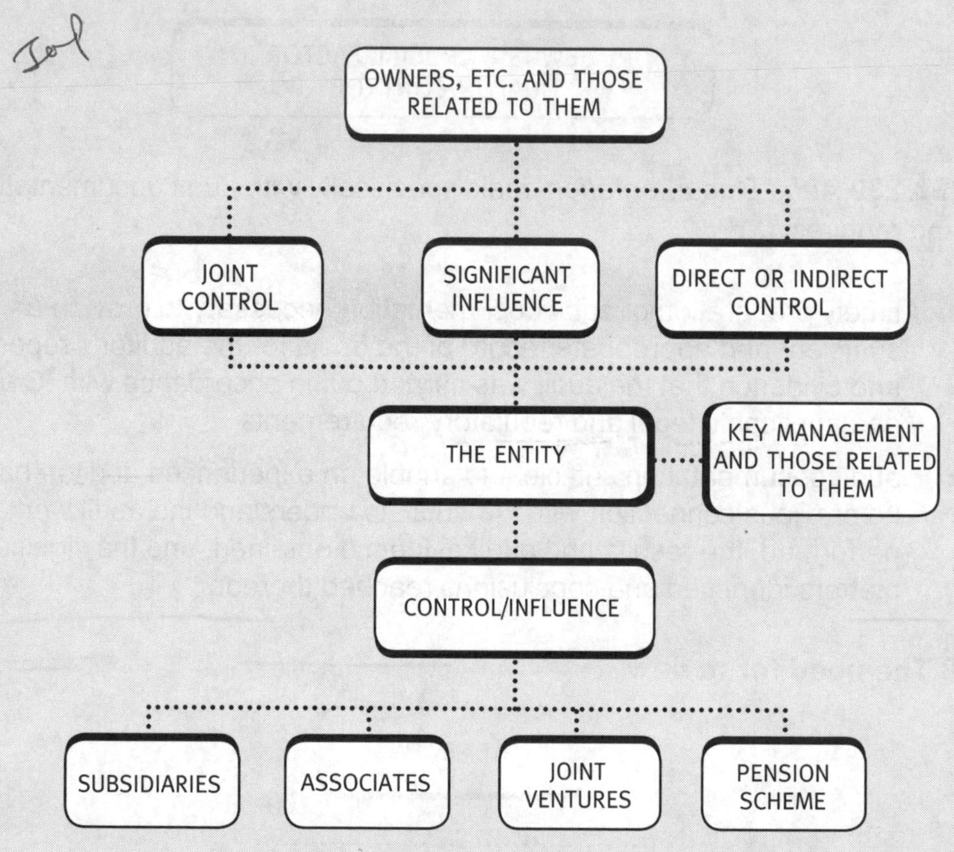

Related Parties to a Business

- Those who control, directly or indirectly, the entity.
- Those related to those who control the entity.
  - Family
  - Entities under their control (including group entities)
  - Parent company management.
- Those who manage the entity.
- Those related to those who manage the entity.
- Those under the control or influence of the entity.
  - Subsidiaries
  - Associates
  - Joint ventures
  - Pension schemes.

Why are related party transactions potentially significant?

There is nothing wrong with an entity dealing with a related party.

However, dealing with related parties increases the potential for transactions to be carried out on a basis other than 'arms length' and for the financial results to be manipulated. In these circumstances it is appropriate for such transactions to be brought to the attention of shareholders.

The Problem With Related Parties

Related parties are often difficult to identify in practice. It can be hard to establish exactly who, or what, are the related parties of an entity.

Furthermore, once related parties have been identified it can be difficult to spot associated transactions with them:

- Directors may be reluctant to disclose transactions, particularly in the case of family members;
- Transactions may not be easy to identify from the accounting systems because they are not separately identified from 'normal' transactions;
- Transactions may be concealed in whole, or in part, from auditors for fraudulent purposes.

Materiality is a difficult concept to apply to related party transactions. **ISA 550** *Related Parties* states that the auditor should consider the effect of a related party transaction on the financial statements. However, it is likely the transaction could occur at an abnormally small, even nil, value. Determining materiality based on monetary value is therefore irrelevant, and the auditor should instead be alert to the unusual nature of the transaction making it material.

Audit procedures for dealing with related party transactions

The degree of difficulty in identifying undisclosed related parties is recognized by **ISA 550** *Related parties.* However, it states that, regardless of whether financial reporting requirements with regard to related parties, the auditor should obtain an understanding of related party relationships and transactions sufficient to be able to:

- Recognise fraud risk factors; and
- To conclude whether the financial statements:
  - achieve a fair presentation; or
  - are not misleading.

In addition, where there are applicable financial reporting requirements relating to related parties, the auditor should obtain sufficient appropriate evidence that transactions have been identified, accounted for and disclosed in accordance with those requirements.

Typical procedures auditors use to identify related party transactions include:

- inspecting prior year working papers ;
- assessing the entity's procedures for identifying, authorising and recording related party transactions;
- enquiring about relationships between those charged with governance and management and other entities;
- inspecting shareholder records for details of principal shareholders;
- inspecting minutes of shareholders' meetings and other relevant minutes and records;
- enquiring of other auditors involved with the audit; and
- inspecting the entity's income tax returns and other information supplied to the regulatory authorities.

Indicators of Related Party Transactions

- transactions with abnormal terms of trade
- transactions that appear not to have a logical business reason
- transactions where substance and form differ
- transactions that are not processed in the usual or routine way
- where there are high volumes of transactions, or high value or otherwise significant transactions with individual customers or suppliers
- unrecorded transactions such as rent free accommodation, or management or other services provided at no cost.

Members of the audit team need to be aware that they should consider the possibility of undisclosed related party transactions while they carry out audit procedures such as examining documents, inspecting minutes of meetings, etc. If the auditor identifies related parties that were not previously indentified or disclosed they shall:

- Communicate that information to the rest of the engagements team;
- Request that management identifies all transactions with the related party and enquire why they failed to identify them;
- Perform appropriate substantive procedures relating to transactions with these entities;
- Reconsider the risk that other, unidentified, related parties may exist; and
- Evaluate the implications if the non-disclosure by management appears intentional.

If the auditor identifies related party transactions outside the entity's normal course of business they should also:

- Inspect the underlying contracts or agreements to establish: the business rationale; the terms of the transaction; and whether appropriate disclosures have been made; and
- Obtain evidence that the transactions were appropriately authorised.

10 Estimates and Fair Values

In accordance with ISA 540 *Auditing Accounting Estimates, Including Fair Value Accounting Estimates and Related Disclosures* auditors need to obtain sufficient appropriate evidence about whether estimates (including fair values) are reasonable and adequately disclosed in the financial statements.

Consideration should first be made when planning and performing risk assessment. In particular the auditor should consider:

- How management identifies transactions and balances requiring estimation;
- How management makes estimates, including:
  - models used;
  - relevant controls;
  - use of an expert;
  - assumptions underlying the estimates;
  - changes since the prior period; and
  - how management assesses the effect of uncertainty.

To assist with this process the auditor should consider the outcome of estimates made in the prior period.

Responses to Risk Assessment

In response to the assessed risk of material misstatement due to estimations the auditor is required to perform one or more of the following procedures with regard to estimates:

- Determining whether events up to the date of the audit report provide additional evidence with regard to the appropriateness of estimates;
- Testing how management made their estimates and evaluating whether the method is appropriate;
- Testing the effectiveness of controls over estimations; and
- Developing a point estimate to use in comparison to management's

If there are significant risks associated with estimates the auditor should also identify whether management considered any alternative assumptions and why they rejected them and whether the assumptions used are reasonable in the circumstances.

Ultimately, due to the uncertainty surrounding estimates, the auditor should obtain written representations from management confirming that they believe the assumptions used in making estimates are reasonable.

Specific Considerations

In accordance with ISA 501 auditors are required to obtain sufficient appropriate evidence with regard to three specific matters, as follows:

(1) The existence and condition of inventory

- Attendance at the inventory count
  - evaluate management's instructions;
  - observe the count procedures;
  - inspect the inventory;
  - perform test counts
- Perform procedures with regard to final inventory records to ensure they reflect actual inventory count results

(2) The completeness of litigation and claims involving the entity

- Enquiry of management and in-house legal counsel;
- Inspecting minutes of board meetings and meetings with legal counsel;
- Inspecting legal expense accounts
- If there is a significant risk of material misstatement due to unidentified litigation or claims the audit should seek direct communication with the entity's external legal counsel

(3) The presentation and disclosure of segmental information

- Understand methods used by management to determine segmental information;
  - evaluate methods;
  - test methods
- Perform analytical procedures.

Exam Focus – Section A Style Question

Study Note: this is an example of a typical section A case study style question. The examiner has indicated that risk assessment and audit procedures are core areas and will be examined in every sitting. The format below represents how these topics have been examined so far.

Your firm has recently been appointed as auditor of Queens Cars Ltd, a new and second hand motor vehicle dealer with six sites. You are currently planning the audit for the year ended 29 February 2008. The draft financial statements show turnover of $23.3mn (2007: $18.1mn), profit before tax of $2.6mn (2007: $1.4mn) and total assets of $15.8mn (2007: $12.6mn).

New cars are purchased on a consignment basis from a single supplier. Queens pays the invoice price (plus a 2% display fee) six months after delivery, or on sale of the vehicle if sooner. Currently Queens records the purchase of the vehicles when the invoice is paid because their supplier legally owns the vehicles and may demand their return at any point prior to settlement. Although, the FD has told you that this has yet to happen.

The value of all new cars held across the various sites at the year end, according to management records, was $2.4mn (2007: $1.9mn). The value of used cars held at the year end, according to inventory records, was $0.6mn (2007: $0.6mn).

Whilst less popular with new cars, many customers like to pay cash, using this as leverage to barter for a "cash discount. In addition, Queens also accept cars in part exchange. One of their current promotions is that they will accept any vehicle for a minimum of $500 trade in value.

The MD of Queens has informed you that he has employed his nephew, a trainee accountant, to manage and record the spare parts inventory across all branches. It was his responsibility to conduct the year end count. However, you have been told that the year end fell during the nephew's reading week and he was on holiday at the time. Therefore he conducted the count the week before the year end and then reconciled the movements on his return. The year end valuation of spare parts inventory was $0.2mn (2007: $0.15mn).

During the year Queens purchased a brand of simple fitting replacement parts that it will now supply on all servicing and repair jobs. As part of this purchase $0.7mn was paid for the brand name "Quick Fit." This has been capitalised as an intangible asset. However, Queens are not amortising the brand following the advice of the MD's nephew, who argued that the brand was so strong that its useful life was indefinite.

All new cars come with a manufacturer's warranty of three years or 30,000 miles, whichever is sooner. Second hand cars are offered with a six month guarantee. At the end of the year the warranty provision was $0.8mn (2007: $0.7mn). The FD believes that despite the increase in the number of cars sold there is no need to increase the warranty provision because the company has focussed more heavily on new car sales this year, which – according to him – require less after sales repairs than used cars.

Required

(a) Prepare a briefing document for the engagement partner that identifies and explains the principal audit risks and other professional issues that need to be considered when planning the final audit of Queens Cars for the year ended 29 February 2008.

Professional marks will be awarded in part (a) for the format of the answer and for the clarity of assessment provided.

(15 marks)

(b) Describe the principal audit procedures that would be carried out in respect of the amortisation of the "Quick Fit" brand.

(5 marks)

Test your understanding 1

Harmonica Ltd owns a portfolio of commercial properties for renting that are valued on an open market basis by a firm of professional valuers of which the senior partner is the brother of Harmonica's Chief Executive. Harmonica's auditors write each year to the valuers and receive confirmation that the market value of the company's properties is as stated in the accounts.

(1) Are there any particular factors the auditors should take into consideration?

(2) If there were reports in the press that property prices were falling in an area where Harmonica owns properties, what implications would there be for the auditors?

(3) If following a visit to some of the company's properties the auditor gained the distinct impression that some were in a poor state of repair, what implications would there be for the auditors?

11 Chapter summary

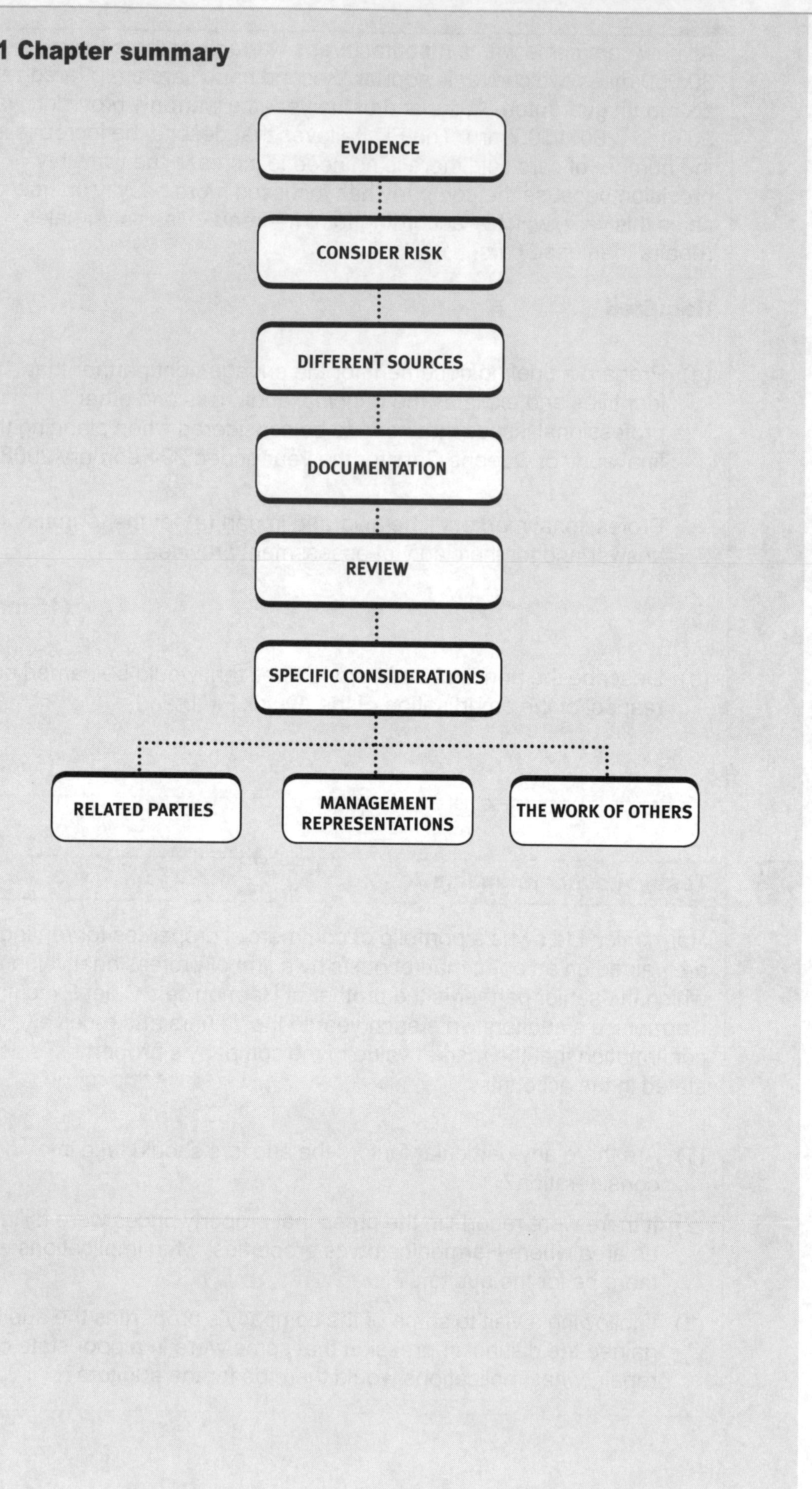

Test your understanding answers

Exam Focus – Section A Style Question

Study Note: throughout your answer you must remain specific to the scenario presented in the question. The vast bulk of the marks are for ***application*** *of knowledge. Simple presentation of definitions and facts will not score enough for a pass.*

Note the use of structure (short paragraphs, headings, report format). This generally leads to more succinct answers, which are easier to mark. There are also professional marks available for use of appropriate formats, introductions, conclusions and the quality of the presentation/flow.

Finally: this is a large question! You must plan your time effectively to answer all parts. Do not simply answer the risk section. It is never going to be enough for a comfortable pass.

Queens Cars Ltd

(a) **Audit Risk**

To: A. Partner

From: A.N. Accountant

Date: 8 April 2008

Subject: Audit Risks to be Considered During the Planning of the Year End Audit of Queens Cars Limited

The audit risks identified during a review of the operations of Queens Cars Limited have been summarised in this report for consideration at the audit planning meeting.

Materiality

The materiality thresholds are as follows:

Turnover:	*½ – 1%*	\$117k – \$233k
Profit before tax:	*5 – 10%*	\$130k – \$260k
Total assets:	*1 – 2%*	\$158k – \$316k

Consignment Inventory

In legal terms Queens Cars do not own the consignment inventory held on site at the year end. However, Queens have never returned a vehicle and in substance they should record the purchase of inventory in their accounting records at the point of delivery. There is therefore a risk that new car inventories, and the consequent liabilities, are understated.

There is also an associated risk that finance costs are understated in the income statement. The 2% display fee should be treated as a finance cost in the income statement.

There is a risk that second hand inventories are overstated. At $0.6mn these are material to total assets. According to IAS 2 inventory should be valued at the lower of cost and net realisable value. The case suggests that it is common for customers to barter for discounts, which could lead to vehicles being sold for less than cost.

Queens also offer a fixed part exchange value for any vehicle and it is therefore likely that they may receive vehicles in part exchange that do not have a resale value of $500 or more. It will be necessary to establish whether such vehicles have a resale value above their part exchange value.

Spare parts inventory total $0.2mn and are therefore material to total assets. There is a risk that these have been incorrectly valued at the year-end due to the fact that the year end count was performed before the year-end. This increases the risk that inventory balances are overstated.

Brand

There is also a risk that the acquired brand, "Quick Fit" is overstated at the year end. The balance of $0.7mn is material to total assets. According to IAS 38 "indefinite" does not mean "infinite." Indefinite suggests the company has sufficient resources to maintain the brand strength. However other factors, such as competition, new technology and substitutes, suggest that this could be difficult to maintain in the long term.

Regardless, according to IAS 38 if Queens Cars rebuts the presumption that the useful life is less than 20 years they must still perform an annual impairment review. Therefore there is further risk that the asset is overstated and impairment charges are understated.

Turnover

There is a risk that turnover is misstated due to discounts for cash sales. There is a risk that the sale may be recorded at the original amount, rather than the renegotiated value. There is also an increased risk of theft by sales persons, who could record a higher cash discount in the accounts and keep some of the cash for themselves.

Provision

There is a risk that the warranty provision is understated on the statement of financial position. $0.8mn is material to total assets. Whereas turnover has increased by 29% the provision has only increased by 14%, which suggests that the provision does not reflect the increased activity of the business. IAS 37 suggests that a provision should be recorded for all probable liabilities and given that all cars are sold with a warranty there is a suggestion that the provision should be increased accordingly.

Other Issues

This is our first year of audit. Given our lack of cumulative audit knowledge and experience there is a greater exposure to audit risk. In response it may be prudent to perform increased substantive procedures this year.

Given the multiple sites it will be necessary to visit at least a sample to assess the accounting/control environment. This could increase the time taken to perform the audit and will have consequences for the budget.

(b) **Audit Work on Useful Life**

- Inspect any purchase agreements/invoices available for the purchase of the brand to confirm the cost to be used in any subsequent impairment tests.
- Review the history of the "Quick Fit" brand. Most importantly assess how long the brand has been trading under that name.
- Inspect advertising invoices to confirm the amount spent on marketing the "Quick Fit" brand during the accounting year.
- Consider the amortisation policies of known competitor brands within the same industry. The accounts should be publicly available and an accounting policy note should be included for amortisation of intangibles.
- Inspect any forecasts/budgets available to assess the level of marketing considered necessary to maintain the brand name.

- Analytically review the performance of the brand since acquisition in comparison to forecasts to identify if performance is as strong as predicted.
- Analytically review the performance of the brand on a month by month basis since acquisition to the present day to identify if performance continues to improve, or at least remain healthy to confirm management's assumption of brand strength.
- Inspect a breakdown of the repairs and maintenance account after the year-end to identify any possible concerns over the quality of the replacement parts.
- Consider industry factors to identify the risk of new entrants or substitute products to the spare parts industry.
- Inspect any impairment tests carried out by management, or make enquiries of management to the same effect.
- Make enquiries of management about the basis of their assumptions with regard to the strength of the brand and their strategy for maintaining its market position.
- Obtain written management representations to corroborate the results of enquiries with management with regard to areas of judgement and estimation.

Test your understanding 1

(1) The service provided by the valuers is a related party transaction and should be disclosed in the financial statements. In the absence of any evidence to the contrary, there is no reason to doubt the valuation, although the auditors should increase the amount of attention they pay to local property prices, etc.

(2) Here there is a conflict between two sources of evidence, which may be exacerbated because of the increased risk due to the involvement of a related party. The auditor should, in the first instance, discuss the matter with management. It is possible that a further valuation from an independent adviser should be sought.

(3) Here there is prima facie evidence of impairment, which again should be discussed with management and that might lead to another independent valuation.

chapter

13

Completion

Chapter learning objectives

Upon completion of this chapter you will be able to:

- explain the purpose of review procedures and assess their role in detecting misstatement;
- evaluate the findings of audit procedures;
- discuss the auditor's responsibility with regard to corresponding figures, comparatives, other information, events after the reporting period and going concern;
- evaluate a range of technical accounting matters.

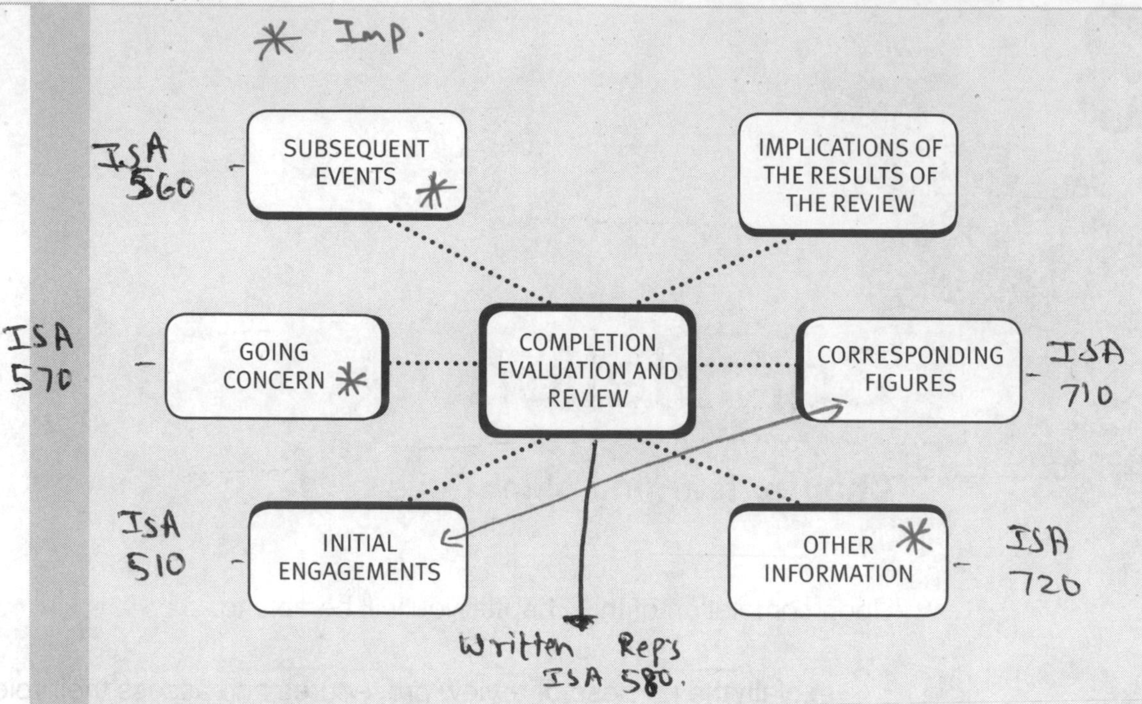

1 Initial engagements – audit considerations

ISA 510 *Initial Engagements – Opening Balances* requires that when auditors take on a new client, they must ensure that:

- opening balances do not contain material misstatements;
- prior period closing balances have been correctly brought forward or, where appropriate, restated; and
- appropriate accounting policies have been consistently applied, or changes adequately disclosed.

Considerations:

- Were the previous financial statements audited
- If the previous financial statements were audited, was the opinion modified?
- If the previous opinion was modified, has the matter been resolved since then?
- Were any adjustments made as a result of the audit? If so, has the client adjusted their accounting ledgers as well as the financial statements?

If auditors are unable to satisfy themselves with regard to the preceding period, they will have to consider modifying the current audit report.

Example

Difficulties may arise where the prior period audit report was modified and the matter is unresolved and the matter has a material effect on the current period financial statements.

For example; if there was a modification on the grounds of a material misstatement or an inability to obtain sufficient appropriate evidence over closing inventory in the prior period, this will affect the current period's profit and loss account. This is because last year's closing inventory is this year's opening inventory and the auditor may need to modify this year's audit report on that basis.

Audit procedures

Where the prior period was audited by another auditor or unaudited, the auditors will need to perform additional work in order to satisfy themselves regarding the opening position. Such work would include:

- consulting the client's management
- reviewing records and accounting and control procedures in the preceding period
- consulting with the previous auditor and reviewing (with their permission) their working papers and relevant management letters
- substantive testing of any opening balances where the above procedures are unsatisfactory.

Some evidence of the opening position will also usually be gained from the audit work performed in the current period.

2 Corresponding figures and comparative financial statements

ISA 710 *Comparative Information – Corresponding Figures and Comparative Financial Statements* requires that comparative figures comply with the identified financial reporting framework and that they are free from material misstatement.

The IASC's Framework for the Preparation and Presentation of Financial Statements and IAS 1 Presentation of Financial Statements both require that financial statements show comparatives.

Two categories of comparatives exist:

- *corresponding figures* where preceding period figures are included as an integral part of the current period financial statements; and
- *comparative financial statements* where preceding period amounts are included for comparison with the current period.

Corresponding figures

Audit procedures in respect of corresponding figures should be significantly less than for the current period and are limited to ensuring that corresponding figures have been correctly reported and appropriately classified. This involves evaluating whether:

- accounting policies are consistently applied; and
- corresponding figures agree to the prior period financial statements.

Corresponding Figures and the Audit Report

The audit report only refers to the financial statements of the current period which encompasses the prior period figures, and does not refer specifically to corresponding figures. However, if a matter in respect of which the prior period audit report was modified is unresolved, the current audit report may also have to be modified in respect of corresponding figures.

Comparative financial statements

Sufficient appropriate evidence should be gathered to ensure that comparative financial statements meet the requirements of an applicable financial reporting framework. This involves evaluating whether:

- accounting policies are consistently applied; and
- corresponding figures agree to the prior period financial statements.

Comparative Figures and the Audit Report

Where comparatives are presented as comparative financial statements the auditor should issue a report in which the comparatives are specifically identified because the auditor's opinion is expressed individually on the financial statements of each period presented.

It is therefore possible for the auditor to express a modified opinion with respect to one or more financial statements while issuing a different report on the other financial statements.

3 Other Information

'Other information' refers to documents and reports contained within the annual report and financial statements that are not subject to audit. For example:

- the Chairman's Report;
- the Operating and Financial Review;
- employee reports; and
- five-year summaries.

ISA 720 *The Auditor's Responsibilities Relating to Other Information in Documents Containing Audited Financial Statements* requires that auditors should read the other information to identify:

- areas of **material inconsistency** between the unaudited information and the audited financial statements; and 
- obvious **misstatements of fact** to other information, unrelated to matters appearing in the audited financial statements.

Further Definitions

A material inconsistency is a statement in the unaudited reports that contradict and therefore undermine the contents of the audited financial statements.

Misstatements of fact are statements in the unaudited reports that the auditor knows to be untrue, whether intended or erroneous.

Material Inconsistency

Upon discovering a material inconsistency the auditor should determine if the audited accounts or the other information needs amending.

The auditor should seek to resolve the matter with those charged with governance.

If, upon further examination, amendment is necessary to the audited financial statements and the entity refuses to make the amendment, the auditor should consider the implication on the audit opinion. This will usually lead to an 'except for' qualification or an adverse opinion.

If, however, the other information is incorrect and the entity refuses to amend it then the auditor should consider including an Other Matter paragraph in the audit report describing the inconsistency, in accordance with ISA 706.

Material Misstatement of Fact

If the auditor concludes that the other information contains a material misstatement of fact then once again they should seek to resolve the matter with those charged with governance.

If, following such discussions, the auditor still considers that there is an apparent material misstatement of fact the auditor shall request management consult with a qualified third party.

If the auditor eventually concludes that there is a material misstatement of fact that management refuses to correct the auditor shall notify those charged with governance and take appropriate further action, which is likely to include seeking legal counsel.

What Next?

Depending on the circumstances, the significance of the issue in question and the advice of any legal counsel sought, the auditor may take further, more severe action, such as:

- Not issuing the auditor's report;
- Withdrawing/resigning from the engagement and making an appropriate statement; and
- Enforcing the auditor's right to be heard at a general meeting of the members.

When taking such action the auditor must consider the severity of the action and the possible financial and reputational repercussions.

4 Events After the Reporting Period

The term 'events after the reporting period' refers to both events occurring between the period end and the date of the auditor's report, and facts discovered after the date of the auditor's report.

To adjust or not to adjust?

IAS 10 identifies two types of event after the reporting period:

- adjusting; and
- non-adjusting.

Discussion of Adjusting and Non-Adjusting Events

Adjusting events

These are events that provide additional evidence relating to conditions existing at the reporting date. Such events cast doubt on whether the period end accounts are correct and, hence, require adjustment.

Non-adjusting events

These are events concern conditions which arose after the balance sheet date, but which may be of such materiality that their disclosure is required to ensure that the financial statements are not misleading. Such events, therefore, will not have any effect on items in the statements of financial position or comprehensive income for the period.

However, in order to prevent the financial statements from presenting a misleading position, some form of additional disclosure is required, by way of note, indicating what effect the events may have.

Illustration 1 – Auditor's responsibilities

Examples of **adjusting** events include:

- provisions for damaged inventory and doubtful debts
- amounts received or receivable in respect of insurance claims which were being negotiated at the balance sheet date
- the determination of the purchase or sale price of non-current assets purchased or sold before the year end
- agreement of a tax liability
- discovery of errors/ fraud revealing that the financials are incorrect.

Illustration 2 – Auditor's responsibilities

Examples of **non-adjusting** events include:

- the issue of new share or loan capital
- major changes in the composition of the group (for example, mergers, acquisitions or reconstructions)
- financial consequences of losses of non-current assets or inventory as a result of fires or floods
- strikes, government action such as nationalisation, and declines in the value of non-current assets or investments
- purchases/sales of significant non-current assets

Auditor's responsibilities

Active duty – up to the date of the audit report:

- the auditor should perform procedures to identify events that might require adjustment or disclosure in the year-end financial statements;
- if the identified adjustments or disclosures are necessary but not adjusted in the financial statements then the auditor should consider the impact on the audit report and whether a modification is necessary to the audit report.

Passive duty – after the date of the audit report:

- the auditor does not have a duty to search for evidence of events after the reporting period;
- however, if after the audit report is signed and the auditor becomes aware of information which might have led him to give a different audit opinion, he should discuss the matter with the directors and take appropriate action;
- this will normally be in the form of amending the accounts, reviewing the amendments and re-issuing the audit report;
- if, however the directors refuse to make necessary amendments the auditor should take necessary steps to prevent reliance on their report. Such action depends upon the advice given by the auditor's lawyer but could involve:
  - resigning from the engagement and issuing a statement;
  - using the auditor's right to make a statement at a general meeting of the members.

Procedures

Procedures include:

- enquiring into management procedures/systems for the identification of events after the reporting period;
- reading minutes of members' and directors' meetings;
- reviewing accounting records including budgets, forecasts, cash flows, management accounts and interim information;
- reviewing the progress of known 'risk' areas and contingencies;
- making enquiries of directors to ask if they are aware of any events, adjusting or non-adjusting, that have not yet been included or disclosed in the financial statements;
- considering relevant information which has come to the auditor's attention, from sources outside the enterprise, including public knowledge, or competitors, suppliers and customers
- obtaining a letter of representation.

Further Considerations

- If financial statements have already been sent to members, directors are permitted in certain circumstances to revise the accounts. In such circumstances, auditors are required to issue a new audit report and also to report on whether the financial statements have been revised correctly in accordance with the legislation.
- Whenever a new audit report is issued, auditors should update their subsequent events review up to the date of the new report.
- Auditors have no duty to enquire specifically into events occurring after the general meeting, but they should inform the directors of any event materially affecting the financial statements. They may also wish to consider taking legal advice on their own position.

5 Going concern

ISA 570 *Going Concern* states that the objectives of an auditor are:

- To obtain sufficient appropriate evidence regarding the appropriateness of management's use of the going concern assumption;
- To conclude, based on the audit evidence obtained, whether a material uncertainty exists; and
- To determine the implications for the audit report.

6 Responsibilities

Management

The going concern is a fundamental principle in the preparation of financial statements, which management are responsible for preparing.

Some financial reporting standards (for example IAS 1) contain an explicit requirement for management to make a specific assessment of the entities ability to continue as a going concern.

This requires management to make judgements about the future outcome of events or conditions which are inherently uncertain.

The Auditor

The auditor's responsibilities can be listed as follows:

- To consider the appropriateness of management's use of the going concern assumption;
- To consider whether there are adequate disclosures regarding the going concern basis in the financial statements;
- To consider the entity's ability to continue for the foreseeable future.

7 Procedures

The auditor should consider whether there are, and remain alert for evidence of, any events, conditions or risks that cast significant doubt on the entity's ability to continue as a going concern.

When events or conditions have been identified which may cast significant doubt on the entity's ability to continue as a going concern, the auditor should:

- review management's plans for future actions based on its going concern assessment

- gather sufficient appropriate audit evidence to confirm or dispel whether or not a material uncertainty exists – this is done by carrying out procedures considered necessary, including considering the effect of any plans of management and other mitigating factors
- seek written representations from management regarding its plans for future action.

Example Procedures

- analysing and discussing cash flow, profit and other relevant forecasts with management
- analysing and discussing the entity's latest available interim financial statements
- reviewing the terms of debentures and loan agreements and determining whether any have been breached
- reading minutes of the meetings of shareholders, the board of directors and important committees for reference to financing difficulties
- enquiring of the entity's lawyer regarding the existence of litigation and claims and the reasonableness of management's assessments of their outcome and the estimate of their financial implications
- confirming the existence, legality and enforceability of arrangements to provide or maintain financial support with related and third parties and assessing the financial ability of such parties to provide additional funds
- considering the entity's plans to deal with unfilled customer orders
- reviewing events after the period end to identify those that either mitigate or otherwise affect the entity's ability to continue as a going concern.

Indicators of Going Concern Risk

Auditors should consider the following indicators as possible reasons for doubt over the going concern presumption:

- rapidly increasing costs;
- shortages of supplies;
- adverse movements in exchange rates;
- business failures amongst customers or suppliers;
- loan repayments falling due in the near future;
- high gearing;

- nearness to present borrowing limits;
- companies financed by loans from directors;
- loss of key staff;
- loss of key suppliers/customers;
- technical obsolescence of product range.
- impact of major litigation; and
- other fundamental uncertainties.

8 The Foreseeable Future

According to ISA 570 the auditor should consider the same period reviewed by management as required by financial reporting requirements. If that period is less than twelve months from the statement of financial position date then the auditor should request that management extend their review to cover that period.

The auditor should remain alert to the possibility of events or conditions that will occur beyond management's period of assessment that may bring into question the appropriateness of the going concern assumption. However, due to the uncertainty surrounding such distant events, the indicator needs to be significant to prompt the auditor into further action. If such an event is identified the auditor should request that management consider the significance of the event of condition. Other than enquiry, the auditor has no other responsibility to perform any other procedures to identify events or conditions beyond the period assessed by management (i.e. at least 12 months from the financial statements date).

9 Audit Conclusions and Reporting

As seen previously, representations do not relieve the auditor of any responsibility. Based on the audit evidence obtained, the auditor should determine if, in their judgement, a material uncertainty exists that may cast significant doubt on the entity's ability to continue as a going concern (ISA 570).

If, in the auditors opinion, the going concern assumption is inappropriate then the accounts should be re-stated on a 'break up' basis. Under this basis of accounting all assets and liabilities are re-classified as ‘current’ and revalued at net realisable value. Further provisions for liquidation costs may also be required.

If the director's were to refuse then an adverse audit opinion would be given.

Where there is a material uncertainty but the going concern assumption is appropriate at the present time, then the accounts should contain disclosures describing the conditions that give rise to the significant doubt. If those disclosures are adequate then the auditor should express an **unmodified opinion** but **modify the audit report** by including an emphasis of matter paragraph highlighting the uncertainty.

10 Review procedures

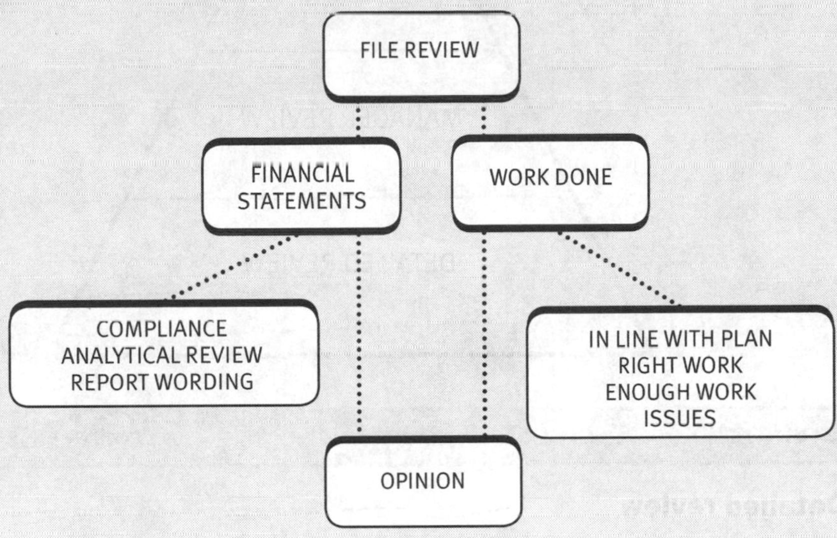

The purpose of review procedures

There are two main purposes for review procedures.

- To ensure that the audit procedures carried out were sufficient and appropriate to reduce the risk of material misstatement to an acceptable level.
- To ensure that the financial statements are in agreement with the known facts and comply with the relevant reporting framework.

Different levels of review

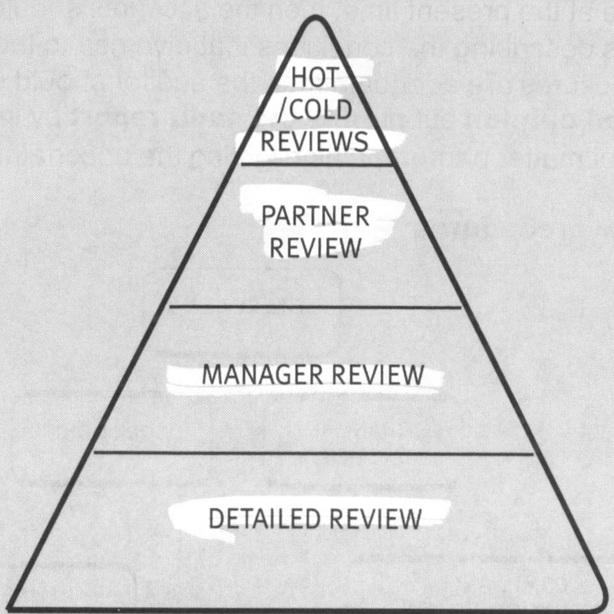

Explanation of Types of Review

Detailed review

- Carried out by senior staff on more junior member's work.
- A review of all work submitted by the assistant.
- Concerned with quality control.
  - Are working papers properly prepared? – proper headings, dates, identity of preparer, cross references, meaning of audit symbols etc.
  - Has the right work been done in accordance with the audit plan?
  - Is the amount of work sufficient?
  - Are there any unresolved issues that can and should be resolved by the person carrying out the work – incomplete tests, queries not followed up etc
- Assessment of matters arising – ensuring that errors found and other issues uncovered are summarised so that they can be brought to the partner's attention.
- Enables a completion memorandum (as recommended by ISA 230) to be produced to facilitate manager and partner reviews.

Manager review

- Will not be a review of every piece of paper (or electronic document) on file – that's the detailed reviewer's job.
- Some quality control aspects:
  - general review to ensure that working papers are properly prepared
  - checklists and programmes completed properly
  - no obvious omissions or gaps
  - has the detailed review been conducted properly?
  - is the file in a fit state to be reviewed by the partner?
- What matters are arising?
  - Are they fully understood?
  - Can they be resolved by the manager?
  - What course of action does the manager recommend?

Partner/Final review

- Top level review, concerned with the issues and finalising the firm's opinion on the financial statements.
- Clearly does have a quality control function, but procedural problems should all really have been resolved by this stage.

Cold review

- Takes place after the audit is finished and the audit report is signed.
- Therefore is the one review dealt with here which is purely concerned with quality control.
- Is not concerned with detecting misstatements in the financial statements (because it is too late), but with ensuring that the firm's procedures were applied properly.

"Hot" or "Independent" reviews

- Compulsory per ISQC (International Standard on Quality Control) 1 for clients which are:
  - listed
  - public interest
- Conducted **before** the audit report is signed.
- Conducted by a partner who is independent of the main audit team.

- Assesses whether:
  - the firm's independence and objectivity is impaired in any way
  - the planning appears to have been carried out properly
  - the file appears to have been reviewed satisfactorily
  - if, in all the circumstances, the audit opinion has been based on valid evidence
  - if, in all the circumstances, the audit opinion is appropriate.

The role of review procedures in detecting material misstatements

It is the review process that enables the decision to be taken by the partner, whether:

- the plan was satisfactory in the light of the audit evidence raised
- the plan was properly flexed to meet any new circumstances
- the audit work was carried out properly
- the evidence gathered has reduced the risk of material misstatement to a satisfactory level
- the audit opinion on financial statements is supported by the audit evidence gathered
- the financial statements comply with the appropriate financial framework.

11 Evaluation of Misstatements

The auditor must consider the effect of misstatements on both the audit procedures performed and ultimately, if uncorrected, on the financial statements as a whole. Guidance on how this is performed is given in ISA 450 *Evaluation of Misstatements Identified During the Audit.*

In order to achieve this the auditor must accumulate a record of all identified misstatements, unless they are clearly trivial. In the first instance they must consider if the existence of such misstatements indicates that others may exist, which, when aggregated with others, could be considered material. If so the audit plan and strategy may need to be revised.

All misstatements identified during the course of the audit should be reported to an appropriate level of management on a timely basis. Importantly, the auditor should request that **all** misstatements are corrected.

If management refuses to correct some or all of the misstatements the auditor should consider their reasons for refusal and take these into account when considering if the financial statements are free from material misstatement.

Evaluation of Uncorrected Misstatement

Before misstatements are evaluated the auditor should revisit their assessment of materiality to determine whether, according to their judgement, it is still appropriate in the circumstances. Following this they can then determine whether the unrecorded misstatements, either individually or in aggregate, are material to the financial statements as a whole.

In so doing the auditor must consider both the size and nature of the misstatements and the effect of misstatements related to prior periods (e.g. on corresponding figures, comparatives and opening balances).

Following this consideration the auditor should report the uncorrected misstatements to those charged with governance and explain the effect this will have upon the audit opinion. At the same time they should request a written representation from those charged with governance that they believe the effects of uncorrected misstatements are immaterial.

12 Overall review of the financial statements

Before forming an opinion on the financial statements and deciding on the wording of the audit report, the auditor should conduct **an overall review**.

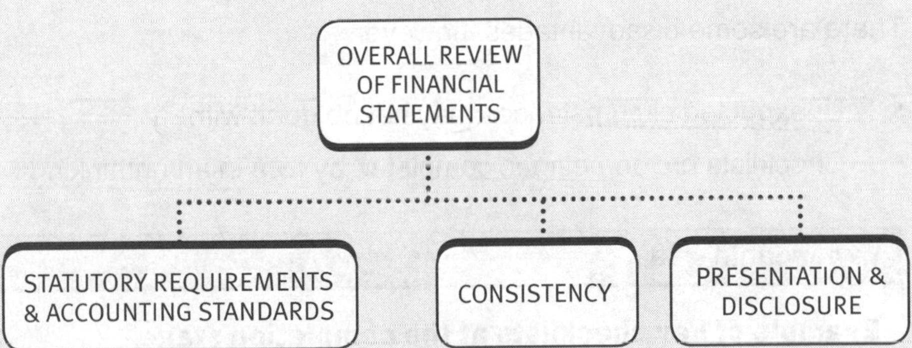

Key methods used to carry out final review include:

- final analytical procedures; and
- checklists.

13 Final analytical procedures

The need for final analytical procedures

Final analytical procedures have to be carried out because:

- they are compulsory according to ISA 520
- they assist the auditor when forming an overall conclusion as to whether the financial statements are consistent with the auditor's understanding of the entity.

What should be done?

Analytical procedures at the final stage of the audit focus on:

- the relationships between figures within the financial statements
- comparisons with figures from previous years
- comparisons with budgets and management information

14 Checklists

Advantages and disadvantages

Many of the procedures to be dealt with at the completion stage of the audit have been set out in checklists which form part of "Audit packs".

The main advantages of this approach are:

- it is clear to the person completing the checklist what needs to be done
- tasks are less likely to be forgotten
- it is clear to the reviewer whether any tasks remain unticked and checklists can therefore be reviewed quickly.

There are some disadvantages, however:

- Unexpected circumstances may not be dealt with
- Checklists are sometimes completed by rote in an unthinking way.

Expandable text

Example of key checklists at the completion stage

- Financial statements disclosures.
- Subsequent events review.
- Going concern review.
- Management Representations.
- Communication with those charged with governance.

15 Statutory requirements & accounting policies

- The auditor will review the compliance with statutory requirements in relation to the presentation of the financial statements.
- Usually focussed on disclosures made within the financial statements.
- A checklist approach is often used by the auditor to ensure all areas have been considered.
- The auditor should review the **accounting policies** adopted by the enterprise to determine whether they:
  - comply with relevant accounting standards
  - are consistent with those of the previous period
  - are consistently applied throughout the enterprise.

Exam Focus

In the exam you will be asked to consider issues that are likely to have some or all of the following conditions in common:

- a critical area of the financial statements
- the subject of an accounting standard which has specific disclosure requirements and recognition and measurement principles
- a contentious or subjective accounting area which has alternative treatments
- a high risk matter
- an area involving a high degree of judgement
- an area where the main source of evidence is that from management.

Many of these conditions will draw upon your detailed knowledge of financial reporting standards from P2. You should use the financial reporting revision chapter at the end of this text to recap the basic principles.

In her article entitled "The Importance of Financial Reporting Standards to the Auditor" (October 2008) Lisa Weaver lists the technical areas that are likely to be tested in detail. She followed this up in the December 2008 exam with questions regarding share options and deferred tax, two of the areas referred to in the article. A well prepared student would be advised to read this article and prepare for the technical areas identified.

The questions at the end of this chapter and in your exam kit provide good practice for this topic area.

Test your understanding 1

Question 1

You are the manager responsible for the audit of Phoenix, a private limited liability company, which manufactures super alloys from imported zinc and aluminium. The company operates three similar foundries at different sites under the direction of Troy Pitz, the chief executive. The draft accounts for the year ended 31 March 2007 show profit before taxation of $1.7m (2006 – $1.5m).

The audit senior has produced a schedule of 'Points for the Attention of the Audit Manager' as follows:

(a) A trade investment in 60,000 $1 ordinary shares of Pegasus, one of the company's major shipping contractors, is included in the balance sheet at cost of $80,000. In May 2007, the published financial statements of Pegasus as at 30 September 2006 show only a small surplus of net assets. A recent press report now suggests that Pegasus is insolvent and has ceased to trade. Although dividends declared by Pegasus in respect of earlier years have not yet been paid, Phoenix has included $15,000 of dividends receivable in its draft accounts as at 31 March 2007.

(6 marks)

(b) Current liabilities include a $500,000 provision for future maintenance. This represents the estimated cost of overhauling the blast furnaces and other foundry equipment. The overhaul is planned for August 2007 when all foundry workers take two weeks annual leave.

(7 marks)

(c) All industrial waste from the furnaces ('clinker') is purchased by Cleanaway Ltd, a government-approved disposal company, under a five-year contract that is due for renewal later this year. A recent newspaper article states that 'substantial fines have been levied on Cleanaway for illegal dumping'. Troy Pitz is the majority shareholder of Cleanaway.

(7 marks)

Required:

For each of the above points:

(i) comment on the matters that you would consider; and

(ii) state the audit evidence that you would expect to find, in undertaking your review of the audit working papers and financial statements of Phoenix.

(Total: 20 marks)

Test your understanding 2

Question 2

You are the manager responsible for the audit of Aspersion, a limited liability company, which mainly provides national cargo services with a small fleet of aircraft. The draft accounts for the year ended 30 September 2006 show profit before taxation of $2.7 million (2005 – $2.2 million) and total assets of $10.4 million (2005 – $9.8 million).

The following issues are outstanding and have been left for your attention:

(a) The sale of a cargo carrier to Abra, a private limited company, during the year resulted in a loss on disposal of $400,000. The aircraft cost $1.2 million when it was purchased in October 1997 and was being depreciated on a straight-line basis over 20 years. The minutes of the board meeting at which the sale was approved record that Aspersion's finance director, Iain Joiteon, has a 30% equity interest in Abra.

(7 marks)

(b) As well as cargo carriers, Aspersion owns two light aircraft which were purchased in 2003 to provide business passenger flights to a small island under a three year service contract. It is now known that the contract will not be renewed when it expires at the end of March 2007. The aircraft, which cost $450,000 each, are being depreciated over 15 years.

(7 marks)

(c) Deferred tax amounting to $570,000 as at 30 September 2006 has been calculated relating to tangible fixed assets at a tax rate of 30% using the full provision method (IAS 12, Income Taxes). On 1 December 2006, the government announced an increase in the corporate income tax rate to 34%. The directors are proposing to adjust the draft accounts for the further liability arising.

(6 marks)

Required:

For each of the above points:

(i) comment on the matters that you should consider; and

(ii) state the audit evidence that you should expect to find, in undertaking your review of the audit working papers and financial statements of Aspersion.

(Total: 20 marks)

Test your understanding 3

Question 3

You are the manager responsible for the audit of Visean, a limited liability company, which manufactures health and beauty products and distributes them through a chain of 72 retail pharmacies. The draft accounts for the year ended 31 December 2006 show profit before taxation of $1.83 million (2000 – $1.24 million) and total assets $18.4 million (2005 – $12.7 million).

The following issues are outstanding and have been left for your attention:

(a) Visean owns nine brand names of fragrances used for ranges of products (e.g. perfumes, bath oils, soaps, etc), four of which were purchased and five self-created. Purchased brands are recognised as an intangible asset at cost amounting to $589,000 and amortised on a straight-line basis over 10 years. The costs of generating self-created brands and maintaining existing ones are recognised as an expense when incurred. Demand for products of one of the purchased fragrances, 'Ulexite', fell significantly in January 2007 after a marketing campaign in December caused offence to customers.

(8 marks)

(b) In December 2006 the directors announced plans to discontinue the range of medical consumables supplied to hospital pharmacies. The plant manufacturing these products closed in January 2007. A provision of $800,000 has been made as at 31 December 2006 for the compensation of redundant employees and a further $450,000 for the three years' unexpired lease term on the plant premises.

(7 marks)

(c) Historically the company's cash flow statement has reported net cash flows from operating activities under the 'indirect method'. However, the cash flow statement for the year ended 31 December 2006 reports net cash flows under the 'direct method' and the corresponding figures have been restated.

(5 marks)

Required

For each of the above issues:

(i) comment on the matters that you should consider; and

(ii) state the audit evidence that you should expect to find, in undertaking your review of the audit working papers and financial statements of Visean.

(Total: 20 marks)

16 Chapter summary

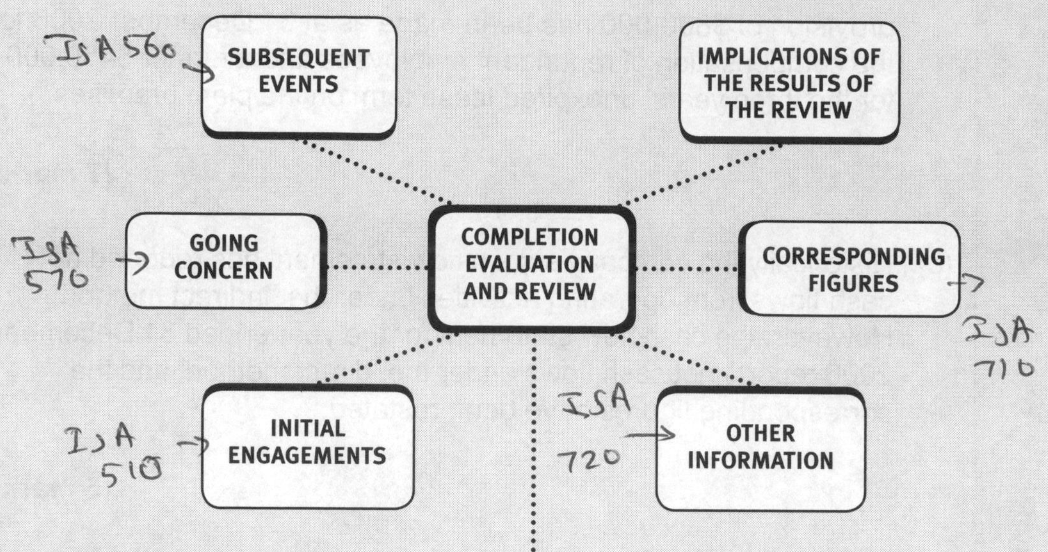

Considering other issues at the review stage

- Inventory
- Standard costing systems
- Cash flow statements
- Changes in accounting policy
- Construction contracts
- Taxation
- Segment information
- Non-current assets
- Fair value
- Leases
- Revenue recognition

- Employee benefits
- Government grants and assistance
- Borrowing costs
- Related parties
- Earnings per share
- Impairment
- Provisions, contingent liabilities and contingent assets
- Goodwill
- Brands

- Research and development
- Other intangible assets
- Capital instruments
- Financial instruments
- Investment properties
- Agriculture
- Transition to IFRS
- Share-based payment transactions
- Business combinations
- Discontinued operations
- Held-for-sale non-current assets
- Exploration and evaluation assets

Test your understanding answers

Test your understanding 1

Answer 1

'Matters' will often encompass considerations of 'risk', 'materiality' and 'accounting treatment' (i.e. the omission of recognition and/ or disclosure as well as benchmark and alternative treatments). A good working knowledge of various accounting standards is essential to the production of a good answer as well as a clear understanding of the relevant financial statement assertions and audit testing techniques as regards the audit evidence.

(a) **Trade investment**

(i) **Matters**

Assuming that Pegasus is insolvent (e.g. a receiver or liquidator has been appointed) this is an adjusting post balance sheet event (IAS 10).

As the recoverable amount is likely to be $nil, $80,000 impairment loss should be recognised in the income statement for the year to 31 March 2007 (IAS 36).

As the likelihood of any distribution of the declared dividends is remote, the $15,000 dividends receivable should be written off.

The total expense of $95,000 represents 5.6% of draft profit before tax and is therefore material. As is it not expected to recur, separate disclosure (IAS 1) may be appropriate to explaining Phoenix's performance for the year.

Before deciding whether or not an 'except for' modified opinion would be reported, if adjustments are not made, materiality should also be assessed in relation to the balance sheet.

The post balance sheet event may also be described in the directors' report with a cross-reference to the investments note.

(ii) **Audit evidence**

- A copy of the press report.
- The audited accounts of Pegasus for the year ended 30 September 2006 showing whether there are assets with market values in excess of book values.

- The receiver's (or liquidator's) statement of affairs indicating whether any distribution is possible.
- If a meeting of the shareholders of Pegasus has been held to consider the company's state of affairs, a copy of the minutes (may be obtained by Phoenix).
- Discussion with client who, if anyone, has replaced Pegasus as one of their major shipping contractors. Also, whether any consignments have been held up while negotiating for an alternative shipping contractor.
- Discussion with client who, if anyone, has replaced Pegasus as one of their major shipping contractors. Also, whether any consignments have been held up while negotiating for an alternative shipping contractor.

(b) **Future maintenance**

(i) **Matters**

The provision represents 29% of draft profit before tax and is therefore material.

The accounting treatment of maintenance costs should be consistent with prior years. However, IAS 37 does not permit the recognition of a provision that does not meet the recognition criteria for liabilities.

Overhaul expenditure to restore or maintain the future economic benefits expected from the plant and equipment should normally be recognised as an expense when it is incurred. However, blast furnaces are of a type of plant and equipment that require relining after a specified period. The components (blast furnace interiors) which require replacement are separate assets that should be depreciated over the replacement cycle. To the extent that the $500k includes the cost of replacing separate assets, it represents future capital cost.

Prudence does not permit the creation of hidden reserves and excessive provisions. This 'provision' does not meet the IAS 37 definition:

- there is no uncertainty about the timing (August);
- there may be relatively little uncertainty about the amounts involved;
- there is no liability as at 31 March 2007.

If the provision is not 'unmade', as being unnecessary, the audit opinion should be qualified 'except for' on grounds of non-compliance with IAS 37.

Draft profit before tax ($1.7m) shows a 13% increase on the previous year. If adjustments are made for points (1) and (2), profit will be increased by at least $400,000 (i.e. (1) $95k decrease plus (2) $500k increase). Profit before tax of $2.1m would be a 40% increase on the prior year.

The management of Phoenix may have decided that $1.7m is what is to be reported. Management may have made the future maintenance provision (which may have been permitted in previous years) as a way of 'setting aside' a reserve. For example, in anticipation of increased costs expected to arise in respect of waste disposal in (3).

Tutorial note: It is a 'higher skill' to be able to demonstrate an ability to stand back from the individual items and take an overall view – in this part of the question, considering the overall impact on the draft PBT.

(ii) **Audit evidence**

- Client's schedule showing make-up of provision.
- Discussion with senior management their reasons for having made the provision and whether any costs have been contracted for.
- External tenders or quotes for sub-contracted work (and/or internal costings).
- Prior year working papers (and/or the permanent audit file) showing the cost and frequency of overhauls in previous periods (whether all sites done at once or on a cyclical basis).

(c) **Cleanaway**

(i) **Matters**

The matter is likely to be material as ALL Phoenix's industrial waste is disposed of by Cleanaway.

Whether Phoenix has been implicated in Cleanaway's illegal dumping (e.g. by Phoenix's clinker having been dumped, or by Troy Pitz's relationship with the two companies).

Whether the integrity of Troy Pitz has been questioned (either by the media or other key personnel in Phoenix) and, if so, its impact on the audit. For example, any assessment of control risk as less than high should be reassessed in the light of his role in the control environment.

Possible consequences for Phoenix of the contract not being renewed:

- a legal alternative will need to be found for disposal of clinker, e.g.:
- another approved provider of waste disposal services
- a suitable landfill site (taxes may be substantial), otherwise
- there may be doubts about going concern.

Possible consequences for Phoenix of the contract being renewed:

- a substantial increase in costs of disposal, e.g. because:
- terms were last agreed five years ago
- Cleanaway will need to pass on the costs of penalties to its customers
- loss of customers' goodwill through associations with Cleanaway
- risk of investigation by a government agency into the company's environmental practices.

Even if doubts about the going concern assumption are resolved, whether or not the contract is renewed in the future amounts to a 'significant uncertainty'. An emphasis of matter paragraph in the auditor's report is likely to be appropriate. The matter must therefore be adequately disclosed (e.g. in the notes to the financial statements).

Cleanaway is a related party. Troy Pitz has authority and responsibility for Phoenix's operational activities (as chief executive) and a controlling interest in Cleanaway. The financial statements of Phoenix should disclose (IAS 24):

- the nature of the related party relationship;
- an indication of the services received including:
- amount (or proportion) of costs involved

- pricing policy (per contract)
- amount outstanding (trade creditor balance)
- credit terms, etc.

(ii) **Audit evidence**

- The terms of the contract, in particular whether:
- early termination could be an option for Phoenix (in the light of Cleanaway's illegal activities);
- any clauses are relevant to its renewal (e.g. restricting price increases).
- Newspaper articles, including any editorial comment or letters from Cleanaway or Troy Pitz.
- Discussions with senior management (Troy Pitz and others) whether a suitable alternative service provider exists.
- Concerning related parties and related party transactions:
- prior year working papers and financial statements;
- review of Phoenix's procedures (e.g. keeping of registers and requiring board approval of certain transactions)
- inquiries of directors, key management and the company secretary
- an extract of principal shareholders from the share register
- minutes of shareholder and board meetings;
- relevant statutory books and records (e.g. register of directors' interests)
- relevant returns supplied to regulatory agencies (e.g. income tax returns)
- extracts from all significant contracts
- third party replies (e.g. bank reports for audit purposes and loan confirmations identifying guarantees).
- A post-year-end review, up to the date of signing the auditors' report, must support the validity or otherwise of the going concern assumption. In particular:
- board minutes should indicate what action, if any, management propose to take to mitigate the adverse publicity surrounding Cleanaway
- order books may reveal the loss of major customers (e.g. if delays experienced consequent on the demise of Pegasus)

– successful negotiations with existing or new shipping contractors, to take on the work of Pegasus, should result in signed contracts

– discussions with management, to ascertain their plans to secure Phoenix's future, may be confirmed by written management representations (assuming there is neither corroborative nor conflicting alternative evidence).

Tutorial note: Taking an overall view on something like the going concern assumption is another example of the higher skill of 'standing back' from the individual items.

Test your understanding 2

Answer 2

(1) 'Matters' will often encompass considerations of 'risk', 'materiality' and 'accounting treatment' (i.e. the omission of recognition and/or disclosure as well as benchmark and alternative treatments).

(2) Many points can only be made as either 'matters' or 'audit evidence' (and there is no 'one-for-one' relationship between the two that would warrant a columnar approach). However, some points could be made as either (or both) although the emphasis would need to be different. For example, a matter to consider is the audit program for the identification of related parties and RPTs, whilst the evidence will include copies of extracts from minutes and company registers and written management representation.

(a) **Related party transaction – sale of cargo carrier**

Matters

The cargo carrier was in use for 8/9 years and would have had a carrying value of $720,000 at 30 September 2005 (assuming nil residual value and a full year's depreciation charge in the year of acquisition and none in the year of disposal). Disposal proceeds were only therefore $300,000 (say).

The $400,000 loss represents 15% of profit before tax and is therefore material. Disclosure as a separate line item may therefore be appropriate (IAS 1).

Abra appears to have a related party with Aspersion as Iain:

- Is one of the key management personnel of Aspersion (being the finance director); and
- has an equity interest in Abra which is presumed to constitute significant influence (being greater than 20%).

This relationship will be further strengthened/closer/more apparent if:

- Iain is also a shareholder of Aspersion and/or a director of Abra;
- any close members of Iain's family are also shareholders of Abra (being a private company).

The reason for the sale e.g. whether this aircraft was:

- surplus to operating requirements (i.e. not being replaced) and
- being replaced with a new model (perhaps more likely as total assets have increased by $600,000 during the year).

The reason for the loss on sale e.g. whether the:

- sale was at an under-value (if the sale to the related party was not at arm's length)
- aircraft had a bad maintenance history (or was otherwise impaired)
- useful life of a cargo carrier is less than 20 years.

If the latter, it is likely that non-current assets are materially overstated in respect of cargo carriers still in use.

How selling price was determined. For example, whether the asset was independently valued or whether this was Abra's best offer. Also whether there were any other unrelated potential purchasers or offers made.

The principal terms of the sale e.g. for settlement of the purchase price.

The board was aware of the related party relationship (as it was minuted) when the sale was approved.

Whether RPTs have been identified and disclosed in prior period financial statements.

The related party relationship and the sale of the cargo carrier to Abra should be disclosed in a note to the financial statements for the year to 30 September 2007. The elements of such a material transaction which are likely to be necessary (for an understanding of the financial statements) are:

- the amount(s) involved (i.e. sale proceeds and loss)
- any outstanding balance of amounts due from Abra
- how price was determined (e.g. by an independent valuation).

If suitable disclosure is not made, the audit opinion would be modified on an 'except for' basis due to a material misstatement with regard to non-compliance with IAS 24 Related Party Disclosures.

(b) **Impairment – light aircraft**

(i) **Matters**

The annual depreciation charge for each of these two aircraft is \$30,000 (1/15 450,000). The aircraft have been depreciated for only 2½ years to 30 September 2006 (assuming time apportionment in 2004 when the aircraft were brought into use) and have a total carrying amount of \$750,000 (2 [450,000 – (2½ 30,000)]). This represents 7.2% of total assets (and some greater % of tangible fixed assets) and is therefore material.

Tutorial note: Alternatively it could be assumed (though less appropriate) that a full year's depreciation was charged in the year to 30.9.04 (i.e. three years' accumulated depreciation to 30.9.06).

The aircraft were purchased for a specific use which will cease six months after the balance sheet date. The value of the aircraft may be impaired and Aspersion should have made a formal estimate of their recoverable amount (IAS 36).

Whether management has estimated net selling price and/or value in use.

Whether Aspersion prepares management accounts and budgets and has experience in projecting cash flows (for determining value in use).

Management's intentions, for example:

- to sell the aircraft
- to find an alternative use (e.g. providing other business or pleasure flights).

The amount of any impairment loss identified and whether or not it is:

- material (say $100,000)
- to be recognised in the financial statements.

Additional point

If the passenger business constitutes a business segment (IAS 14), cessation of the contract may result in a discontinued operation (IFRS 5).

(ii) **Audit evidence**

- A copy of the service contract confirming expiry in March 2007.
- Physical inspection of aircraft (evidence of existence and condition at 30 September 2006).
- Notes of discussions with Aspersion's management concerning negotiations for:
- the sale of the aircraft or
- obtaining new service contracts.
- Extracts from any correspondence.
- A copy of any (draft) agreement for:
- the sale of the aircraft after the contract expires;
- new business or pleasure contracts.
- Discounted cash flow projections for any proposed new venture/contracts (i.e. value in use).
- Comparison of projected cash flows with budgets and assumptions (e.g. aircraft days available and average daily utilisation per aircraft).

(c) **Deferred tax – change in tax rate**

(i) **Matters**

The total provision amounts to 21% of PBT and its therefore material. (However the deferred tax expense/income for the year may not have been material.)

Under IAS 12 deferred tax should be provided for if the transactions or events that give rise to an obligation to pay more tax in the future have occurred by the balance sheet date. Accelerated capital allowances are a timing difference calculated as the difference between the tax written down value and the net book value of assets.

The increase in liability if calculated at 34% ($570,000 (34/30 – 1) = $76,000) represents 2.8% of PBT. Considered in isolation, this amount is not material.

The tax rate that should be used is the rate that is expected to apply to the period when the liability is settled, based on tax rates that have been (substantively) enacted by the balance sheet date (IAS 12). The increase in tax rate announced on 1 December is a non-adjusting post balance sheet event (IAS 10).

Also, the extra 4% does not meet the definition of a liability ('a present obligation arising from past events') and no provision should be recognised (IAS 37).

If the directors adjust the draft accounts there will be non-compliance with IASs 10, 12 and 37 which may be regarded as material 'by nature'.

(ii) **Audit evidence**

- A copy of the computations of:
- deferred tax liability (balance sheet)
- current tax expense (income statement)
- deferred tax expense/income.
- Agreement of tax rate(s) to tax legislation.
- A numerical reconciliation between tax expense and accounting profit multiplied by the applicable tax rate.
- Schedules of carrying amount (i.e. cost of revalued amounts net of accumulated depreciation) of fixed assets agreed to:
- the asset register (individual assets and in total)
- general ledger account balances (totals).
- Completed audit program for non-current assets (e.g. inspecting invoices for additions, agreeing depreciation rates to prior year account policies, etc).
- Client's schedules of tax base agreed, on a test basis, to:
- the asset register (for completeness)
- prior year working papers (completeness and accuracy of brought forward balances).

Test your understanding 3

Answer 3

(1) 'Matters' will often encompass considerations of 'risk', 'materiality' and 'accounting treatment' (i.e. the omission of recognition and/or disclosure as well as benchmark and alternative treatments).

(2) Many points can only be made as either 'matters' or 'audit evidence' (and there is no 'one-for-one' relationship between the two that would warrant a columnar approach). However, some points could be made as either or both – although the emphasis would need to be different. For example, a matter to consider in (1) is the fall in demand which may provide evidence of impairment, whilst the evidence will include the level of after-date sales, by month, by fragrance.

(a) **Brand names**

(i) **Matters**

'Ulexite' is one of the four purchased brands and therefore has a net book value in the balance sheet.

The cost of the purchased brands represents 3.2% of total assets and 32% of PBT (net book value will be less). Annual amortisation amounts to 3.2% of PBT. Brands as a whole are therefore material. If the net book value of 'Ulexite' at the year end is greater than $91,500 (i.e. 5% PBT) its total write-off (e.g. due to impairment) is likely to be regarded as material.

The fall in demand in January 2007 is an adjusting post balance sheet event (IAS 10) providing evidence about the valuation of assets as at 31 December 2006 as a result of the marketing campaign.

In particular:

- the net realisable value of inventory of 'Ulexite' products may be less than cost
- the value of the brand name 'Ulexite' itself may be impaired
- by association, the value of other brand names and their associated products may be similarly affected
- there could be loss of customer goodwill to Visean as a whole if, by the association of 'Ulexite' with Visean, there is a boycotting of Visean's products (as has been the case with Benetton and Nestlé).

Each purchased brand is likely to be regarded as a cash-generating unit as the revenues flowing from each brand are largely independent of each other (IAS 36). Also, decisions can be made about individual fragrances (e.g. to discontinue use of the 'offending' fragrance). It is likely that the recoverable amount of an individual purchased brand name can be assessed.

Whether management consider the 'Ulexite' brand value to be impaired and, if so:

- the amount they propose to recognise as an impairment loss and
- how the recoverable amount (the higher of net selling price and value in use) has been determined.

Net book value of 'Ulexite' as at the year-end will provide a 'ceiling' for the amount of any impairment loss recognised.

What action, if any, management propose to take (e.g. to discontinue the fragrance, sell the name or promote it).

If management is taking legal action against the advertising consultants (if external to Visean) – there may be a disclosable contingent gain.

Whether 10 years is a reasonable period over which to amortise purchased brand names. It is appropriate that the straight line method should be used (as an alternative pattern of consumption of economic benefits cannot be determined reliably) – IAS 38

(ii) **Audit evidence**

Year-end cost/net book value of 'Ulexite' agreed to prior year working papers, less current year's amortisation charge.

Analytical review of actual after-date sales (and/or inventory turnover) against budget, month on month, and by fragrance to identify:

- the significance of the fall in demand of 'Ulexite'
- whether other fragrances have been similarly affected
- if demand is 'picking up' again (in February to June).

Monthly sales analysis returns received from retail pharmacies.

The advert, promotional literature or 'slogan' relating to 'Ulexite' which caused the offence. (And media reports, if any, arising from bad publicity.)

If the 'Ulexite' brand name has been written down:

- to net selling price – a binding agreement to sell 'Ulexite'
- to value in use – cash flow projections for the next five years (or the remaining useful life of 'Ulexite' if shorter).

Board minutes reflecting any decisions taken (e.g. to discontinue the fragrance).

Expenses, if any, incurred since April (reflected in the cash book and/or after-date invoices) to rectify the damage done (e.g. a new marketing campaign).

Amortisation rates and periods used in the 'cosmetics' industry.

Copy correspondence and notes concerning any pending legal action and possible quantified outcomes.

(b) **Discontinued operation**

(i) **Matters**

The provisions have reduced PBT by 40% (i.e. 1.25 ÷ [1.83 + 1.25]) and now represent 68% of PBT and are therefore considered to be material.

The plan to close the plant facility is likely to result in a discontinued operation if hospital medical consumables are a separate line of business which can be distinguished operationally and for financial reporting purposes (IFRS 5).

If hospital medical consumables were reported as a business segment in the notes to the financial statements for the prior year (under IAS 14) this will satisfy the 'separate line of business' criterion.

The initial disclosure event will be the earlier of:

- the directors' announcement in December (that the factory closed in January strongly suggests that a formal detailed plan existed and was approved before it was announced);
- a binding sale agreement for substantially all the related assets (I.e. equipment and inventory – not the plant itself, as it is leased).

Tutorial note: The announcement is the more likely in the context of the given scenario.

The disposal of any assets (e.g. equiptment) arising from the plant closure in January is a non-adjusting post balance sheet event (IAS 10) which may require disclosure in the financial statements (if material).

No provision should be made for the loss on sale of related assets after the year end unless a binding sale agreement was entered into before the year end. However:

– plant assets (plant and equipment) should be reviewed for impairment (IAS 36); and
– inventory of hospital consumables should be measured at the lower of cost and net realisable value (IAS 2).

Assuming that the announcement in December raised valid expectations (in employees and customers) that a detailed formal restructuring plan would be carried out, a constructive obligation to restructure arises (IAS 37). The provision made should include:

– redundancy costs (but not any costs of retraining or relocating continuing staff);
– present obligations under onerous contracts (e.g. for the unexpired lease term on the factory premises).

If products other than medical consumables were supplied to hospitals, Visean may lose hospital customers altogether (as the hospitals turn to other suppliers for the medical consumables).

Tutorial note: Presumably this was taken into account when making the decision to discontinue the activity.

Further provision may be necessary for onerous contracts with customers (and possibly suppliers). For example, hospitals (as public sector bodies) are likely to have contracts with Visean containing penalty clauses for non-performance (breach of contract, etc).

(ii) **Audit evidence**

Segmental information in the prior year financial statements showing hospital medical consumables to be a business segment (e.g. if this activity accounted for 10% or more of Visean's turnover, result or net assets).

Initial disclosure of:

- carrying amounts of assets being disposed of (if any) and
- revenue, expenses, pre-tax profit (or loss) and income tax expense attributable to the discontinuing of medical consumable supplies.

Agreement of initial disclosure to underlying financial ledger accounts (management reports, etc).

Comparison of separate disclosure with budgeted amounts and prior year.

Board minutes approving the formal plan to discontinue the product range, close the factory and make staff redundant.

Copies of announcements (e.g. press releases and letters to hospitals (i.e. as customers) and employees).

The binding sale agreement (if any) for plant, equipment and stock.

The contractual terms of the factory lease and correspondence with the lessor (e.g. to negotiate the surrender of the lease, sub-leasing, etc).

Penalty clauses, if any, in contracts with hospitals (also contracts with suppliers).

Calculations of the provisions (and assumptions made).

Redundancy terms for employees (both contractual and statutory).

Past redundancy settlements (as compared with statutory and contractual obligations).

After-date sales of hospital medical consumables.

(c) **Cash flow statement**

(i) **Matters**

The cash flow statement should be prepared in accordance with IAS 7, Cash flow statements i.e. reporting cash flows classified under the standard headings (including operating activities, returns on investments, taxation, capital expenditure, etc). IAS 1 requires comparative figures for all items in the primary statements (and therefore for the cash flow statement).

Cash flows from operating activities may be reported using either:

- the 'direct' method (i.e. showing relevant constituent cash flows) or
- the 'indirect' method (i.e. calculating operating cash flows by adjustment to the operating profit reported in the profit and loss account).

IAS 7 encourages reporting under the direct method because it provides information which is not available under the indirect method. Because the provision of such additional information may be more time-consuming and costly, the direct method is not required – however, the change from indirect to direct is clearly permitted.

It is appropriate, in the interest of comparability that the corresponding figures have been restated. The reason for reclassification should also be disclosed.

The restatement only affects the amounts which make up cash generated from operating activities (i.e. a part of 'Net cash inflow from/outflow for operating activities').

The auditor's responsibility for corresponding figures (ISA 710) is to obtain sufficient appropriate audit evidence that they have been correctly reported and appropriately classified.

The auditor's report should not specifically identify the comparatives because the audit opinion is on the current period's financial statements as a whole, including the corresponding figures.

There should be no specific reference to the corresponding figures in the auditor's report merely because they have been restated (ISA 710). However, if the corresponding amounts have not been properly restated (or appropriate disclosures have not been made – e.g. the reason for restatement) the report should be modified with respect to the corresponding figures.

(ii) **Audit evidence**

Agreement of 'Net cash from operating activities' downwards in the cash flow statement corresponding amounts to the prior year cash flow statement in the financial statements.

For the prior year, agreement (or reconciliation) of net PBT as adjusted for non-cash items (e.g. depreciation) and working capital changes to cash receipts from customers less cash paid to suppliers and employees.

Schedules of cash receipts (per analysis of cash book receipts) agreed to the debtors ledger control a/c.

Schedules of cash payments to suppliers and employees (per analysis of cash book payments) agreed to the creditors ledger and payroll control a/cs (respectively).

Analytical procedures such as the comparison of trade debtor (and creditor) days (i.e. average credit periods given to customers and received from suppliers) with prior year.

chapter

14

Auditors' reports

Chapter learning objectives

Upon completion of this chapter you will be able to:

- justify an audit opinion
- assess whether or not a proposed audit opinion is appropriate
- discuss 'a true and fair view'
- describe special purpose auditors' reports

1 The Objectives of the Auditor

According to **ISA 700** *Forming an Opinion and Reporting on Financial Statements,* the auditor's objectives are twofold:

- To form an opinion on the financial statements based on an evaluation of the conclusions drawn from the audit evidence obtained; and
- To express clearly that opinion through a written report that also describes the basis for that opinion.

2 The written report

To ensure consistency and clarity in the reporting of the audit opinion, ISA 700 prescribes the following structure for the audit report:

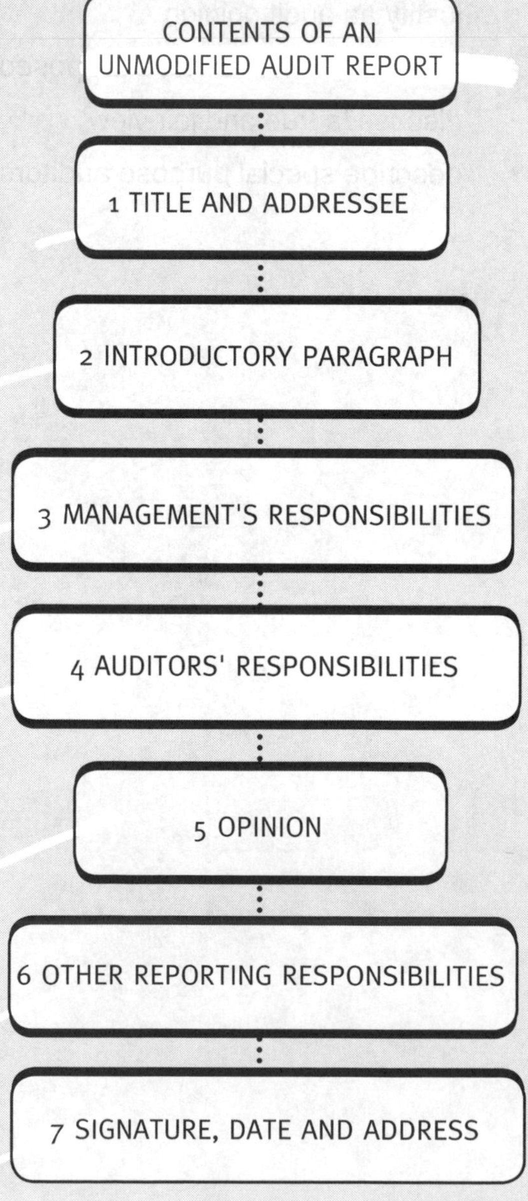

The 'Expectations Gap'

Background

The seven sections of the audit report are set out in **ISA 700**.

Over time the wording of the audit report has grown longer in an attempt to counteract what has become known as the **expectation gap**, i.e. the difference between what an auditor's responsibility actually is (and can reasonably be expected) and what the public perceives the auditor's responsibility to be.

The audit report is not:

- a certificate of the accuracy of the contents of financial statements;
- a guarantee against fraud; and/or
- confirmation that an entity is being run in accordance with the principles of good corporate governance.

The wording recommended by ISA 700 is intended to ensure that users of the accounts understand what level of assurance they are being given and how much reliance they may place on a set of audited financial statements.

The standard wording Per ISA 700

Illustration 1

INDEPENDENT AUDITOR'S REPORT

(APPROPRIATE ADDRESSEE)

Report on the financial statements

We have audited the accompanying financial statements of the ABC Company, which comprise the balance sheet as of December 31, 20X1, and the income statement, statement of changes in equity, and cash flow statement for the year then ended, and a summary of significant accounting policies and explanatory notes.

Management's responsibility for the financial statements

Management is responsible for the preparation and fair presentation of these financial statements in accordance with International Financial Reporting Standards, and for such internal control as management determines necessary to enable the preparation of financial statements that are free from material mis-statement, whether due to fraud or error.

Auditor's responsibility

Our responsibility is to express an opinion on these financial statements based on our audit. We conducted our audit in accordance with International Standards on Auditing. Those Standards require that we comply with ethical requirements and plan and perform the audit to obtain reasonable assurance about whether the financial statements are free from material mis-statement.

An audit involves performing procedures to obtain audit evidence about the amounts and disclosures in the financial statements. The procedures selected depend on the auditor's judgment, including the assessment of the risks of material mis-statement of the financial statements, whether due to fraud or error. In making those risk assessments, the auditor considers internal control relevant to the entity's preparation and fair presentation of the financial statements in order to design audit procedures that are appropriate in the circumstances, but not for the purpose of expressing an opinion on the effectiveness of the entity's internal control. An audit also includes evaluating the appropriateness of accounting policies used and the reasonableness of accounting estimates made by management, as well as evaluating the overall financial statement presentation.

We believe that the audit evidence we have obtained is sufficient and appropriate to provide a basis for our audit opinion.

Opinion

In our opinion, the financial statements present fairly, in all material respects (or *give a true and fair view of*) the financial position of ABC Company as at December 31, 20X1, and *(of)* its financial performance and its cash flows for the year then ended in accordance with International Financial Reporting Standards.

Report on other legal and regulatory requirements

(Form and content of this section of the auditor's report will vary depending on the nature of the auditor's other reporting responsibilities.)

Auditor's signature

Date of the auditor's report

Auditor's address

The illustration above is provided by ISA 700 as an example of the wording of an unmodified report, i.e. when the auditor concludes that the financial statements are prepared, in all material respects, in accordance with the applicable financial reporting framework. In essence, this is the report an auditor gives when there are no concerns about the financial statements prepared by management.

The reasons for the various sections are as follows:

Title and addressee

- The title differentiates the audit report from the rest of the financial statements and other matter included.
- The word 'independent' in the title reminds the reader of the value of the audit.
- Specifying the addressee of the report, clarifies its purpose.
- This may also be regarded as an attempt to restrict to a defined category, those people to whom the auditor acknowledges a duty of care.

Introductory paragraph

- Identifying the financial statements on which the auditor is reporting.
- It may also serve to restrict the scope of the auditor's implied responsibility.
- There is often a reference to the accounting convention or the applicable financial reporting framework in the introductory paragraph, which clarifies the basis on which the financial statements are prepared.

Management's responsibilities

- This is clearly an attempt to manage the expectation gap, by making it clear to the reader what management is responsible for.

Auditor's responsibility

- Principally aimed at managing the expectation gap.
- Includes a technical information that could be accused of being jargon:
  - ethical requirements
  - reasonable assurance
  - the risk-based approach
  - true and fair (see below)
  - no opinion on the effectiveness of internal control.
- Clear statement that the auditor believes that sufficient, appropriate evidence has been obtained.

Opinion

- The only issue here is the meaning of 'true and fair' (or present fairly).

Other nationally determined reporting requirements

- Given the potential for variety in these requirements across the world, these are unlikely to be examined in depth.
- Examples are:
  - requirement to report on the consistency of the directors' report with the financial statements (UK)
  - requirement to report on the remuneration report for listed companies (UK)
  - requirement to report on capital adequacy (Ireland).

Signature, date, and address

- Further emphasis on who has responsibility for what.
- There is some debate currently about whether the report should be signed by the firm, or whether the individual taking responsibility for the audit within the firm should be identified.
- There is clearly scope for debate about the relative merits of collective v personal responsibility:
  - Collective responsibility puts the whole weight of the firm behind the audit opinion.
  - Collective responsibility arguably allows an individual to hide behind the anonymity of the firm's name.
  - Personal responsibility of the individual potentially allows 'scapegoating.'

The meaning of true and fair

Introduction

True and fair has never been defined as a concept by the courts and yet it appears in legislation, financial reporting standards, and auditing standards throughout the world.

Possible definitions

Auditors should attempt to ensure that the financial statements that are the subject of the audit present clearly and equitably the financial state of affairs of the enterprise. This suggests that in order to achieve the statutory true and fair view, it is necessary not only:

- to present certain information impartially, but also
- that this data is shown in such a way that it is clearly understood by the user.

'Truth' in accounting terms can be taken to mean not factually incorrect.

The word **fair** can have the following meanings:

- clear, distinct, and plain, and
- impartial/unbiased, just, and equitable.

'You Can't Handle the Truth!'

Truth in accounting is quite different from scientific truth because:

- costs and revenues for an accounting period (that is less than the full life of the enterprise involved) can never be determined with precision (e.g. the use of estimations – useful lives, provisions etc);
- in accounting, only cash draws close to the concept of scientific truth, but since the real value of cash changes with time, it lacks total correspondence with the precision of scientific truth; and
- the financial statements may contain error (immaterial) and still be considered to be 'true.'

Views on 'True and Fair'

The following quotations represent authoritative views on the meaning of true and fair view although they all predate the era of IFRS and ISAs.

- A true and fair view implies that all statutory and other information is not only available but is presented in a form in which it can be properly and readily appreciated. (Sir Russell Kettle – former president of ICAEW in the 1950s.)
- A true and fair view implies appropriate classification and grouping of items … (and) consistent application of generally accepted principles. (The Institute of Chartered Accountants in Australia – Recommendations on Accounting Principles 1964.)
- … the meaning attached to (the words true and fair) has been built up over the years by standards of presentation specifically required by the Act; established accounting techniques; case law decisions; the natural desire of responsible directors of companies and auditors to ensure that the facts and figures that are presented to the public properly reflect the position, and last but not least common sense. (Sir Henry Benson, 1962. Senior partner, Coopers and Lybrand, now part of PWC.)
- … true and fair has become a term of art. It is generally understood to mean a presentation of accounts drawn up according to accepted accounting principles using accurate figures as far as possible and reasonable estimates otherwise, and arranging them so as to show within the limits of current accounting practice as objective a picture as possible free from wilful bias, distortion, manipulation, or concealment of material facts. (Lee – academic)

So why is 'true and fair' a problem?

Financial statements represent a summarized version of what may be quite complex events.

- Items such as brands and partly developed software that need to be valued
- modern complex financial instruments
- the impact of inflation and currency fluctuations.

it might be possible to state that an individual transaction is accurately recorded, but this becomes more difficult when a number of such transactions are aggregated. Different accounting policies may be equally acceptable but produce different results.

Illustration 2

The treatment of financing costs for supermarkets

At one time the UK supermarket chains Sainsbury and Tesco used different accounting policies for dealing with the interest payable on borrowings used to finance the cost of constructing new stores.

- One company treated the borrowings as finance for the business as a whole and expensed the interest charge directly.
- The other company regarded the interest on the borrowings as a part of the cost of developing the site and opening the store. As a result the interest was capitalized as part of the cost of the store and then amortized over the store's expected useful life.

Whilst leading to massive differences in the reported profits and positions of the businesses both treatments were permitted by accounting standards and could be argued to give a true and fair view. (It should be noted that under IAS 23 revised the choice of accounting treatments is no longer permitted. See chapter 22 for further clarification).

3 Forming an opinion

Recap from earlier studies

ISA 700 provides illustrations of the wordings of the standard, or unmodified, audit report. There are two ways that the audit report can be modified:

- By modifying the audit opinion; or
- By drawing users' attention to certain issues by way of an additional communication.

To clarify the reasons for and the impacts of the above departures from the standard, unmodified audit report, guidance has been split into two further **ISA's**, namely: **705** *Modifications to the Opinion in the Independent Auditor's Report* and **706** *Emphasis of Matter Paragraphs and Other Matter Paragraphs in the Independent Auditor's Report.*

Modifications of the audit opinion

The auditor may decide that it is inappropriate to give a 'true and fair' opinion when they conclude that:

- Based upon the evidence obtained the financial statements as a whole are not free from material misstatement

- They have been unable to gather sufficient appropriate evidence to be able to conclude that the financial statements as a whole are free from material misstatement.

In such circumstances the auditor has to modify their opinion, of which there are three broad types:

- Qualified opinions;
- Adverse opinions; and
- Disclaimers of opinions.

The nature of the modification depends upon whether the auditor considers the matter to be material and, if so, whether it is pervasive to the financial statements.

The term 'pervasive' is defined by ISA 705 as those effects that, in the auditor's judgement:

- Are not confined to specific elements, accounts or items of the financial statements;
- If so confined, represent or could represent a substantial proportion of the financial statements; or
- In relation to disclosures, are fundamental to users' understanding of the financial statements.

In brief, a pervasive matter must be fundamental to the financial statements, therefore rendering them unreliable as a whole. A simple material matter, whilst itself significant to users' decision making, can be isolated whilst the remainder of the financial statements may be relied upon.

The following table illustrates how the auditor's judgement about the nature of the matter effects the type of opinion to be given in the audit report:

	Material but Not Pervasive	**Material & Pervasive**
Financial statements are materially misstated	Qualified "Except for..." Opinion	"Adverse Opinion" (accounts are unreliable as a whole)
Inability to obtain sufficient appropriate audit evidence	Qualified "Except for..." Opinion	"Disclaimer of Opinion" (unable to form an opinion)

Wording for modified reports

Example Wording of Qualified Opinion (a)

Below is an example of a qualified opinion where the auditor concludes that inventories have been materially misstated but the matter is not pervasive to the financial statements:

Basis for Qualified Opinion

The company's inventories are carried in the balance sheet at xxx. Management has not stated the inventories at the lower of cost and net realisable value but has stated them solely at cost, which constitutes a departure from International Financial Reporting Standards. The company's records indicate that had management stated the inventories at the lower of cost and net realisable value, an amount of xxx would have been required to write the inventories down to their net realisable value. Accordingly, cost of sales would have been increased by xxx, and income tax, net income and shareholder's equity would have been reduced by xxx, xxx and xxx respectively.

Qualified Opinion

In our opinion, except for the effect on the matter described in the Basis for Qualified Opinion paragraph, the financial statements present fairly in all material respects (*or give a true and fair view of*) … (remaining words are the same as illustrated in the opinion illustrated by ISA 700).'

(ISA 705)

Example Wording of Qualified Opinion (b)

Below is an example of a qualified opinion where the auditor was unable to obtain sufficient appropriate evidence regarding an investment in a foreign affiliate. The possible effects are deemed to be material but the matter is not pervasive to the financial statements:

Basis of Opinion Paragraph

ABC Company's investment in XYZ Company, a foreign associate acquired during the year and accounted for by the equity method, is carried at xxx on the balance sheet as at December 31, 20X1, and ABC's share of XYZ's net income of xxx is included in ABC's income for the year then ended. We were unable to obtain sufficient appropriate evidence about the carrying amount of ABC's investment for the year because we were denied access to the financial information, management, and the auditors of XYZ. Consequently we were unable to determine whether any adjustments to these amounts were necessary.

Qualified Opinion

In our opinion, except for the possible effects of the matter described in the Basis for Qualified Opinion paragraph, the financial statements present fairly in all material respects (*or give a true and fair view of*) … (remaining words are the same as illustrated in the opinion illustrated by ISA 700).'

(ISA 705)

Example Wording of an Adverse Opinion

Below is an example of an adverse opinion where the auditor has concluded that the financial statements are misstated due to the non-consolidation of a material subsidiary that was deemed pervasive to the financial statements:

Basis for Adverse Opinion

As explained in Note X, the company has not consolidated the financial statements of subsidiary XYZ Company it acquired during 20X1 because it has not yet been able to ascertain the fair values of certain of the subsidiary's material assets and liabilities at the acquisition date. The investment is therefore accounted for on a cost basis. Under International Financial Reporting Standards, the subsidiary should have been consolidated because it is controlled by the company. Had XYZ been consolidated, many elements in the accompanying financial statements would have been materially affected. The effects on the consolidated financial statements of the failure to consolidate have not been determined.

Adverse Opinion

In our opinion, because of the significance of the matter discussed in the Basis of Adverse Opinion paragraph, the consolidated financial statements do not present fairly (or *do not give a true and fair view*) of the financial position of ABC Company and its subsidiaries as at December 31 20X1, and their financial performance and their cash flows for the year then ended in accordance with International Financial Reporting Standards.

(ISA 705)

Example Wording of a Disclaimer of Opinion

Below is an example of a disclaimer of opinion where the auditor was unable to obtain sufficient appropriate evidence about a single element of the financial statements. The auditor has concluded that the possible effects of this matter are both material and pervasive to the financial statements:

Basis for Disclaimer of Opinion

The company's investment in its joint venture XYZ (Country X) Company is carried at xxx on the company's balance sheet, which represents over 90% of the company's net assets at December 31 20X1. We were not allowed access to the management and the auditors of XYZ, including XYZ auditor's audit documentation. As a result, we were unable to determine whether any adjustments were necessary in respect of the company's proportional share of XYZ's assets that is controls jointly, its proportional share of XYZ's income and expenses for the year, and the elements making up the statement of changes in equity and cash flow statement.

Disclaimer of Opinion

Because of the significance of the matter described in the Basis for Disclaimer of Opinion paragraph, we have not been able to obtain sufficient appropriate audit evidence to provide a basis for an audit opinion. Accordingly, we do not express an opinion on the financial statements.

(ISA 705)

4 Additional Communications in the Audit Report

In certain circumstances auditors are required to make additional communications in the audit report. Issues requiring communication include:

- Matters already communicated in the financial statements that are of fundamental importance to users' understanding of the financial statements; and
- Any other matters relevant to the users' understanding of the audit, the auditor's responsibility and the auditor's report.

These matters are communicated either through use of an 'Emphasis of Matter' paragraph or and 'Other Matter' paragraph.

It is important to note that these **do not impact the wording of the opinion** and do not constitute either a qualified, adverse or disclaimer of opinion.

The Emphasis of Matter Paragraph

Emphasis of matter is used to refer to a matter that has been adequately presented or disclosed in the financial statements by directors. The auditor's judgement is that these matters are of such fundamental importance to the users' understanding of the financial statements that the auditor should emphasis the disclosure.

Examples of such fundamental matters includes:

- An uncertainty relating to the future outcome of exceptional litigation or regulatory action;
- Early application of a new accounting standards; and
- Major catastrophes that have had a significant effect on the entity's financial position.

For P7, fundamental matters tend to be uncertainties that, if and when they crystallise, could damage the entity's ability to continue as a going concern. **ISA 570** *Going Concern,* in fact, requires the auditor to include an emphasis of matter paragraph in certain circumstances.

Example Wording of an 'Emphasis of Matter Paragraph'

Below is an example of the wording of an emphasis of matter paragraph included in an otherwise unmodified audit report in response to exceptional pending litigation:

Emphasis of Matter

We draw attention to Note X to the financial statements which describes the uncertainty related to the outcome of the lawsuit filed against the company by XYZ Company. Our opinion is not qualified in respect of this matter.

(ISA 706)

Other Matter Paragraphs

If the auditor considers it necessary to communicate to the users regarding matters that are not presented or disclosed in the financial statements that, in the auditor's judgement, are relevant to understanding: the audit; the auditor's responsibilities; or the audit report, the auditor includes an "Other Matter" paragraph in the audit report.

Examples of its use include:

- When a pervasive inability to gather sufficient appropriate audit evidence is imposed by management but, due to regulatory restrictions, the auditor is unable to withdraw from the engagement;
- Where an entity prepares one set of accounts in accordance with a general purpose framework and another set in accordance with a different one (e.g. one according to UK and one according to International standards) and engage the auditor to report on both sets;
- When restricting the use of the auditor's report when the financial statements are prepared for a specific purpose; and
- When the auditor has identified a material misstatement of fact in the 'Other Information' in the annual report (in accordance with ISA 720).

5 The implications of International Financial Reporting Standards (IFRS)

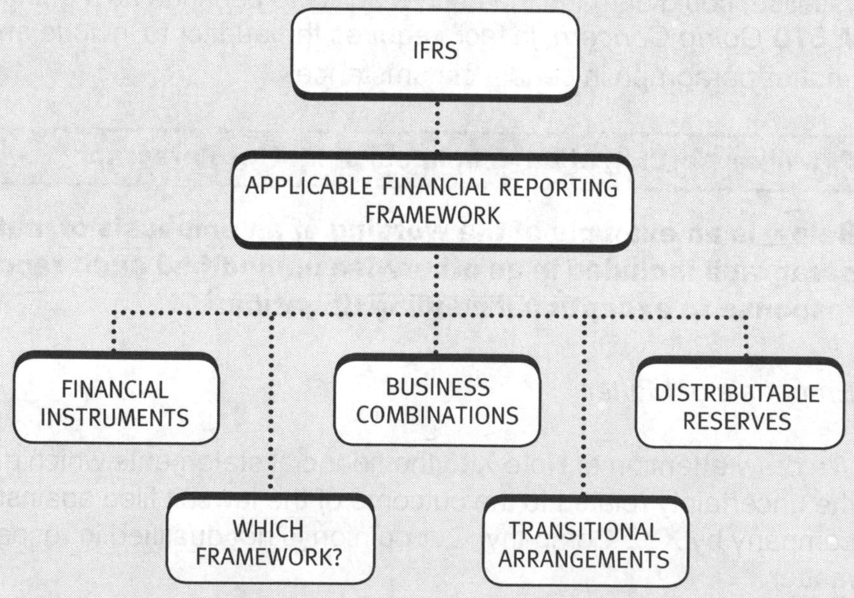

IFRS as the applicable financial reporting framework

Audit reports prepared under ISAs include an opinion on whether the financial statements give a true and fair view in accordance with the **applicable financial reporting framework**.

Since January 1 2005 the financial statements for all listed companies throughout the European Union (EU) have been prepared in accordance with International Accounting Standards and IFRS, for those companies have therefore become the applicable financial reporting framework.

In some jurisdictions national GAAP will still apply. In others, as for example in the UK, unlisted companies may choose between IFRS and national GAAP.

As long as the auditor is familiar with reporting requirements under IFRS, this may seem to have no further implications for the audit report. However, there are nevertheless, specific implications of IFRS that may require particular care by auditors.

Issues Raised by IFRS

- Financial instruments:
  - May lead to reclassification between debt and equity that may affect companies' borrowing covenants and that could, in extreme circumstances, raise questions about going concern.
  - Using fair values for certain instruments could cause similar problems as well as making decisions about what actually is 'fair value' more difficult.
- Distributable reserves
  - The above issues with financial instruments may have implications for distributable reserves if dividends are reclassified as interest.
  - Under IFRS, dividends are recognized in the period when they are paid, a change for some jurisdictions where dividends proposed but unpaid in the year were also recognized.
- Business combinations
  - National GAAP may permit the pooling of interests method that is not allowed under IFRS 3.

- The applicable financial reporting framework itself
  - In the EU, for example, parts of IFRS 39 have been 'carved out' and are therefore not applicable to EU companies. This means that the applicable financial reporting framework references in the audit report may have to refer to IFRS as adopted in the EU.
  - While the financial statements of a listed group in the EU must be prepared under IFRS, it is theoretically possible for the parent company to prepare its financial statements under national GAAP. If the auditor is required to report on both the financial statements of the group and the parent company, these will need to be separated in the brochure in which they are published and separate audit reports issued.

6 Special Considerations

The majority of auditing standards consider the auditor's responsibilities with regard to an audit of statutory financial statements. There are, however, a number of special considerations that need to be made for:

- **ISA 800** *Audits of Financial statements Prepared in Accordance with Special Purpose Frameworks;*
- **ISA 805** *Audits of Single Financial Statements and Specific Elements, Accounts or Items of a Financial Statement; and*
- **ISA 810** *Engagements to Report on Summary Financial Statements.*

The objective of the auditor under each of the above standards is to address appropriately the special considerations that are relevant to accepting the engagement, planning and performing the engagement, and forming an opinion and reporting on the financial information under review.

Special Purpose Frameworks

A special purpose framework is one that is designed to meet the needs of specific users.

In deciding whether to accept the engagement the auditor should obtain an understanding of: the purpose of the financial statements; the intended users; and the steps taken by management to determine whether the applicable framework is acceptable.

When planning the engagement the auditor needs to consider whether the application of ISA's requires special consideration in the circumstances.

When forming an opinion the auditor still has to consider the requirements of ISA 700. However, the following amendments are necessary to the report:

- It should describe the purpose for which the financial statements are prepared and, if necessary, the intended users, or refer to a note in the special purpose financial statements that contains the information; and
- If management has a choice of financial reporting frameworks in the preparation of such financial statements, the explanation of management's responsibility for the financial statements shall make reference to its responsibility for determining that the applicable financial reporting framework is acceptable in the circumstances.

Specific Elements, Accounts or Items

The application of ISA's is necessary whether the auditor is auditing a complete set of financial statements or, in this case, a specific element, item or primary statement. Therefore, when considering whether to accept the engagement, the auditor must consider if this is practicable.

The auditor must also consider whether the application of financial reporting requirements, which are applied in the preparation of the financial statements as a whole, will result in the presentation of a specific element, account or item that is understandable to the user.

ISA 200 states that ISAs are written in the context of an audit of financial statement and that, where necessary, they are to be adapted to the audits of other historical financial information. Therefore in planning and performing the audit of a single financial statement or of a specific element of a financial statement, the auditor shall adapt all ISAs relevant to the audit as necessary in the circumstances of the engagement.

When forming an opinion and reporting on specific elements the auditor shall apply the requirements of ISA 700 and adapt them, as necessary.

Summary Financial Statements

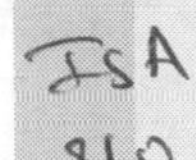

Different jurisdictions have different requirement with regard to what is included in a set of summary financial statements but, in basic terms, it is historical financial information derived from the financial statements but containing less detail.

Where company law permits a public company whose shares are listed to send summary financial statements to their shareholders instead of the full annual report (for example, in the UK), there are two main areas of work for auditors:

- determine whether the statement is consistent with the annual accounts and the directors' report; and
- determine whether it complies with statutory requirements.

With summary financial statements the objectives of the auditor are:

- To determine whether it is appropriate to accept the engagement to report on summary financial statements. This requires the auditor to consider if the summary information criteria are acceptable;
- To form an opinion on the summary financial statements based on an evaluation of the conclusions drawn from the evidence obtained; and
- To express clearly that opinion through a written report that also describes the basis for that opinion.

In order to fulfil these objectives the auditor is required to evaluate whether:

- The nature of the summary information is adequately disclosed;
- The summary information adequately discloses from whom or where the full financial statements are available;
- The summary criteria have been adequately disclosed;
- The summary information is prepared in accordance with those criteria;
- The summary contains the information necessary so as not to be misleading;
- The financial statements are available without undue difficulty; and
- The summary information agrees to, or can be recalculated from, the audited financial statements

The auditor has to form an opinion on whether the financial statements are consistent, in all material respects, with (or *are a fair summary of*) the audited financial statements. This is not the same as the standard wording of the opinion from ISA 700.

Exam Focus: Reporting "Holly & Ivy"

This question is typical of the style and wording of an audit reporting question. In order to ensure a good mark you must discuss relevant accounting guidance, why there appears to be a departure from that guidance, whether you are able to gather sufficient appropriate evidence to support an opinion and how these issues affect your opinion.

Ultimately you will have to suggest an opinion. You must reach a specific conclusion (i.e. the wording of your report) based upon your discussion. Do not offer a range of possible solutions as there is very rarely a range of possible opinions to these questions. The examiner has indicated that she would like to see students be able to draw conclusions from their work.

You are a partner of Finbar & Sons, a firm of accountants. You are conducting a review of the draft financial statements of a major client, Holly & Ivy Ltd, for the year ended 30 April 2008. According to the draft accounts turnover for the year was $125mn, profit before tax was $9mn and total assets were $100mn. You also identify the following issues:

(1) The accounting policies note state that all development costs are expensed as incurred. The audit work performed shows that these costs totalled $6mn during the year and that of these $1.3mn should have been capitalised as development assets in accordance with relevant financial reporting standards.

The audit senior has suggested a qualified audit opinion with a disclaimer paragraph, given the highly material nature of the matter above in comparison to profit before tax. She has also included and emphasis of matter paragraph, due to the perceived significance of the issue.

(2) The directors of Holly & Ivy have, for the first time, stated their intention to publish the annual report on the company's website.

Required

Identify and comment upon the implications of the above matters and the impact they will have on the final audit report for the year ended 30 April 2008.

(10 marks)

Delphinius

Question 1

(a) Explain the importance of comparatives to the conduct of an audit.

(5 marks)

(b) Libra & Leo, a small firm of certified accountants, has provided audit services to Delphinus Ltd for many years. The company, which makes hand-crafted beds, is undergoing expansion and has recently relocated its operations. Having completed the audit of the financial statements for the year ended 31 December 2006 and issued an unmodified opinion thereon, Libra & Leo have now indicated that they do not propose to offer themselves for re-election.

The chief executive of Delphinus, Mr Pleiades, has now approached your firm to audit the financial statements for the year to 31 December 2007. However, before inviting you to accept the nomination he has asked for your views on the following extracts from an auditors' report:

'However, the evidence available to us was limited because we were not appointed auditors of the company until (date 2007) and in consequence we were not able to attend the inventory count at 31 December 2006. There were no satisfactory alternative means that we could adopt to confirm the amount of inventory and work- in-progress included in the preceding period's financial statements at $ ....

'In our opinion, the financial statements give a true and fair view of the state of the company's affairs as at 31 December 2007 and, except for any adjustments that might have been found to be necessary had we been able to obtain sufficient evidence concerning inventory and work-in-progress as at 1 January 2007, of its profit [loss] for the year then ended ....

'In respect alone of the limitation on our work relating to inventory and work-in-progress:

we have not obtained all the information and explanations that we considered necessary for the purpose of our audit, and we were unable to determine whether proper accounting records had been maintained.'

Mr Pleiades has been led to understand that such a qualified opinion must be given on the financial statements of Delphinus for the year ended 31 December 2007, as a necessary consequence of the change in audit appointment. He is anxious to establish whether you would issue anything other than an unmodified opinion.

Required

Comment on the proposed auditors' report. Your answer should consider whether and how the chief executive's concerns can be overcome.

(10 marks)

(Total: 15 marks)

Avid

Question 2

(a) Explain, with reasons, how a member of The Association of Chartered Certified Accountants should respond to a request to provide a 'second opinion'.

(5 marks)

(b) Avid, a limited liability company, is a wholly-owned subsidiary of Drago. As a result of Drago divesting its non-core activities, Avid ceased to trade in the year to 31 March 2006 when its trade and assets were sold to a competitor.

At 31 March 2006, Avid's remaining assets (including amounts due to group companies, current investment, cash and cash equivalents) were sufficient to meet Avid's provisions which totalled $9.7 million in respect of:

- year 2000 product liability;
- staff redundancies;
- claims for unfair dismissal;
- property leases;
- breach of contracts with distributors and suppliers.

The audit opinion on the financial statements for the year ended 31 March 2006 was unmodified.

All known claims and liabilities have since been settled. The draft financial statements for the year ending 31 March 2007 show the balance on the provisions account to be $3.9 million.

Avid's finance director, Marek, has approached you, as a personal friend, to discuss the following extract from the draft auditor's report which he received yesterday.

'As more fully explained in note 7 an amount of $3.9 million has been included in 'Provisions' in respect of general risks facing the Company. The directors consider that such a provision is prudent in the light of the impending liquidation of the Company. In our opinion future liabilities should be recognised in accordance with the International Accounting Standard 37 Provisions, Contingent Liabilities and Contingent Assets. If liabilities had been so recognised, the effect would have been to increase the profits brought forward in the financial statements to 31 March 2007 by $3.9 m.

'In our opinion, because of the effects of the matters discussed above, the financial statements do not give a true and fair view of the financial position of the Company as at 31 March 2007, and of the results of its operation and its cash flows for the year then ended …'

Required:

Comment on the suitability or otherwise of the proposed auditor's report. Your answer should discuss the appropriateness of alternative audit opinions.

(10 marks)

(Total: 15 marks)

Test your understanding 1

Harp Ltd is a house builder, which builds a small number of exclusive and expensive houses each year and expects to make a gross profit of $1m on each sale. Its accounting policy is to recognize the revenue from sales in the period when the sale is completed.

At the end of the year under review, Harp Ltd was very close to its borrowing limits with its bankers, but in spite of incurring heavy overhead expenditure during the year has managed to produce a profit of $500,000 according to its draft financial statements.

The audit file reveals that for one property, the sale was recognized when contracts were exchanged, two weeks before the year end, even though the sale was not completed until one month after the year end.

As the engagement partner for the audit of Harp Ltd, what implications do the above circumstances have for your audit opinion?

Draft the relevant paragraph(s) of your report.

Test your understanding 2

Timpani Ltd has a subsidiary in the USA and another in Canada, which this year together account for 15% of the group's revenue, profits and net assets. Last year they together accounted for no more than 5%. Neither subsidiary is audited although both use external professional accountants to compile their financial statements for submission to the tax and other authorities.

Timpani's management are unwilling to ask the local accountants to conduct a full audit, and although your firm and both the local firms have all the authorizations needed to communicate with each other, the US and Canadian firms are unable to give your firm assurance about the subsidiaries' figures beyond the fact that they have compiled the accounts diligently from the information supplied to them, without carrying out an audit.

What are the implications for your audit opinion?

Draft the relevant paragraph(s) of your report.

7 Chapter summary

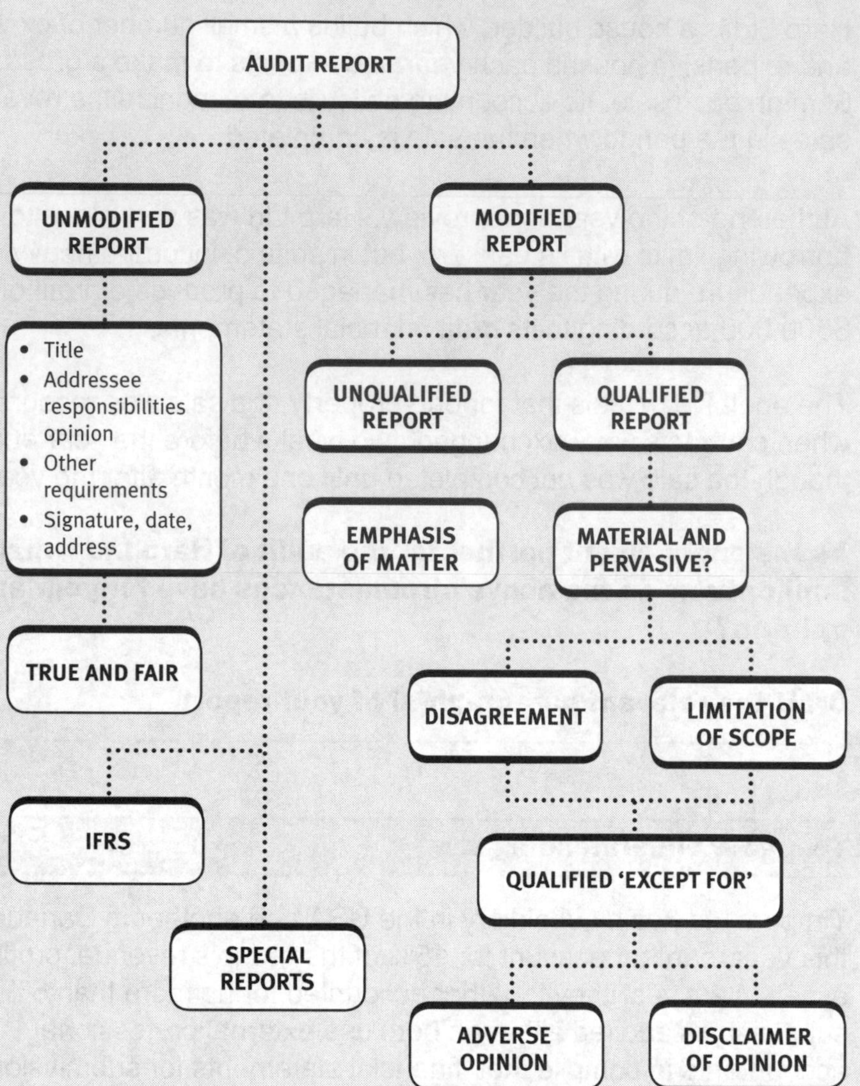

Test your understanding answers

Exam Focus: Reporting "Holly & Ivy"

Development Costs

The expensing of development costs is in direct contravention of IAS 38 “Intangible Assets.” According to the standard if the costs of a project can be measured separately and reliably, if the project is commercially viable and technically feasible and if an overall profit is expected then the development costs MUST be capitalised.

It is the auditor’s responsibility to express an opinion on whether the financial statements are prepared, in all material aspects, in accordance with an identified financial reporting framework.

In this instance the error of $1.3mn represents 14.4% of profit before tax and is clearly material to the financial statements. Therefore an adjustment should be proposed and the director’s of Holly & Ivy should be given the opportunity to amend the financial statements. To achieve this the directors must restate the accounts, removing the $1.3mn from the income statement and capitalising them as intangible development costs on the balance sheet, as per IAS 38.

In addition the directors will be required to update the accounting policy notes. If this policy were adopted in the prior year, and development costs expensed again, then a restatement of opening reserves may be required. This would require an explanatory note in the accounts discussing the nature of the prior year adjustment.

With regard to the audit opinion the first matter is that disclaimers of opinion are given when the auditor is unable to gather sufficient appropriate audit evidence, which is not the case here. In this instance the auditor has identified a material misstatement in the financial statements.

The second matter is that the use of a disclaimer suggests that the matter is being treated as a pervasive issue. This means that the misstatement is so significant to the users' understanding of the financial statements that it renders them unreliable on the whole. If this were the case then an adverse opinion would be given.

However, whilst the error represents 14% of profit before tax and 1.3% of total assets and is clearly material, it is unlikely to be pervasive. With full knowledge of the error the users should still be able to rely on the other information contained in the financial statements as there is no indication of further misstatement.

Therefore, in this instance, an 'except for' qualification would be made on the basis of a failure to comply with relevant financial reporting guidelines for capitalising development costs.

The emphasis of matter paragraph is not required in these circumstance. These are usually required when uncertainty exists that is so fundamental it could cast doubt on the entity's ability to continue trading as a going concern in the future. That is clearly not the case here. Emphasis of matter paragraphs should not be used to refer to the nature of a modification to the audit opinion. That information is contained in the 'Basis of Opinion' paragraph.

Internet Report

There is no extension to the auditor's duty of care simply because the report is being published electronically as well as in hard copy. All accounts are publically available. The main concern is the extent to which audited information is published on the web. The directors may choose to exclude some parts of the financial statements and there will need to be some sort of upload onto the internet, where information may be corrupted.

The auditor must check the following:

(a) that the information uploaded is derived from the information contained in the manually signed financial statements (e.g. conversion to PDF or HTML);

(b) that the electronic copy agrees to the hard copy, by proof reading;

(c) that the auditor's signature copied onto the electronic document is protected from modification;

(d) that the conversion has not distorted the information in any way.

Most importantly, the auditor needs to make it clear in the audit opinion which information has and has not been audited (e.g. by use of page numbers if PDF version).

A point should be raised in the management representation letter that the directors sign asking them to acknowledge their responsibility for implementing a security system that prevents the deliberate corruption or manipulation of the electronic financial statements.

Delphinius

Answer 1

It is important that you should not make issues out of information given in a question which is not relevant to answering the question set. For example, this question requires a predecessor auditor.

Addressing or speculating upon the reasons for the change will not earn marks because (i) it is not relevant; (ii) the tone of the introductory paragraph ('expansion', 'relocation', 'unqualified opinion') does not suggest anything untoward about the change.

(a) **Corresponding figures**

Amounts and disclosures derived from preceding financial statements are included with (and are intended to be read in relation to) the current period figures. When comparatives are presented as corresponding figures they are not specifically identified in an auditor's report because the auditor's opinion is on the current period financial statements as a whole, including the corresponding figures. (ISA 710)

For initial engagements (ISA 510) the auditor seeks to obtain sufficient, appropriate audit evidence to confirm that:

- opening balances do not contain misstatements that materially affect the current period's financial statements;
- prior period's closing balances have been properly brought forward as the current period's opening balances;
- accounting policies have been consistently applied (or changes properly accounted for per IAS 8).

An auditor must be satisfied with the opening position, in particular, to form an opinion on the current year's profit (or loss). A new auditor, however, does not have previously obtained audit evidence to support transactions and accounting policies of the prior period.

To obtain the necessary assurance on the opening position, additional procedures can be performed, for example:

- a review of working papers and accounting records for the previous year end kept by the client's management;
- audit work on the current year's transactions and balances will also provide some evidence to support the completeness, valuation, existence and rights or obligations of the opening balances.

Also, a predecessor auditor may make their audit working papers available to a new auditor.

In rare circumstances, if these procedures are unsatisfactory, some of the opening balances may need to be substantively tested in order to form an opinion on them.

If the scope of a new auditor's work (with respect to the opening position) is effectively limited, the lack of audit evidence may result in a modification.

(b) **Proposed auditors' report**

If it is not possible to form an opinion on a material matter, due to lack of evidence, a modified opinion ('except for' qualification or disclaimer) will be required.

The mere fact that an auditor was not previously appointed to perform procedures on the prior period closing balances is not grounds for modification. For example, a new auditor does not obtain direct confirmations in respect of prior period trade receivable balances, but that does not mean that he cannot form an opinion about the opening trade receivables balance.

ISAs 510 and 710 both use inventory as an example of an opening balance where lack of evidence may result in a qualified 'except for' opinion – such as the one proposed – or a disclaimer.

Inventory is certainly likely to be a very significant balance in a manufacturing business such as Delphinus. It will be more difficult to form an opinion on the opening balance if:

- inventory is not accounted for in the double-entry bookkeeping system
- inventory records are not maintained
- quantities are ascertained by a year-end physical count and
- values of work-in-progress, slow-moving and damaged items are a matter of judgement.

Where a modification is warranted (e.g. because sufficient evidence regarding opening stock quantities cannot be ascertained by alternative means) the 'except for' opinion is a modification of the opinion on the current period's result (i.e. profit or loss) only and not its financial position (i.e. balance sheet).

For Delphinus, it is likely that sufficient evidence will be available to a new auditor in respect of inventory. In particular:

- stock quantities as at 31 December 2006 and the valuation thereof should be available from Delphinus (if Delphinus does not have, Mr Pleaides would be able to request a copy from Libra and Leo);
- hand-crafted beds are not small, inexpensive items and the auditor will be able to compare quantities as at 31 December 2007 with those of the prior year;
- gross profit margins might be expected to be relatively stable, so if opening stock was materially overstated (say) the current year margin would be deflated (and the prior year inflated).

How to overcome chief executive's concerns

Such audit procedures (as outlined above) should be undertaken, as necessary, to confirm the opening position. In particular:

- reviewing prior year end inventory sheets and comparing quantities of raw materials, WIP and finished beds
- analytically reviewing key ratios (e.g. gross profit percentages and inventory turnover) and the relative proportions of raw materials, WIP and finished beds.

Such analytical procedures would take into account known fluctuations which, in the case of Delphinus, would arise through recent acquisitions.

It is highly unlikely that there would be a need to substantively test opening stock or make specific enquiries of the prior year auditors, Libra & Leo.

To assist the audit, Mr Pleaides should ensure that the following information is readily available:

- records of physical inventory taking at 31 December 2006
- full details of write-downs and provisions
- adjustments, if any, requested to be made by Libra & Leo
- statements of inventory acquired on purchase of unincorporated businesses
- an analysis of turnover by business segment.

Although Libra & Leo have no legal or ethical obligation to make their working papers, or other information, available to their successor, they may do so as the reason for the change in audit appointment (re-location of client) should not affect reasonable co-operation.

Whether the chief executive's concerns can be overcome

The change in audit appointment does not necessitate a modified auditor's report. For a company such as Delphinus, minimal additional procedures should confirm, to the auditor's satisfaction, the opening position including that of inventory.

However, it is not possible to state, unequivocally, that an unmodified opinion will be issued (since the audit has yet to be performed). If, for example, a matter of material misstatement were to arise in respect of the current year, the auditor would be duty-bound to report this to the members.

Tutorial note: To agree that the proposed modification is unavoidable or, at the other extreme, promising an unmodified opinion without any reservation would not be a professional stance.

Avid

Answer 2

(a) **Responding to a request**

How?

When asked to provide a 'second opinion' (i.e. concerning the application of accounting standards or principles to specific circumstances or transactions of an entity which is not an audit client) a member should seek to minimise the risk of giving inappropriate guidance, by ensuring that they have access to all relevant information.

The member should therefore:

– ascertain why their opinion is being sought

– contact the auditor to provide any relevant facts

– with the entity's permission, provide the auditor with a copy of their opinion.

If asked to give an opinion in a hypothetical situation the member should make it clear that their response is not based on specific facts or circumstances relating to a particular organisation.

Reasons

The member who is not the entity's auditor must be alert to the possibility that their opinion – if it differs from that of the auditor – may create undue pressure on the auditor's judgement and so threaten the objectivity of the audit.

The member's opinion is more likely to differ if it is based on information which is different (or incomplete) as compared with that available to the auditor. The member should decline to act if permission to communicate with the auditor is not given.

(b) **Comment on suitability**

The proposed auditor's report gives an adverse opinion on the grounds of a material and pervasive misstatement. The financial statements appear not to have complied with IAS 37 and that $3.9 million shown as a liability does not meet the criteria for recognition as a provision.

The auditor agreed with the setting up of the provision (as the prior year audit opinion was not modified). However, in reviewing the unutilised provision at 31 March 2007, it should be adjusted to reflect the current best estimate. This appears to be zero (as all known claims, etc have since been settled). As a provision should only be used for expenditure for which the provision was originally recognised, the balance on the provision should be reversed (IAS 37) and disclosed separately within profit from ordinary activities (as it is likely that the expenses for which the provision was originally set up were disclosed separately per IAS 1).

The directors' argument of prudence does not appear to be justified. That the proposed audit modification is one of misstatement means that the auditor has sufficient evidence to support his opinion that the provision is not required. If the directors wish to draw the users of financial statements attention to uncertainties and possible contingent liabilities (e.g. for claims not received) they should do so by way of disclosure in a note to the accounts.

The provision is an accounting estimate. $9.7 million should have been the directors' best estimate at 30 March 2006. Assuming it is now nil, the $3.9 million balance should be included in the determination of profit or loss in the year to 31 March 2007 (IAS 1).

However, the auditor is proposing a prior period adjustment (i.e. restating the opening balance of retained earnings) which is covered by IAS 8. This suggests that the auditor considers that there was a fundamental error in the determination of the prior period provision (and not merely that the approximation was inaccurate). For example, mathematical mistakes may have occurred in estimating the Y2K product liability or facts about the contracts or leases may have been misinterpreted (to suggest that liabilities existed which did not). In proposing a prior period adjustment the auditor is implying that they would have modified their previous year's opinion (had they known of the error before they issued it).

As 40% of the provision was not utilised and should be written back (in some way) it is clearly material (as the balance sheet contains relatively little else).

In proposing an adverse opinion the auditor is concluding that the non-compliance (with IAS 37) is 'so material and persuasive' that a qualified opinion is not adequate to disclose the misleading nature of the financial statements. However, the adjustment proposed is to restate the retained profits brought forward which has no impact on the results of operation or cash flows for the current year.

Alternative audit opinions

It is unlikely, given the amount involved, that Avid can avoid modification without adjusting for the provision. Therefore, an unmodified opinion would NOT be appropriate.

A disclaimer of opinion would also be inappropriate (as there is nothing to suggest a lack of evidence).

It is not certain from the information available whether the audit opinion should be modified on grounds of non-compliance with IAS 37 and/or IAS 8. In either case provisions (in current liabilities) should be reduced and either:

- profit for the year increased by $3.9 million (if non-compliance with IAS 37) or
- retained profit brought forward increased by $3.9 million (as per the proposed report if non-compliance with IAS 37).

In either case the matter is material but not pervasive and the auditor should express an 'except for' opinion.

Test your understanding 1

The profit on the sale is material, not least because it makes the difference between the company showing a profit rather than a loss.

If the company decides to change its accounting policy and discloses the effect of the change properly, including the impact on prior periods, in the financial statements you might well, given the impact of the change, make reference to it in the audit report.

If management refused to disclose the change in policy, you would need to consider modifying your report. As the sale was completed, apparently successfully, shortly after the year end, it is probable that an 'except for' rather than an adverse opinion would be given.

Possible 'except for' modification

As stated in Note X to the financial statements, the Company recognizes the income from sales of properties on completion. In the year ended xxxx income from one sale was recognized on exchange of contracts that increased the profit for the year by $1m.

In our opinion, except for the effect on the financial statements of the matter referred to in the preceding paragraph, the financial statements give a true and fair view of … (remaining words are the same as illustrated in the opinion paragraph – see paragraph 60 of ISA 700).

Test your understanding 2

The amounts are material and there appears to be an inability to gather sufficient appropriate audit evidence.

It is possible, that by carrying out certain key procedures – attending an inventory count, confirming receivables, obtaining a bank confirmation letter, and testing the bank reconciliation, for example – that you might be able to reduce the risk of material mis-statement in the context of group accounts to an acceptable level.

It is more probable that an 'except for' qualification would be given.

Possible 'except for' qualification

The Company's Subsidiaries X and Y were not subject to audit, and we were unable to undertake the necessary procedures to satisfy ourselves that the amounts included in the group's financial statements deriving from these subsidiaries that are separately disclosed in Note Z to the accounts (if not summarize the figures here) are free from material mis-statement.

In our opinion, except for the effects of such adjustments, if any, as might have been determined to be necessary had the financial statements for Subsidiary X and Subsidiary Y been audited, the financial statements give a true and fair view of … (remaining words are the same as illustrated in the opinion paragraph of ISA 700).

chapter

15

Reports to management

Chapter learning objectives

Upon completion of this chapter you will be able to:

- draft suitable content for a report to management.
- critically assess the quality of a management letter
- advise on the content of reports to those charged with governance
- explain the need for timely communication, clearance, feedback, and follow up

1 Communication between the auditor and the client

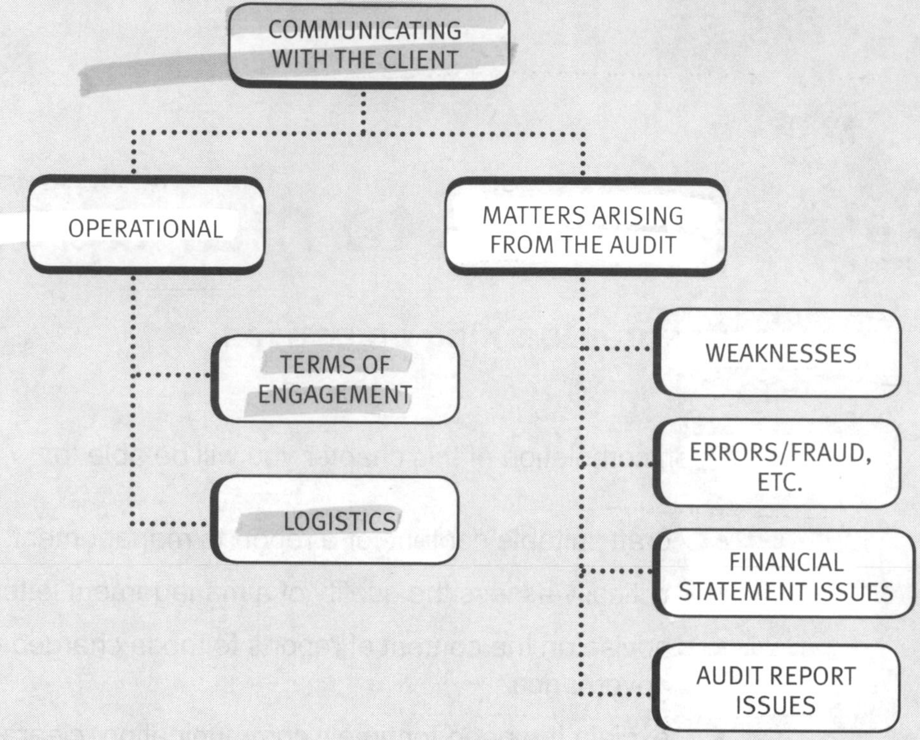

There are two standards requiring the auditor to engage in communication with the client, other than the audit report. These are:

- **ISA 260** *Communication With Those Charged With Governance; and*
- **ISA 265** *Communicating Deficiencies in Internal Control to Those Charged with Governance and Management.*

2 Management and those charged with governance

According to ISA 260 'those charged with governance' can be defined as

"The persons with responsibility for overseeing the strategic direction of the entity and obligations related to the accountability of the entity."

In contrast management are defined as:

"The persons with executive responsibility for the conduct of the entity's operations."

Problems with these definitions

One of the areas of difficulty with ISA's 260 and 265 is that they assume that there is a distinction between management and those charged with governance. For small and medium-sized entities and particularly for owner-managed businesses, this is often not the case.

There is a possibility, therefore, that the auditor could find themselves reporting to the owners of the business, matters already discussed with them in their capacity as management.

3 Communicating with those charged with governance

According to ISA 260 the matters that should be reported to those charged with governance include:

- The auditor's responsibilities in relation to the financial statements audit;
- The planned scope and timing of the audit including, for example;
  - the auditor's approach to internal control relevant to the audit;
  - the extent to which the auditor is planning to use the work of internal audit and the arrangements for so doing;
  - business risks that may result in material misstatements;
  - communications with regulators.
- Significant findings from the audit, such as:
  - the auditor's views about qualitative aspects of the entity's accounting practices/policies;
  - significant difficulties encountered during the audit;
  - significant matters arising during the audit that were discussed with management;
  - written representations the auditor is requesting;
  - other matters that, in the auditor's opinion, are significant to the oversight of the reporting process.
- Matters of auditor independence.

4 Communicating Deficiencies in Internal Control

According to ISA 265 the auditor should also communicate identified deficiencies in internal control that, in the auditor's judgement, are of sufficient importance to merit attention by the entity.

The first task of the auditor, therefore, is to distinguish between simple deficiencies, which do not require communication, and significant ones that do. This is a matter of judgement. Deficiencies, however, have been defined as occurring when:

- A control is designed, implemented or operated in such a way that it is unable to prevent, or detect and correct misstatements in the financial statements on a timely basis; or
- A control necessary to prevent, or detect and correct, misstatements in the financial statements on a timely basis is missing.

In their communication the auditor includes:

- A description of the deficiencies and their potential effects;
- An explanation of the purpose of the auditor (i.e. to express an opinion on the financial statements, not to help redesign internal systems);
- An explanation of why consideration of internal control is relevant to the audit; and
- An explanation that the matters being reported are only those identified during the audit and considered to be significant enough to report.

As well as reporting to those charged with governance, ISA 265 requires auditors to communicate deficiencies to management on a timely basis (include those significant ones reported to those charged with governance and other, less significant ones, meriting the attention of management).

Matters to be Communicated (in Detail)

Ultimately what constitutes a matter requiring the attention of those charged with governance is a matter of professional judgement. However, typical examples include:

- Expected limitations on the audit, either imposed by management or other circumstances'
- The selection of, or changes in, significant accounting policies and practices that have, or could have, a material effect on the entity's financial statements;

- The potential effect on the financial statements of any material risks and exposures, such as pending litigation, that are required to be disclosed in the financial statements;
- A summary of identified errors, whether corrected or not by the entity;
- Material uncertainties related to events and conditions that may cast significant doubt on the entity's ability to continue as a going concern.
- A request that uncorrected material misstatements be adjusted in the financial statements;
- The nature and wording of expected modifications to the auditor's report;
- Any other matters agreed upon in the terms of the audit engagement.

5 Means of communication with those charged with governance

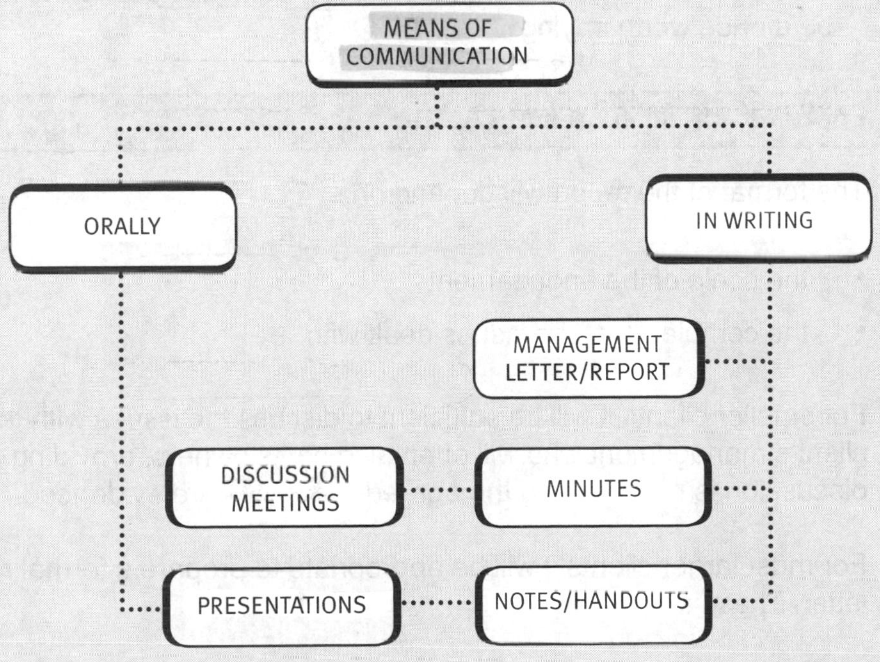

6 The management report

Auditing standards simply require that the auditor communicates the form, timing and expected general content of communications with those charged with governance. In addition, communications should, generally, be in written form and presented on a 'timely' basis.

The standard recognises that effective communication may involve many methods, such as: presentations; discussions; and written reports. However, the typical form of communication is the 'management report' or 'management letter.'

The management letter (or any other form of communication with those charged with governance) is not a substitute for modifying the audit report if the circumstances demand it.

Common failings

The major failings in management letters tend to be:

- the failure to assess the impact of significant deficiencies in controls (hence the newly created ISA 265);
- the failure to assess the real costs of implementing the auditor's recommendations;
- the failure to recognize that the client's experience of his own business is likely to be longer and of greater depth than the auditor's; and
- the failure to understand that some inconvenience during the audit may be a price worth paying.

Format of the Management Letter

The format of the report will depend on:

- the scale of the engagement
- the complexity of the issues dealt with.

For smaller clients it will be sufficient to discuss the issues with the client's management who will often also be its owners, providing the discussion is minuted and the agreed outcomes are evidenced.

For most larger clients it will be appropriate to prepare a formal report or letter. These may be:

- In paragraph format with each issue and relevant recommendations dealt with under separate headings, or
- In tabular format with a column for:
  - the issue
  - the recommendations
  - client's response.

Every management letter should have a covering letter or opening paragraphs dealing with:

- the scope of the report
- its limitations (including a disclaimer that the audit may not reveal all weaknesses that may exist)
- arrangements for feedback from the report.

Exam Focus

Management letters formed the basis of a 17 mark question in June 2008. To clarify the examination perspective on such audit outputs Lisa Weaver published an article entitled "Auditor's Reports to Those Charged with Governance" (April 2008).

This can be found on the P7 section of the ACCA website.

Test your understanding 1

The following issues have been highlighted by the audit team during the audit of Mandolin Limited, an unlisted medium-sized company. It has eight directors including two non-executives. The directors together own 60% of Mandolin's share capital.

For each issue draft suitable paragraphs for inclusion in the management letter or, if appropriate, explain what other action, if any, you would take.

(1) The passwords that enable the finance director to access the accounting system when Ms Z needs to are written on a sticky label on the inside of the top right-hand drawer of Ms Z desk. Ms Z office is usually locked and access to Ms Z office is usually observable by the two personal assistants who assist the directors.

(2) The person who runs the payroll each month has access to all aspects of the payroll system and is responsible for processing changes to salary rates, tax deduction codes, and all other payroll items. No one reviews the payroll in detail, although the directors do review the management accounts that are produced promptly each month. The finance director is an experienced, qualified accountant and the CEO and one of the non-executive directors also have financial expertise.

(3) The company has used the same freight company for despatching its goods to customers for many years. The audit team has noticed that freight costs have increased considerably as a proportion of sales revenue over the past two years.

(4) The company's inventory includes a material amount of spares inventory against which provisions are made based on a formula calculated on the basis of the period since the last inventory movement. Broadly, the longer the period since the last movement, the higher the provision. It has emerged that any adjustments to the inventory files, whether or not they represent valid sales, are interpreted by the system as if the inventory is active and therefore current. Such adjustments might include changes of location, the scrapping of small amounts of damaged inventory, or the correction of errors.

(5) The audit team, when testing purchases, found it difficult to locate particular invoices because once approved for payment, they are scanned and held digitally in a sequence which depends upon when they were scanned. The originals are kept for the statutory period, off site in a remote location and there is no reason to believe that access there would be any easier. The client's staff very rarely need to have access to the original invoices because all the necessary checks to validate the invoice happen prior to approval for payment, and in the event of any dispute, copies can be obtained from the supplier.

(6) The client's system for segregating expenditure on non-current assets from repairs is haphazard. The client's staff are happy to correct mistakes uncovered by the audit team, but seem unconcerned by the distinction between capital and revenue expenditure.

7 Chapter summary

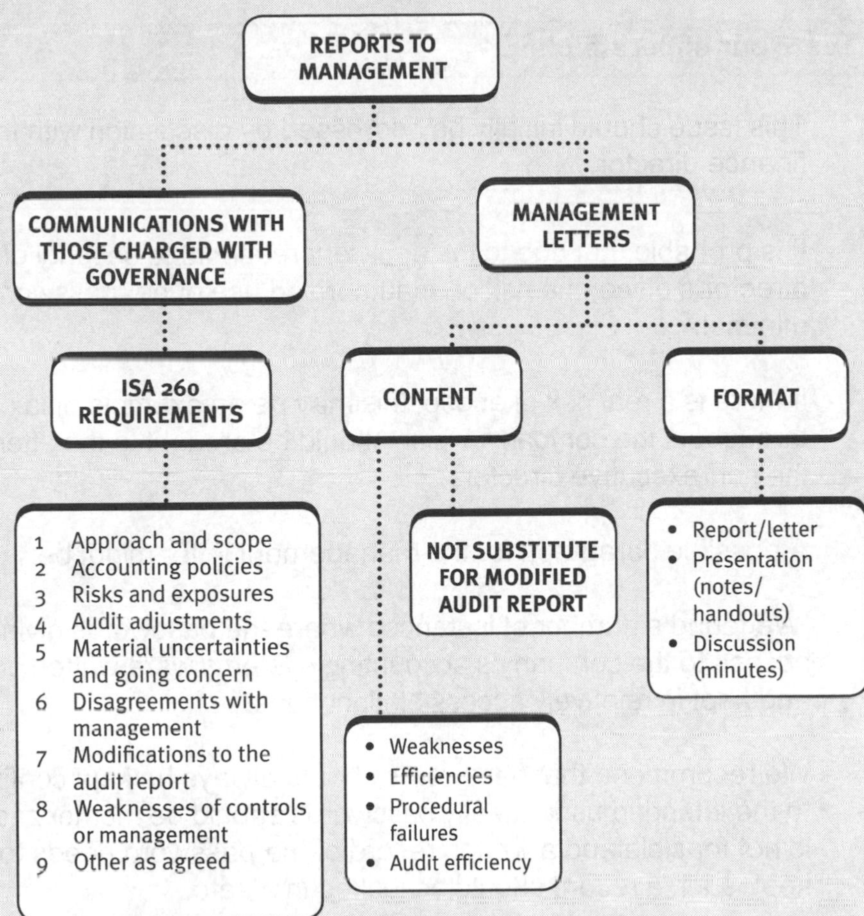

Test your understanding answers

Test your understanding 1

(1) This issue should initially be addressed by discussion with the finance director.

It is probable that due to the apparent reasonable security of the director's office, the risk of unauthorized use of her passwords is minimal.

If there is a real risk of abuse, this may be an example of lax controls throughout the company, which should be brought to the attention of the non-executive directors.

A possible paragraph for the management letter might be:

'We found a number of instances where the passwords giving access to the company's accounting systems were written down and kept in relatively accessible locations.

We recommend that passwords should always be kept confidential to the intended user. Ideally passwords should be memorized. If this is not feasible and a written record of the password needs to be kept, such a record should be locked in a safe.'

(2) It is possible that the budgetary controls operated by the board in reviewing the management accounts are sufficient for the detection of possible abuse of the payroll system. If not the following might be appropriate.

'Mr X has sole control of the payroll system and puts all changes into effect. While we have no reason to doubt Mr X's integrity in any way, he or his successors in post have the capability to introduce dummy employees onto the payroll or manipulate their own or other staff members' rates of pay.

In our view, the monthly review of the management accounts conducted by the board is insufficiently detailed to detect modest abuses of the system, which, although unlikely to be material on an individual basis, could amount, over time, to substantial sums.

We recommend that before the instruction to make the monthly transfers is given to the bank, the payroll should be reviewed in detail by either Mr Y the financial controller or Ms Z the finance director.'

(3) 'We draw your attention to the fact that ABC Ltd has been the sole contractor for the company's outward freight business for a number of years.

We have noted that freight charges as a proportion of sales revenue have increased at the rate of x% per annum on average over the past five years and may not be giving best value for money.

We recommend that you should consider asking ABC Ltd to review their charges, or else invite tenders for the business from other companies.'

(4) We have identified a flaw in the operation of the spares Inventory provisions system, which has led to an overstatement of spares inventory that we estimate to be $Xm at the year-end (PY $Ym). The impact on net profit for the current year was $Ak (PY $Bk).

The errors have arisen because the system recognizes any adjustment to spares inventory as a movement on inventory and therefore treats the relevant inventory lines as being current, even though the movements may be minor technical adjustments or, even, write downs.

Although the impact of profits is not material year on year, it is possible that the cumulative overstatement of spares inventory values is material.

We recommend that the company should investigate further the actual level of the overstatement of spares inventory, and should take immediate steps to ensure that only valid sales of inventory are recognized as movements for the purpose of deciding whether or not a particular line of inventory is current.

(5) It is possible that the company is in breach of statutory rules concerning the accessibility of accounting records, but may well not be.

If not, this should almost certainly not be dealt with in the management letter.

Instead, the impact on the audit fee should be explained to the client. It is possible that the client will agree to give administrative assistance in retrieving relevant invoices, and the precise terms of these arrangements should be set out in the engagement letter.

The auditors will need to take care that such arrangements do not limit the scope of the audit in some way.

(6) Misallocations between capital and revenue expenditure tend to have tax implications, so the concept of audit materiality may not be relevant.

Possible wording might be:

'We have identified $Xk of capital expenditure which has been incorrectly treated as repairs. Such errors have an equal impact on the company's profits for the year, which in turn affects its tax liability.

We recommend that your accounts staff should receive training about the impact of tax sensitive expenditure so that such misallocations do not occur in the future.'

chapter

16

Audit-related services

Chapter learning objectives

Upon completion of this chapter you will be able to:

- describe the nature of audit-related services and the levels of assurance provided by accountants
- explain the difference between audit-related services and audits of historical financial statements
- explain the importance of and apply enquiry and analytical procedures in review engagements
- describe and apply the general principles relating to 'compilation' and 'agreed upon procedures' engagements

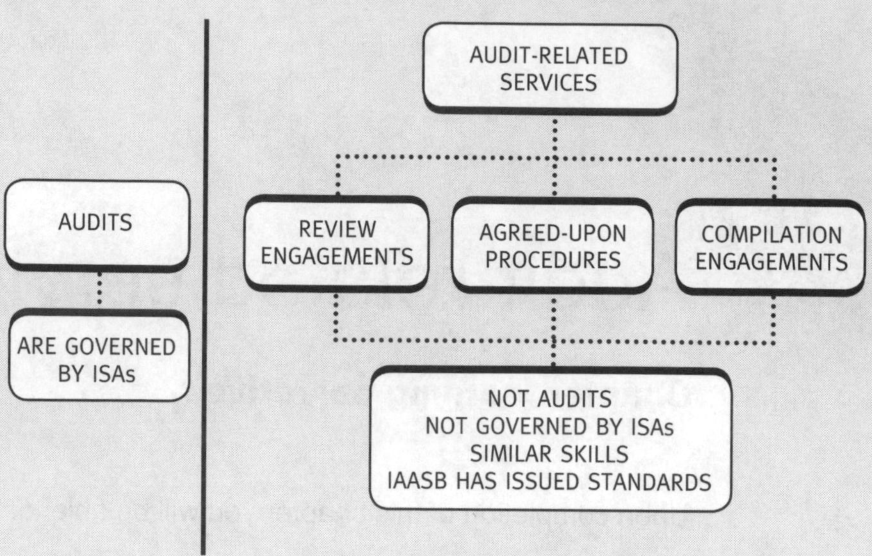

1 The nature of audit-related services

What are audit-related services?

Audit-related services are those services that professional accountants offer but which are not statutory audits, although they are conceptually related and use similar skills.

You must be familiar with three types of audit-related services.

(1) review engagements

(2) agreed-upon procedures

(3) compilation engagements.

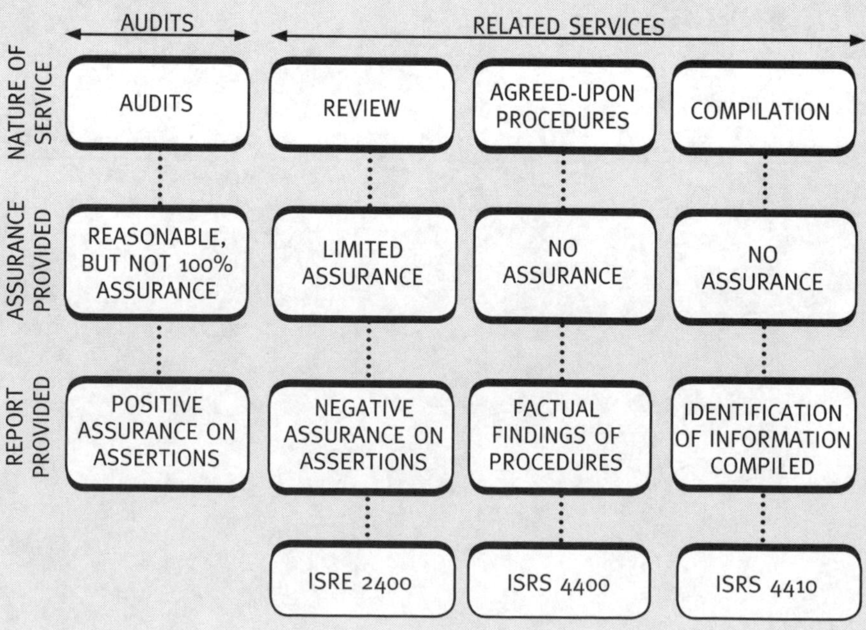

IFAC standards for non-audit services

IFAC has issued specific International Standards on Review Engagements (ISREs) and International Standards on Related Services (ISRSs) in relation to each of the types of audit-related service.

- ISRE 2400 Engagements to Review Financial Statements.
- ISRE 2410 Review of Interim Financial Information Performed by the Independent Auditor of the Entity.
- ISRS 4400 Engagements to Perform Agreed-upon Procedures Regarding Financial Information.
- ISRS 4410 Engagements to Compile Financial Information.

The circumstances in which audit-related services are required

The usual types of audit-related work are tabulated below:

Reviews	**Agreed-upon procedures**	**Compilations**
• Reviews of financial statements that do not have to be audited (e.g. small companies). • Interim financial information reviews. • 'Due diligence' assignments.	• Forensic accounting investigations. • Verifying insurance claims. • Reporting on non-financial data.	• Preparing accounts. • Preparing tax computations. • Special tax enquiries.

Illustrations of Audit Related Services

The nature of audit-related services

Review

A small private company, with turnover below mandatory audit thresholds, might use their financial statements to support an application for a bank loan.

Rather than pay for a full audit to be carried out, it may engage an accountant to review the financial statements to offer some limited assurance to the bank and others that the financial statements give an accurate picture.

Although only limited assurance will be given, this is much better than no assurance at all, and the bank is more likely to place reliance on the financial statements if they know that a professional accountant has reviewed them.

Agreed-upon procedures

A small private company may want help in substantiating its receivables figure at the balance sheet date and may engage an accountant to carry out a receivables circularization. The accountant will carry out the necessary procedures and will report the results of the procedures that have been carried out.

Compilation

A small private company may want help in drawing up its financial statements for the accounting period that has just ended. It engages an accountant to compile the statements from the accounting records. The accountant does not test the accuracy of these records, so no assurance is given that the financial statements produced give a fair presentation.

Levels of assurance provided

The International Framework for Assurance Engagements (the Framework) provides the overall guidance for carrying out assurance engagements such as audits and reviews. It permits only two types of assurance engagement to be performed:

- A 'reasonable level of assurance' refers to the professional accountant having obtained sufficient appropriate evidence to conclude that the subject matter conforms in all material respects with identified suitable criteria. The accountant provides a report in the form of positive assurance, giving an opinion on whether the subject matter is free from material misstatement.
- A 'limited level of assurance' refers to the professional accountant having obtained sufficient appropriate evidence to be satisfied that the subject matter is plausible in the circumstances. The accountant provides a report in the form of negative assurance, stating that their procedures have not identified any material misstatement of the subject matter.

Statutory audit is a 'reasonable' assurance engagement. A review engagement is a typical example of a 'limited' assurance engagement.

Agreed-upon procedures and compilation engagements

- Agreed-upon procedures engagements and compilation engagements are **not assurance engagements** since no assurance is given by the professional accountant.
- In an agreed-upon procedures engagement the accountant carries out specified procedures and reports their findings; it is then up to the readers of the report to draw their own conclusions.
- In a compilation engagement the accountant draws up (i.e. compiles) financial documents for their client (such as tax computations) from information made available to them, but offers no assurance as to their validity.

Differences between an audit and audit-related services

	An Audit	Audit related Services
Level of assurance	Reasonable assurance	Either limited or no assurance
Scope of work	Established by the auditor in accordance with auditing standards.	Established in consultation with client, in accordance with assurance and related services standards.
Wording of assurance/other reports	positive assurance	Negative or no assurance
Required by	Law in many countries	Usually not required by law

Attestation Engagements and Direct Reporting Requirements

To 'attest' something is to certify that it is true or valid, for example attested cattle are certified as being free from particular viruses.

- In an attestation engagement, the accountant's conclusion relates to an assertion made by the party who is responsible for the subject matter.
- The accountant can either express a conclusion about this assertion, or can provide a conclusion about the subject matter.
- Attestation engagements are alternatively called 'assertion-based engagements.'

In a direct reporting engagement, the accountant expresses a conclusion on the subject matter based on identified criteria, regardless of whether the responsible party has made a written assertion on the subject matter.

Illustration of Attestation Services

A professional accountant may be engaged to report on a company's internal financial controls.

Structured as an attestation engagement:

- management would first make a written assertion about the effectiveness of the company's control structure; and
- the accountant would then give an opinion on management's assertion.

Care must be taken to ensure that management's assertion is clearly understandable and is not subjective. For example, an assertion that the control structure is 'very effective' would be unacceptable since this is a subjective opinion.

Alternatively the engagement could be structured as a direct reporting engagement and the accountant would simply report directly on the effectiveness of the control structure.

2 Review engagements

What is a review engagement?

ISRE 2400 *Engagements to Review Financial Statements* states that:

'The objective of a review of financial statements is to enable an auditor to state whether, **on the basis of procedures that do not provide all the evidence that would be required in an audit**, anything has come to the auditor's attention that causes the auditor to believe that the financial statements are not prepared, in all material respects, in accordance with an identified financial reporting framework.'

A review involves less work than an audit and the review report is worded to offer negative assurance.

The work required for a review engagement

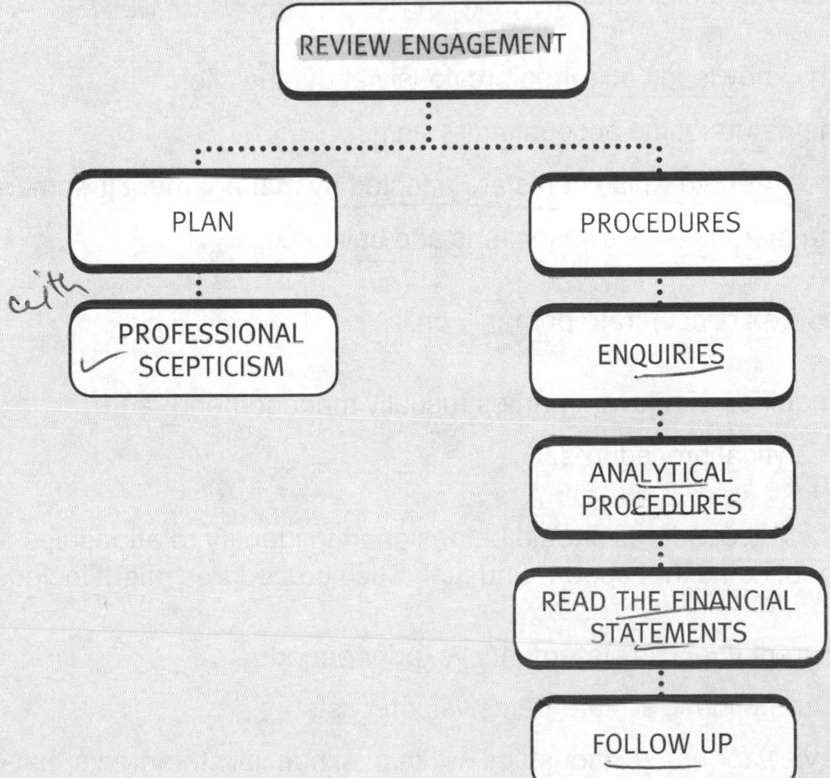

Engagement Terms and Planning Considerations

- Once the terms of the engagement have been agreed, the accountant should send an engagement letter to the client to confirm the accountant's acceptance of the appointment and to avoid misunderstandings over the scope of the work to be done and the extent of the accountant's responsibilities.
- The engagement letter is the starting point for planning the engagement.
- In planning the engagement, the accountant should update their knowledge of the business including the client's:
  - organisational structure
  - accounting systems
  - operating characteristics
  - assets, liabilities, revenues, and expenses.

Appropriate procedures in review engagements

The accountant must carry out sufficient work to enable them to express negative assurance on the financial statements.

In deciding on the scope of the review (i.e. the procedures deemed necessary in the circumstances), the accountant will consider:

- any knowledge acquired previously about the client
- the nature of the accounting systems
- the extent to which items are affected by management judgment
- the materiality of transactions and balances.

Procedures concentrate primarily on:

- enquiries of relevant parties (usually management); and
- analytical procedures.

Analytical procedures should be designed to identify relationships and individual items that appear unusual. Such procedures might include:

- current financial statements vs. prior periods.
- current financial statements vs. forecasts
- review for any relationships within the financial statements that would be expected to conform to a predictable pattern based on previous patterns for the entity or industry norms

Work Performed During a Review Engagement

The work of the review should incorporate the following features:

- The auditor should plan and perform the review with an attitude of professional scepticism, obtain knowledge and obtain sufficient appropriate evidence on which to base conclusions.
- Detailed procedures will comprise:
  - making enquiries concerning the entity's accounting principles, practices, recording procedures, and material financial statement assertions
  - performing analytical procedures designed to identify relationships and individual items that appear unusual
  - enquiries concerning actions taken at meetings of shareholders, the board of directors, and other meetings that may affect the financial statements
  - reading the financial statements to consider whether they appear to conform with the basis of accounting indicated
  - obtaining reports from other auditors who have been engaged to audit or review the financial statements of components of the entity
  - enquiries of persons having responsibility for financial and accounting matters concerning such matters as, for example, completeness of recording transactions, basis of preparation of financial statements, accounting policies, etc.
  - enquiries into subsequent events
  - suspected mis-statements should be further investigated.

The review report

The review report must contain a clear written expression of negative assurance.

Illustration 1 – Example of an unqualified review report

REVIEW REPORT TO ... ...

We have reviewed the accompanying balance sheet of Company X at December 31 20XX, and the related statements of income and cash flows for the year then ended.

These financial statements are the responsibility of the company's management. Our responsibility is to issue a report on these financial statements based on our review.

We conducted our review in accordance with the International Standard on Review Engagements 2400 (or refer to relevant national standards or practices applicable to review engagements). This Standard requires that we plan and perform the review to obtain moderate assurance as to whether the financial statements are free of material mis-statement. A review is limited primarily to enquiries of company personnel and analytical procedures applied to financial data and thus provides less assurance than an audit. **We have not performed an audit and, accordingly, we do not express an audit opinion.**

Based on our review, nothing has come to our attention that causes us to believe that the accompanying financial statements are not presented fairly, in all material respects, (or 'do not give a true and fair view') in accordance with International Accounting Standards.

AUDITOR

Date

Address

Review of interim financial information

ISRE 2410 Review of Interim Financial Information Performed by the Independent Auditor of the Entity gives guidance to the accountant in carrying out a review of interim financial information.

- In many countries, listed companies are required to publish a half-yearly interim report containing a summarized income statement for the first six months of the financial year as well as certain balance sheet information and notes.
- Companies may choose to, or be required to, have this report reviewed by professional accountants (normally the company's auditors).
- Where a review has been performed, the review report must typically be published with the interim report.
- The review report will offer negative assurance, i.e. the reviewer reports that he is not aware of any material modifications that should be made to the financial information as presented.

Due diligence assignments

Due diligence can be defined as a "fact finding exercise" usually conducted to reduce the risk of poor investment decisions. Whilst it has a range of applications it is normally conducted in relation to potential company mergers and acquisitions.

The term can be used to describe a wide range of services, including financial, legal and operational investigations. Depending upon the client's requirements a professional opinion may be expressed, although in practice it is more likely that such investigations result in the presentation of factual findings. Therefore it may **either be conducted as an assurance assignment or an agreed upon procedures assignment**.

Typical due diligence procedures include:

- Gathering of financial, operational, legal, taxation and commercial data;
- Verification of representations that the vendor has made to the potential acquirer, for example: future order levels and current finance agreements;
- Identification of the reported assets and liabilities of the target company. It is particularly important that the potential acquirer identifies internally generated intangibles (i.e. those not included on the statement of financial position but vital to purchasing decisions, such as internal brands) and contingent liabilities that may crystallise in the future;
- Risk assessment of the target company, particularly with regard to possible contractual disputes following a takeover;
- Identification of possible post-acquisition synergies and economies of scale and the potential further costs of merger, such as redundancy/restructuring;

Comparison to External Audit

The objective of an audit is to form an opinion regarding whether the financial statements are free from material misstatement. In contrast the main aim of due diligence is fact finding to assist a specific decision. Therefore due diligence tends to draw upon wider informational resources that include: historical financial statements; forecasts; management accounts; business plans; and the results of enquiries with management.

Unless there are specific issues that cause concern, or specific tests have been requested by the client, no detailed audit procedures will be performed on a due diligence investigation. The type of work conducted tends to focus primarily on analytical procedures and enquiry. It will also focus more heavily on forecasts and projections, rather than just historical data. Finally, it is unlikely that any internal control assessment/testing will be performed on a due diligence exercise unless specifically requested by the client.

Example of Due Diligence Services

Due diligence prior to a flotation

Company A has decided to float part of its share capital on the stock market, so it engages its auditors to conduct a due diligence review. The auditors will investigate:

- the structure of the business – how it is currently owned and constituted
- the financial health of the business – looking at past financial statements
- the credibility of the senior management of the business – looking at the career histories of the directors and ensuring that a balance of skills is available
- the future potential of the business – planned products and likely future earnings
- the risk involved in the business
- the business plan – whether it is realistic.

3 Agreed-upon procedures

ISRS 4400 *Engagements to Perform Agreed-upon Procedures Regarding Financial Information* governs occasions when an accountant is engaged to carry out procedures of an audit nature but is only required to report their factual findings. For example, reports on insurance claims to insurance companies.

Where procedures are agreed upon between the accountant and the client, and the accountant is to report on factual findings, no assurance is expressed. The accountant simply reports their findings in a pre-defined manner.

Ultimately, the users of the accountant's report assess for themselves the findings reported by the accountant and draw their own conclusions.

Terms of Engagement

- The distribution of the report should be restricted to those parties that have agreed to the procedures as others may misinterpret the results.
- The terms of the engagement should be formalized in an engagement letter and should involve consideration of the following matters:
  - the nature of the engagement and the fact that neither an audit nor a review is being carried out
  - the purpose of the engagement
  - the information to which the procedures will be applied
  - the procedures to be applied
  - the form of report to be issued (a proforma report may be attached to avoid any misunderstandings)
  - limitations on the distribution of the report.
- The accountant should plan and document the work to perform an effective engagement. The actual procedures involved may well be very similar to many typical audit procedures.

Illustration 2 – Example of report of findings following agreed-

REPORT OF FACTUAL FINDINGS

To (those who engaged the auditor)

We have performed the procedures agreed with you and enumerated below with respect to the accounts payable of Goliath plc as at (date), set forth in the accompanying schedules (not shown in this example). Our engagement was undertaken in accordance with the International Standard on Related Services (or relevant national standards or practices) applicable to agreed-upon procedures engagements. The procedures were performed solely to assist you in evaluating the validity of the accounts payable and are summarized as follows.

(1) We obtained and checked the addition of the list of balances of accounts payable as at (date) prepared by Goliath plc, and we compared the total to the balance in the related general ledger account.

(2) We compared the attached list (not shown in this example) of major suppliers and the amounts owing at (date) to the related names and amounts in the list of balances.

(3) We obtained suppliers' statements or requested suppliers to confirm balances owing at (date).

(4) We compared such statements or confirmations to the amounts referred to in item 2. For amounts that did not agree, we obtained reconciliations from Goliath plc. For reconciliations obtained, we identified and listed outstanding invoices, credit notes, and outstanding checks, each of which was greater than $XXX. We located and examined such invoices and credit notes subsequently received and checks subsequently paid and we ascertained that they should in fact have been listed as outstanding on the reconciliation.

We report our findings below:

(a) With respect to item 1 we found the addition to be correct and the total amount to be in agreement.

(b) With respect to item 2 we found the amounts compared to be in agreement.

(c) With respect to item 3 we found there were suppliers' statements for all such suppliers.

(d) With respect to item 4 we found the amounts agreed, or with respect to amounts that did not agree, we found Goliath plc had prepared reconciliations and that the credit notes, invoices, and outstanding checks over $XXX were appropriately listed as reconciling items with the following exceptions:

(Detail the exceptions)

Because the above procedures do not constitute either an audit or a review made in accordance with International Standards on Auditing (or relevant national standards or practices), we do not express any assurance on the accounts payable as at (date).

Had we performed additional procedures or had we performed an audit or review of the financial statements in accordance with International Standards on Auditing (or relevant national standards or practices), other matters might have come to our attention that would have been reported to you.

Our report is solely for the purpose set forth in the first paragraph of this report and for your information and is not to be used for any other purpose or to be distributed to any other parties. This report relates only to the accounts and items specified above and does not extend to any financial statements of Goliath plc, taken as a whole.

Accountant
Date
Address

4 Compilation engagements

In a compilation engagement an accountant uses their accounting expertise (not their auditing skills) to collect, classify, and summarize financial information. The typical compilation engagement is where an accountant is asked to compile a set of financial statements from underlying accounting books and records.

ISRS 4410 *Engagements to Compile Financial Information* regulates this work.

- When financial information is compiled by an accountant, no assurance is given on the financial information.
- This should be made clear in the report.
- The benefit is derived from the accountant's professional competence and due care.
- An engagement letter should be issued to ensure there is a clear understanding of the terms of the engagement.

Engagement Letter Contents

The letter should include:

- the nature of the engagement – that it is not an audit nor a review, that no assurance will be provided, that it will not detect fraud, etc.
- that it will be based on client-supplied information
- that management is responsible for the accuracy and completeness of the information supplied and the compiled financial information

- the basis of accounting on which the financial information is to be compiled and the fact that it, and any known departures therefrom, will be disclosed
- intended use and distribution of the information, once compiled
- form of report to be given.

Management should acknowledge responsibility for the appropriate presentation of the financial information and of their approval of the financial information before the accountant prepares and signs the compilation report.

The accountant should:

- obtain a general knowledge of the business and operations of the entity
- be familiar with the accounting principles and practices of the industry in which the entity operates
- be familiar with the form and content of the financial information that is appropriate in the circumstances.

This information will usually be obtained through experience and/or by discussion with the management of the entity.

The accountant should read the compiled information and consider whether it appears to be appropriate in form and free from obvious material misstatements.

The financial information compiled by the accountant should contain a reference such as 'Unaudited' or 'Compiled without Audit or Review' on each page of the financial information or on the front of the complete set of statements.

Illustration 3 – Example of a compilation report

COMPILATION REPORT TO … … …

On the basis of information provided by management we have compiled, in accordance with the International Standard on Related Services (or refer to relevant national standards or practices) applicable to compilation engagements, the balance sheet of Kaplan Ltd at December 31 20XX and statements of income and cash flows for the year then ended. Management is responsible for these financial statements. We have not audited or reviewed these financial statements and accordingly express no assurance thereon.

ACCOUNTANT
Date
Address

5 Chapter summary

You must be able to discuss the differences between:

- audits, and
- audit-related services
- reviews
- agreed-upon procedures engagements

	Audits	Reviews	Agreed-upon procedures	Compilations
Assurance provided	Reasonable but not absolute assurance	Limited assurance	No assurance	No assurance
Guidance given in ...	ISAs	ISRE 2400	ISRS 4400	ISRS 4410
Scope of work decided by ...	Auditor, as much as he deems necessary to give positive opinion	Reviewer, as much as he deems necessary to give negative opinion	The party engaging the accountant's services (to carry out the procedures)	The party engaging the accountant's services (to compile the accounts)
Type of report provided	Positive assurance	Negative assurance	Factual findings of the procedures carried out	Identification of the information compiled

chapter

17

Assurance services

Chapter learning objectives

Upon completion of this chapter you will be able to:

- describe, and assess the benefits of, the main categories of assurance services that audit firms can provide
- justify a level of assurance for an engagement
- explain the difference between positive and negative assurance opinions
- recognise the ways in which different types of risk may be identified and analyzed
- recommend operational measures
- describe a value for money audit
- select procedures for assessing internal control effectiveness

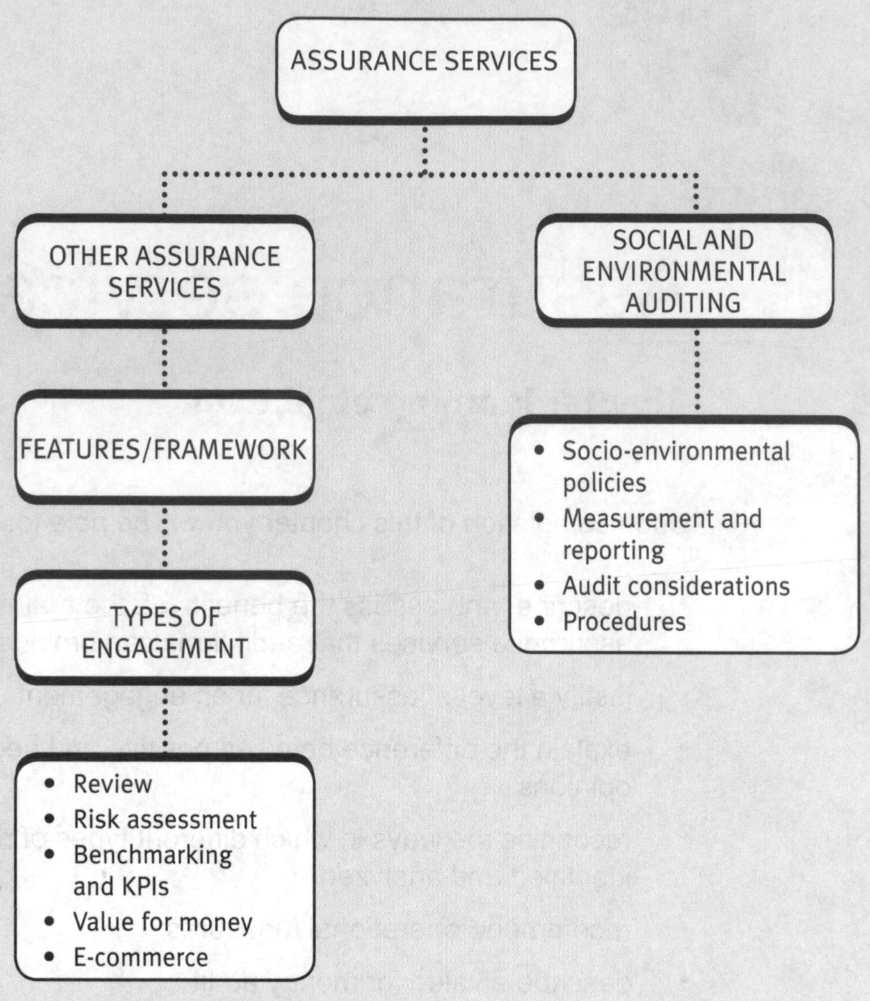

1 The nature of assurance engagements

An assurance engagement is an engagement in which a practitioner expresses a conclusion designed to enhance the degree of confidence of the intended users other than the responsible party about the outcome of the evaluation or measurement of a subject matter against criteria.

2 The framework for assurance engagements

The International Framework for Assurance Engagements (the Framework) provides the overall guidance for carrying out assurance engagements. It states that the objective of an assurance engagement is:

"for a professional accountant to evaluate or measure a subject matter, that is the responsibility of another party, against identified suitable criteria and to express a conclusion that provides the intended user with a level of assurance about that subject matter."

Levels of assurance that can be provided

The framework permits only two types of assurance engagement to be performed:

- reasonable assurance, typified by an audit of historical financial information; and
- limited assurance engagement, typified by review engagements.

Not absolute assurance!

It is not possible to give an absolute level of assurance because of:

- the lack of precision often associated with the subject matter
- the nature, timing, and extent of procedures
- the sufficiency and appropriateness of the evidence available to support a conclusion
- the use of sampling procedures
- the inherent limitations of internal control.

The Elements of an Assurance Engagement

The five elements of an assurance engagement are:

- A 'tripartite' relationship between the practitioner (i.e. accountant), the responsible party (usually directors) and the users of the report
- A subject matter (the items about which assurance is being sought, e.g. compliance with environmental requirements).
- Suitable criteria (the benchmarks against which the subject matter is being evaluated, e.g. compliance with International Financial Reporting Standards).
- Sufficient appropriate evidence.
- A written assurance report.

The engagement process usually involves:

- agreeing the terms of the engagement in an engagement letter
- deciding on a methodology for evidence gathering, and evaluation and measurement to support a conclusion
- agreeing on the type of report to be produced at the end of the engagement.

International Standard on Assurance Engagements (ISAE) 3000 provides guidance as to the conduct of assurance engagements. Accordingly reporting accountants must apply the following concepts:

Practitioners should comply with the ethical code of conduct;

Practitioners should apply appropriate quality controls;

The terms of engagements should be recorded in an engagement letter;

Practitioners should: plan the engagement so that it will be performed effectively; consider materiality and engagement risk; and sufficient appropriate evidence should be obtained on which to base the conclusion; and

The assurance report should be in writing and should contain a clear expression of the practitioner's conclusion about the subject matter information.

3 The main categories of assurance services

As well as the traditional audit (offering reasonable assurance on financial statements) and review (offering limited assurance on financial statements), audit firms offer assurance services in the following areas:

- risk assessment
- business performance measurement
- systems reliability
- electronic commerce; and
- social and environmental audit.

The benefits of assurance services

Businesses need to know if their systems are reliable and their business procedures are sound. They may need to demonstrate this to third parties, e.g. a company may wish to persuade influential shareholders that their business plans are sensible and are supported by sound infrastructure. It would be desirable if a third party with the necessary skills and reputation reassured the shareholders.

The assurance services listed above bridge the gap between traditional audit and the problem solving activities of management consultancy. This recognises that decisions are not based on financial information alone, but incorporate a wide range of commercial factors.

The incumbent auditor is in a strong position to carry out these additional assurance services for their clients. They are professionally trained and already familiar with the business systems in operation at the company. Although this does raise a number of questions regarding the objectivity of the reporting accountant.

In practice, the skills required to offer a comprehensive suite of assurance services mean that it is only the largest firms that can straddle the market to offer a complete range of services to clients. Other firms still offer these services and many specialise in certain areas, such as due diligence.

The implications of assurance services being provided by auditors are wide-ranging.

- There will be further pressures on the audit firm to maintain its independence as the proportion of fees earned from non-audit work continues to grow.
- Practitioners specializing in a range of disciplines (e.g. IT systems, public sector specialists, etc.) will be needed in the firm as well as traditional financial auditors.
- Many assurance services involve reporting on risk (operational, financial, environmental, etc.) Reporting on such matters will increase the auditor's exposure to professional liability claims.
- The pressures on traditional audit fees will continue to drive them down, since clients will be willing to pay for value-adding assurance services but correspondingly less willing to pay for the statutory audit where they perceive less value for their money.

Article Focus

In October 2007 Lisa Weaver published an article entitled "Continue to be Rest Assured."

The purpose of the article was to identify how assurance has been examined in the past. Lisa indicates that similar methods will be adopted in future exam sittings.

In addition, the articles "How to Tackle Audit and Assurance Case Study Questions 1 & 2" provide vital guidance regarding the practical implications of answering assurance questions in the exam.

All of these articles can be found on the ACCA website.

4 Risk assessment engagements

Corporate governance best practice requires that boards of directors conduct, at least annually, a review of the effectiveness of the group's system of internal controls.

The entity's risk assessment process is an essential component of an effective internal control system.

Management must therefore have a process for identifying and responding to business risks. Possible responses are:

- transfer the risk to someone else, e.g. by insurance or by outsourcing the risky activity or by requiring third parties to sign indemnities
- avoid the risk, e.g. terminate the risky operation and move the resources to a less risky activity
- establish controls to manage the risk
- accept the risk, particularly if it is of low impact and/or low likelihood.

The auditor may be engaged to report on the effectiveness of the company's internal controls, especially where evident criteria exist such as the company applying a specific control framework.

Risk assessment is a core element of internal auditing. As such the nature of internal risk assessment exercises is considered in more detail in chapter 20.

Article Focus

Risk audit is also an integral element of P1 *The Professional Accountant*. The P1 examiner, David Campbell, has published an article entitled "Risk and Environmental Auditing" that may also be of use to candidates studying P7.

5 Business Performance Measurement

Key Performance Indicators (KPI's)

KPIs are financial and non-financial statistical measures that are chosen and monitored to determine the strategic performance of an organization.

KPIs should be: 

- Specific
- Measurable

- Achievable
- Realistic
- Timely

(NB Use the mnemonic SMART to remember these characteristics.)

The monitoring of KPIs is part of the performance information system that management should establish. In this way actual performance can be evaluated in comparison to benchmarked performance criteria.

Rather than look at their progress in isolation, management may also wish to benchmark their own progress against the results of their competitors.

Example KPI's

Remember KPI's have to be SMART. Examples include:

Operational

- To despatch, over a twelve month average, 95% of customer orders within 1 day of receipt of the order.
- To reduce waste raw materials from the production process by 10% over the next twelve months.

Financial

- To increase gross profit margin by 5% every year over the next three years.
- To reduce total wages and salary costs to 50% of total costs in the next two years.

Social

- To increase spending on staff training by 10% in the next twelve months.
- To increase the monetary valuation of charitable donations by 10% over the next twelve months.

Environmental

- To reduce energy concumption by 10% over the next two years.
- To increase the recycling of waste by 10% over the next twelve months.

Providing assurance on KPI's

Auditors may be engaged to report on the fairness and validity of KPI benchmarking exercises. This will give assurance to external users that the progress claimed by a company's management is in fact real progress.

This poses a number of problems for the reporting accountant though and it is unlikely that auditors will ever be able to offer anything other than limited assurance – and even this may not be feasible. Reasons include:

- KPI's may not be specific enough to measure accurately. Take, for example: "To increase the monetary value of charitable donations by 10% over the next 12 months."

  Although this appears easy enough to assess in principle, what would happen if the company chose to donate goods and human resources? How would you value donated goods (cost vs. sales price) and how would you value human resources (i.e. wage cost vs. value of skills contributed)? This becomes much more difficult to measure in practice.

- The concepts involved may lack precise definition.

  Consider the concepts of 'sustainability,' 'being green,' 'customer satisfaction,' and 'serious workplace accidents.' All of these are common terms form KPI's but none of them have a standard definition and for that reason may lack credibility. For example: what do you consider being 'green' means?

- Evidence may not be sufficient or appropriate for the purposes of providing an assurance opinion.

  It is unlikely that companies will establish sophisticated measuring and recording systems to gather the data used for all KPI's. For example: if a company donates goods to charity it is unlikely that there will be invoices, orders, goods despatched notes, remittances, cash transactions etc. In this case how does the auditor determine the quantity and value of goods donated?

Test your understanding 1

You are the manager responsible for the audit of The National Literary Museum (NLM), a museum focusing on famous literary works.

Entry to the museum is free for all visitors and many visitors make repeat visits to the museum.

NLM receives funding from government departments for culture and education, as well as several large charitable donations. The amount of funding received is dependent on three key performance indicator (KPI) targets being met annually. All three of the targets must be met in order to secure the government funding.

Extracts from NLM's operating and financial review are as follows:

	KPI target	Draft KPI 2007	Actual KPI 2006
Number of annual visitors:	100,000	102,659	103,752
Proportion of total visitors of school age:	25%	29%	27%
Number of educational programmes run:	4	4	4

Your firm is engaged to provide an assurance opinion on the KPIs disclosed in NLMs operating and financial review.

Required

Discuss why it may not be possible to provide a high level of assurance over the stated key performance indicators ?

Value for money auditing

A value for money audit is an investigation into whether proper arrangements have been made for securing economy, efficiency, and effectiveness in the use of resources.

Value for money obviously considers measures that cannot ordinarily be determined by the statutory financial statements but are still significant in assessing the performance of the business.

This is a technique often adopted in the public sector and with charities. These institutions differ from private businesses in that profit is not their strategic objective. Instead they have other social, cultural, philanthropic, or environmental aims and are not owned by external shareholders.

For this reason traditional profit based measures of performance appear irrelevant and the focus of external scrutiny generally concerns whether resources are being used to meet the objectives of the organisation.

The Three E's

Value for money is usually defined in terms of the three Es – economy, efficiency, and effectiveness.

- Economy – the ability of the organisation to optimise the use of its productive resources (often assessed in relation to cost containment);
- Effectiveness – the extent to which the organisation achieves its objectives; and
- Efficiency – the 'output' of the organisation per unit of resource consumed.

Audits of public sector organizations are normally carried out by a government organization or by approved firms of accountants. The approach to achieving value for money includes:

- undertaking studies that make recommendations for improving economy, efficiency, and effectiveness
- preparing statistical profiles of each organization that contrast cost and other data with national averages. These may be published in national newspapers in order to inform consumers. Examples would be league tables ranking universities or schools in terms of pass rates
- encouraging organizations to learn from each other, thus disseminating best practice
- undertaking local projects
- assessing the effectiveness of management arrangements.

Test your understanding 2

Identify suitable measures of economy, efficiency, and effectiveness that could be used by a hospital.

6 Systems reliability

All businesses/organisations begin life with a specific objective (or objectives) in mind: to make profit; to exploit a technological niche in a market; to provide free health care to the population; to provide free education to the population etc. In order to achieve these objectives businesses and organisations have to establish systems to enable:

- the sourcing of required resources;
- the application of those resources to producing relevant goods and services; and
- the production of information for monitoring of performance.

In an audit of financial statements the auditor assesses the effectiveness of those internal systems for measuring, recording and reporting financial data. This is only a small part of the overall systems of internal control of an organisation. Therefore further assurance engagements may be provided to assess the effectiveness of other systems of internal control relevant to achieving the objectives of a business.

Systems reliability and assurance

Practitioners may be engaged to provide assurance about the nature of internal systems. This usually involves considering:

- whether the design of the system is appropriate for meeting its objectives; or
- whether current systems are being operated effectively.

The nature of the assurance report depends upon the requirements of management. However it is likely to include some discussion of:

- The effectiveness of controls within the system;
- Any deficiencies identified in the system;
- The risks applicable to those deficiencies;
- Cost vs. benefit analysis; and
- Whether the overall design of the system is sufficient to meet its objectives.

7 Demands on the modern audit – e-commerce

Introduction

Technological development means that increasingly sophisticated information systems are available to businesses at a steadily decreasing cost. This has led to a demand for reliable and more timely reporting on financial information.

Illustration 1

For example, banks used to be happy to draw up internal management accounts for each quarter that were available a month after the end of the quarter. Nowadays banks have moved to a weekly availability of KPI-related data and sometimes to a daily analysis. This has increased the demand for timely assurance on the information provided.

Continuous auditing

Continuous auditing enables independent auditors to give written assurance on a subject matter (e.g. inventory levels, receivables balances, etc.) by issuing audit reports simultaneously with (or a short time after) the events that underlie the subject matter.

Continuous auditing clearly increases the frequency of reporting. Where a traditional audit report is issued annually on the year's financial statements, continuous auditing generates audit reports much more frequently, e.g. weekly or daily.

Continuous audit reports are generally (but not exclusively) produced automatically through the use of auditing software packages that are either installed onto or linked to the client's system.

The risks and benefits of auditing software

Auditing software has obvious benefits:

- It allows continual auditing of processes and delivery of more frequent reports;
- Once software has been written for a client it can then be applied to their system with few further costs;
- Reduced need for audit staff to perform procedures, hence further cost savings for clients; and
- Reduced need for paper audit trails (hence reduced environmental impact of the audit process).

However, there are many concerns that need to be addressed before an audit firm actually implements computer based auditing techniques:

- There is an initial high cost of designing the software package;
- Software may interfere with the client's system (and what about viruses and corruption of data?);
- Clients may fear for the security of their data;
- Audit firms will need to recruit increasingly from an IT, rather than an accounting, background; and
- Software has to be tested on a 'live' system before the auditor knows whether it will work or not (i.e. high risk of corrupting that system).

The audit of core technologies

The modern auditor must be confident in auditing his client's use of today's core technologies, e.g.:

- Electronic Data Interchange (EDI)
- Electronic mail (email)
- The internet
- The World Wide Web.

Test your understanding 3

What risks arise from a company's adoption of new technologies such as maintaining a comprehensive website and carrying out business transactions on the internet?

Electronic commerce: Effect on the Audit of Financial Statements

E-commerce is conducting business over the internet and therefore by electronic rather than paper-based methods.

- EDI or electronic data interchange is a standard method of exchanging documents, such as invoices, between companies that may have incompatible hardware and/or software.
- SET or secure electronic transactions is an extension of EDI so that monies can be transferred primarily through credit card payments.

Risk Management Procedures for E-Commerce

Risk management procedures for e-commerce may include:

- risk assessment – essential
- creating a good control environment – there should be an information systems security policy
- subscribing to nationally set standards
- having an internal audit facility
- maintaining systems access control, such as passwords, and physical security
- using encryption
- backups for data but also for service providers and other links in the e-commerce chain
- having good website design – many websites are still in their infancy and are difficult to navigate or are not kept up to date. Loss of customers and/or reputation can follow
- minimizing exposure to risk of legal liability in some areas of web page design
- maintaining audit trails – it should be possible (and service level agreements should provide this) to have the ability to retrieve and review audit trails/logs on demand for a date or range of dates
- registering with WebTrust or a similar organization.

IAPS 1013

The IAASB has issued **IAPS 1013** *Electronic Commerce – Effect on the Audit of Financial Statements* to give guidance to auditors when performing the audit of an entity that undertakes e-business

E-commerce and all forms of advanced computerization of complex systems present a number of challenges to the auditor:

- The need for technical expertise in the audit firm.
- Increased audit risk.
- The going concern problem needs more attention than usual.
- Internal audit is especially important in these areas.
- Some parts of the system may be outsourced (e.g. to ISPs or in connection with Secure Electronic Transactions of funds).

- The focus of controls may be different. Most systems concentrate on recording and storage of transactions. In e-commerce the focus may be on the actual execution of the transactions.
- Audit firms may be involved in an advisory or consultancy role in setting up systems for clients engaging in e-commerce. This may imply a conflict of interest in carrying out the audit.
- In the early stages of e-commerce, the auditor may find that analytical review is not an option as the business is changing so rapidly.

Test your understanding 4

Many companies now put their financial statements on the web. Does this action have any implications for auditors?

8 Environmental and social auditing – introduction

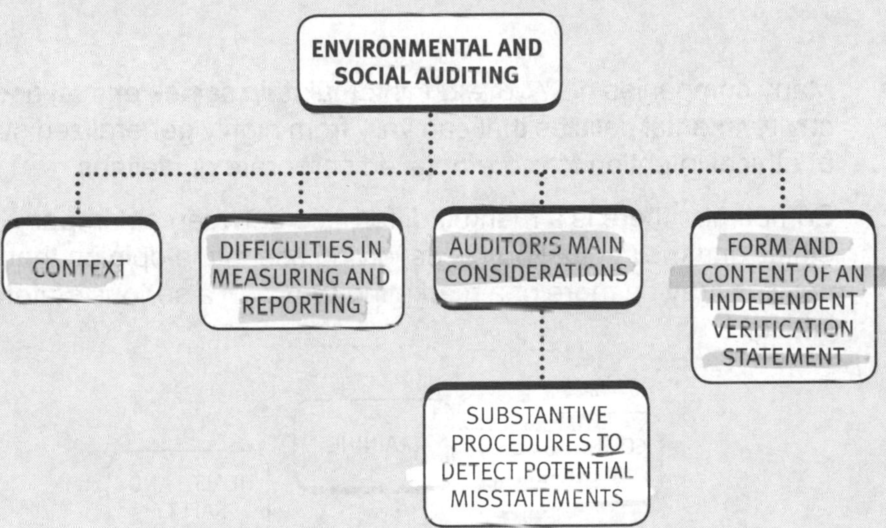

Socio-environmental policies

Today's heightened interest in the role of businesses in society has been promoted by increased sensitivity to and awareness of environmental and ethical issues.

The Importance of Society and the Environment

- Issues like environmental damage, improper treatment of workers, and faulty production that inconveniences or endangers customers are highlighted in the media.
- In some countries government regulation regarding environmental and social issues has increased.
- Some investors and investment fund managers have begun to take account of a corporation's social and environmental policies in making investment decisions.
- Some consumers have become increasingly sensitive to the social and environmental performance of the companies from which they buy their goods and services.
- These trends have contributed to the pressure on companies to operate in an economically, socially, and environmentally sustainable way.

- Many companies now develop and maintain social, ethical and environmental policies that can vary from highly generalized statements of ethical intention to more detailed corporate guidelines.
- Sometimes there is a marked difference between a company's code of ethics and their actual practices, giving rise to the opinion that such policies may be more of a marketing tool than a serious statement of intent.

9 Environmental and social auditing – reporting and measurement

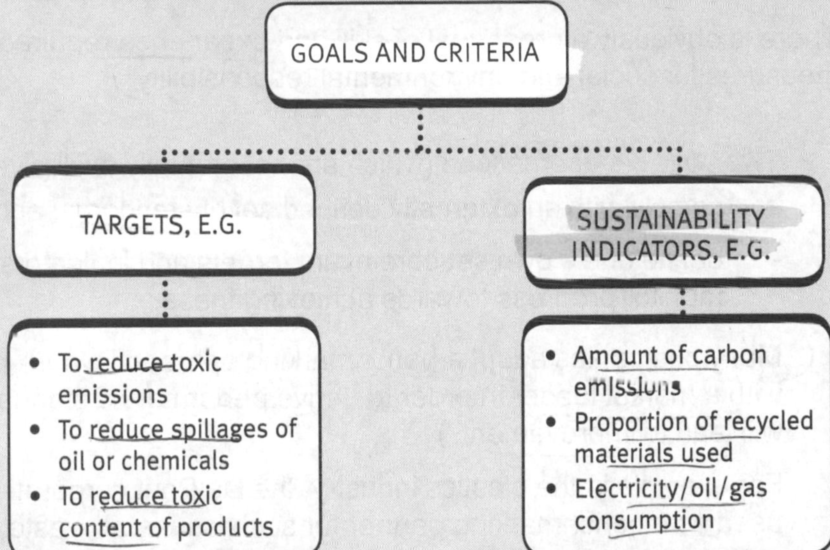

Due to the individual and often subjective nature of economic, environmental, and social matters within organizations, measurement and reporting can be a difficult task.

Reporting

Many companies now publish social and environmental reports but few attach audit reports to them. However, it is possible:

- to conduct an audit on social, environmental, or health and safety issues; and/or
- to attest to the report to add assurance to its authenticity.

Whether an audit firm is the right agent for such an audit is doubtful and there are specialized firms that can conduct such audits. It would be difficult for any firm of accountants to provide assurance over social and environmental KPIs, for example; carbon emissions. There is also a significant amount of subjectivity with regard to environmental reporting, for example; what is 'environmentally friendly?'

Whilst an accountant's powers in this field are limited they can still provide a relevant service. Namely, auditors can review internal processes and systems for measuring and reporting social and environmental data. They can provide recommendations for improvement and, if required, can provide assurance reports regarding the operation of the systems based on client assertions.

The Problem of Measurement

There is obviously a great deal of skill and experience required to derive measures for social and environmental responsibility.

- Two possible approaches (which are not mutually exclusive):
  - comply with an externally defined set of standards; and/or
  - define one's own set of relevant targets and indicators and monitor progress towards achieving these.
- Many companies adopt a benchmarking approach where they work with a market leader in order to derive performance standards that will lead to improvement.
- For example in the plastics industry, the Du Pont corporation is often used as a benchmarking partner for such issues as waste disposal and energy conservation.

The statutory auditor's considerations

Auditors must appreciate that their clients' social and environmental obligations may lead to liabilities that must be recognized in the financial statements.

- Certain types of enterprises are 'high risk' bodies in terms of social and environmental reporting.
- Typical examples are companies engaged in oil and gas exploration, shipping, and nuclear waste reprocessing.

Possible areas that might lead to the risk of material mis-statements include the following:

- provisions, e.g. for site restoration costs
- contingent liabilities, e.g. arising from pending legal action
- impairment of asset values, e.g. non-current assets or inventories that may be subject to environmental concern or contamination
- accounting for capital or revenue expenditure on cleaning up the production process or to meet legal or other standards
- product redesign costs
- product viability/going concern considerations.

When an auditor realizes that his client may have environmental issues that could have an impact on the financial statements, additional procedures should be designed and carried out to detect any potential mis-statements.

The following substantive procedures might be appropriate to detect potential mis-statements in respect of socio-environmental matters:

- Obtain an appropriate understanding of the company, its operations, and, in particular, its environmental issues.
- Enquire of management as to any systems or controls that are in place to identify risk, evaluate control, and account for environmental matters.
- Obtain written representations from, and seek corroborative evidence of any statements by, management on any environmental matters.
- Obtain evidence from environmental experts where necessary.
- Use professional judgment to consider whether the evidence in relation to environmental matters is sufficiently persuasive.
- Review available documentation (board minutes, expert's reports, correspondence with authorities or lawyers etc)
- Review all assets for impairment.
- Review liabilities and provisions to ensure all have been included and contingencies to ensure adequate disclosure.
- Include environmental issues in the review of the appropriateness of going concern.

10 Independent verification statements

Where a review is carried out by an independent third party into the environmental matters of an organization, an **independent verification statement** may be issued.

- Some companies conduct an internal audit on environmental matters and have the internal audit verified by external assessors.
- Some companies may contract for a third party independent review of their environmental matters.

Regardless of the type of review undertaken, the report will have some common features:

- the methodology is stated
- the matters reviewed are spelled out precisely
- reference is made to other documents where applicable
- an opinion is given.

Illustration of an independent verification statement

Here is an example of a report by an external assessor who might be a Registered Environmental Impact Assessor and/or a member of the Institute of Environmental Assessment or other recognized bodies.

External verification statement

AB & Company has conducted a formal independent verification of the internal audit undertaken by CD Construction plc.

Method and scope of the verification

The verification was conducted by reviewing the internal audit report and by interviewing the senior staff responsible for the audit. The verification examined the audit findings against 50 of the 64 targets in detail. The targets selected were those that had been awarded a maximum score for target achievement (10/10).

Internal audit's role related to auditing progress against targets reported by CD Construction plc's businesses and internal audit's findings are included in the section on Environmental Performance Targets (we have not verified other sections of this report).

Opinion

We are satisfied that the internal audit was conducted against an appropriate methodology. We have reviewed the statements made about progress against targets and confirm that they accurately reflect the audit findings.

Signed

AB & Company

Wolverhampton erh

March 3 20X6.

11 Chapter summary

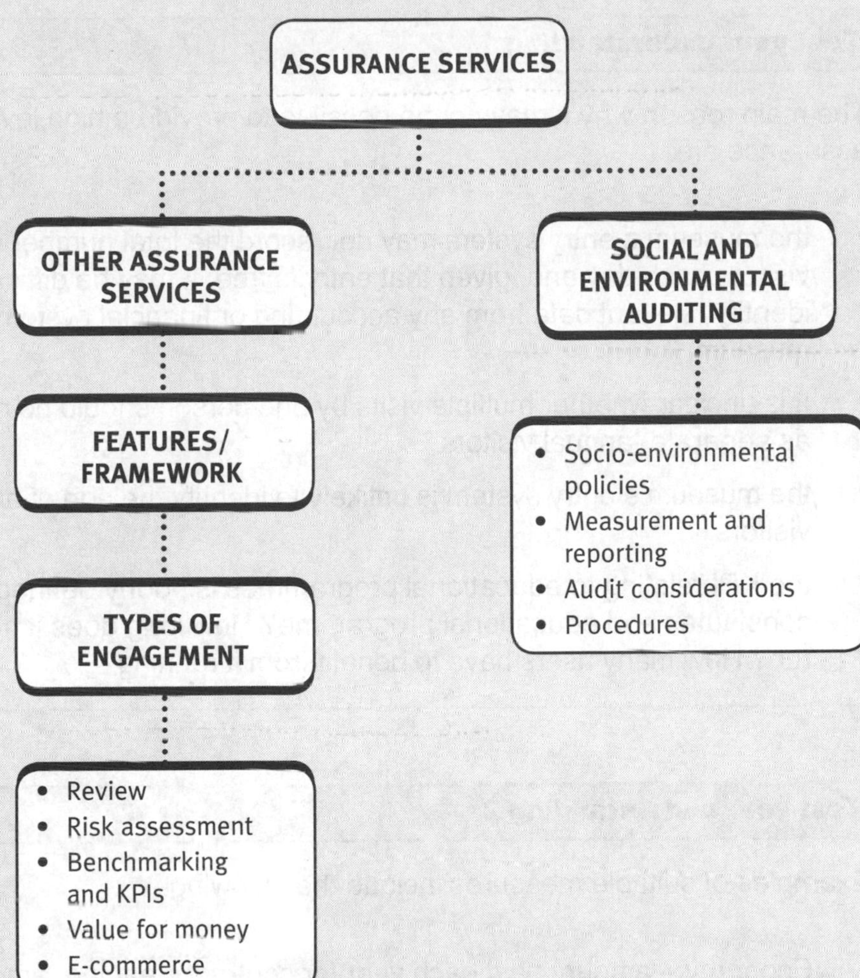

Test your understanding answers

Test your understanding 1

The main reason why it may not be possible to provide a high level of assurance are:

- the museum's entry system may not record the total number of visitors each day and, given that entry is free, it may be difficult to identify relevant data from any accounting or financial systems of the museum.
- It is unclear whether multiple visits by one person should be counted as separate 'annual visitors'
- the museum's entry system is unlikely to identify the age of all visitors
- the KPI relating to educational programmes is poorly defined – what constitutes and educational programme? How long does it have to run? How many users have to benefit from it running?

Test your understanding 2

Examples of suitable measures include the following.

- Economy – amount paid each year for contract cleaning, amount paid per meal provided by caterers, total cost per hip-replacement operation.
- Efficiency – percentage utilization time of operating theatres, number of nurses employed per patient treated.
- Effectiveness – percentage of heart transplant patients who survive 12 months after the operation, annual number of patients who are infected by hospital 'superbugs' while admitted as a patient.

Test your understanding 3

There are many risks associated with companies using these new technologies. They might be as follows.

- Exposure to competitors – website monitoring is now a regular exercise in business enterprises, as competitors can react quickly to price changes.
- Risk of acts of malice – attempts may be made to corrupt websites and help to damage marketing strategy.
- Loss of earnings – parties to a transaction can deny their contractual duties.
- Corruption of financial data – frauds can be committed via the web whereby people/organizations can misappropriate money. Credit card fraud is a multi-million dollar activity and the victims are ultimately the insurance companies who indemnify the intermediaries for loss by fraud.
- Theft of intellectual property – performing rights of artists such as musicians can be stolen and widely distributed via the web.

Test your understanding 4

The auditor must take care to ensure that he is not linked or associated with unaudited information on clients' websites. He should therefore check that his audit report as reproduced on the website clearly identifies what material has been audited and what has not.

chapter

18

Prospective financial information

Chapter learning objectives

Upon completion of this chapter you will be able to:

- define 'prospective financial information' (PFI) and distinguish between a 'forecast,' a 'projection,' a 'hypothetical illustration,' and a 'target'
- explain the principles of useful PFI
- identify and describe the matters to be considered before accepting a specified engagement to report on PFI
- discuss the level of assurance that the auditor may provide and explain the other factors to be considered in determining the nature, timing, and extent of examination procedures
- describe examination procedures to verify forecasts and projections
- compare the content of a report on an examination of PFI and reports made in providing audit-related services.

ISAE - 3400.

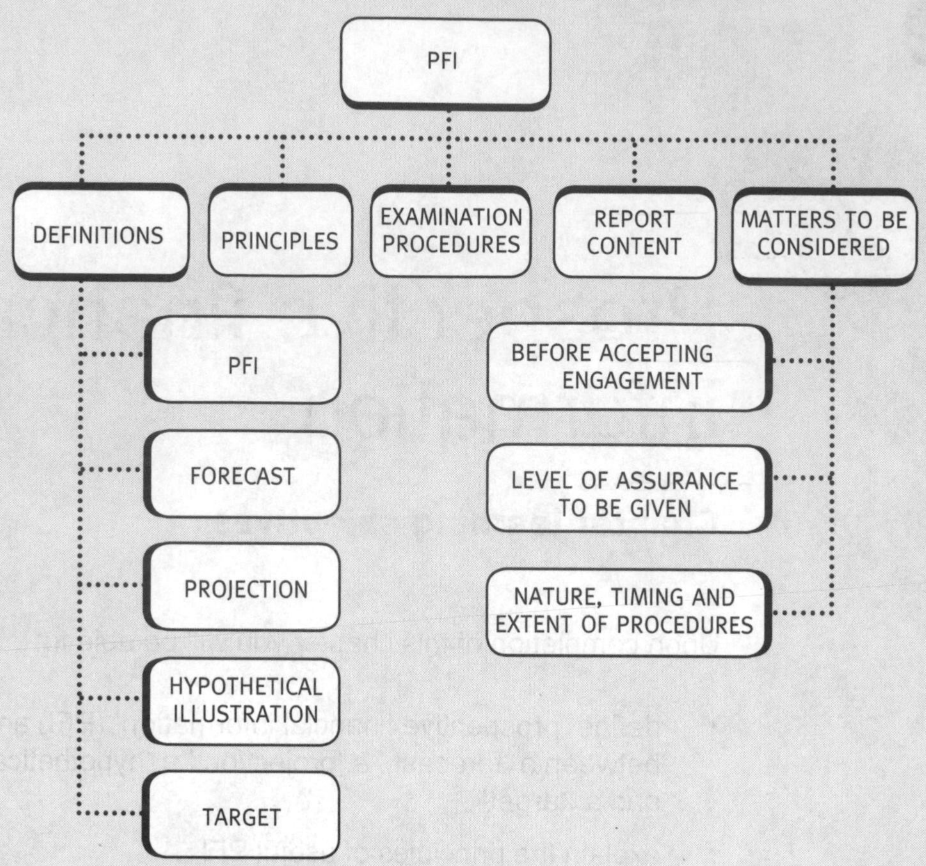

1 What is 'prospective financial information'?

A reporting accountant may be asked to give an assurance opinion on prospective (i.e. future) financial information. The authoritative source covering this activity is **ISAE 3400** *The Examination of Prospective Financial Information*.

Definitions

Prospective financial information (PFI) means financial information based about events that may occur in the future and possible actions by an entity. It may be in the form of a forecast or a projection, or a combination of both.

A forecast is:

- PFI prepared on the basis of assumptions as to future events that management expects to take place and the actions management expects to take (best-estimate assumptions).

A projection is:

- PFI prepared on the basis of hypothetical assumptions about future events and management actions that are not necessarily expected to take place.

A hypothetical illustration is a depiction of anticipated outcomes based on uncertain future events and actions.

A target is a desired future outcome aimed for by an organisation.

Principles of useful PFI

PFI can be issued:

- as an internal management tool, e.g. to support a possible capital investment; or
- for distribution to third parties, for example:
  - in a prospectus
  - in an annual report
  - to inform lenders or to support an application for finance.

What are they interested in?

- How the information has been prepared.
- What reliance they can place on it.
- Material issues only – too much information reduces the effectiveness.
- Mixture of presentation styles – i.e. tables, diagrams, charts, etc.

Ultimately the usefulness of PFI depends on the informational requirements of the end user. Consdider, for example, the different decisions and information needs of a prospective lender and shareholder. The unifying qualities of good PFI are that reports must:

- address the specific needs of the user; and
- be prepared on a timely basis to enable decisions to be taken.

2 Acceptance of PFI engagements – matters to consider

In general, like an audit engagement, the reporting accountant must consider the risk of involvement with the PFI. The greater the risk of giving an inappropriate report, the greater the risk of legal claims and loss of reputation. Ultimately, if the risk profile is too high the engagement should be politely declined.

More specifically the reporting accountant should consider the following:

Matter under consideration	Reason
The intended use of the information, such as internal management or external users	Information for external use will be relied upon by third parties, potentially for making investment decisions. This makes it riskier for the accountant because the consequences of inappropriate reports will be more severe.
Whether the information will be for general or limited distribution.	Information for general distribution will result in the assignment being potentially more risky to the accountant as a larger audience will be relying on it.
The nature of the assumptions (e.g. best-estimate or hypothetical).	Forecasts and projections cannot be verified with any certainty – because the outcome is unknown, however: • If information is best-estimate, it should be a reasonable approximation to what might actually happen. • Where the assumptions are hypothetical, they will be much more difficult for the auditor to validate – as there is likely to be little to support them – and therefore the assignment holds higher risk.
The elements to be included in the information.	Inclusion of elements that the auditor has little knowledge of, that are extremely complex or highly subjective increase the risk to the accountant of accepting the engagement.
The period covered by the information.	Short-term forecasts are likely to be more easily verified than projections looking out over a longer period.

3 Level of assurance

Due to the uncertainty surrounding forecasts and projections, and due to the limited nature of the procedures performed during the accountant's review, only limited assurance can be offered for PFI engagements.

4 Verification procedures

In order to provide assurance that forecasts and projections are reasonable, the auditor will need to determine the timing, nature and extent of procedures.

As PFI is a form of limited review engagement and due to the lack of evidence to support forecasts and assumptions, the bulk of procedures will be limited to analytical review and enquiry. More detailed testing will normally only be required if potential misstatements are identified.

Some areas of a projection/forecast are capable of more specific procedures, for example, verifying that loan or lease repayments agree to existing contractual terms.

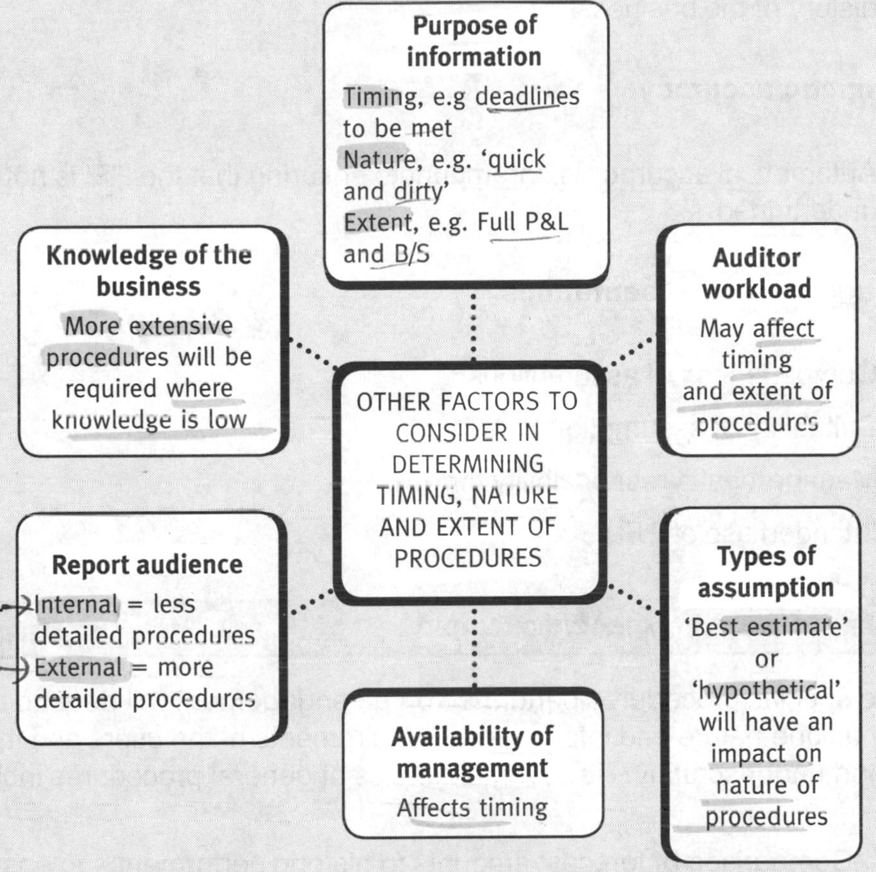

Knowledge of the business (KOB)

- The assurance firm needs to have, or obtain, sufficient knowledge of the client's business and the environment in which it operates in order to design appropriate procedures and reach an appropriate opinion.

Management's assumptions

- Management is responsible for the assumptions in the PFI.
- However, the assurance firm has to satisfy itself that the assumptions are:
  - reliable
  - realistic.

Consistency with known information

- The auditor must ensure that the PFI is consistent with their knowledge of the business and known information (e.g. business plans, recent history of the business.

Arithmetic accuracy

- Arithmetical accuracy is paramount to ensuring that the PFI is not undermined.

Management representations

- Completeness of assumptions.
- Suitability of assumptions.
- Management's responsibility for PFI.
- Intended use of PFI.

PFI procedures – specific examples

The specific procedures performed on an engagement will depend on the unique nature and informational requirements of the users and the report under scrutiny. However, examples of general procedures include:

- Comparison of forecast amounts to historic performance to ensure consistency. Whilst future results will not always follow previous trends historical patterns give an indication of the capacity of the business. It is also important to consider that rapid growth is unlikely and potentially damaging to a business (overtrading!!).
- Comparison of forecast amounts to actual results. It is likely that by the time that a PFI review is actually conducted some of that period may have elapsed. Internally produced management accounts may therefore be available to use to assess actual performance for the first few months of the forecast period.

- Forecasts for previous periods may also be assessed in comparison to actual results to assess how accurately management have forecast in the past.
- Reasonably certain incomes and costs (such as loan interest) may be verified by comparison of forecast amounts to documents such as orders, contracts, loan agreements, lease contracts etc.
- Comparison of accounting policies/estimates used in forecasts in comparison to financial statements, e.g. depreciation method;
- Inspection of the non-current asset note to identify if assets are approaching the end of their useful lives and require replacement;
- Comparisons of working capital amounts/liquidity to assess whether liabilities can be met and the company can finance its short term resourcing requirements.
- Comparison of the relationships between the reported figures, for example is a significant increase in revenue supported by increased production costs, advertising costs and distribution costs?
- Typical enquiries may include:
  - whether the client requires investment in non-current assets;
  - when loan agreements expire;
  - whether further forms of finance are being sought;
  - whether any new customer/supplier contracts have been agreed since the year-end;
  - have any new capital purchases been agreed;
  - have the company invested in any product research/development and if so what are the results;
  - have they conducted any market research and again what are the results;
  - have there been any new competitors/products in the market place.

This list is by no way exhaustive and is very general in nature. The purpose of the examples is that they all consider events or circumstances that will have an impact on the business in the future. Note that none of the enquiries are vague, such as "how do you forecast sales?" They try and identify issues that will directly impact management's forecasts.

In the exam you will be required to suggest procedures that are relevant to the specific financial forecasts in the scenario.

5 Final report

The report following an examination of PFI will be significantly different to a traditional audit report. The key elements are summarised below:

- Title, date and addressee
- Reference to any applicable laws or standards (e.g. ISAE 3400)
- Basis of opinion
- Identification of what is included in the prospective forecast information;
- A statement that it is management's responsibility to prepare the PFI;
- A reference to the purpose and distribution of the report;
- A clear written expression of limited (or negative) assurance as to whether anything has come to light to suggest that:
  - the assumptions are not a reasonable for the purposes of the PFI;
  - the report is not prepared on the basis of those assumptions; and
  - the report is not in accordance with a relevant financial reporting framework;
- Appropriate caveats about the nature of assumptions and the inherent limitations in the forecasting process
- Reporting accountant's name, signature, and address.

FIXED TEST 3 – 'Imperiol'

Imperiol, a limited liability company, manufactures and distributes electrical and telecommunications accessories, household durables (e.g. sink and shower units) and building systems (e.g. air-conditioning, solar heating, security systems). The company has undergone several business restructurings in recent years. Finance is to be sought from both a bank and a venture capitalist in order to implement the board's latest restructuring proposals.

You are a manager at Hal Falcon, a firm of Chartered Certified Accountants. You have been approached by Paulo Gandalf, the chief finance officer of Imperiol, to provide a report on the company's business plan for the year to 31 December 2010.

From a brief telephone conversation with Paulo Gandalf you have ascertained that the proposed restructuring will involve discontinuing all operations except for building systems, where the greatest opportunity for increasing product innovation is believed to lie. Imperiol's strategy is to become the market leader in providing 'total building system solutions' using new fibre optic technology to link building systems. A major benefit of the restructuring is expected to be a lower on-going cost base. As part of the restructuring it is likely that certain of the accounting functions, including internal audit, will be outsourced.

You have obtained a copy of Imperiol's Interim Report for the six months to 30 June 2009 on which the company's auditors, Discorpio, provide a conclusion giving negative assurance. The following information has been extracted from the Interim Financial Report:

(1) **Chairman's statement**

The economic climate is less certain than it was a few months ago and performance has been affected by a severe decline in the electrical accessories market. Management's response will be to gain market share and reduce the cost base.

(2) **Statement of Financial Position**

	30 June 2009 (unaudited)	**31 December 2008**
	$m	$m
Intangible assets	83.5	72.6
Non-current assets	69.6	63.8
Inventory	25.2	20.8
Trade receivables	59.9	50.2
Cash	8.3	23.8
Total assets	246.5	231.2
Non-current liabilities – borrowing	65.4	45.7
Current liabilities	55.6	57.0
Equity and liablities:		
Share capital	30.4	30.4
Reserves	6.0	9.1
Accumulated	89.1	89.0
	246.5	231.2

(3) **Continuing and discontinuing operations**

	Six months to 30 June 2009 (unaudited)	**Year to 31 December 2008**
	$m	$m
Turnover		
Continuing operations		
Electrical and telecommunication accessories	55.3	118.9
Household durables	37.9	77.0
Building systems	53.7	94.9
Total continuing	146.9	290.8
Discontinued	–	65.3
Total turnover	146.9	356.1
Operating profit before interest and taxation – continuing operations	13.4	32.2

Required:

(a) Identify and explain the matters Hal Falcon should consider before accepting the engagement to report on Imperiol's prospective financial information.

(8 marks)

(b) Describe the procedures that a professional accountant should undertake in order to provide an assurance report on the prospective financial information of Imperiol for the year to 31 December 2010.

(10 marks)

(Total: 18marks)

6 Chapter summary

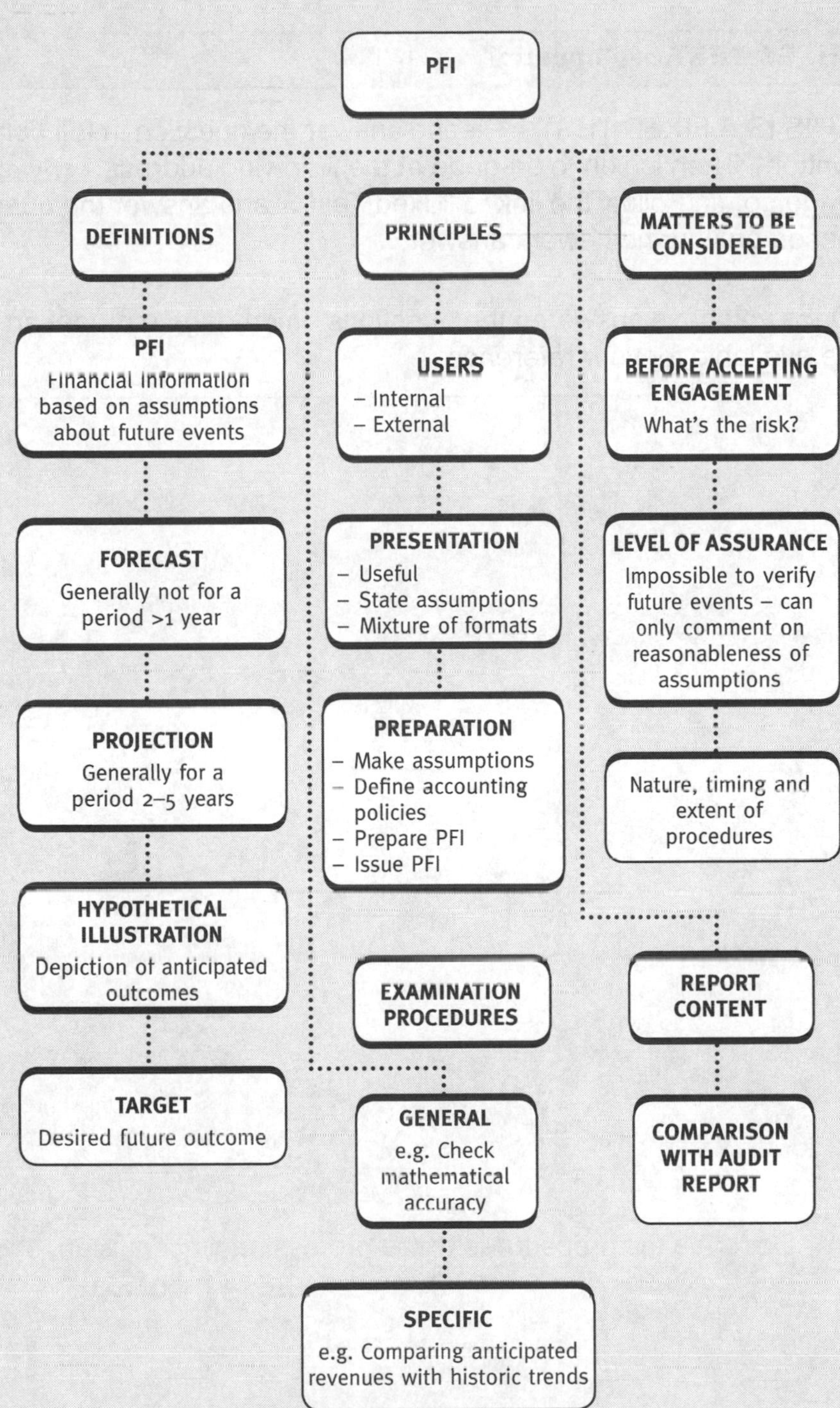

Test your understanding answers

FIXED TEST 3 – 'Imperiol'

THIS IS A FIXED TEST – Please answer the question in full (long form written). Then log on to en-gage at the following address: www.en-gage.co.uk. Follow the link to 'Fixed Test 3' and answer the questions based on your homework answer.

Once you have answered the questions on en-gage a model answer will be available for your reference.

chapter

19

Forensic audits

Chapter learning objectives

Upon completion of this chapter you will be able to:

- define the terms 'forensic accounting', 'forensic investigation' and 'forensic audit'
- describe the major applications of forensic auditing (e.g. fraud, negligence, insurance claims) and analyse the role of the forensic auditor as an expert witness
- apply the fundamental ethical principles for professional accountants engaged in forensic audit assignments
- explain the application of the fundamental ethical principles in given circumstances
- select investigative procedures and evaluate evidence appropriate to determining the loss in a given situation
- explain the terms under which experts make reports.

1 What is 'forensic accounting'?

The field of forensic accounting is a specialist branch of the profession carried out by forensic accountants and encompassing forensic auditing and investigation.

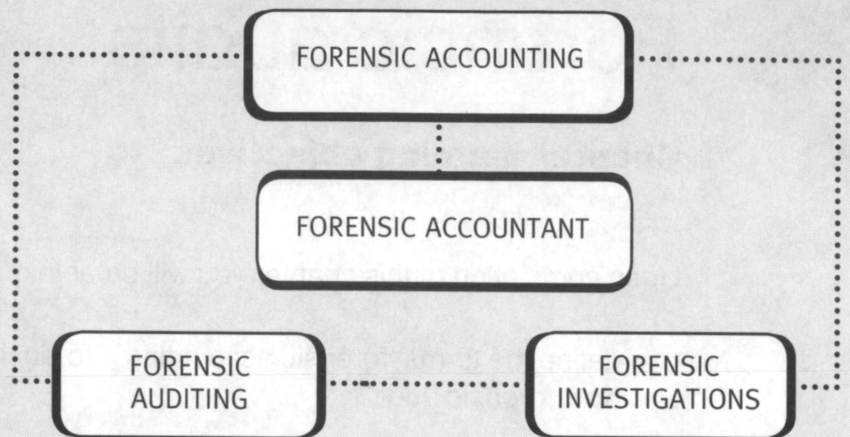

Forensic accounting

- Uses accounting, auditing, and investigative skills to conduct an examination into a company's financial affairs.
- It is often associated with investigations into alleged fraud.
- It involves the whole process of conducting an investigation, including acting as an expert witness.

Forensic investigations

- This refers to the practical steps that the forensic accountant takes in order to gather evidence relevant to the alleged fraudulent activity.
- Such investigations involve a planning phase, a phase of gathering evidence, a review phase and a report to the client.

Forensic audit

- This refers to the specific procedures adopted in order to produce evidence.
- From an accountancy perspective, this usually requires the adoption of traditional financial auditing skills and techniques.

2 What do forensic accountants do?

Forensic accountants become involved in a wide range of investigations, spanning many different industries. Some of the major applications of forensic auditing are shown below.

Application	Examples	Type of work performed
Fraud investigations	Theft of company funds, tax evasion, insider dealing	Funds tracing, asset identification and recovery, forensic intelligence gathering, due diligence reviews, interviews, detailed review of documentary evidence
Insurance claims	Business interruptions, property losses, motor vehicle incidents, personal liability claims, cases of medical malpractice, wrongful dismissal	Detailed review of the policy from either an insured or insurer's perspective to investigate coverage issues, identification of appropriate method of calculating the loss, quantification of losses
Professional negligence	Loss suffered as a result of placing reliance on professional adviser	Advising on merits of a case in regards to liability, quantifying losses
Shareholder, partnership and matrimonial disputes	Determination of funds to be included in settlements, as benefits or distributions	Detailed analysis of numerous years accounting records to quantify the issues in dispute, tracing, locating and evaluation of assets

As part of their assignments forensic accountants will:

- communicate their findings in the form of reports, exhibits and collections of documents; and
- assist in legal proceedings, including testifying in court as an expert witness and preparing visual aids to support trial evidence.

The forensic accountant may be used as an expert witness where:

- it is relevant to a matter that is in dispute between the parties;
- it is a reasonable requirement to resolve proceedings;

- they have the expertise relevant to the issue on which an opinion is sought; and
- they have experience, expertise, and training appropriate to the value, complexity, and importance of the case.

3 Fundamental Ethical Principles

Implications for Forensic Assignments

Integrity

Given the nature of their work forensic professionals are likely to deal frequently with individuals who lack integrity, or may even be involved in criminal behaviour. It is imperative that the investigator recognises this, and does nothing to damage their own reputation, such as accepting bribes or giving in to other forms of coercion/intimidation.

Objectivity

The professional accountant must always be – and be perceived to be – entirely neutral.

This is particularly important if the forensic report is going to be submitted to a court of law. Any threat to objectivity could undermine the credibility of the evidence provided.

In particular the accountant must safeguard against self-review and advocacy threats.

- Advocacy threat arises because the firm may feel pressured into promoting the interests and point of view of their fee paying client, which breaches the concept of objectivity in court proceedings.
- Self-review threat arises when an auditor also becomes involved in some form of forensic work because the investigation is likely to involve some form of fraud or potential misstatement to the accounts.

Professional competence and due care

Forensic investigations involve very specialist skills, including:

- Detailed knowledge of the relevant legal framework,
- An understanding of how to gather specialist evidence,
- Skills in the safe custody of evidence, including maintaining a clear 'chain' of evidence, and
- Strong personal skills: interview techniques, presentation of material at court.

Confidentiality

During legal proceedings the court will require the investigator to reveal information discovered during the investigation. There is an overriding requirement for the investigator to disclose all of the information deemed necessary by the court.

Outside of the court, the investigator must maintain confidentiality, especially because much of the information they have access to will be highly sensitive.

Professional behaviour

Fraud investigations can become a matter of public interest, and much media attention is often focused on the work of the forensic investigator. A highly professional attitude must be displayed at all times, in order to avoid damage to the reputation of the firm, and of the profession. Any lapse in professional behaviour could undermine the credibility of the investigator, especially when acting in the capacity of expert witness.

4 Gathering and evaluation of evidence

Forensic engagements are general conducted as 'agreed upon procedures' assignments and, as seen above, cover a wide variety of scenarios. The nature of the procedures are therefore entirely dependent upon the requirements of the client. However, the auditor can select from the normal variety of available procedures used in traditional audits.

With most fraud investigations the basic objectives of a forensic engagement include:

- identification of:
  - the type of fraud that has occurred;
  - how long it has been occurring for;
  - how the fraud was concealed;
  - the main suspects.
- quantification of the financial losses;
- gathering of evidence to support legal action/recovery of losses; and
- providing advice to prevent fraud.

The most common procedures include:

- enquiries/interviews of key staff, including the ultimate interview with the suspect/s;
- detailed inspections and analysis of documentary evidence;
- substantive procedures including reconciliations and cash counts;

- controls tests to identify weaknesses and, hence, opportunity to commit fraud;
- analytical procedures to compare trends over time or between business segments; and
- computer assisted audit techniques, for example to identify the timing and location of alterations.

To evaluate the results of procedures the forensic auditor can use a range of techniques including:

- recalculation of economic damages;
- regression and sensitivity analysis;
- summarising of large volumes of data;
- present value calculations;
- computerised analysis of large volumes of data; and
- charts/graphs to aid analysis/explanation.

5 The report

Once a forensic investigation is complete, the forensic accountant will write and submit a report of their findings.

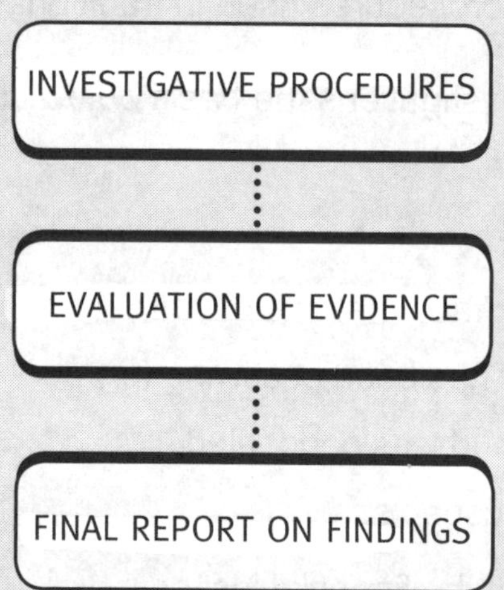

As an agreed upon procedures the most important factor of a forensic report is that the practitioner adequately addresses the requirements of the client, as established in the engagement letter.

A basic report will include:

- a summary of the procedures performed;
- a summary of the results of procedures;
- any limitations in the scope of the engagement; and
- a conclusion regarding the amount of any losses suffered.

It is also likely that the report will discuss how the fraudster set up the scheme, and which controls, if any, were circumvented. In addition, the reporting accounting may provide recommendations to improve the controls within the organisation to prevent any similar frauds occurring in the future.

It is possible that an investigation will lead to legal proceedings. If so it is important to note that the accountant's findings may be used as evidence and the accountant may be required to act as an expert witness.

Forensics: Exam Focus

Forensic investigation is a new area of the syllabus. To date there have been a number of questions on the topic:

- the Paper 7 pilot contained a 30 mark case style question based upon a forensic investigation ('Efex Engineering')
- the December 2007 paper contained 5 marks with regard to forensic audit; and
- the December 2008 paper contained a 26 mark compulsory case style question about a payroll fraud investigation ('Crocus').

In order to enhance understanding of this new topic Lisa Weaver has published an article entitled "Forensic Auditing" (September 2008). This can be downloaded from the P7 section of the ACCA website.

Test Your Understanding

Forensic Audit

(a) Define the following:

(i) Forensic accounting

(ii) Forensic investigations

(iii) Forensic audit

(3 marks)

(b) You have been asked by the management of The Marvellous Manufacturing Company to carry out an investigation into a suspected expenses fraud within the marketing department.

During a routine annual spend review, management noticed that the expenses budget for year ended 30 June 2007 of $300,000 had been exceeded by nearly $30,000, with no known increase in activity.

Required

(i) Set out the matters you would consider and procedures you would carry out in planning such an audit

(10 marks)

(ii) Identify the preliminary tests you might carry out to determine whether or not an expenses fraud has taken place.

(7 marks)

(Total: 20 marks)

6 Chapter summary

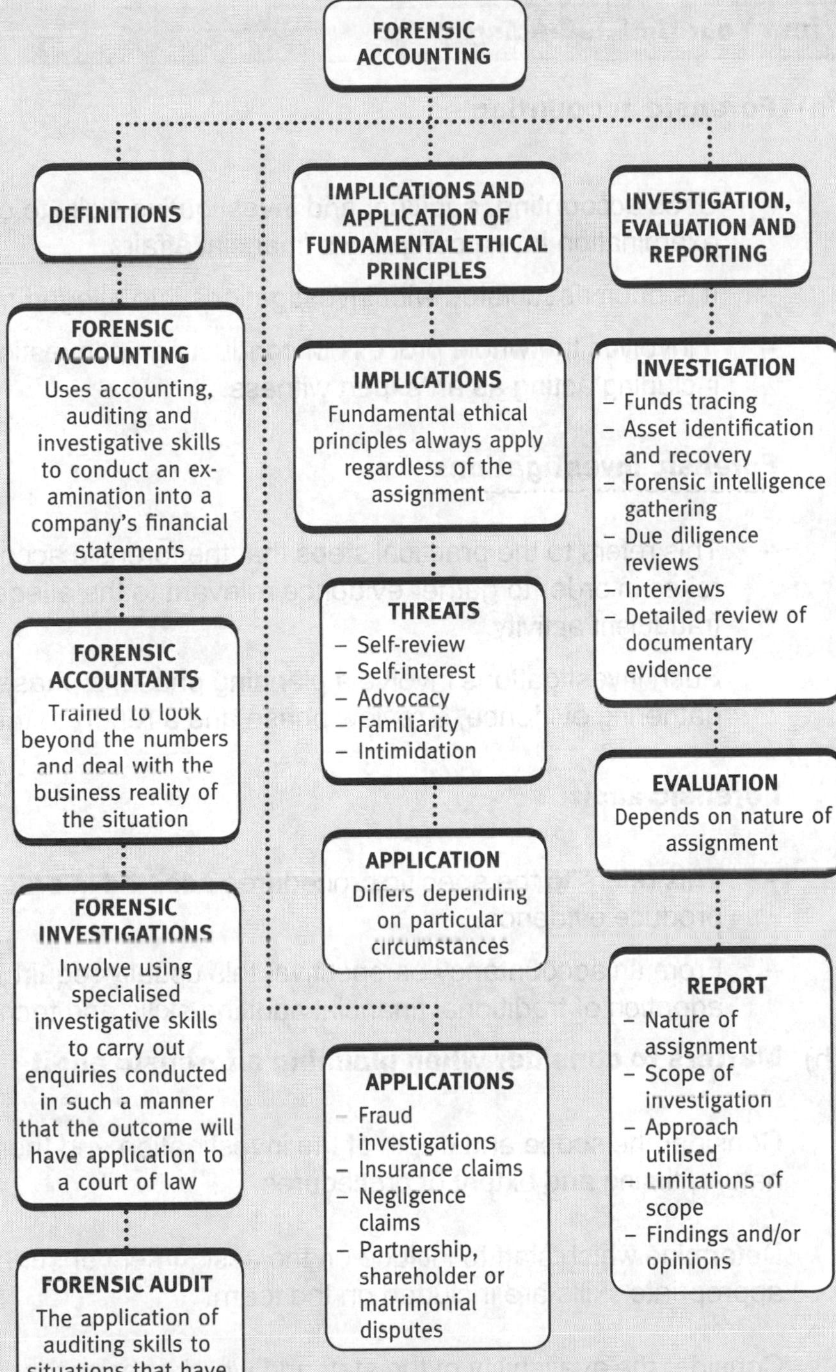

Test your understanding answers

Test Your Understanding

(a) **Forensic accounting**

- Uses accounting, auditing, and investigative skills to conduct an examination into a company's financial affairs.
- It is often associated with investigations into alleged fraud.
- It involves the whole process of conducting an investigation, including acting as an expert witness.

Forensic investigations

- This refers to the practical steps that the forensic accountant takes in order to gather evidence relevant to the alleged fraudulent activity.
- Such investigations involve a planning phase, a phase of gathering evidence, a review phase and a report to the client.

Forensic audit

- This refers to the specific procedures adopted in order to produce evidence.
- From an accountancy perspective, this usually requires the adoption of traditional financial auditing skills and techniques.

(b) **Matters to consider when planning a forensic audit**

Consider the scope and depth of the investigation and therefore the nature, timing and extent of procedures

Determine which staff to include on the assignment ensuring the appropriate skills are included on the team.

Consider the availability of the staff and whether any other work needs to be rescheduled and whether this is possible.

Prepare the budget for the assignment of hours, grades of staff and costs.

Calculate the fee for the assignment based on the budget.

Discuss with management why they believe the overspend is through fraudulent behaviour

Consider who the intended users of the report will be as this will affect risk and liability levels and therefore the amount of work undertaken.

Identify risk areas that would provide opportunities for fraud to take place e.g. lack of segregation of duties, poor control environment, etc

Develop an assignment plan that focuses on the areas where fraud could have taken place.

Ensure the team are fully briefed on the client and the assignment.

Preliminary tests to determine whether an expenses fraud has taken place

Obtain management accounts and perform analytical procedures to see if any other significant variances have occurred.

Speak with the marketing director to identify if there have been more trips required this year that could explain the reason for the increase.

Enquire if any new customers/contracts have been won in the year that might explain an increase in marketing expenses e.g. entertaining to win new business.

Enquire with the marketing director whether expenses are authorised and what the authority limits are.

Enquire if there has been any change in expenses policy that might explain the increase e.g. an increase in the standard of hotels used, meal allowances, etc.

Enquire when the spending increase was first identified and what measures were taken by the client to find reasons why.

Analyse expense claims by individual to try to identify who might be the culprit.

Analyse expenses by type to identify which category of expenses has seen the biggest rise. For example, if fuel costs the rise might be due to fuel price increases rather than fraud.

chapter

20

Internal audit

Chapter learning objectives

Upon completion of this chapter you will be able to:

- compare the objectives and principal characteristics of internal audit with other assurance engagements
- compare and contrast operational and compliance audits
- justify a suitable approach (e.g. cyclical compliance) to specified multi-site operations
- discuss outsourcing internal auditing services.

1 Internal audit and assurance engagements: how do they compare?

Definition

'Internal audit' is an appraisal activity established by management for the review of accounting and internal control systems as a service to the entity.

Internal audit activities

The function may perform many different activities, many of which might also be the focus of assurance engagements.

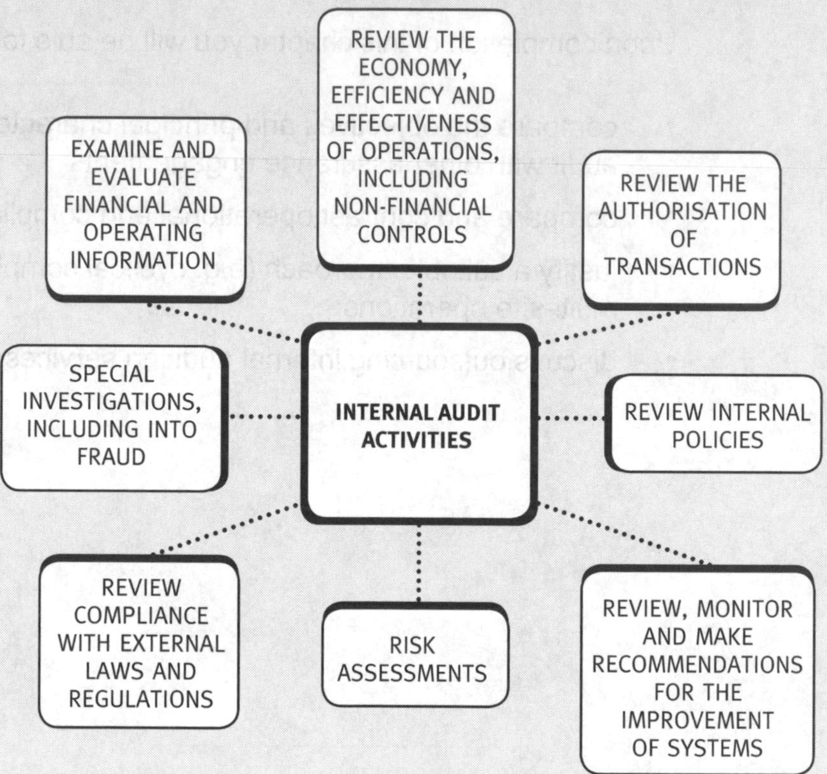

It should be noted that many of the activities performed by internal audit are similar to, or the same as, those activities discussed in chapter 17 'Assurance Services.' Risk assessment, benchmarking, value for money audits and e-commerce assessments are all important tools for internal performance analysis and decision making. These are also fundamental aspects of corporate governance and, therefore, the primary responsibility to perform these assessments rests with internal management.

Comparison of internal audit with assurance engagements

Internal audit has many similarities to assurance engagements that may be undertaken by a professional firm.

- Evaluation of an area against predetermined criteria.
- Conclusion required by end user.
- Carried out by party external to the area under review.
- Can be applied to many different areas of the business.

Differences between internal audit and other assurance engagements might include:

	Internal audit reviews	**Assurance engagements**
Objective	To add value and improve an organization's operation	To provide assurance on a particular area of business operations
Regularity	Ongoing, regular reviews	One-off/annual exercise
Scope	Flexible, as dictated by management	Focused on specific area. Audit dictated by statute.
Legal Basis	Recommended in UK by Turnbull report. Some industry specific guidance	Audit required in national law, e.g. Companies Act 2006
Reviewers	Internal team (unless function outsourced)	External experts
Output	Highlight areas of weakness, make recommendations for improvement	Assurance report
Intended audience	Management team and responsible parties	Shareholders, management or other intended recipient
Approach	Risk based	Risk based

Further Comparisons

Internal auditing

The institute of internal auditors defines internal auditing as: 'An independent, objective assurance and consulting activity designed to add value and improve an organization's operations. It helps an organization accomplish its objectives by bringing a systematic, disciplined approach to evaluate and improve the effectiveness of risk management, control, and governance processes.'

Assurance engagements

Those in which a practitioner expresses a conclusion designed to enhance the degree of confidence of the intended users other than the responsible party about the outcome of the evaluation of a subject matter against predetermined criteria.

For example, management may seek more information on other matters on which auditors can provide some assurance and thus credibility:

- performance measures
- internal controls
- systems reliability
- e-commerce assurance, etc.

2 Operational and compliance audits

Comparison

Two of the main types of work undertaken by an internal audit department can be categorized as operational or compliance audits.

	Operational	Compliance
Main focus	Effectiveness, operation, and adherence of business to internal controls	Compliance of business with external laws, rules, and regulations
Risk addressed	Failure of internal controls could lead to financial loss, operational inefficiency, etc. Ways to improve operational economy, efficiency and effectiveness.	Compliance failures could result in criminal penalties, fines and costs, executive time in defending actions, legal fees, investigations, bad publicity, etc.
Other areas of review	Ways to improve operational economy, efficiency and effectiveness.	Appropriateness of, and adherence with, internal processes and procedures supporting compliance Maintenance of documentation supporting compliance Management responsibilities

Specific Objectives of Operational and Compliance Audits

Questions that a business might seek to answer through internal audit are:

Operational audits

- what are the operational risks within the business?
- are sufficient internal controls in place to ensure operational risks are minimized?
- are the internal controls in place being adhered to?
- do the existing internal controls perform as intended?
- have there been any changes to operations that impact on internal control requirements?
- are there any control weaknesses that need to be addressed?
- are there any improvements to operational efficiency, economy, or effectiveness that have been identified?

Compliance audits

- what laws, rules, and regulations apply to the business?
- what are the potential penalties for non-compliance?
- what processes and procedures do we have in place to ensure compliance?
- are the processes and procedures sufficient to ensure compliance?
- is the business following the processes and procedures?
- is the business compliant?

Multi-site operations and internal audit

Many companies today have branches, subsidiaries, and multiple sites on a global basis. Such companies find internal audit is an essential tool for effective management.

The problem for internal audit departments in such situations is how to be in many places at once. The solution may be as follows:

Option	Good for	Why not?
Regular visits to each location	• Small number of locations • Locations sited close together • Large audit teams • Coverage	• Regularly visiting geographically disparate sites: • Will require large numbers of staff • Expensive? • Can be difficult to co-ordinate
Random or surprise visits to each location	• As above (still visiting all locations) • Seeing how operations really work	• As above • View that internal audit are 'checking up' might harm relations and limit co-operation
Cyclical visits to each location such that each location is visited over a small number of years	• Achieving complete coverage of a large number of locations • Small audit teams compared with number of locations	• Not all locations visited every year • If intervals between visits are too long, issues can be missed • No consideration of size/complexity of locations • Requires long- term planning

Weighting the visits so that more frequent visits are paid to large locations and problem locations	• Making the most efficient use of time: risk focus! • Planning and co-ordination • Good audit team vs. location ratio • Businesses with many locations	• Full coverage not achieved on a regular basis • Problems at small locations may not be identified on a timely basis
Maintaining internal audit presence in all locations or in the larger or main regional centres	• Coverage of all areas • Visible presence may encourage 'good' behaviors • Large audit teams	• Expensive!

3 Outsourcing

Many companies now outsource their internal audit work to a professional firm, whose experience of different company systems and procedures provides added benefit to the client.

The advantages of outsourcing internal audit

- Professional firms are independent of the client.
- Professional firms should have qualified staff who receive regular development.
- Professional firms can be employed on a flexible basis, i.e. when they are required, whereas internal audit departments cannot easily be expanded or contracted.
- Professional firms are responsible for their activities and hold insurance.
- Professional firms follow an ethical code of conduct.
- Professional firms should not be coerced by management.
- The flexibility and expertise of a professional firm may prove more cost effective.

The disadvantages of outsourcing internal audit

- Professional firms cannot have the intimate knowledge that internal audit will have.
- Engagements with professional firms are constrained by contractual terms and cannot be instructed as flexibly as internal employees.
- Professional fees tend to be high.

4 Chapter summary

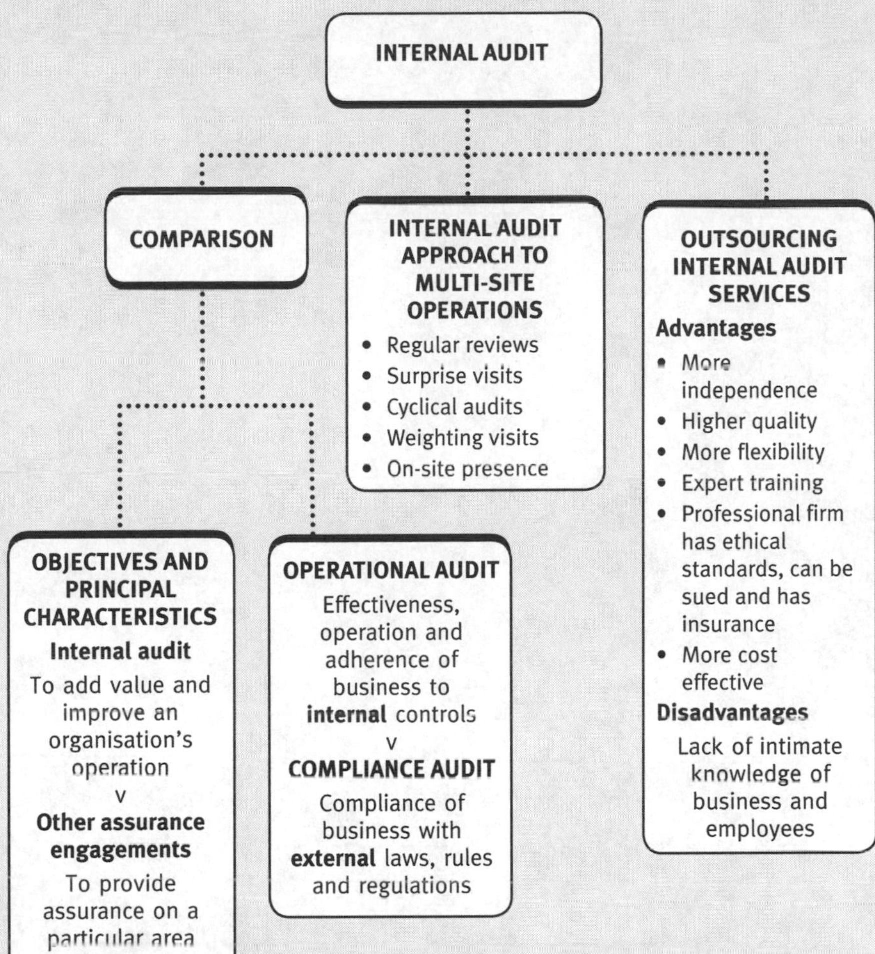

hapter

21

Outsourcing

Chapter learning objectives

Upon completion of this chapter you will be able to:

- explain the different approaches to 'outsourcing' and compare with 'insourcing'
- discuss and conclude on the advantages and disadvantages of outsourcing finance and accounting functions including:
  - data (transaction) processing
  - pensions
  - information technology (IT)
  - internal auditing
  - due diligence work
  - taxation services
- recognize and evaluate the impact of outsourced functions on the conduct of an audit.

1 What is 'outsourcing'?

- Outsourcing means using outside specialist organizations to perform functions that would otherwise be performed 'in-house.'
- The opposite of outsourcing is 'insourcing,' where a business performs a service in-house.

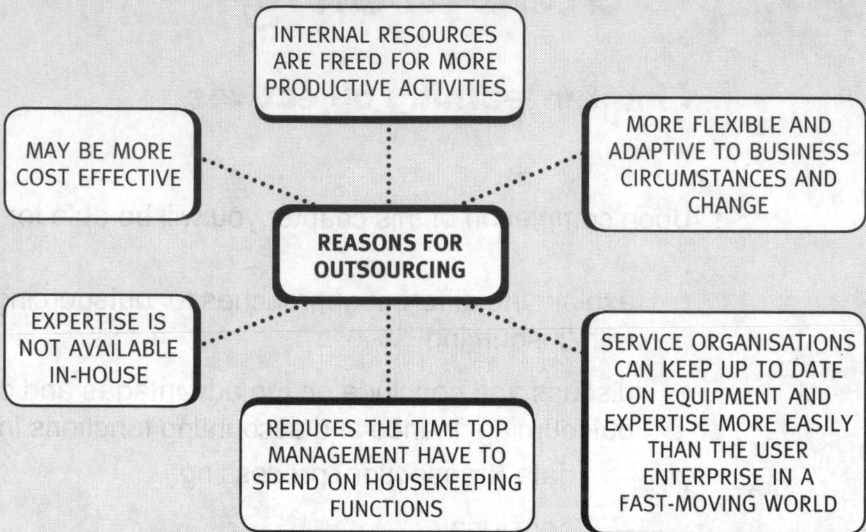

2 Outsourcing – advantages and disadvantages

Certain areas of finance and accounting are some of the most widely outsourced functions within the business community.

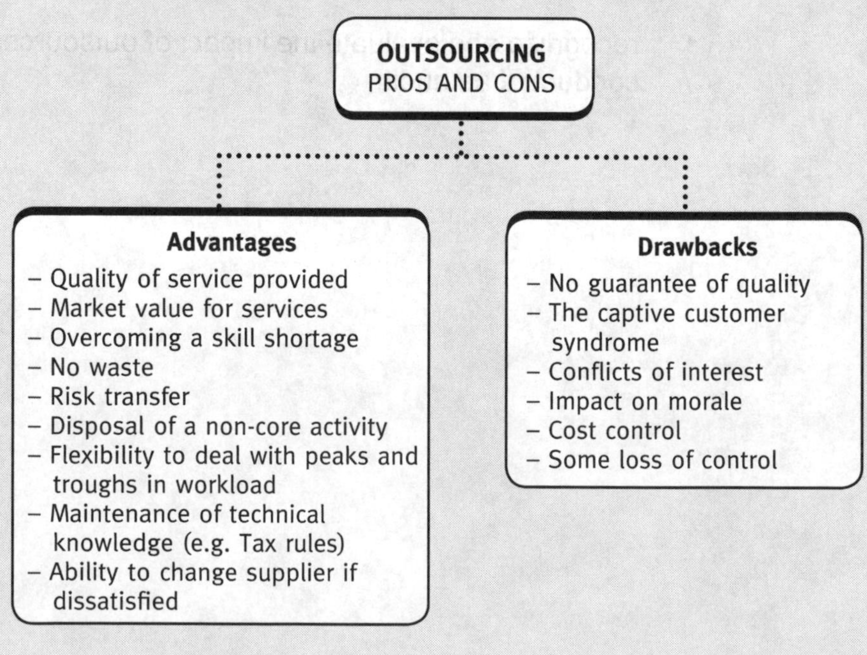

Reasons for selecting a particular area for outsourcing include:

- Area of the business is entirely objective in nature, therefore no judgment or knowledge of the business required e.g. monthly processing of payroll
- Largely transactional in nature – just 'turning the handle.' e.g. invoice processing and debt collection
- Requires specialist knowledge that is difficult or expensive to maintain in-house e.g. internal audit function
- Infrequent, but necessary, business exercises where maintaining an in-house team would prove expensive and inefficient e.g. due diligence

Examples

Common examples of outsourcing arrangements include:

- Data processing
  - Company advises external service organization of the transactions it has undertaken (e.g. sales made).
  - Service organization operates a transaction processing system on the company's behalf, raising invoices, etc. for the company.
- Pensions
  - Many businesses offer a pension scheme to their employees.
  - Rather than employ pension specialists in a human resources department, many companies will select an external pension scheme provider and advise employees to join that provider's scheme if they wish.
- Information technology
  - As an extension of outsourcing the transaction processing, a company could outsource the entire IT function.
  - This would allow the company access to all the latest technological advances without having to buy the hardware itself.
  - Would also provide expertise to deal with one-off projects, such as systems implementation or software upgrades.
- Internal auditing
  - Rather than setting up its own internal audit department, a company could buy in the service from an external provider such as a firm of accountants.

- Due diligence work
  - A Stock Exchange will typically require listed companies to obtain due diligence (special investigations undertaken by professional firms) assurance when they are considering large transactions, e.g. buying another company.
  - This is specialist work where the necessary high level of expertise can be bought in from an external provider.
  - Additional benefits are increased independence and objectivity, professional cachet and indemnity for negligence.
- Tax management
  - Main benefit would be the availability of skilled expertise without having to pay the ongoing employment costs for such an individual.

3 Impact of outsourcing on audit practice

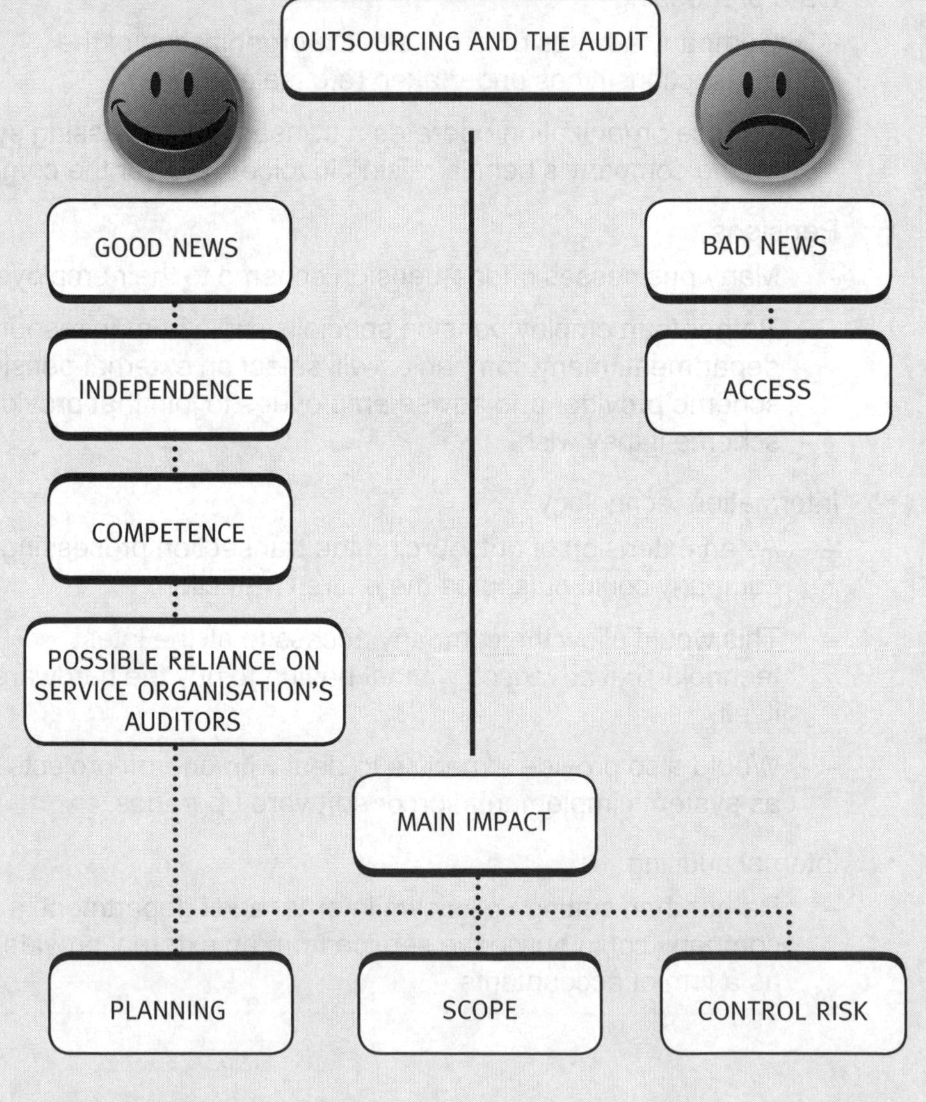

Discussion of the 'Good News'

- Independence – because the service organization is external to the client, the audit evidence derived from it is regarded as being more reliable than evidence generated internally by the client.
- Competence – because the service organization is in business to provide the services it provides, it may be more competent in executing its role than the client's internal department.
- Possible reliance on the service organization's auditors – it may be possible for the client's auditors to confirm balances directly with the service organization's auditors.

Discussion of the 'Bad News'

The main disadvantage of outsourced services from the auditor's point of view concerns access to records and information.

Auditors generally have statutory rights of access to the client's records and to receive answers and explanations that they consider necessary to enable them to form their opinion.

They do not have such rights over records and information held by a third party such as a service organization.

Test your understanding 1

Your client uses a payroll bureau to operate its payroll. Describe the benefits this may have in the auditors assessment of inherent and control risk. What potential additional risks or pitfalls does this arrangement present to the auditor?

Main impact on the audit

Planning

The service organization is an additional element to be taken into account when planning the audit and may require:

- confirmation letters to be arranged
- visits to the service organization's offices to be organized.

Scope

If access to records and other information is denied by the service organization, this may impose a limitation on the scope of the auditor's work. This may lead to the auditor being unable to gather sufficient appropriate evidence, which in turn could result in a modified audit report.

Control risk

The use of a service organization may well result in reduced control risk, and a reduction in the amount of detailed substantive testing required.

ISA 402 Audit Considerations Relating to an Entity Using a

ISA 402 provides guidance to auditors on the audit impact of outsourcing.

Use of service organisations

The auditor should identify whether the client uses service organizations and assess the effect of such use on the procedures necessary to obtain sufficient appropriate audit evidence to determine with reasonable assurance whether the user's financial statements are free from mis-statement.

Procedures

The auditor should, as always, obtain a knowledge and understanding of the client's business. They should consider how an entity's use of a service organization affects the entity's internal control so as to identify and assess the risk of material misstatement and to design and perform further audit procedures. Specifically they should perform the following procedures:

- Obtain a Type 2 report, if available. This is a report on the description, design and operating effectiveness of controls at the service organisation. It contains a report prepared by management of the service organisation and a reasonable assurance report by the service auditor;
- Perform tests of control at the service organisation;
- Use another auditor to perform tests of control at the service organisation on their behalf.

If the auditor intends to use a report from a service auditor they should perform procedures to ensure they are satisfied with the competence and independence of the service auditor and that the service auditor's report provides sufficient appropriate evidence about the effectiveness of controls.

Contractual terms

The auditor should obtain and document an understanding of:

- the contractual terms that apply to the relevant activities;
- the way the user monitors those activities so as to ensure that it meets is fiduciary duty.

Relevant points here include the following:

- right of access to records held by the outsourcer;
- whether the terms take proper account of statutory requirements (e.g. proper accounting records) or regulatory body requirements;
- performance standards; and
- the extent of reliance on controls operated by the service organisation.

Lack of access to records may mean that the auditor has to qualify their report on the grounds of limitation of scope.

Inherent risk

The auditor should determine the effect on their assessment of inherent and control risk. The following issues should be considered.

- The reputation of the service organization.
- The existence of external supervision.
- The extent to which indemnities offered by the outsourcer can be honoured.

Control risk

The auditor should consider the following issues:

- the extent of controls operated by service provider
- the experience of errors and omissions
- the degree of monitoring by the user
- the extent of information on controls provided by the outsourcer
- the quality assurance in the outsourcer, e.g. ISOs or internal audit.

Audit procedures

The auditor must:

- assess the sufficiency and appropriateness of audit evidence
- assess the quality and quantity of audit evidence available.

Accounting records

If accounting records are kept by a service organization then the auditor has to assess whether the records comply with relevant law and regulations.

The requirements of statutes and of regulatory authorities are relevant here. The auditor specifically has to have evidence that proper accounting records have been maintained.

Audit evidence

The auditor needs to assess whether sufficient appropriate audit evidence concerning the relevant financial statements assertions is available from the records held at the user, or whether effective procedures for obtaining evidence necessary for the audit can be obtained directly from the service organization or their auditors.

Exam Focus – Other Engagements: 'Thomas Trends'

Please note that with questions of this nature there is usually a more straight forward element coupled with a tougher, more scenario specific, element. Simpler questions tend to focus on definitions, pros and cons and common sense discussions. The more scenario specific question usually focuses on issues you would consider during a planning meeting, what evidence you would gather during the engagement and what the impact on your report might be.

You are a partner of Finbar & Sons, a firm of accountants. You have been approached by a potential client, Thomas Trends Ltd. They recently notified you of their intention to outsource their internal audit function. The company operates a small, high street based, chain of clothes outlets.

They set up the internal audit department some years ago based on advice given them by their external auditors, Suckit & Sea. However, given that most employees use internal audit as a springboard to management positions, the staff turnover is high and the FD believes it may be more effective to use an external provider of this service.

They are interested in some form of evaluation of organisational risks, financial compliance, IT systems and fraud risks. He has asked you if you would be interested in offering this service and, with this in mind, has set up a breakfast meeting with you to discuss the role.

Required:

(a) **Briefly describe the advantages and disadvantages of outsourcing an accounting function.**

(6 marks)

(b) **Describe the principal matters relating to the assignment to be discussed during you meeting with the FD of Thomas Trends Ltd.**

(10 marks)

4 Chapter summary

OUTSOURCING

DEFINITION AND APPROACHES

OUTSOURCING
Using outside organisations to perform functions that would otherwise be performed 'in-house'

INSOURCING
Where a business performs a service in-house

REASONS FOR OUTSOURCING
- Internal resources are freed for more productive activities
- Reduces time top management spend on housekeeping functions
- Service organisations keep up to date on equipment and expertise
- Expertise not available in-house
- More flexible and adaptive to business circumstances and change
- May be more cost effective

IMPACT ON CONDUCT OF AN AUDIT

THINGS TO CONSIDER
- Planning and audit procedures
- Inherent risk and user entity's control environment
- Sufficient appropriate audit evidence available

ADVANTAGES AND DRAWBACKS

ADVANTAGES
- Quality of service provided
- Market value for services
- Overcoming a skill shortage
- No waste
- Risk transfer
- Disposal of a non-core activity

DRAWBACKS
- No guarantee of quality
- The captive customer
- Conflicts of interest
- Impact on morale
- Cost control

Test your understanding answers

Test your understanding 1

The auditors may also decide that:

- inherent risk in this area is reduced, because of the service organization's experience and competence
- control risk is also reduced because of the independence of the service organization.

Possible pitfalls

- Independence may not be all it seems if the client's business represents a major contract to the service organization.
- Similarly, it may not always be safe to assume competence on the part of the service organization. There may be a possibility that the organization may give misleading responses to the auditors' enquiries to cover up its own failures.

Exam Focus – Other Engagements: 'Thomas Trends'

(a) **Advantages**

There should be some form of time or cost efficiency made when outsourcing a previously 'in-house' function.

An outsourced internal audit function may improve controls in the eyes of the external auditors, thus reducing the need for substantive testing.

Reduce turnover of staff for Thomas Trends and improve continuity – and perhaps morale – of human resource.

An external source should provide a wider range of industry knowledge. They will also provide an independent perspective. This should lead to recommendations that improve internal procedures. Outsourcing should provide more flexibility in terms of access to experienced staff at all times throughout the year, even busy periods.

The outsourced firm will be technically up to date and will therefore be able to update management about changes in financial reporting requirements.

Management will be able to focus on core competencies.

Disadvantages

Loss of 'springboard' for junior managers trying to work their way in to more senior managerial positions. Future "stars" will have to be identified and trained in other ways.

Over time the outsourced function may increase their charges if they perceive the company is becoming reliant on their expertise.

Whilst the outsourced company may have relevant industry knowledge they will lack understanding of Thomas Trends' internal processes and policies. This issue will be further exaggerated if the audit team used by the outsourced company changes each year.

The outsourced audit staff will not have any allegiance to the Thomas Trends. Therefore the management of Thomas Trends may not buy into any suggestions made as readily.

(b) **Principle Matters to be discussed**

Firstly you would introduce your firm, including details of the functions undertaken, the office locations and the experience of the internal audit department and its partners. You would discuss which office would be responsible for providing the services and who the main points of contact would be.

You would incorporate a discussion of how Finbar & Sons services relate to the specific functions requested, namely: organisational risk analysis; financial compliance; IT systems analysis; and fraud risk analysis.

You would discuss Finbar & Sons' approach to assessing the needs for audit and the approach involved. For example:

- Preliminary – review of business and industry characteristics;
- Planning – needs analysis and co-ordination with external auditors;
- Post audit – assurance that activities were effectively executed;
- Review – of services provided, reports and management's responses.

You would discuss the tools/methods adopted for internal audit tasks. Most importantly you would discuss the use of any computer aided audit techniques, namely embedded audit software.

The installation of embedded audit software could require some training for the staff/management of Thomas Trends. You would discuss the provision of any training services offered.

You might discuss any insurance taken out covering, for example, public liability and professional indemnity.

You would probably discuss how your firm ensures quality, namely through the use of the standards you follow (such as the Institute of Internal Auditors).

You might provide sample report templates to help Thomas Trends understand the nature of the reports they will receive in return. Examples might include: risk analysis reports and reports to the audit committee.

You might offer a list of current clients who you provide internal audit services to so that Thomas Trends can take up references if they so wish.

Although Thomas Trends is not an audit client you would discuss any potential conflicts of interest. An important area would be identifying any possible competitors to Thomas Trends that are also clients.

You would also have to discuss fee levels. You would identify the charge out rates for different levels of staff and the firms policy with regard to recharging travel and others expenses. You would give an indication of possible future increases (e.g. inflationary) and invoicing/credit terms offered, e.g. payable on demand or 30 days credit.

Finally you would discuss performance targets to be bet, such as deadlines for completing fieldwork and submission dates for the various reports.

chapter

22

Financial reporting revision

Chapter learning objectives

This chapter is designed to assist you with revision of key financial reporting topics. Given the inter-relationship between financial reporting and auditing it is inevitable that the auditing exam will encompass many aspects of financial reporting that you have encountered in previous studies.

For further clarification with regard to the importance of financial reporting standards please refer to Lisa Weaver's article entitled "The Importance of Financial Reporting Standards to Auditors" (Nov 2008).

This can be found on the P7 section of the ACCA website.

IAS 1 Presentation of Financial Statements

IAS 1 provides standard formats for the Statement of Comprehensive Income, Statement of Financial Position, Statement of Cash Flows and Statement of Changes in Equity as well as setting out six overall accounting principles that should be applied:

- going concern
- accruals
- consistency of presentation
- materiality and aggregation
- offsetting
- comparative information.

Accounting policies should be selected so that the financial statements comply with all international standards and interpretations.

An entity must make an explicit statement in the notes to the accounts that the financial statements comply with IFRS.

IAS 2 Inventories

IAS 2 Inventory valuation requires that inventories should be valued at the lower of cost and net realisable value.

At this level, the examiner might be more interested in your ability to determine cost in a complex case than to be able to describe the rules.

Cost includes all of the costs associated with bringing items of inventory to their present condition and location.

Cost includes:

- purchase price including import duties, transport and handling costs
- any other directly attributable costs, less
- trade discounts, rebates and subsidies
- costs which are specifically attributable to units of production, e.g. direct labour,
- direct expenses and subcontracted work
- production overheads (which must be based on the normal level of activity)

- other overheads, if any, attributable in the particular circumstances of the business to bringing the product or service to its present location and condition.

Cost excludes:

- abnormal waste
- storage costs
- administrative overheads which do not contribute to bringing inventories to their present location and condition
- selling costs.

Some businesses can identify individual units of inventory (e.g. vehicles can be identified by a chassis number). Those that cannot should keep track of costs using either the first in, first out (FIFO) or the weighted average cost (AVCO) assumption.

The main disclosure requirements of IAS 2 are:

- accounting policy adopted, including the
- cost formula used
- total carrying amount, classified appropriately
- amount of inventories carried at NRV
- amount of inventories recognised as an expense during the period
- details of any circumstances that have led to the write-down of inventories to their NRV.

IAS 7 Statement of Cash flows

The statement of cash flows provides an important insight into the ways in which the entity has created and applied cash during the period. The fact that a business generated profit during a period means that it has created wealth, but wealth is not necessarily reflected by cash. The fact that a business is liquid according to the Statement of Financial Position at the year-end does not say a great deal about the cash movements that occurred during the year.

IAS 7 requires the provision of a statement of cash flows that classifies cash flows into:

- operating activities
- investing activities
- financing activities

This approach to calculating cash generated from operations is known as the "indirect method". It starts with profit before tax from the income statement and:

- adjusts for interest to get back to profit from operations
- adjusts for non-cash items such as depreciation
- adjusts for increases and decreases in working capital.

It is possible to get the same result by means of the 'direct method', which states the actual cash flows associated with operations:

- cash received from customers
- cash paid to suppliers
- cash paid for expenses
- cash paid for wages and salaries.

This approach works equally well to the other operating figures.

The balancing figure approach can also be invaluable in obtaining figures for any of the other cash flows under other headings (transactions involving non-current assets, tax paid, etc).

Interpreting statements of cash flow

The statement of cash flows is a vital supplement to the other statements.

Arguably, there is no point in a business existing if it cannot produce an adequate profit. However, cash can be more important in the short term because a business that runs short of cash could fail even if it has the capacity to generate profits and even return to a cash surplus in the longer term.

The statement provides another dimension to the liquidity position spelt out in the Statement of Financial Position.

IAS 8 Accounting policies, changes in ....

.... accounting estimates and errors.

IAS 8 is an important standard because it clarifies the accounting treatment of a variety of accounting issues, including:

- selection of accounting policies
- changes in accounting policies
- changes in accounting estimates
- correction of prior period errors.

Accounting policies

Accounting policies are the principles, bases, conventions, rules and practices applied by an entity which specify how the effects of transactions and other events are reflected in the financial statements.

IAS 8 requires an enterprise to select and apply appropriate accounting policies complying with International Financial Reporting Standards (IFRSs) and Interpretations to ensure that the financial statements provide information that is:

- relevant to the decision-making needs of users
- reliable in that they:
  - represent faithfully the results and financial position of the enterprise
  - reflect the economic substance of events and transactions and not merely the legal form
  - are neutral, i.e. free from bias
  - are prudent
  - are complete in all material respects.

Changes in accounting policies

Changes in accounting policies are rare. However, on occasions changes in policy are enforced due to changes/updates to financial reporting standards. It can be difficult to introduce these into a question. Take care not to treat a simple change in an estimate as a rather more complicated change in accounting policy.

Accounting policies should remain the same from period to period in order to allow for consistency of treatment.

In order to preserve the appearance of consistency, a change in accounting policies is accounted for as follows: the new policy will be applied retrospectively, with the opening balance on retained earnings recalculated on the basis that the new policy had always been in force the resulting change in the retained earnings brought forward will be shown as a prior period adjustment in the statement of changes in equity comparatives will be restated as if the new policy had been in force during the previous period.

The change and its effects must be described in the notes to the accounts.

Accounting estimates

Many of the figures in the financial statements rely on estimates.

Inevitably, some estimates will be revised in the light of unfolding events and new information.

Changes in accounting estimates are recognised in the income statement in the same period as the change occurs and included under the same classification as for the original asset. If the change is material then it should be disclosed in the notes to the financial statements.

Prior period errors

Prior period errors are omissions from, and misstatements in, the financial statements for one or more prior periods arising from a failure to use, or misuse of, reliable information. The errors must be ones that were reasonably identifiable when the financial statements were authorised for issue.

Prior period errors are dealt with by:

- restating the opening balance of assets, liabilities and equity as if the error had never occurred, and presenting the necessary adjustment to the opening balance of retained earnings in the statement of changes in equity
- restating the comparative figures presented, as if the error had never occurred.

These adjustments should be disclosed in full in the notes to the accounts.

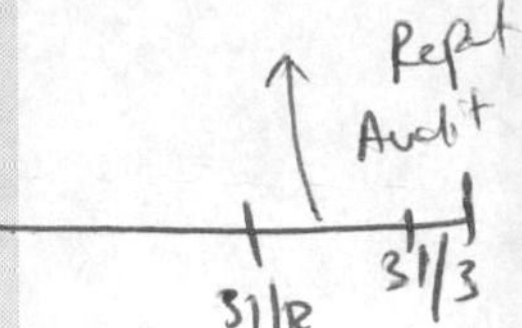

IAS 10 Events after the Reporting Period

- Events after the Reporting Period are those events, favourable and unfavourable, that occur between the Statement of Financial Position date and the date when the financial statements are authorised for issue.
- Adjusting events after the Reporting Period are those that provide evidence of conditions that existed at the Statement of Financial Position date.
- Non-adjusting events after the Reporting Period are those that are indicative of conditions that arose after the Reporting Period.

Accounting treatment

- Adjusting events affect the amounts stated in the financial statements so they must be adjusted.
- Non-adjusting events do not concern the position at the Statement of Financial Position date so the accounts are not adjusted. If the event is material then the nature and its financial effect must be disclosed.

Examples of adjusting events

- The sale of inventory after the date which gives evidence about the inventory's net realisable value at the date.
- The bankruptcy of a customer after the date that confirms that a provision is required against a receivable balance at the date.
- The discovery of fraud or errors that show that the financial statements are incorrect.
- The settlement after the Reporting Period of a court case that confirms that the entity had a present obligation at the Statement of Financial Position date. This would require a provision to be recognised in the financial statements (or an existing provision to be adjusted).

Examples of non-adjusting events that would require disclosure

- A major business combination after the date or disposing of a major subsidiary.
- Announcing a plan to discontinue an operation.
- Major purchases and disposals of assets.
- Destruction of a major production plant by a fire after the date.
- Announcing or commencing a major restructuring.
- Abnormally large changes after the date in asset prices or foreign exchange rates.

Dividends

- Ordinary dividends declared after the date are not recognised as liabilities at the date.
- If the liability did not exist at the date, then it cannot be recognised.
- This is consistent with IAS 37 and the definition of a liability in the Framework.

IAS 11 Construction contracts

IAS 11 Construction contracts deals with the recognition of revenues and balances associated with long-term projects carried out for clients.

The logic behind IAS 11 is that long term contracts are deemed to be "sold" to clients throughout the course of each contract.

If, say, 75% of a potentially profitable contract has been completed to date then 75% of the profit anticipated on that contract should have been recognised during the income statement(s) covering the period(s) since work on the contract commenced.

Cumulative revenues and costs that have already been recognised are deducted from the total as at the year end to give the revenue and cost for the year.

Any expected losses on contracts should be recognised as expenses immediately.

Contract revenue comprises:

- the initial revenue agreed with the client
- any additional variations or claims that are probably going to result in revenue and that can be measured reliably

Contract costs comprise:

- costs that relate directly to the specific contract
- costs that are attributable to contract activity in general and can be allocated to the contract
- such other costs as are specifically chargeable to the customer under the terms of the contract.

The statement of Financial Position will include the gross amount due from/to customers as an asset/ liability. This can be determined as:

	$
Costs incurred	X
Add: recognised profit	X
Less: recognised losses	(X)
Less: progress billings	(X)
Gross amount due to/from customers	X

Any unpaid progress billings will be treated as trade receivables.

IAS 12 Income taxes

- IAS 12 covers both current and deferred tax, but deferred tax is the most examinable and will be reviewed here.
- Temporary differences are differences between the carrying amount of an asset or liability in the Statement of Financial Position and its tax base.
- Tax base is the amount attributed to an asset or liability for tax purposes.

Temporary differences can be either:

(i) taxable temporary differences, when the carrying amount of an asset exceeds its tax base and deferred tax must be provided for.

(ii) deductible temporary differences, when the tax base of an asset exceeds the carrying value of that asset.

Sources of taxable temporary differences

- Interest revenue received in arrears, which is accounted for on an accruals basis in the income statement but taxable on a cash basis.
- Deferred tax is the estimated tax payable in future periods in respect of taxable temporary differences.
- Depreciation of an asset is accelerated for tax purposes.
- Development costs that were capitalised and amortised in the accounts, but deducted as incurred for tax purposes.
- Non current assets are revalued upwards for accounting purposes but no adjustment was made for tax purposes.

- Pension liabilities that are recognised in the financial statements but only allowable for tax when the contributions are made to the scheme in the future
- Losses in the income statement where tax relief is only available against future profits.
- Short term timing differences where amounts are included in the income statement on an accruals basis but only allowed for tax on a cash basis (e.g. royalty income)
- Intra-group profits in inventory that are unrealised for consolidation purposes but taxable in the individual company that made the unrealised profit.
- A revaluation surplus on non-current assets as the carrying value of the asset increases but the tax base of the asset has not changed. Deferred tax is provided on the revaluation.

Sources of deductible temporary differences

- Accumulated depreciation of an asset in the Statement of Financial Position is greater than the cumulative depreciation for tax purposes
- Research expenses are recognised as an expense in determining accounting profit but not deductible for tax until a later period
- Income is deferred in the Statement of Financial Position but has already been included in taxable profit.

Other points

- Unremitted earnings of group companies: a temporary difference arises when the carrying value of subsidiaries, associates and investments is different from the tax base. The accounting base for subsidiaries and associates will be based on net assets value, whilst the tax base will be cost of investment. A deferred tax liability should be recognised unless the investor can control the timing of the reversal of the temporary difference or it is probable that the temporary difference will not reverse. As an associate is not controlled, a deferred tax liability should be recognised. It would be unlikely that deferred tax would be recognised for a subsidiary. A trade investment would only give rise to deferred tax if it was revalued.
- Business combinations: temporary differences can arise on acquisition if assets or liabilities are increased to fair value but the tax base of the asset remains at cost. Deferred tax is recognised on these differences and is included as part of net assets acquired. The exception is for non tax-deductible goodwill.

Accounting treatment

- IAS 12 requires full provision for all taxable temporary differences (except for goodwill) using the Statement of Financial Position liability method.
- Deferred tax assets can be recognised for all deductible temporary differences to the extent it is probable that taxable profits will be available for these differences to be utilised.
- IAS 12 does not permit the discounting of deferred tax liabilities.
- The charge for deferred tax is recognised in the income statement account unless it relates to a gain or loss that has been recognised in equity e.g. revaluations, in which case the deferred tax is also recognised in equity.
- Deferred tax should be measured at the rates expected to be in force when the temporary differences reverse, although usually the current tax rate is used.

IAS 16 Property, plant and equipment

An asset's cost is its purchase price, less any trade discounts or rebates, plus any further costs directly attributable to bringing it into working condition for its intended use.

- IAS 23 Borrowing costs (revised 2007) requires finance costs to be capitalised providing they are directly attributable to the asset being constructed. Capitalisation commences when construction expenditure is being incurred and ceases when the asset is ready for use.
- Subsequent expenditure on non current assets may be capitalised if it:
  - enhances the economic benefits of the asset e.g. adding an new wing to a building
  - replaces part of an asset that has been separately depreciated and has been fully depreciated; e.g. furnace that requires new linings periodically
  - replaces economic benefits previously consumed, e.g. a major inspection of aircraft.
- The aim of depreciation is to spread the cost of the asset over its life in the business.
- The depreciation method and useful life of an asset should be reviewed at the end of each year and revised where necessary in accordance with IAS 8. This is not a change in accounting policy.

- If an asset has parts with different lives, (e.g. a building with a flat roof), the component parts of the asset should be capitalised and depreciated separately. It is not acceptable to provide for the cost of replacing the asset.

Revaluation of tangible non-current assets

- Revaluation of non-current assets is optional.
- If one asset is revalued, all assets in that class must be revalued, i.e. no cherry-picking.
- Where an entity adopts a policy of revaluation it need not be applied to all classes of tangible non-current assets held by the entity
- Valuations should be kept up to date to ensure that the carrying amount does not differ materially from the fair value at each Statement of Financial Position date.
- Revaluation gains are credited to the revaluation reserve in equity unless the gain reverses a previous revaluation loss of the same asset previously recognised in the income statement.
- Revaluation losses are debited to the income statement unless the loss relates to a previous revaluation surplus, in which case the decrease should be debited to the revaluation reserve to the extent of any credit balance existing in the revaluation reserve relating to that asset.

Accounting for revaluations

Steps:

(1) Restate asset from Dr Non-current cost to valuation. asset cost (valuation – cost)

(2) Remove any existing Dr Accumulated depreciation provision. depreciation

(3) Include increase in Cr Revaluation carrying value in reserve (valuation revaluation reserve. – old carrying value)

Depreciation is charged on the revalued amount less residual value (if any) over the **remaining useful life** of the asset.

A **reserves transfer** of the **excess depreciation** is taken from the revaluation reserve to retained earnings annually and disclosed in the Statement of Changes in Equity.

Note that assets **held for sale** are recognised at fair value less costs to sell in accordance with IFRS 5.

IAS 17 Leases

IAS 17 Leases deals with a complicated area that was frequently used to disguise liabilities in the Statement of Financial Position.

The point of IAS 17 is to identify those leases that are effectively financial instruments used to acquire the rights and benefits associated with a particular asset. These are then classified as liabilities in the Statement of Financial Position.

Not all leases have to be treated in this way. Some leases do not give the lessee the rights and benefits of ownership (e.g. when a business hires a van for a week).

A **finance lease** is a lease that transfers substantially all the risks and rewards incidental to ownership of an asset to the lessee.

An **operating lease** is any lease other than a finance lease.

Questions incorporating Leases will ask you to explain why a particular agreement should be treated as a finance lease or an operating lease.

The question will imply one or the other in terms of whether the lessee has the risks and rewards of ownership.

In general, a lease is a finance lease if:

- the leased asset is likely to become the property of the lessee at the end of the agreement (either automatically or because there is an option that is likely to be exercised)
- the lease (including any secondary term that is likely to be taken up) is likely to run for most of the asset's useful life
- the present value of the minimum lease payments is close to the fair value of the asset at the commencement of the lease
- the asset is of a specialised nature that makes it particularly suited to the lessee.

This list is not intended to be exhaustive.

Substance over form

The treatment required by IAS 17 effectively accounts for the economic substance of finance leases rather than their legal form.

The economic substance is that the lessee has borrowed an amount equivalent to the fair value of the asset and used that sum to purchase the asset itself. The fact that the lessee may never become the legal owner of the asset is ignored.

Accounting for finance leases

At the start of the lease:

- the fair value (or, if lower, the present value of the minimum lease payments) should be included as a non-current asset, subject to depreciation
- the same amount (being the obligation to pay rentals) should be included as a loan, i.e. a liability.

In practice, the fair value of the asset or its cash price will often be a sufficiently close approximation to the present value of the minimum lease payments and therefore can be used instead.

The asset is depreciated over the shorter of the asset's useful life and the term of the lease (including any secondary term that is likely to be taken up).

Each lease payment is split between:

- a repayment of the lease liability
- a finance charge.

IAS 18 Revenue recognition

Provides detailed guidance on accounting for revenue.

Revenue is the gross inflow of economic benefits during the period arising from the ordinary activities of the entity.

Recognition

- Revenue from the sale of goods can be recognised when the seller transfers the risks and rewards of ownership to the buyer.

- Revenue from the rendering of services is recognised by reference to the stage of completion at the Statement of Financial Position date.
- In both cases above, the amount of revenue and costs incurred must able to be measured reliably and it is probable that economic benefits will flow to the entity as seller.
- Revenue from interest, royalties and dividends should be recognised when receipt is probable and revenues are measurable, as follows:
  - interest is recognised using the effective interest method;
  - royalties are accrued in accordance with the relevant contract;
  - dividends are recognised when the shareholders right to receive payment is established.

Measurement

- Revenue should be measured at the fair value of consideration received or receivable.
- In most cases this will be the amount agreed between the two parties as the price, adjusted for discounts if necessary.

If the time value of money is material, then the revenue should be discounted to present value and the unwinding of the discount treated as interest income in the income statement. In this case, there are effectively two transactions –the sale of the goods and the provision of finance.

IAS 19 Employee benefits

Deals with accounting for pensions in the employer's accounts.

- The accounting issues lie with defined benefit schemes where an employer guarantees that an employee will have a specific pension on retirement, usually a percentage of final salary.
- To estimate the fund required, an actuary will have to calculate the contributions required to ensure the scheme has enough funds to pay out its liabilities.
- This involves estimating what may happen in the future, such as the age profile of employees, retirement age etc.
- A pension scheme consists of a pool of assets (cash, investments, shares etc) and a liability for pensions owed to employees when they are at retirement age. The assets are used to pay out the pensions.

Measurement of pension assets and liabilities

IAS 19 requires that

- assets are measured at their fair value at the date
- liabilities are measured on an actuarial basis and are discounted to present value to reflect the time value of money.

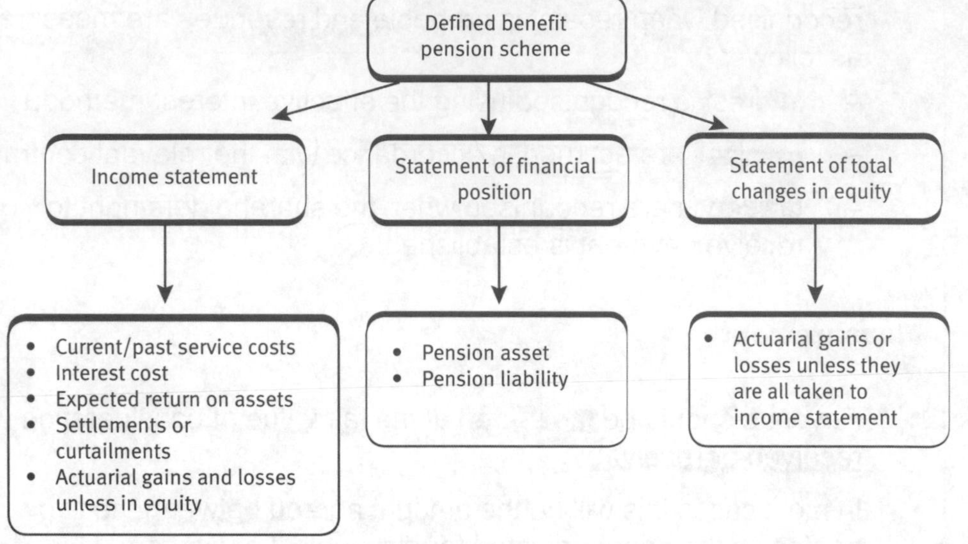

IAS 20 Accounting for government grants and disclosure of ....

Government grants are transfers of resources to an entity in return for past or future compliance with certain conditions.

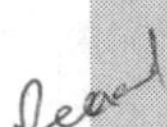

Accounting treatment

Grants should not be recognised until the conditions for receipt have been complied with and there is reasonable assurance that the grant will be received.

- Grants should be recognised in the income statement so as to match them with the expenditure towards which they are intended to contribute.
- Income grants given to subsidise expenditure should be matched to the related costs.
- Income grants given to help achieve a non-financial goal (such as job creation) should be matched to the costs incurred to meet that goal.
- Grants for purchases of non-current assets should be recognised over the expected useful lives of the related assets.

There are two acceptable accounting policies for this:

- deduct the grant from the cost of the asset and depreciate the net cost; or
- treat the grant as deferred income. Release the grant to the income statement over the life of the asset. This is the method most commonly used.

IAS 21 The effects of changes in foreign exchange rates

Provides the accounting guidance on foreign currency transactions.

Its main points are detailed below.

Functional and presentation currencies

A company must determine both its functional and presentation currency. Presentation currency is the currency in which the entity presents its financial statements.

In determining **functional currency**, the following must be considered.

- The currency that mainly influences sales prices for goods and services.
- The currency of the country whose competitive forces and regulations mainly determine the sales price of goods and services.
- The currency that mainly influences labour, material and other costs of providing goods and services.

If the company is a foreign owned subsidiary, the following must be considered to determine whether it is has the same functional currency as the parent.

- Whether the activities of the foreign operation are carried out as an extension of the parent, rather than with a significant degree of autonomy.
- Whether transactions with the parent are a high or low proportion of the of the foreign operation's activities.
- Whether cash flows from the foreign operation directly affect the cash flows of the parent and are readily available for remittance to it.
- Whether cash flows from the activities of the foreign operation are sufficient to service existing debt obligations without funds being made available by the parent.

Once determined, functional currency should not be changed.

Presentation currency can be any currency and can be different from functional currency.

This is particularly the case if the company is foreign-owned as the presentation currency may be that of the parent. If the presentation currency is different from the functional currency, then the financial statements must be translated into the presentation currency.

Individual transactions in foreign currency

If a company enters into **foreign currency transactions** the results of these transactions should be translated and recorded in the accounting records in the functional currency:

- at the rate on the date the transaction occurred; or
- using an average rate over a period of time providing the exchange rate has not fluctuated significantly.

At subsequent Statement of Financial Position dates, the following process must be applied.

- At subsequent Statement of Financial Position dates, the following Foreign currency monetary items (receivables, payables, cash, loans) must be translated using the closing rate.
- The closing rate is the exchange rate at the Statement of Financial Position date.
- Foreign currency non-monetary items (non-current assets, investments, inventory) are not retranslated. They are left at the exchange rate that was used at the date of the transaction (called the historic rate).
- Exchange differences on settlement of monetary items or on retranslating monetary items are recognised in the income statement process must be applied.

Hedging loans

It is not unusual for entities making overseas equity investments to raise the funds locally, in an overseas currency. Such a loan is known as a hedging loan as it will **hedge** against foreign currency movements.

- The investing entity holds both an asset (the investment) and a liability (the loan) denominated in foreign currency. As the exchange rate moves, so the values of the asset and liability will move.

- If the functional currency value of the loan increases, this exchange loss is set off by an increase in the functional currency value of the asset (and so an exchange gain).

- If the functional currency value of the loan increases, this exchange loss is set off by an increase in the functional currency value of the asset (and so an exchange gain).

The hedging provisions of IAS 39 state that the exchange differences arising on a foreign currency hedge of an entity's investment in a foreign entity should be recognised directly in equity until such time as the investment is sold. At that stage they should be recognised in the income statement alongside any gain or loss on disposal of the investment.

Example

USCO holds:

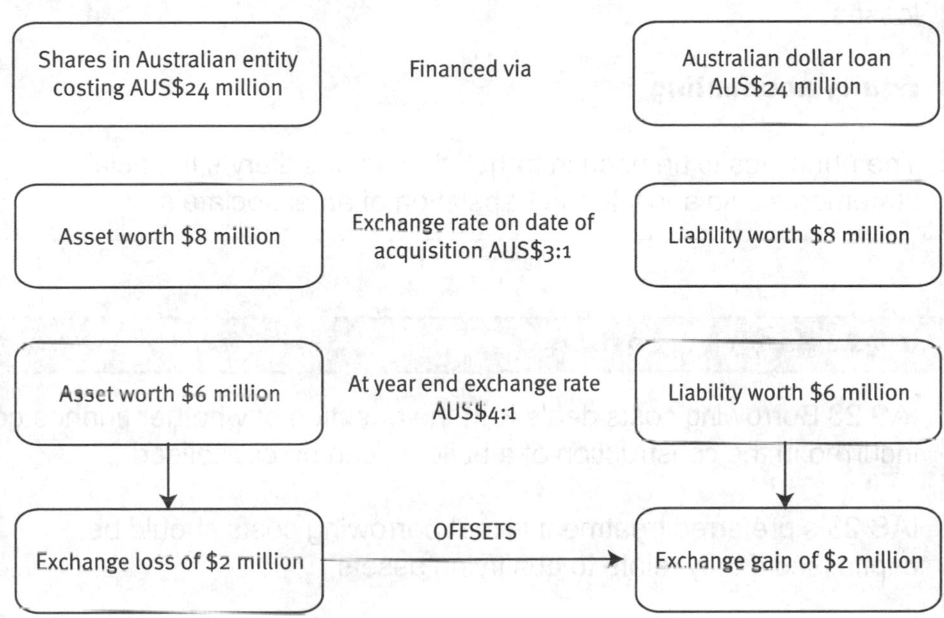

Foreign subsidiaries

If a company has foreign subsidiaries whose functional currency is their local currency, their financial statements must be translated into the parent's presentation currency.

- All assets and liabilities are translated into the parent's presentation currency at the closing rate at the Statement of Financial Position date.
- Goodwill is treated as an asset of the subsidiary and is also translated at the closing rate.
- Income and expenses in the income statement must be translated at the average rate for the period.

- Exchange differences arising on consolidation are recognised in reserves until disposal of the subsidiary when they are transferred to the income statement.
- Exchange differences arise from:
  – the retranslation of the opening net assets using the closing rate
  – retranslation of the profit for the year from the average rate (used in the income statement) to the closing rate (for inclusion in the Statement of Financial Position).

Disposal of overseas subsidiaries

On disposal of a subsidiary that has been translated into presentational currency, the cumulative exchange differences that have previously been recognised in reserves become realised. The foreign exchange reserve is taken to the income statement on the disposal of the subsidiary as part of the gain or loss on disposal. This is called recycling of gains and losses.

Equity accounting

The principles to be used in translating a subsidiary's financial statements also apply to the translation of an associate's.

IAS 23 Borrowing costs

IAS 23 Borrowing costs deals with the question of whether finance costs incurred in the construction of a building can be capitalised.

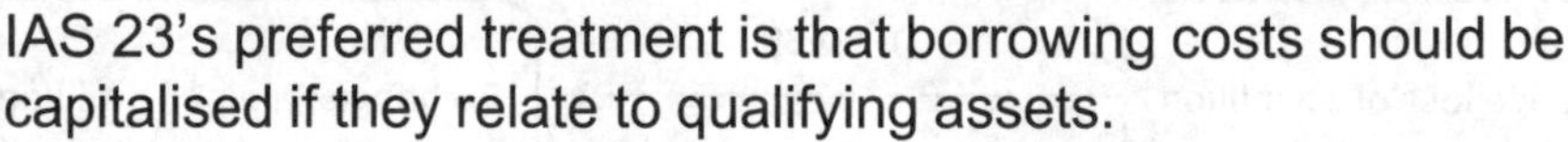

IAS 23's preferred treatment is that borrowing costs should be capitalised if they relate to qualifying assets.

The examiner might expect you to offer opinions or justifications for the accounting treatment required by particular IASs or IFRSs.

It might make sense to capitalise interest associated with the construction of a building (or any other asset that takes a long time to get ready). Arguably, the borrowing costs could be seen as part of the cost in exactly the same way as the cost of the materials or labour applied.

On the other hand, it might be difficult to identify the actual costs of borrowing associated with this asset (unless the company took out a loan that was specifically for this purpose). It can also lead to inconsistencies (such as two identical buildings having different carrying values because one was financed with debt and the other with equity).

If you do have to justify the treatment adopted by a standard then think about its impact on the financial statements.

Will it increase reported profit?

What will it do to the Statement of Financial Position?

Do you believe that these are improvements?

It is permissible to capitalise borrowing costs incurred during the period when work is in progress on the asset. Costs incurred after the asset has been completed or while work is suspended must be written off as revenue expenditure.

It is also necessary that expenditure on the asset and associated borrowing costs are being incurred.

Capitalised borrowing costs are those actually incurred, although this might have to be estimated if the entity is financing the cost out of general borrowings.

The disclosures required by IAS 23 are:

- the accounting policy adopted for
- borrowing costs
- the amount of borrowing costs
- capitalised during the period
- the capitalisation rate used

IAS 24 Related party disclosures

A party is related to an entity if:

(a) directly or indirectly through one or more intermediaries, the party
  - (i) controls, is controlled by, or is under common control with the entity
  - (ii) has an interest in the entity that gives it significant influence over the entity
  - (iii) has joint control over the entity.

(b) the party is an associate of the entity (as defined in IAS 28 Associates)

(c) the party is a joint venture in which the entity is a venturer

(d) the party is a member of the key management personnel of the entity or its parent

(e) the party is a close member of the family of any individual referred to in (a) or (d)

(f) the party is an entity that is controlled, jointly controlled or significantly influenced by, or for which significant voting power in such an entity resides with, directly or indirectly, any individual referred to in (d) or (e)

(g) the party is a post-employment benefit plan for the benefit of employees of the entity, or of any entity that is a related party of the entity.

A related party transaction is the transfer of resources, services or obligations between related parties regardless of whether a price is charged.

Disclosures

- Relationships between parents and subsidiaries irrespective of whether there have been transactions between the parties.
- The name of the parent and the ultimate controlling party (if different).
- Key management personnel compensation in total and for each short term employee benefits, post employment benefits, other long term benefits, termination benefits and share based payment.
- For related party transactions that have occurred, the nature of the relationship and detail of the transactions and outstanding balances.
- The disclosure should be made for each category of related parties ((a) to (g)
- above) and include:
  - (a) the amount of the transactions
  - (b) the amount of outstanding balances and their terms
  - (c) allowances for doubtful debts relating to the outstanding balances
  - (d) the expense recognised in the period in respect of irrecoverable or doubtful debts due from related parties.

IAS 27 Consolidated and Separate Financial Statements

Definition of a subsidiary

Both IAS 27 and IFRS3 define a subsidiary in the same way.

Subsidiary – an entity that is controlled by another entity (known as the parent)

Control – the power to govern the financial and operating policies of an enterprise so as
to obtain benefits from its activities.

Control can be established in a number of ways:

- ownership of more than 50% of voting power
- control of more than half the voting rights by virtue of an agreement with other investors
- the ability to govern the financial and operating policies of the entity under a statute or an agreement
- the right to appoint or remove the majority of the members of the board of directors
- the right to cast the majority of votes at a meeting of the board of directors.

The definition of the holding company/ subsidiary company relationship is complicated because there have been scandals in the past with holding companies attempting to exclude subsidiaries from the consolidated accounts.

The main reason for wanting to exclude a subsidiary is the desire to engage in off Statement of Financial Position financing (OSFPF).

One form of OSFPF involves a "non-subsidiary" borrowing in order to pay for assets which are then made available to the group. That means that neither the assets or liabilities appear in the group accounts and the group's gearing and return on capital employed ratios look better than they otherwise would.

It is generally not acceptable to exclude a subsidiary from the consolidated financial statements. The only exceptions are highly unlikely to occur in practice:

- the holding company might not have effective control
- the subsidiary might be held for resale.

IAS 28 Investments in associates

IAS 28 defines an **associate** as:

An entity over which the investor has significant influence and that is neither a subsidiary nor an interest in joint venture.

Significant influence is the power to participate in the financial and operating policy decisions of the investee but is not control or joint control over those policies.

The definition of significant influence is very broad. You might have to read the question very carefully in order to decide whether an investment creates an associate.

It is normally assumed that significant influence exists if the holding company has a shareholding of 20% to 50%. That does not, however, guarantee that the holding company has any real influence. For example, a 40% shareholding might actually offer very little real influence if the remaining 60% is in the hands of another individual shareholder.

Equity accounting

Acquisition accounting is used to account for subsidiaries.

Equity accounting is used to account for associates.

Unlike acquisition accounting, which combined the holding company's figures with those of the subsidiary or subsidiaries, equity accounting involves single figure adjustments to the consolidated income statement and the consolidated Statement of Financial Position.

Statement of Financial Position

The consolidated income statement includes the **investor's share** of the associate's results.

The consolidated includes the **investor's share** of the associate's net assets.

The holding company is not required to produce consolidated statements unless it has at least one subsidiary. Associates are accounted for using equity accounting within the consolidated financial statements, but the existence of an associate does not, in itself, require the preparation of group accounts.

Consolidated

The initial investment in the associate is shown at cost, identifying any goodwill on acquisition.

The carrying amount is then adjusted to include the group share of any profits arising post-acquisition, less any goodwill written off through impairment.

Alternatively, the same figure can be determined by taking the group's share of the associate's net assets at the date and adding any goodwill that is not yet impaired.

Sundry points

The accounting treatment of associates has some similarities to accounting for subsidiaries, but there are also some significant differences.

Associates are not members of the group in the same way that subsidiaries are.

Always remember that subsidiaries are **controlled** by the holding company, whereas associates are subject to no more than **significant interest**.

Fair values

If the fair value of the associate's net assets at acquisition are materially different from their book value the net assets should be adjusted in the same way as for a subsidiary.

Balances with the associate

Generally the associate is considered to be outside the group. Therefore balances between group companies and the associate will remain in the consolidated.

If a group company trades with the associate, the resulting payables and receivables will remain in the consolidated

Sales to and from associates

Sales between group members and associates are left in the consolidated income statement. The only adjustments are in respect of any closing inventory that remains from such transactions.

Unrealised profit in inventory

Unrealised profit in closing inventory arising from sales between group members and associates should still be cancelled.

If the sale was made to the associate then the amount of the unrealised profit should be added back to group cost of sales.

If the sale was made by the associate then it would be more appropriate to deduct the unrealised profit from the group's share of the associate's profit. However, it would be acceptable to make the adjustment to the group cost of sales for the sake of simplicity.

Dividends from associates

Dividends from associates are not included in the consolidated income statement. This is because the dividend is effectively being paid out of the group's share of the associate's profit, which has already been recognised in the group accounts.

IAS 29 Financial Reporting in Hyperinflationary Economies

Hyperinflation is a very high rate of inflation.

- Hyperinflation is deemed to exist when the cumulative inflation rate over three years is approaching or exceeds 100%.
- Such high inflation renders financial information useless unless it is expressed in terms of current prices.

Therefore, IAS 29 requires that non monetary assets (inventory, investments and non-current assets) and income and expenses are restated by applying the change in the general price index from the date of the transaction to the Statement of Financial Position date. (If a general price index is not available then use an estimate based on the exchange rate movements between the functional currency and a stable currency.)

- Monetary assets and liabilities are not restated as they are already expressed in terms of amounts owed or owing at the Statement of Financial Position date.
- Corresponding figures must also be restated to improve comparability.

IAS 31 Interests in Joint Ventures

A joint venture is a contractual arrangement whereby two or more parties undertake an economic activity that is subject to joint control.

IAS 31 identifies three basic types of joint venture.

- Jointly controlled operations – involves the use of assets and resources of the venturers rather than establishing a separate entity.
- Jointly controlled assets – the venturers jointly control an asset dedicated to be used within the joint venture rather than establishing a separate entity.
  - Jointly controlled entities – this involves the establishment of a separate entity in which each venturer has an interest.

Jointly controlled operations

It is rare for a jointly controlled operation to have its own financial statements. The individual financial statements of each individual venturer will recognise:

- the assets that it controls and the liabilities that it incurs
- the expenses that it incurs and its share of the revenue that it earns from the sale of goods or services by the joint venture.

Jointly controlled assets

It is unlikely that there is a full set of accounts for this type of joint venture so the individual venturers will set up a joint venture account in their own records for the income and expenses incurred in respect of the joint venture and a memorandum income statement is prepared periodically to calculate the amount payable to or receivable from the other venturers.

Jointly controlled entities

A jointly controlled entity keeps its own accounting records.

In the individual financial statements of the venturers, the investment in the joint venture is recorded at cost. In the consolidated financial statements, IAS 31 gives a choice of treatment:

Proportionate consolidation – the venturer includes its share of the assets, liabilities, income and expenses of the jointly controlled entity.

- Equity method – as used for associates (IAS 28).

IAS 32 Financial Instruments: Disclosure and Presentation

IAS 32 Financial Instruments: Presentation classifies financial instruments as debt or equity according to the substance of the contractual arrangement.

It does not matter whether a financial instrument is called a 'share' or 'equity'. IAS 32 might still classify it as a liability if it has the characteristics of debt.

A financial instrument is classified as **debt** if the issuer has a contractual obligation either to deliver cash or another financial asset to the holder or to exchange another financial asset/liability with the holder under conditions that are potentially unfavourable to the issuer.

A financial instrument is classified as **equity** if it does not give rise to such a contractual obligation.

For example, preference shares:

- are classified as equity if they are irredeemable
- are classified as debt if they are redeemable.

Compound instruments

A compound instrument is one which has both a liability and an equity component.

For example, a convertible bond pays interest for the first part of its life, at which time it is redeemed or converted into ordinary share capital. The interest paid during the debt phase is usually lower than the rate offered on equivalent debt capital that does not carry conversion rights.

Compound instruments must be broken down between their liability element and equity element and each is shown in the appropriate part of the Statement of Financial Position. This is usually accomplished by subtracting the net present value of the cash payments associated with the debt element from the fair value of the proceeds of issuing the instrument. That remainder is the equity element.

IAS 33 earnings per share

- Earnings per share is an important ratio that is used as a comparison for company performance and forms part of the Price / Earnings ratio.
- IAS 33 applies to all listed companies. Private companies must follow the standard if they disclose an EPS figure.

Basic earnings per share is:

$$\frac{\text{Profit or loss for the period attributable to the ordinary shareholders}}{\text{Weighted average number of ordinary shares outstanding in the period}}$$

- Basic earnings are profit after tax less minority interest and preference dividends
- Weighted average number of ordinary shares must take into account when the shares were issued in the year.
- Partly paid shares are treated as a fraction of an ordinary share to the extent that they were entitled to participate in dividends relative to a fully paid share.

Changes in share capital

- Issue at full market price – as this share issue will bring cash into the business and increase earnings from the date the shares were issued, the weighted average number of shares must be calculated to ensure that the increase in earnings is matched with the increase in shares.
- Bonus issue – as there is no cash received; there is no effect on earnings.
- Therefore a bonus issue reduces EPS as share capital increases but earnings do not. The bonus issue is treated as if it has always been in issue, so share capital is adjusted at the beginning of the year and the comparative figures are adjusted for the effect of the bonus issue for comparability.
- Rights issue – the rights issue will bring cash into the business but not full price per share as the shares are issued below full market price. This share issue is treated as a combination of a bonus issue and a rights issue. Firstly, the bonus element must be dealt with by adjusting the opening capital by the rights issue bonus fraction:

$$\frac{\text{Fair value of share before exercise of rights}}{\text{Theoretical ex rights price}}$$

The theoretical ex rights price is the average price of the shares after the rights issue has taken place.

Secondly, the weighted average no of shares is calculated by time apportioning the shares according to the date of issue to match the increase in earnings with the increase in shares.

As there is a bonus element with a rights issue, the comparative must be adjusted.

Diluted earnings per share

- IAS 33 requires diluted earnings per share to be disclosed as well as basic EPS
- Diluted EPS shows the effect on the current EPS if all the potential ordinary shares had been issued under the greatest possible dilution.
- Potential ordinary shares consist of:
  - convertible loan stock
  - convertible preference shares
  - share warrants and options
  - partly paid shares
  - rights granted under employee share schemes
  - rights to ordinary shares that are conditional.
- The profit used in the basic EPS calculation is adjusted for any expenses that would no longer be paid if the convertible instrument was converted into shares, e.g. preference dividends, loan interest.
- The weighted average number of shares used in the basic EPS calculation is adjusted for the conversion of the potential ordinary shares. This deemed to occur at the beginning of the period or the date of issue if they were not in existence at the beginning of the period.

Other DEPS considerations

- Options and warrants are included in the DEPS calculation by calculating the number of shares that were issued for no consideration. Calculate the number of shares that would be issued if the cash has been used to buy shares at the fair value in the period. The remainder of the shares are treated like a bonus issue (i.e. for no consideration) and are included in the DEPS calculation.

- If there is more than one source of potential ordinary shares, then the DEPS calculation must be done in two stages as only potential ordinary shares that are dilutive can be included in the DEPS calculation. Firstly, calculate earnings per incremental share and then rank each potential share with the most dilutive being first. Secondly, starting with basic EPS, add in each potential share, with the most dilutive being added in first, giving a DEPS figure calculated in stages. DEPS is the most diluted figure – any potential share that increases EPS must be ignored as it is anti-dilutive.

Disclosure of EPS

- Basic and diluted earnings per share for continuing operations should be presented on the face of the income statement for each class of ordinary share.
- Basic and diluted earnings per share for discontinued operations should be presented on the face of the income statement or in the notes to the accounts for each class of ordinary share.
- If a company discloses an EPS using a different earnings figure, the alternative calculation must show basic and diluted EPS with equal prominence.

These alternative calculations must be presented in the notes to the financial statements, not on the face of the income statement.

IAS 34 Interim financial reporting

Objective: to prescribe the minimum content of an interim financial report (IFR) and the recognition and measurement principles for an IFR.

Definitions:

Interim period is a financial reporting period shorter than a full financial year

Interim financial report means a financial report containing either a complete set of financial statements or a set of condensed financial statements for an interim period.

Contents of an interim report:

The minimum contents prescribed by the standard are:

- a condensed Statement of financial position
- a condensed income statement
- a condensed cash flow statement

- a condensed statement of changes in equity
- a selected explanatory notes

The condensed information must at least have the same headings and subtotals as were in the latest annual financial statements published.

Comparative figures in the condensed financial statements should be those of the immediately preceding financial year.

Basic and diluted EPS should be presented in the interim report.

IAS 36 Impairment of assets

An impairment loss is the amount by which the carrying amount of an asset or cash generating unit exceeds its recoverable amount.

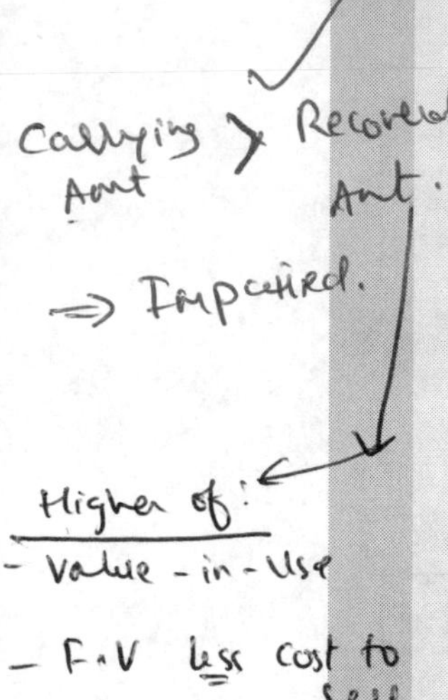

- Impairment is measured by comparing the carrying value of an asset with its recoverable amount.
- If the carrying value exceeds the recoverable amount, the asset is impaired and must be written down.

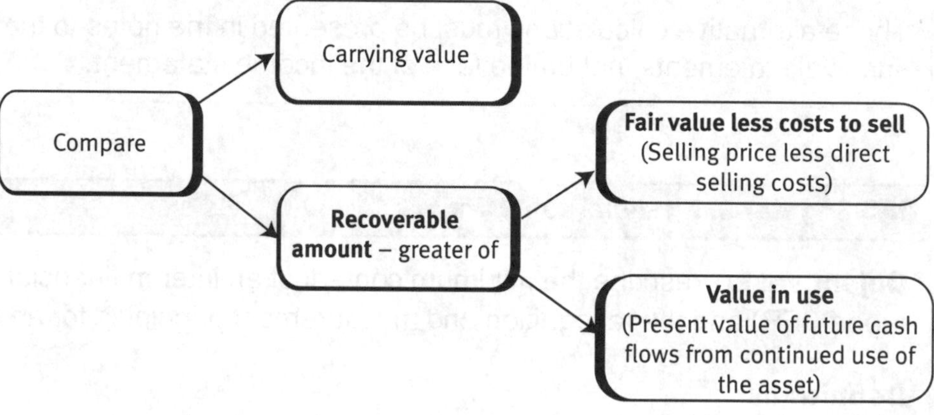

Indicators of impairment

Unless an impairment review is required by another standard (e.g. IAS 38 for intangible assets not amortised of IFRS 3 for purchased goodwill), then impairment reviews are required where there is an indicator for impairment.

Examples

Internal

- Physical damage to the asset.
- Management committed to reorganisation of the business.
- Obsolete assets.

- Idle assets.
- Major loss of key employees..
- Operating losses in the business where the assets are used.

External

- Competitor actions.
- Increasing interest rates (affect value in use).
- Market values of assets falling.
- Change in the business or market where assets are used (e.g. govt action).

Cash-generating units (CGU)

A **cash-generating unit** is the smallest identifiable group of assets that generates cash inflows from other assets or group of assets.

- It will not always be possible to base the impairment review on individual assets as an individual asset may not generate a distinguishable cash flow. In this case the impairment calculations should be based on a CGU.
- The impairment calculation is done by comparing the carrying value of the CGU to the recoverable amount of the CGU. This is done by allocating an entity's asset including goodwill, to CGUs.
- Impairment losses are allocated to assets with specific impairments first, then allocated in the following order:
  (1) goodwill
  (2) remaining assets on a pro rata basis. No asset can be written down below the higher of fair value less costs to sell, value in use and zero.

Recognition of impairment losses

Assets held at cost: The amount of the impairment is charged to the income statement for the period int which the impairment occurs.

Revalued assets: The impairment is charged to the revaluation reserve to reverse any previous surplus on that asset in the same way as a downword revaluation.

IAS 37 Provisions, contingent liabilities and contingent assets

- A provision is a liability of uncertain timing or amount.
- A contingent liability is a possible obligation arising from past events whose existence will only be confirmed on the occurrence of uncertain future event outside of the entity's control.
- A contingent asset is a possible asset that arises from past events and whose existence will only be confirmed on the occurrence of uncertain future events outside of the entity's control.

Provisions

Recognition

Recognise when:

- an entity has a present obligation (legal or constructive) as a result of a past event,
- It is probable that an outflow of resources embodying economic benefits will be required to settle the obligation, and
- a reliable estimate can be made of the amount of the obligation.

Measurement

- The amount recognised as a provision should be the best estimate of the expenditure required to settle the present obligation at the balance sheet date.
- Where the time value of money is material, the provision should be discounted to present value.

Contingent liabilities should not be recognised. They should be disclosed unless the possibility of a transfer of economic benefits is remote.

Contingent assets should not be recognised. If the possibility of an inflow of economic benefits is probable they should be disclosed.

Specific guidance

Future operating losses

- Provisions should not be recognized for future operating losses.

No provision, For future losses.

Onerous contracts

- Provisions should be recognized for the present obligation under the contract.
- E.g. non-cancellable lease, provide for the unavoidable lease payments.

Must provide for (P.V)

Restructuring

Provisions can only be recognised where an entity has a constructive obligation to carry out the restructuring.

- A constructive obligation arises: when there is a detailed formal plan, identifying at least:
  - the business concerned,
  - the principal location, function, and approximate number of employees being made redundant,
  - the expenditures that will be incurred,

  when the plan will be implemented; and

  There is a valid expectation that the plan will be carried out by either implementing the plan or announcing it to those affected.

Contingent liabilities should not be recognised. They should be disclosed unless the possibility of a transfer of economic benefits is remote.

Contingent assets should not be recognised. If the possibility of an inflow of economic benefits is probable they should be disclosed.

IAS 38 Intangible Assets

An **intangible asset** is an identifiable non-monetary asset without physical substance.

Accounting treatment

- An intangible asset is initially recognised at cost if all of the following criteria are met.

  (1) It is identifiable – it could be disposed of without disposing of the business at the same time.

  (2) It is controlled by the entity

  – the entity has the power to obtain economic benefits from it, for example patents and copyrights give legal rights to future economic benefits.

(3) It will generate probable future economic benefits for the entity

- this could be by a reduction in costs or increasing revenues.

(4) The cost can be measured reliably

- this is straightforward if the asset was purchased outright. If the asset was acquired in a business combination then the initial cost will be the fair value.

- If an intangible does not meet the recognition criteria, then it should be charged to the income statement as it is incurred. Items that do not meet the criteria are internally generated goodwill, brands, mastheads, publishing titles, customer lists, research, advertising, start-up costs and training.
- Intangible assets should be amortised, normally using the straight line method, over the term of their useful lives.
- If it can be demonstrated that the useful life is indefinite; no amortisation should be charged but an annual impairment review must be carried out.
- Goodwill and intangible assets can be revalued but fair values must be determined with reference to an active market. This will have homogenous products, willing buyers and seller at all times and published prices.
- The recognition of internally generated intangible assets is split into a research phase and a development phase. Costs incurred in the research phase must be charged to the income statement as they are incurred. Costs incurred in the development phase should be recognised if they meet the following criteria:

  (a) the project is technically feasible

  (b) the asset will be completed then used or sold

  (c) the entity is able to use or sell the asset

  (d) the asset will generate future economic benefits (either by internal use or there is a market for it)

  (e) the entity has adequate technical, financial and other resources to complete the project

  (f) the expenditure on the project can be reliably measured.

- Amortisation over the useful life of the new product or process will commence once the project is complete.

IAS 39 Financial instruments: Recognition and Measurement

Financial instruments

This standard requires the recognition of financial instruments in the financial statements.

Initial recognition

Financial assets and liabilities should be recognised at fair value which is usually their cost.

Subsequent measurement

For the purpose of subsequent measurement, financial instruments have to be classified into four categories and remeasured as shown below.

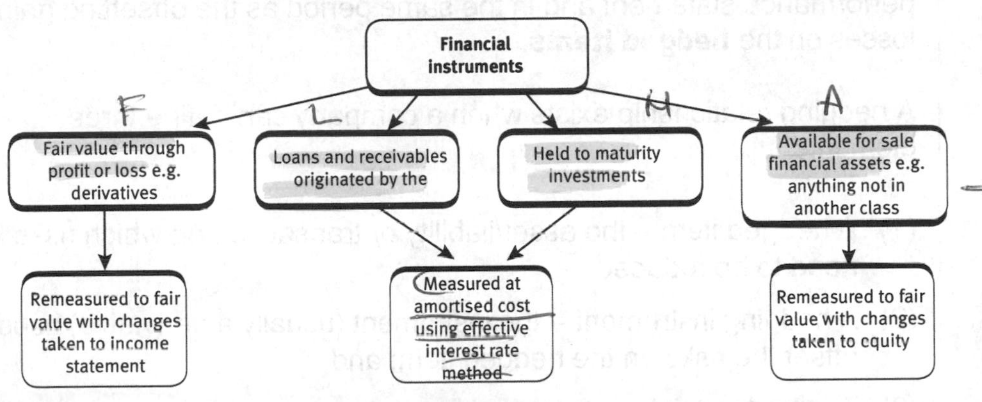

Derivatives

A derivative is a financial instrument with all three of the following characteristics:

(1) its value changes in response to the change in a specified interest rate, security price, commodity price, foreign exchange rate or similar variable

(2) it requires little or no initial investment

(3) it is settled at a future date.

Derivatives include:

- options
- forward contracts
- futures
- swaps.

As seen previously, derivatives are measured at fair value with changes recognised in the income statement. However, if a derivative is used as a hedge, then changes in value are recognised in equity.

Hedge accounting

Hedge accounting is the accounting treatment where the gains or losses on the **hedging instruments** are recognised in the same performance statement and in the same period as the offsetting gains or losses on the **hedged items**.

A hedging relationship exists when a company can define three elements.

(1) A hedged item – the asset/liability or transaction on which risks need to be reduced;

(2) A hedging instrument – the instrument (usually a derivative) used to offset the risks on the hedged item; and

(3) The hedged risks – the specific risk (currency, interest rate etc) that is being hedged.

In order to follow the hedge accounting rules in IAS 39, the following criteria need to be met.

(1) The hedge must be documented at inception and the elements of the hedging relationship defined (hedged item and instrument).

(2) The hedge is expected to be highly effective

(3) The effectiveness of the hedge can be measured reliably.

(4) Forecast transactions must be highly probable in order to be hedged'.

(5) The effectiveness of the hedge must be able to be assessed and measured on an on-going basis.

Types of hedge

There are three types of hedge:

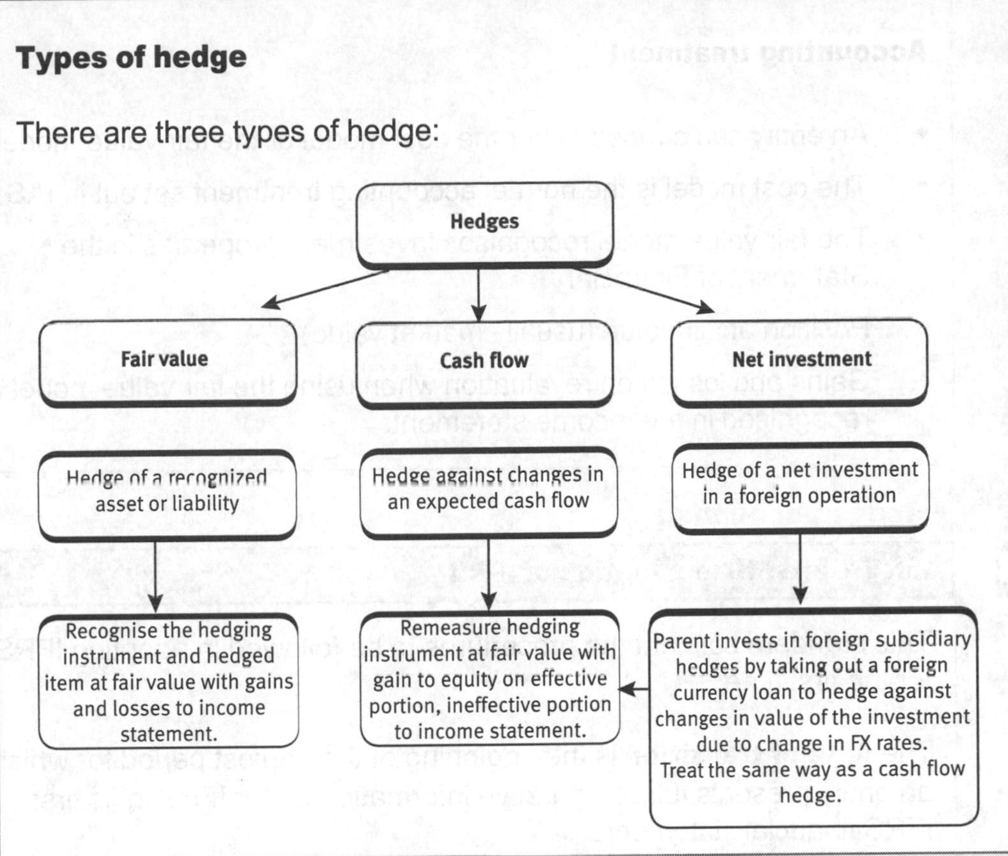

IAS 40 Investment property

Investment property is property (land or a building - or part of a building) held to earn rentals or for capital appreciation or both, rather than for:

- use in the production or supply of goods or services or for administration purposes; or
- sale in the ordinary course of business.

Investment property is not:

- owner occupied property (deal with under IAS 16)
- property held for sale in the normal course of business (deal with under IAS 2 inventories)
- property being constructed for third parties (deal with under IAS 11 Construction contracts)
- property being constructed or developed for future use as investment property (deal with under IAS 16 until it is complete).

Accounting treatment

- An entity can choose either the cost model or the fair value model.
- The cost model is the normal accounting treatment set out in IAS 16.
- The fair value model recognises investment properties in the Statement of Financial
- Position at fair value (usually market value).
- Gains and losses on revaluation when using the fair value model are recognised in the income statement.

IFRS 1 First time adoption of IFRS

This standard sets out the procedures to be followed in adopting IFRS for the first time.

The **date of transition** is the beginning of the earliest period for which an entity presents full comparative information under IFRS in its first IFRS financial statements

Example

If an entity adopts IFRS for the first time in its 31 December 2007 financial statements and presents one year of comparative information, the transition date will be 1 January 2006.

Adoption of IFRS

- The entity should use the same accounting policies for all the periods presented; these policies should be based solely on IFRS in force at the reporting date.
- A major problem for entities preparing for the changeover is that IFRS themselves keep changing, although the IASB have said there will be no more standards to adopt until 2009.
- Entities will have to collect information enabling them to prepare statements under previous GAAP, current IFRS and any proposed new standards or amendments.

- IFRS 1 states that the opening IFRS Statement of Financial Position must:
  - recognise all assets and liabilities required by IFRS
  - not recognise assets and liabilities not permitted by IFRS
  - reclassify all assets, liabilities and equity components in accordance with IFRS
  - measure all assets and liabilities in accordance with IFRS

Disclosures

- Entities must explain how the transition to IFRS affects their reported financial performance, financial position and cash flows. Two main disclosures are required, which reconcile equity and profits.

The entity's equity as reported under previous GAAP must be reconciled to the equity reported under IFRS at two dates:

- the date of transition. This is the opening Statement of Financial Position date
- the last Statement of Financial Position prepared under previous GAAP.

The last annual profit reported under previous GAAP must be reconciled to the same year's profit prepared under IFRS.

- Any material differences between the previous GAAP and the IFRS cash flows must also be explained.

IFRS 1 allows exemptions for certain items where it is considered the cost of complying would outweigh the benefit.

Examples are:

- Previous business combinations do not have to be restated (e.g. if merger accounting had been applied which is not allowed under IFRS).
- Past currency translation reserves do not have to be shown separately from retained earnings.
- Convertible debt that has been repaid does not have to be split into debt and equity component.

IFRS 2 Share based payments

A **share based payment** transaction is one where an entity obtains goods or services from other parties with payment taking the form of shares or share options issued by the entity.

There are two types of share based payment transactions:

(1) equity-settled share based payment transactions where a company receives goods or services in exchange for equity instruments (e.g. shares or share options).

(2) cash-settled share based payment transactions, where a company receives goods and services in exchange for a cash amount paid based on its share price.

Accounting

- IFRS 2 requires that all share-based payments are recognised in the accounts.
- When a share based transaction is entered into, the goods or services received and corresponding increase in equity should be measured at fair value.
- If a company issues share options (e.g. to employees), the fair value of the option at the grant date should be used as the cost of the services received.
- For cash settled share based payments, the fair value of goods and services is measured and a liability recognised. The, liability is re-measured at each Statement of Financial Position until it is settled with changes in value being taken to the income statement.
- The expense in relation to the share based transaction must be recognised over the period in which the services are rendered or goods are received.

Grant date: the date a share based-payment transaction is entered into.

Vesting date: the date on which the cash or equity instruments can be received by the other party to the agreement.

IFRS 3 (revised) Business Combinations

IFRS 3 requires that on acquisition both the cost of investment and the net assets acquired are recorded at their fair value. Assets and liabilities must be recognised if they are separately identifiable and can be reliably measured. The future intentions of the acquirer must not be taken into account when calculating fair values.

Fair value is the amount for which an asset could be exchanged, or a liability settled, between knowledgeable, willing parties in an arm's length transaction.

Type of asset/ liability	**Fair value**
Tangible non-current/assets	(a) land and buildings – market value (b) plant and equipment – market value or if not available, depreciated replacement cost.
Intangible assets	Recognise at market value if there is an active market or estimated value if not (see IAS 38).
Inventory and work-in-progress	Finished goods – the selling price less the cost of disposal and a reasonable profit allowance Work in progress – the selling price of finished goods less costs to complete, the cost of disposal and a reasonable profit allowance Raw materials – current replacement cost
Quoted investments	Quoted investments should be valued at market price.
Contingencies	Contingent assets and liabilities should be measured at fair values where these can be determined (reasonable estimates of the expected outcome may be used).
Pensions and other post retirement benefits	The fair value of a deficit or surplus in a pension or other post retirement benefits scheme should be recognised as a liability or an asset of the acquiring group.
Deferred tax	Deferred tax on adjustments to record assets and liabilities at their fair values should be recognised in accordance with the requirements of IAS 12 Income taxes.

Fair value of the cost of acquisition

The cost of acquisition is:

(a) the amount of cash paid; plus

(b) the fair value of other purchase consideration given by the acquirer; plus

Note:

- If payment of cash is deferred it should be discounted to present value using a rate at which the acquirer could obtain similar borrowing.
- If the acquirer issues shares, fair value is normally the market price at the date of acquisition.
- The revised IFRS 3 requires the acquirer to recognise the acquisition-date fair value of contingent consideration as part of the consideration.

Goodwill and the non-controlling interest

The standard now allows the acquirer (parent) to measure any non-controlling interest (NCI) in one of two ways:

- either at fair value (the 'new' method); or
- at the NCI's proportionate share of the acquiree's (subsidiary's) identifiable net assets (this is the 'old' method)

Negative goodwill

If the net assets acquired exceed the fair value of consideration, then negative goodwill arises.

After checking that the calculations have been done correctly, negative goodwill is credited to the income statement immediately.

Other adjustments

Don't forget that there are other adjustments that you may be required to make. These have been seen in previous studies and include:

- dividends declared by the subsidiary or associate and not accounted for by the parent
- interest on intercompany loans that has not been accounted for by the receiving party

- intercompany management charges that have not been accounted for by the receiving party
- intercompany sales, purchases and unrealised profit in inventory
- intercompany transfer of non-current assets and unrealised profit on transfer
- intercompany receivables, payables and loans that need eliminating.

IFRS 5 Non-current assets held for sale and discontinued

A **discontinued operation** is a component of an entity that either has been disposed of, or is classified as held for sale; and

- represents a separate major line of business or geographical area of operations
- is part of a single coordinated plan to dispose of a separate major line of business or geographical area of operations
- is a subsidiary acquired exclusively with a view to resale.

An entity should classify a non-current asset or a disposal group as held for sale if its carrying value will be recovered principally through a sale transaction rather than continued use in the business.

A **disposal group** is a group of assets to be disposed of, by sale or otherwise, together as a group in a single transaction, and liabilities directly associated with those assets that will be transferred in the transaction.

Assets can only be classified as held for sale (and therefore a discontinued operation) if they meet all of the criteria below:

- management commits itself to a plan to sell
- the asset (or disposal group) is available for immediate sale in its present condition
- sale is highly probable and is expected to be completed within a year from date of classification
- the asset (or disposal group) is being actively marketed for sale at a reasonable price compared to its fair value
- it is unlikely that significant changes will be made to the plan or it will be withdrawn.

If there are events outside the entity's control that mean that the sale cannot be completed within one year and there is evidence that the entity remains committed to the plan to sell, then the asset or disposal group can still be classified as held for sale.

If the criteria are met after the Statement of Financial Position date but before the accounts are authorised for issue, the assets should not be classed as held for sale but the information should be disclosed.

Measurement

- A non-current asset (or disposal group) classified as held for sale should be measured at the lower of its carrying value and fair value less costs to sell.
- Assets classified as held for sale should not be depreciated, regardless of whether they are still in use by the reporting entity.

Presentation

Information about discontinued operations should be presented in the financial statements.

- On the face of the income statement, a single amount comprising:
  - the total of the post tax profit or loss of discontinued operations
  - the post tax gain or loss on the measurement to fair values less costs to sell or the disposal of the discontinued operation.
- Either on the face of or in the notes to the income statement an analysis of the single amount described into:
- the revenue, expenses and pre tax profit or loss of discontinued operations
- the related tax expense
- the gain or loss recognised on the measurement to fair value less costs to sell or on the disposal of the discontinued operations
- the related tax expense.

IFRS 7 Financial instruments: Disclosures

IFRS 7 requires the following disclosures:
The two main categories of disclosures required are:

(1) information about the significance of financial instruments

(2) information about the nature and extent of risks arising from financial instruments.

The qualitative disclosures describe:

- risk exposures for each type of financial instrument
- management's objectives, policies, and processes for managing those risks
- changes from the prior period.

The quantitative disclosures provide information about the extent to which the entity is exposed to risk, based on information provided internally to the entity's key management personnel. These disclosures include:

- summary quantitative data about exposure to each risk at the reporting date
- disclosures about credit risk, liquidity risk, and market risk as further described below
- concentrations of risk.

IFRS 8 Operating segments

IFRS 8 Operating segments requires an entity to disclose information about each of its operating segments.

An **operating segment** is a component of an entity:

- that engages in business activities from which it may earn revenues and incur expenses;
- whose operating results are regularly reviewed by the entity's chief operating decision maker to make decisions about resources to be allocated to the segment and assess its performance; and
- for which discrete financial information is available.

A **reportable segment** is an operating segment that is used in an entity's internal management reports. Therefore management identifies the operating segments

Reporting thresholds

An entity must separately report information about an operating segment that meets any of the following quantitative thresholds:

- sales, is 10 per cent or more of the combined revenue of all operating segments.

- its reported profit or loss is 10 per cent or more of the greater, in absolute amount, of
- the combined reported profit of all operating segments that did not report a loss and
- the combined reported loss of all operating segments that reported a loss.
- Its assets are 10 per cent or more of the combined assets of all operating segments.

At least 75% of the entity's external revenue should be included in reportable segments. So if the quantitative test results segmental disclosure of less than this 75%, other segments should be identified as reportable segments until this 75% is reached.

Disclosures

IFRS 8 requires detailed disclosures, including:

- factors used to identify the entity's reportable segments, including the basis of organisation (for example, whether segments are based on products and services, geographical areas or a combination of these).
- the types of products and services from which each reportable segment derives its revenues.

For each reportable segment an entity should report:

- a measure of profit or loss
- a measure of total assets
- a measure of total liabilities (if such an amount is regularly used in decision making).

Index

Index

Index